Bennion
on
Statute Law

Third Edition

F A R Bennion MA (Oxon), Barrister

Research Associate, University of Oxford
Centre for Socio-Legal Studies.
Former UK Parliamentary Counsel and
Lecturer and Tutor in Law, St Edmund Hall, Oxford.
Chairman, Statute Law Society 1977–1979.

© Longman Group UK Limited, 1990

Published by
Longman Law, Tax and Finance
Longman Group UK Ltd
21–27 Lamb's Conduit Street
London WC1N 3NJ

First published in 1980
Second edition 1983
Third edition 1990

Associated Offices
Australia, Hong Kong, Malaysia, Singapore, USA

A CIP catalogue record for this book is
available from the British Library

ISBN 0 85121 580 7   Po 3293

Printed and bound in Great Britain by
Mackays of Chatham Plc

£ 25.00
2F
f 28

Bennion
on
Statute Law

Dedicated to the memory of
Sir John Rowlatt KCB, KCIE, QC
First Parliamentary Counsel 1953–1956

What he would have thought of
this, I cannot say, but he knew
how to encourage, and he
knew how to inspire.

Contents

Preface to the Third Edition

In the preface (see below) to the 1983 edition, I acknowledged that this book was then still incomplete. It did not deal adequately with a central topic, namely statutory interpretation. My full-scale treatment of this, set out in a textbook of around a thousand pages, was published in the following year under the title *Statutory Interpretation* (Butterworths). As a result of the reassessment carried out for that book, I am able in this new edition of *Statute Law* to include five additional chapters on the topic. They form the new Part II of the book, and drastically condense the treatment in the larger work. I hope this will make it more accessible both to students and practitioners.

The essence of my new treatment of statutory interpretation is to anchor the subject firmly within the main currents of law. Instead of attempting to get by with rules of thumb like the so-called 'mischief rule', 'golden rule' and 'literal rule', it appears that the law really requires the matter to be treated more seriously and thoroughly. Legislative enactments bring in by implication all relevant rules and principles of law, and must be interpreted accordingly. In a particular case it may be necessary to apply numerous interpretative criteria (which may be otherwise called guides to legislative intention). A balancing exercise must then be carried out.

It is a disquieting fact, constantly exposed in the law reports, that applicable interpretative criteria are commonly overlooked by those concerned with arguing or deciding a point of statutory interpretation. My aim is that the new Part II included in this edition will help to remedy that state of affairs.

The natural wish of the publishers to minimise the number of additional pages has meant the omission of some developments in statute law arising from cases decided since the last edition. I should mention in particular a case in which I myself appeared as counsel, *R v Horseferry Road Magistrates' Court, ex p Independent Broadcasting Authority* [1986] 3 WLR 132; [1986] 2 All ER 666, which revolutionised the law relating to the common law offence known as contempt of statute (on this see my remarks in (i) [1986] All ER Annual Review, pp 268–270 and (ii) the Supplement to my book *Statutory Interpretation*, pp 3–5). Another case worthy of mention is *R* v *Hunt* [1987] AC 352 (on this see my article 'Statutory Exceptions: A Third Knot in the Golden Thread?' in [1988] Crim LR 31).

The need to keep down the length of the text has led to some excisions from the previous edition. In particular the treatment of Composite Restatement has had to be drastically shortened. For a more detailed account of this topic, see chapter 27 of the second edition.

I should finally mention that in this edition I have made a belated gesture to the feminists (at risk of offending the purists) by changing 'draftsman' to 'drafter' throughout.

Francis Bennion
2 January 1990

Preface to the Second Edition

This is a book about the need people feel to know where they stand. Having this recognised could be numbered among human rights, but few lawyers seem to take it seriously. I ask readers, if they are kind enough to study these pages with attention, to look out for signs of this object. They will find many, and perhaps will feel moved to do something about them. We should, as has been said, take rights seriously.

In the preface to the first edition, I invited criticisms and suggestions. There have been few of these, but I am grateful that the book was well received. The only substantial objection was to the effect that, while the demolition of received ideas effectively cleared the way for some new system of statutory interpretation, this was not forthcoming. True indeed, but it needed a book to itself. This is nearing completion, and should appear in 1984.

My disappointment mainly springs from the apparent reluctance of some expert readers to grapple with the *ideas* in the first edition. They are still there in the second (with a few more), and may in time sink in. Time is always needed; and this is not after all an area in which one expects new ideas.

The first edition was generously praised for its 'wealth of examples'. There seemed little understanding of what these were examples *of*. If there is a wealth of examples (as is most kindly suggested) it is only because there is a wealth of ideas which they illustrate. Ideas are usually more important than examples.

It is time for heads to go down, and for close attention to be paid to this subject. There is more to it than most people seem to think. It concerns the way our lives are lived, and merits concentrated care for that reason. Theories about rules in general are all very well, but statutory rules matter in a special way. They also possess special characteristics. If we are to take rights seriously, it is time we took statutes seriously. We can only do this if we look very carefully at them as they are.

The book has not been much altered in this edition. Reviewers have been kind enough to indicate that the arrangement was right to start with, so what is the point of changing it? Accordingly, the second edition has the same number of chapters and the same chapter headings as the first. That was the product of a lifetime's practical experience, and the passing of a year or two is not likely to alter it much.

I am glad to be able to record in this edition an improvement in the Law Commissions' output of consolidation Acts. Against that is the regrettable failure to implement their promise (noted in the first edition) to produce a plan for statute law revision. This plan has been abandoned, we are told, because of staff shortage—one more indication of the low priority given by our masters to the people's statute book. Another Law Commission failure since the first edition was the reiterated refusal of Parliament to enact their 1969 Interpretation Bill. It is time we had a Statute Law Commission, or at least a Statute Law Institute.

Many new cases have been noted in this edition. Perhaps the most significant is the House of Lords decision in *Wills* v *Bowley* [1982] 2 All ER 654, which sounded the death knell of the so-called literal rule of statutory interpretation and finally disposed of the suggestion (always absurd) that there are no implied meanings in statutes.

There is quite a lot of new commentary in this edition. By far the most important is that dealing with interstitial articulation and selective comminution. If only this were taken seriously it would indeed mark a break-through.

I should add to the acknowledgments in the preface to the first edition the editors of the *Law Society's Gazette*, the *Statute Law Review*, the *British Tax Review* and the *Criminal Law Review*.

Francis Bennion
8 April 1983

Preface to the First Edition

Statute law interests few people. Yet it is of vital concern to us all. I have tried to make this presentation lively, and to engage the reader's attention. I have also sought to avoid overlap with existing treatments, and to present a constructive appproach original in concept. The approach is that of a legislative draftsman (which I have been for nearly thirty years).

Some of the material derives from articles of mine in legal journals, though it is all rewritten for this book. I am grateful to the editors of *British Journal of Law and Society*, *Computers and Law*, *New Law Journal*, and *Solicitors Journal* for permission to reproduce the substance of work which first appeared in their journals. I am also grateful to the publishers for venturing to back a work which, because its treatment of the subject is novel, perhaps carries more than the usual publishing risks. In view of this novelty, I shall particularly welcome constructive criticisms and suggestions.

Francis Bennion
26 May 1980

THE MIKADO: Unfortunately the fool of an Act says 'compassing the death of the Heir Apparent'. There's not a word about a mistake . . . That's the slovenly way in which these Acts are always drawn.

The Mikado, Act 2.

Table of Cases

Table of Statutes

Table of Statutory Instruments

Table of EEC Regulations

Table of EEC Treaties

Introduction

This book, written from a drafter's viewpoint, has two purposes. One is expository, the other reforming. The first seeks to help people who have to understand statute law under the present system. The second suggests new techniques, by which their needs might be better met. Throughout, the approach is realistic.

The book deals with legislative texts on the British model, as found generally in the Commonwealth. But since 1972, a new element has been added in Britain itself. Community law now forms part of our body of law, and an overriding part. Here, if not everywhere else in Europe, Community law is acknowledged to be what the European Court says it is. Thus in the United Kingdom two systems of statute law dwell uneasily side by side. The implications of this are explored.

The main difference between the British and Continental systems of statute law lies in the way the text is regarded. The British system (*pace* Lord Denning) on the whole requires the text to be literally observed. The European system treats the text as merely a guide. When a British court processes a text of uncertain meaning by handing out a decision, this is reported and from then on used as an authoritative ruling. Europe has no such doctrine of *stare decisis*.

The difference is important for the person who seeks to find out the law. Is it fully stated in the text as enacted (or as subsequently processed)? If so the enquirer has his answer. Or does it depend finally on the discretion of a judge or official? If so, the enquirer will be without an answer unless he activates that judge or official. To do so will cause the enquirer trouble and may involve him in expense. It will certainly defer his enlightenment. What is more, one judge or official may differ from another. The law becomes subjective. That is a widespread defect of the Continental system, though no system of statute law can altogether avoid it.

In Britain, and in other Commonwealth countries which follow the British model, the good drafter seeks to word his text so that wherever possible it gives the answer. This makes the text complicated. Even the skilled reader needs help in unravelling it. But the answer is there.

The texts

The book begins by describing the texts of which statute law consists. A person who does not know how they are drafted and arranged, and how they come into existence as law, cannot expect to understand them. They are not like other literary texts. The reasons for this are discussed. There is an explanation of the way our statutes are consolidated and revised. The system of official publication of Acts, statutory instruments and European law is described.

Statutory interpretation

Having described the legislative texts, the book goes on in Part II to explain how they are interpreted.

The purpose of our system of statutory interpretation is to find the intention of the legislator as expressed in the text. For this the law lays down various guides or criteria, which can be identified as: six common law *rules*, a varying number of *rules* laid down by statute, eight *principles* derived from a legal policy, ten *presumptions* arising from the nature of legislation, and a collection of linguistic *canons*.

A rule of construction is of binding force, but in cases of real doubt rarely yields a conclusive answer. A principle embodies the policy of the law, and is mainly persuasive. A presumption affords a *prima facie* indication of the legislator's inferred or imputed intention as to the working of the Act. A linguistic canon of construction reflects the nature or use of language and reasoning generally, and is not specially referable to legislation. The unit of enquiry where a problem of interpretation arises is a legislative statement or *enactment* whose legal meaning in relation to a particular factual situation falls to be determined. The sole purpose of an enactment is to achieve a particular legal effect. The enactment lays down a legal rule in terms showing that the rule is triggered by the existence of certain facts. The enactment indicates these facts in outline form (the factual outline). All sets of facts that fall within the outline activate the legal thrust of the enactment. Problems of statutory interpretation concern either the exact nature of the factual outline, or the exact nature of the legal thrust, or both.

The interpreter's duty is to arrive at the *legal* meaning of the enactment, which is not necessarily the same as its grammatical (or literal) meaning. This must be arrived at in accordance with the rules, principles, presumptions and canons mentioned above, which are in this book referred to as the interpretative criteria or guides to legislative intention. By applying the relevant interpretative criteria to the facts of the instant case, certain interpretative factors will emerge. These may pull different ways. For example, the desirability of applying the clear grammatical meaning of the enactment under enquiry may conflict with the fact that in the instant case this would not remedy the mischief that Parliament clearly intended to deal with. In such cases a balancing operation is called for.

There are no fixed priorities as between various factors, since much depends on the wording of the enactment and the particular facts of the case under consideration. For example, in some cases the adverse consequences of a particular construction may be very likely to arise whereas in others they may be unlikely. They may be very grave, or comparatively minor. It is for the court, assisted by the advocates on either side, to identify the relevant interpretative factors correctly and exhaustively, and then carry out any necessary balancing exercise to determine which of the opposing constructions put forward correctly embodies the legal meaning of the enactment. The technique required for this takes the interpreter to the heart of our legal system.

Processing of legislative texts

As a consequence of the predominantly *literal* treatment of statutory texts on the British model, it is possible to regard them as parts of a whole. They are not drafted or arranged that way, but conceptually that is how they can and should be treated. This falls within the realm of *processing*. For reasons partly historical and partly due to the way the drafter carries out his task, legislative texts cannot be understood as they stand. Not even the experienced practitioner can comprehend the texts without help. For the citizen they are a closed book.

Part III begins by analysing the difficulties of the statute user in seeking to apply the basic text. Chapter 13 gives a concise account of these, and may be referred to as a handy summary. The difficulties can be reduced to four heads.

Text-collation is necessitated by the fact that the law on a particular topic is likely to be contained in a number of different sources. *Text-comprehension* concerns the difficulty of understanding the peculiar prose of the legislative drafter. *Doubt-resolving* refers to the fact that statute drafting necessarily produces areas of uncertainty, deriving from the deliberate adoption of techniques for shortening the text, from deliberate uncertainty, the passage of time, or from error. Finally there is the problem of *differential readings*. Different minds reach different views, though each regards the meaning as plain.

Methods of processing

Having described the problems experienced in understanding and applying the basic texts, we pass to the methods which are or could be employed to help. A description of the methods now employed can assist current users. A description of possible improvements may aid reform.

The term processing is used in this book as a blanket expression to mean treatment of the basic text in ways which elucidate its meaning and effect. We take the text as given. We are only incidentally concerned with improving the original production of legislative texts, which is another subject. It is necessary to distinguish two kinds of processing. One provides assistance without affecting meaning, and may be called *static processing*. The other develops meaning by resolving doubts authoritatively, and may be called *dynamic processing*.

Part IV describes the various techniques involved in each kind of processing. While static processing is an indispensable aid, dynamic processing is of greater theoretical interest.

Dynamic processing

Because the legislator cannot as a practical matter impose his will down to the last detail, it is necessary to interpose official functionaries who will do this in particular cases. These may be either administrative or judicial. The result of their work, provided it is made public, is to elucidate the texts for the future. Part IV describes how this is done. Government officials, charged with administering regulatory Acts, settle by the exercise of their judgment in particular cases how the texts are to operate. Decisions are promulgated. Circulars, leaflets and other guides are issued. In practice these are authoritative, though occasionally they are upset on appeal to the courts.

An unofficial form of processing is carried out by academic and professional commentators, whose views have an important influence in determining how the law actually operates. Judges in particular are guided by their opinions.

Judicial processing is the most important. Doubt-resolving is carried out by the courts at the instance of individual litigants. Where there are differential readings, the highest court to which the matter is taken has the final say. The opinions of judges on legislative intent carry great weight in problems of text-comprehension. Yet the dynamic function of the courts has been obscured by judicial reluctance to recognise this aspect of their role.

The obvious function of the court is to decide the dispute before it. The fact that the decision may illuminate for future litigants and others the meaning of the statutory text in question is irrelevant to this function. But it is vital to statute processing. That courts should more openly accept and act upon this truth is advocated. So is a more refined approach to statutory interpretation. By recognising that doubt may arise through the adoption by the drafter of any one of a number of specific techniques, the court could perform its task of interpretation more efficiently. In other cases, the court would be aided by acknowledging that it was perfecting a text vitiated by a particular type of error. Adoption of these judicial practices may need authorisation from Parliament. The draft of a Bill for this purpose is included.

Static processing

This may be official or unofficial, and includes publication of indexes, textbooks and other aids. It also includes *text manipulation*, by which the legislative text, without being essentially altered, is processed to make it more readily available and comprehensible. The computer has an important part to play here.

The book ends by describing in detail a novel form of text manipulation known as *composite restatement*. This is akin to consolidation, but is more sophisticated. It takes the relevant texts on a topic (whether derived from Acts or statutory instruments) and presents them in a rearranged coherent structure, to which annotations can be added. Typographical devices aid comprehension. This system, which has already been successfully employed by the author, has the advantage of using the official text (rather than a summary, as in the normal textbook). At the same time problems of text-collation and text-comprehension are eased.

Conclusion

Our system of statute law has grown up piecemeal and it would be useful now to stand back and regard it afresh. It is a basic element in the social and economic regulation of a modern state, performing functions undreamt of by early legislators. Its techniques need to be re-examined in this light, and made more scientific.

As Sir Rupert Cross pointed out just before his lamented death, academic analysis and synthesis are required here. It is satisfactory that since the first edition of this book appeared in 1980 academics have increasingly come to recognise this, and to direct their attention accordingly.

Part I

Statutory Texts

Chapter One

What Statute Law is

Not inappropriately, we meet at the outset a term with a core of firm meaning and a penumbra of uncertainty. We are concerned mainly however with the core meaning of the term statute law, that is the primary legislation of a parliament or other legislature together with subordinate legislative instruments made under powers delegated by the primary legislation. In Britain, until the coming into operation of the European Communities Act 1972 (and ignoring the complications of Northern Ireland), this broadly meant Acts of the Westminster Parliament and statutory instruments as defined by the Statutory Instruments Act 1946. Our discussion, though mostly conducted in relation to these Acts and instruments, will be applicable generally to other instances of statute law in Britain and the remainder of the Commonwealth. We shall need to take account however of special factors arising in connection with the European Communities and other federal or quasi-federal systems.

The statute law of a modern legislature on the British model displays certain key features. It is largely promoted and wholly administered by the government (or executive), enacted by a parliament broadly supporting the government (senatorial quirks of an upper house being set aside), and interpreted by, and enforced on the orders of, an independent judiciary. The judiciary however lacks any *general* interpretative power. Statute law, piecemeal rather than systematic, is produced over the years in response to needs as they arise in society. It is inert, tending to remain stranded after the needs have passed or changed. Parliament, too congested with business to keep its legislation updated, is forced to rely on law reform agencies. These however are not organised and financed on a scale sufficient for the task.

Statute law is universally binding (subject only to the doctrine of *ultra vires* in the case of subordinate instruments). Nevertheless it is not self-operative but, if it is to be effective, needs to be continuously applied and enforced. It is not however subject to any doctrine of desuetude. Deductive in character (whereas case law is inductive), it lays down general rules for application to particular facts. In this it suffers acutely from the drawbacks of language as a medium of precise communication. Here we come to the nub.

Modern statute law consists of a set of written texts which (in themselves) are difficult to understand if you are a lawyer and impossible if you are not. Yet misapprehension will not avail as a shield: *ignorantia juris non excusat.*

It is strange that free societies should thus arrive at a situation where their members are governed from cradle to grave by texts they cannot comprehend. The democratic origins are impeccable; the result far from satisfactory. While minor improvements in the basic texts are always possible, the real answer to this problem lies in adequate processing.

Categories of law

There are many ways of dividing up the Acts on the statute book. One is to sort them into groups according to subject-matter. This is done by the official publication *Statutes in Force* and the private compilation *Halsbury's Statutes* (published by Butterworths). It is significant that there are wide differences between the two editions over the titling of the groups. As the government-appointed Renton Committee found, it is a major problem to settle a generally acceptable division of the corpus of the statute law into subjects (Renton 1975, para 14.7). For this reason (among others) they rejected the idea that Britain, like other Commonwealth countries, should have a statute book on a one Act-one subject basis arranged under titles (Renton 1975, para 20.2(47)). This denied the strong preference shown in a survey of users' wishes (Statute Law Society 1970, para 68).

In evidence to the Renton Committee I had argued strongly for a statute book divided under titles, with one Act for each title. I suggested that there might be 300 to 400 Acts, each with a convenient scope and title, adding:

This is meant to amount to what the 1835 Statute Law Commissioners referred to as Acts 'framed as part of a system', to which the Select Committee of 1875 added the proposition that it should involve a 'proper classification of public statutes'. This was the system adopted in this country for colonies. It has been retained, in much more sophisticated form, by all the independent countries which were formerly British colonies (Bennion 1979(4), p 86).

The Renton Committee were not moved by this argument. Yet they found words of praise for the new official edition *Statutes in Force* which, as stated above, is arranged under titles (Renton 1975, para 20.2(88)).

There is a great difference between printing a number of separate Acts in chronological order under one title (as is done in *Statutes in Force*) and drafting an Act as one comprehensive title (on the modern Commonwealth pattern). The 1835 Commissioners complained that the statutes had been 'framed extemporaneously, not as parts of a system, but to answer particular exigencies as they occurred' (Statute Law Society 1974, para 78). The modern practice of repealing some Acts and re-enacting them in consolidated form meets only very inadequately this ancient criticism.

The Marshall Committee set up by the Statute Law Society graphically remarked in 1974: 'The statute law of the United Kingdom at the present time can be likened to a large number of Gordian knots located in an Augean stables situated at the centre of a labyrinth'. They advocated as a first step that all concerned in the legislative process should adopt a fresh outlook towards statutes, regarding them not as individual Acts dealing with particular situations but as, potentially, parts of a coherent whole 'which for convenience can be divided up under a number of subject-headings but which are nevertheless interrelated' (Statute Law Society 1974, para 79). A year later the Renton Committee echoed this plea for a fresh outlook when they said that little could be done to improve the quality of legislation 'unless those concerned in the process are willing to modify some of their most cherished habits' (Renton 1975, para 1.10). Yet, as we have seen, the Renton Committee rejected the plea for a statute book arranged systematically under titles. It remains as far from being implemented as ever.

Text creation and validation

This book is written from a drafter's standpoint, but is not primarily concerned with drafting technique or its improvement. It takes the basic texts as given. Nevertheless some knowledge of how the basic texts come into existence is needed if statute processing, and the possibilities of its development, are to be understood. Processing is concerned with curing *incomprehensibility* and elucidating *doubt* as to the meaning of a text—either in general, or in its application to a particular set of facts. The general meaning may be sought by a teacher or student, or by some person involved in changing the law. The particular meaning is needed by a person concerned with the factual situation in question. He may wish to resolve the doubt in his favour (the litigant) or have the duty of deciding between conflicting views (the judge). Whether general or particular meaning is in question, some knowledge of the method by which the text comes into existence is essential.

On the model chiefly taken for this book the basic legislative text gains its validity, under the relevant 'rule of recognition' (Hart 1961, pp 92-6), from enactment by Parliament, from a procedure followed by some other body (eg the Privy Council) or person (eg a Minister of the Crown), or by a combination of the two (eg a ministerial order requiring confirmation by affirmative resolution in Parliament). Whichever the method, validating procedures have to be followed if the text is to be recognised as law. We are not here concerned with difficulties that arise if it appears that these procedures may not have been followed correctly. Such cases are extremely rare and can be studied in specialist textbooks (eg Bennion 1984(1), pp 124–129).

It is necessary to distinguish carefully between the validating procedures and the text creation procedures. Under modern systems a text is first created by a legislative drafter and then put through the validating procedures (in the course of which it may or may not be altered). Since the drafter is a technician and not a legislator, the validating procedures embody the concept of a legislator who consciously approves the text as finally authenticated. This may or may not correspond with fact. Either way, the text is officially taken to represent the *intention* of the legislator.

The typical course of events in legislating can be represented as follows:

POLICY DECISION
|
PREPARATION OF DRAFTING INSTRUCTIONS
|
TEXT CREATION
|
VALIDATION AS LAW

Policy decision   This is the political decision, taken by or on behalf of the government, to initiate the proposed legislation. The reasons for taking such decisions vary widely. The persons involved are politicians and their advising administrators (civil servants). The source of the initiative may lie with the politicians (say a general election pledge), or with the administrators (reform of some area of government for which their department is responsible), or outside the public service altogether (a lobby or vested interest). Sometimes outside interests carry their initiative to the point of persuading a non-government politician to introduce a measure they desire to become law. In such a case the policy decision becomes one of whether the government is to support or resist the measure, or remain neutral. Usually this decision is crucial to the success or failure of the promoters.

Whatever the origin of a government's decision to legislate, the administrative civil servants concerned are active in shaping the policy. When the main outline is settled (with ministerial approval) they call in colleagues from the relevant legal department of the civil service to help in working out how the policy is to be given legal effect, and precisely what modifications of existing law are required.

Preparation of drafting instructions   If an outside drafter is to be used, as is usual with Acts of Parliament (and also with statutory instruments of unusual importance or difficulty), the departmental lawyer will prepare written instructions. These should not contain legislative drafts, but convey in ordinary language the details of the policy and the legal changes required.

Text creation Either an outside drafter or the departmental lawyer, as the case may be, will now create the text which is to form the new law. He may need to hold many discussions, and revise his draft frequently, before he satisfies the politicians, and the other civil servants, who are his clients.

Validation If the legislator is a Parliament, the text will need to go through successive stages, at one or more of which it may be amended. It is of crucial importance whether the practice is for MPs themselves to draft amendments to the Bill or whether (as is the modern British system) the original drafter also drafts the amendments. Only on the latter basis can there be any hope of preserving a coherent structure and internal consistency. Furthermore a government tends to lose control of the policy of a Bill where its officer does not draft the amendments made to it. Each substantive amendment requires stages corresponding to those shown in the diagram. There must be a policy decision on whether to make or allow the amendment, then the working out of policy details and legal repercussions, then the instructing of the drafter, then the drafting of the amendment, and finally its addition to the Bill by consent signified in the required manner.

Validation differs according to whether 'the legislator' is one or more groups of persons or one individual. In the former case it again differs according to whether or not the text is capable of amendment. For our purpose validation can be categorised as follows:

Full parliamentary validation On the British model, the text is presented successively to two Houses of Parliament and is debated and amended in each (the debates being reported). It is then finally validated by the royal assent procedure (or a comparable procedure in the case of a republic).

Parliamentary non-amendable validation The text is presented successively to two Houses of Parliament and may be debated in each but not amended (any debate being reported). If approved by both houses it is validated without further action.

Non-parliamentary group validation The text is presented to a body such as the Privy Council or the former Board of Trade, and may be debated but not amended (any debate *not* being reported). In practice debate does not occur. On approval the text is validated without further action (unless *ultra vires*).

Non-parliamentary individual validation The text is presented to a minister and approved by him. On approval it is validated without further action (again unless *ultra vires*).

In the light of this analysis what are we to make of the usual judicial pronouncement that what matters when doubts arise is 'the intention of the lawgiver' (*Sussex Peerage Claim* (1844) 11 Cl & F 85, 143) or 'the intention of the legislature' (*Warburton v Loveland* (1832) 2 D & Cl (HL) 480, 489)? Who is the lawgiver or legislature? Whose intention really counts? Very little detailed attention has been paid to this question. The tendency is to murmur 'myth' or 'fiction' and hurry past. Thus Dr JA Corry says 'The intention of the legislature is a myth' (Corry 1935, p 205).

Legislation is a process central to democracy. We should not have to resort to fictions to explain it, and this is not in fact necessary. We cannot properly impute to modern judges construing democratic legislation anything but a desire to proceed in strict accordance with reality. What is the reality here?

The duplex approach

I have tried to spell out the essential dichotomy which is relevant whenever doubts as to meaning arise. Broadly it is a dichotomy between the official approach and the political approach. The official approach provides the actual text, based on a thorough working out of policy, a full assessment of the practical considerations and a detailed foresight of consequences. The political approach combines ministerial policy and the views of the nation's representatives in the legislature. The elected politician tells the civil servant what the public will not stand for, and also what the public want. The parliamentarian validates the result or not as (subject to the whipping procedure) he thinks fit.

In construing legislation it is necessary to bear both these aspects constantly in mind and produce a synthesis between them. We have gone beyond the crudities of early Acts and early judicial attitudes. A sophisticated modern society demands a sophisticated approach to its laws. This requires a full awareness of how the validated text comes into existence as law, and a precise weighing of the relevant factors.

This may be called the duplex approach to legislative meaning because it is composed of two parts. It is necessary to bear in mind the text creation process, but also to remember that the drafter is merely a technician. The validating process is usually a genuine one, and not a question merely of administering a rubber stamp. Between the two the answer lies. The drafter is fallible, and invariably inadequate to his imposing task. The legislator is armed with the people's vote and speaks in their name. That Parliament in one sense should err, and bungle its commands, is acceptable (and must be accepted) provided it is recognised that in the other sense Parliament is infallible. It was in the latter sense that Grove J remarked in *Richards* v *McBride* (1881) 8 QBD 119, 122, that we cannot assume a mistake in an Act of Parliament.

Although the duplex approach has not been worked out as such by the courts, it is implicit in many judgments. For example in referring to the provisions of an Interpretation Act, Lord Morris of Borth-y-Gest said 'Prima facie it can be assumed that in the processes which lead to an enactment both draftsman and legislators have such a provision in mind' (*Blue Metal Industries Ltd* v *RW Dilley* [1970] AC 826, 846).

The working out of this dichotomy between text-creation and validation, and the definition of how the duplex approach to legislative meaning operates (or should operate) are principal themes of this book and will be fully explored. But first we consider some further aspects of the question of what statute law is.

Historical

The Chronological Table of the Statutes, a most valuable official work, lists all the public Acts, and says what happened to them in the way of amendment and repeal. It starts with Statutes of the Parliaments of England, beginning with the Statute of Merton (1235). This starting point may cause surprise, because we think of Magna Carta as the earliest statute and that was first promulgated 20 years earlier. The answer is that the Chronological Table records Edward I's confirmation of Magna Carta, dated 1297. It was thought in medieval times that a statute lapsed on the death of the king who made it. If it was to endure, it had to be confirmed by the next king. That no longer applies of course. An Act now remains in force until it is repealed, or (if it is a temporary Act) expires.

The Chronological Table also includes Acts of the Parliaments of Scotland beginning with James I of Scotland (1424), though there were earlier Scottish Acts. Statutes of the Parliaments of Great Britain start in 1707, following the union of England and Scotland. Statutes of the Parliaments of the United Kingdom start in 1801, following the temporary union with Ireland. Acts of the Parliaments of Northern Ireland are not included in the table, but do of course form part of the statute law of the United Kingdom. Stormont, consisting of a Senate and House of Commons, was set up in 1920 and abolished in 1973. Northern Ireland is now regulated by a combination of Westminster Acts and Orders in Council.

Our earliest statutes are not Acts of Parliament at all. They are royal decrees or ordinances or charters (such as Magna Carta). Usually they were drawn up in consultation with the king's principal subjects, the great barons and prelates. The statutes are in Latin for the first two centuries after the Norman Conquest. For the next two centuries they are in Norman French. They are not printed, for printing has not been invented. The labour of copying them by hand keeps the text short.

Ancient statutes, that is those of the period commencing with Magna Carta in 1215 and ending with the death of Edward II in 1327, are known as *vetera statuta* or *antiqua statuta*. They include some which are described as *incerti temporis* (of uncertain date). Acts passed between 1327 and 1483 are known as *nova statuta*.

By the middle of the fourteenth century it is established that the assent of the Commons as well as the assent of the Lords and the king is necessary to the validity of a statute. Editors begin to put together collections of statutes. With the introduction of printing late in the fifteenth century these editions are printed, many of the statutes being translated into English. Often things are included which are not statutes at all, for example bits of lawyers' commonplace books. This is because the editions are working manuals for lawyers. (As to later published editions see chapter 7 below.).

Some of these early statutes remain of everyday interest and concern to us. The law of treason is still centred on the Treason Act 1351. Binding-over in magistrates' courts is done every day under the Justices of the Peace Act 1361. The Forcible Entry Act 1381 was repealed only as recently as 1977.

Categories of Acts

A declaratory Act is presumed not to change the law. A penal Act must be strictly construed. On the latter point Blackstone cites the example of the statute 1 Edw 6 c 12, which enacted that those convicted of stealing 'horses' should not have benefit of clergy. The judges held that this did not apply to him who should steal but one horse (Blackstone 1765, I 63).

While there is little point in dividing up the entire statute book according to subject matter, we can usefully distinguish some further categories in addition to those mentioned above.

Financial Acts   These are subject to a special enactment procedure, which reflects the constitutional principle that grants of supply for public expenditure, and the raising of taxation ('ways and means'), are within the province of the House of Commons alone.

Adoptive Acts   While they have a place on the statute book they do not apply in a particular area or for a particular purpose unless they have been adopted for that area or purpose by some appointed machinery. The Town Police Clauses Act 1847 is one of the category of adoptive Acts known as Clauses Acts. These were a nineteenth-century phenomenon. Parliament does not pass them nowadays. By setting out once and for all common form provisions, Clauses Acts greatly shortened the language needed in individual local or personal Acts. They incidentally produced a useful standardisation in the law.

In the days of the so-called railway mania, when entrepreneurs such as George Hudson were promoting one new company after another, Parliament was asked to pass, by the private Bill procedure, a great many authorising Acts. They were seen to be all on the same lines. So Parliament passed the Railway Clauses Consolidation Act 1845. This contained the common form provisions, and could be incorporated in each special Act promoted by an individual company. The same was true of the Lands Clauses Consolidation Act 1845, and the Companies Clauses Consolidation Acts, and of others—for example the Harbours, Docks and Piers Clauses Act 1847. All these are still on the statute book.

This idea of the adoptive Act had other applications. Local authorities could adopt an Act for their area or not, as they chose. There were the Baths and Washhouses Acts 1846 to 1899—the days before almost every house had its own bathroom and kitchen. There were the Burial Acts 1852 to 1906, and the Public Libraries Acts 1892 to 1919. When the cinema came in, it was left to each locality to decide whether it wanted Sunday cinemas, notwithstanding the Lord's Day Observance Acts. This local option was provided for by the Sunday Entertainments Act 1932. Although Clauses Acts are no longer passed, the adoptive system, which may appply to a part of an Act as well as to a whole Act, is still very much alive today. Thus the Highways Act 1980, provides for the adoption of an advance payments code for private street works (see s 204(2)). A list of adoptive and clauses Acts is given in the official Index to the Statutes (see headings Adoptive Acts and Clauses Acts and Clauses Consolidation Acts).

Acts of indemnity, amnesty or oblivion   These are passed to relieve named individuals or groups from penalties imposed for the transgression of some public law. The statute 12 Car 2 c 11, known as the Act of Oblivion, was passed on the restoration of Charles II in 1660 to give certain persons an indemnity for illegal acts done during 'the late interruption of government'. Modern indemnity Acts have relieved government ministers from inadvertent breaches of law, MPs from sitting and voting while disqualified, servicemen from dubious activities in defence of the realm, and so on. (For an example see the Housing Finance (Special Provisions) Act 1975.)

Validation Acts   These declare some specified action or procedure to have been valid even though it is known or suspected that it was in fact invalid or otherwise legally defective. (For an example see the National Health Service (Invalid Direction) Act 1980, reversing the decision in *R* v *Secretary of State for Social Services, ex parte Lewisham, Lambeth and Southwark London Borough Councils* (1980) *The Times*, 26 February.)

Public and private Acts

Section 3 of the Interpretation Act 1978 tells us that 'Every Act is a public Act to be judicially noticed as such, unless the contrary is expressly provided by the Act'. This seems to be saying something quite straightforward. Every Act is a public Act. Unfortunately it is not true. Every Act is not a public Act. There are public Acts and private Acts, according to the procedure by which they were enacted by Parliament.

A public Act results from a public Bill, ie one introduced by a Member of the House of Commons or the House of Lords. A private Act results from a private Bill, ie one introduced in a quite different way on the petition of its promoter (who may be anyone except a member of the House of Commons or the House of Lords). Brief details of the various types of Bill are given below (for a fuller treatment see Miers and Page 1982, chapter 5).

A public Bill goes through various stages in each House of Parliament, always under the wing of a member of that House. If at any stage no member can be found who is interested, the Bill drops.

A private Bill goes through a different procedure. It must be advertised, and its promoter must satisfy a Parliamentary committee that it deserves to be enacted. It changes the law in a limited way purely for the benefit of its promoter, and Parliament has to make sure no one else will be unfairly prejudiced by it. Usually the promoter appears by counsel, who is a member of the Parliamentary Bar and is instructed by parliamentary agents. This is a vestige of the ancient idea that a Bill is a petition presented to the king in Parliament by his subjects, craving some benefit.

A hybrid Bill is a public Bill which has something of the nature of a private Bill because it affects a particular private interest in a way different from its effect on such private interests generally, for example because it regulates a named industrial or commercial undertaking. Bills of this kind have first to go through a modified form of private Bill procedure so that objections can be heard. (For a judicial reference to this procedure see the remarks of Lord Diplock in *Jones* v *Wrotham Park Settled Estates* [1980] AC 74, 106.)

So why does s 3 of the Interpretation Act say that every Act is a public Act when it is not? The key lies in the phrase 'to be judicially noticed as such'. We get a clue from the sidenote, which refers only to judicial notice. So the section which appears to be so general is in fact concerned with nothing else but the doctrine of judicial notice.

All s 3 means is that no Act, whether public or private, need be proved in court. Unless, that is, the final limb of the section applies, and the Act otherwise provides. To account for this it needs to be explained that private Acts are divided into *local* and *personal* Acts. There are a great many local Acts, usually promoted by local authorities. They regulate matters such as behaviour in public parks or the licensing of coffee bars or massage parlours. They are local and private Acts, but for the purpose of judicial notice only they are by virtue of s 3 of the Interpretation Act 1978 public Acts— because they do not say otherwise.

Personal Acts do say otherwise. They only concern named individuals, for example by regulating their family trusts or estates, or granting them naturalisation, or allowing them to marry within the prohibited degrees of affinity. Here the practice is for the personal Act to declare itself not to be a public Act. Judicial notice is not taken of it. It requires to be proved in court.

The two meanings of 'statute law'

Lord Hailsham of St Marylebone LC pointed out that nine cases out of ten reaching the House of Lords concern statutory interpretation (*Johnson* v *Moreton* [1980] AC 37, 53). A similar proportion no doubt prevails in respect of reported cases generally. This justifies the statement that every lawyer now needs to be a statute lawyer (see Bennion 1982(1) and (2)). What does this involve?

We see that the term 'statute law' really has two meanings. The older and perhaps more established meaning is that statute law is the body of *enacted law* or legislation (as opposed to unwritten law consisting of common law, equity and custom), together with the accompanying body of judicial decisions explanatory of the individual statutes. Statute law in this sense forms a very large proportion of the whole *corpus juris*. It is from that point of view that we have so far discussed it in this chapter. (For a very interesting study of the impact of modern statutes on the society they regulate see Miers and Page 1982, Chapter 8.)

The other meaning of statute law is that it is the body of knowledge or expertise which tells people how to handle the statute law (in the first meaning of the term). This covers the legislative processes, the nature of the various types of enacted law, and the principles governing the interpretation and operation of statutes. It is in this second sense that lawyers of today need to be, or to become, competent and efficient statute lawyers.

Chapter Two

The Drafting of Legislation

As I have said, this book is not primarily concerned with drafting technique. Yet it is difficult to understand an Act without some knowledge of how it comes to be the way it is. The work of the drafter is crucial to statute processing, but is little understood outside the drafting office. It seems necesary to spend a little time on this therefore. I propose here to single out four aspects relevant to our theme: the drafter's function, the drafting office, the controversy over whether civil-law drafting on the continental model is superior to common-law drafting on the English model and the question of standardisation. Later I shall also discuss what I call the drafting *parameters*, the factors behind the special techniques of British drafters.

The drafter's function

By saying in chapter 1 that the drafter is merely a technician, denigration of his function was not intended. When helping to frame the report of the Heap Committee I ventured to write: 'Although, like the plumber or the electrician, the draftsman provides a necessary service for the user, he is not employed, as they are, by the consumer' (Statute Law Society 1970, p 17). I said this to make the point, thereafter spelt out, that the needs of the statute user are in practice subordinated to governmental interests. My reference to the plumber or electrician has at times been misunderstood. For example, the former New Zealand legislative draftsman and anti-positivist, NJ Jamieson wrote that if the drafter of legislation is treated as a plumber or electrician then 'open societies are likely to be doomed' (Jamieson 1976, p 550). He argued that if the drafter is to be considered as a craftsman at all he should be seen as an industrious clockmaker who never makes the same clock twice. In his view the drafter is 'engaged in an infinitely more venturesome and skilful enterprise than the judge who accepts by his own judicial doctrine of Parliamentary sovereignty that he is being at the most taught, and at the least merely told, how to tell the time by it' (*ibid* p 546). He later wrote (*ibid* p 558) that to compare drafting with plumbing 'naturally results in inadvertent clowning more tragic than funny'.

20

Describing the drafter as a technician, I adverted to the skill he must undoubtedly possess. Only because the capacity to acquire the skill is rarer than that needed by an apprentice plumber or electrician can it be inapt to make the comparison. But Jamieson is right to feel uneasy: the legislative drafter's function is basic to democracy. Though merely a technician he should not be an unaware technician. He operates only as a technician, but the democratic process requires that he does so as an ardent democrat. He needs to be fired by a sense of the public importance of his function. The drafter who is a wage-slave, seeing the job as just another well-paid occupation, is a disaster. (See further Bennion 1962, pp 339–346.)

The drafting office

Drafting can be organised in various ways. In early times the judges did it, hence the famous rebuke to counsel by Hengham CJ in 1305: *'Ne glosez point le Statut; nous le savoms meuz de vous, qar nous les feimes'* ('Do not gloss the statute; we understand it better than you do, for we made it', YB 33–35 Edw I (RS) 82, 83). Six hundred years later judges were still making comments in court about their drafting of statutes (now very rare), but the sublime confidence had evaporated. In 1902 Lord Halsbury LC abstained from delivering judgment because the case concerned an Act he had drafted himself. He said: 'I believe the worst person to construe it is the person who is responsible for its drafting' (*Hilder v Dexter* [1902] AC 474, 477). For a rejoinder by the present author see Bennion 1962, p 346. Sir Courtenay Ilbert, a former head of the Parliamentary Counsel Office, also sided with Hengham CJ: '. . . the Parliamentary Counsel can often, from his knowledge of the history and intention of an enactment, give a clue to its true construction' (Ilbert 1901, p 93).

Between 1487 and 1869, when the Parliamentary Counsel Office was established in Whitehall, drafting of Westminster Acts was done either by Chancery barristers or by counsel attached to the government department in question. Lord Thring, who in 1869 became the first to be appointed as Parliamentary Counsel (with one assistant), had drafted Acts of Parliament during his private practice at the Bar till 1861, when he was appointed draftsman to the Home Office (Thring 1902, p 5). The Parliamentary Counsel Office, where all government Bills (except purely Scottish ones) are now drafted, grew in size but very slowly. A third draftsman was added in 1917. It was only in 1930 that the number of counsel was increased to four, when a more formal system became necessary. Up till about 1935 it was the practice to allow unestablished draftsmen in the Office to undertake outside drafting work for a fee. At the same time outside practitioners were also employed to carry out drafting assignments. Currently the Office employs around 20 drafters.

The Parliamentary Counsel Office has raised the technical efficiency of legislative drafting to a standard far superior to that prevailing when it was set up in 1869. A corresponding drawback is thus expressed by Lord Renton: 'But the trouble is that the need to achieve certainty of legal effect causes the brilliant men who have to draft the Bills to resort to skilfully compressed phrases which are nothing like ordinary language' (Renton 1980, p 6). I discuss this question of compression in detail below (chapters 3 and 14) and conclude that it is inescapable and can be dealt with only through subsequent processing by text-manipulation methods such as Composite Restatement (chapter 23).

The Office was set up as the Office of Parliamentary Counsel to the Treasury though the last three words have now been dropped. Although answerable to the Law Officers on technical matters of drafting, it is in practice an adjunct of the Cabinet Office. This is because its primary function is to serve the government of the day, the head of which is still First Lord of the Treasury. The government must get its Bills on time and they must be in a form which will first stand up in Parliament and then stand up in court. This is difficult enough to achieve without worrying too much about users' chronic complaints of obscurity (or such is the Office's traditional attitude). My own view on this is discussed elsewhere (see Bennion 1980(1) and (5)) where I criticise in detail the characteristics identified by Twining and Miers at the end of the following passage

. . . the Parliamentary Counsel Office appears, at least to outsiders, to have developed a rigorous, arcane and somewhat inflexible craft-tradition. They have an enviable reputation for technical proficiency and, in some of their relatively rare public pronouncements, a less enviable reputation for *hubris* (Twining and Miers 1981, p 203; for a choice example of this *hubris* see (1982) *Times Lit Supp* 1009).

Other defects which the heads of the Office have collectively displayed since the death of Sir Granville Ram in 1952 are timidity, reluctance to innovate and lack of leadership. It was regrettable that when the Law Commission was set up in 1965 it was found necessary to include statute law among its functions in addition to the reform of lawyer's law. This betrayed my ideal of the drafter as the keeper of the statute book — an ideal which Ram certainly subscribed to. He established a separate consolidation branch in the Parliamentary Counsel Office and instigated the passing in 1949 of an Act that considerably aided the process of consolidation (see chapter 6). He was a man full of resource who never lost his nerve and was a doughty champion of the Office (Kent 1979, p 73).

Two examples may be given of the reluctance to innovate. In 1974–75, in conjunction with the Central Computer Agency I conducted in the Office an experiment in the use of a computer for legislative drafting (see Bennion 1975(4)). This was done in relation to what subsequently became the Children Act 1975 and the Sex Discrimination Act 1975. It was the first time a computer had been used in the drafting of British legislation, but, except for the late Sir Anthony Stainton, my colleagues in the Office displayed little interest.

The other example concerns the Interpretation Act 1978. A disgracefully long period had elapsed since the passing of the previous Act (the Interpretation Act 1889). Much complaint had been expressed over this quite unnecessary delay, which meant that many obsolete provisions continued to encumber the statute book. Other countries had developed this useful tool to a considerable degree. Even Northern Ireland, with exiguous resources, had been able to produce a very sophisticated model (the Interpretation Act (Northern Ireland) 1954 — see Leitch and Donaldson 1955 and Leitch 1965). The adoption of these improvements by the United Kingdom Parliament was confidently looked forward to. The Renton Committee for example, after pointing out that without the 1954 Act subsequent Northern Ireland statutes would, upon a conservative estimate, be one-third larger than they are, called for a comprehensive revised Interpretation Act (Renton 1975, paras 19.4–19.11, 19.31, 19.32). What happened? The 1978 Act, produced under the inspiration (if that is the word) of the Parliamentary Counsel Office, amounted to little more than straight consolidation of existing British enactments.

My own belief is that, while legislative drafting is a difficult art requiring a lengthy apprenticeship, it is not the best arrangement to make it what Sir Noël Hutton has called 'a life engagement' (Hutton 1979, p 253). Most drafters join the Office in their 20s and remain involved in its work until well past the official retirement age. They do little else but drafting. Alec Samuels has commented that under our present system the drafter 'gets further removed from the day-to-day application and use of statutes in legal practice' (Samuels 1974, p 532). For a Canadian view see Bennion 1980(7).

Common-law drafting *v* civil-law drafting

In Canada, where they have a bilingual legal system in English and French, the British style of complex drafting has been dubbed 'common-law drafting'. Professor Clarence Smith of Ottawa University had this to say about its relation to civil-law drafting:

. . . if we take any random example of this drafting of either side we do not seem to be even in the same world. A civil-law draft is likely to be simple and short — a common lawyer is inclined to say disdainfully, conversational — so that at least you think you understand it easily. A common-law draft is likely to be a writhing torrent of convoluted indigestion (Clarence Smith 1972, pp 158–9).

Clarence Smith is not impressed by the argument (to which I

subscribe) that the complications of common-law drafting are justified by its much greater degree of certainty and democratic control. He does however admit the danger that drafting in wide terms may encourage the litigation which detailed precision makes absolutely hopeless (*ibid* p 162; for examples see Bennion (1971(2), pp 140–1).

The theme is taken up by Sir William Dale in a book published in 1977, *Legislative Drafting: A New Approach.* He supports the view that the British should go over to the continental system of drafting. The book, commissioned by the Commonwealth Secretary General to help developing countries draft their laws, compares recent United Kingdom statutes on copyright, divorce, adoption, labour law and other topics with corresponding statutes in France, Sweden and West Germany. Dale holds that a statute should be drafted so that it can be understood by all affected by it. An author should be able to understand a statute on copyright, a family man a statute on family law, a landowner a statute on land law, and so on (Dale 1977, p 331).

This sounds fine until we look more closely. Copyright law applies to every sort of creator or performer, down to the writer of an article in a parish magazine and the man who does lightning sketches on the pier. We are all family men or women and most of us at some time own or rent a dwelling. Thus Dale's thesis really means that statutes should be drafted so that they can be understood by all. Though many people hold this view, and it has the ring of fairness, it could be achieved only by giving to judges and officials a degree of discretion unlikely to be aceptable in a democracy. Even then, the law would not really be 'understood by all'. Only the very broad principles would be understood. Their application to particular cases would depend on how the discretion happened to be exercised. The Code Napoleon enacted the whole law of tort in two sentences:

Any act whatsoever by a man that causes damage to another obliges the person at fault to make good the damage. Everyone is responsible for the damage he causes not only by his act but also by his negligence or imprudence.

It left the aggrieved citizen uninformed as to whether in a particular case he might receive compensation from a tortfeasor, and to what amount (Renton 1980, p 6). Dale quotes approvingly a sample of civil-law drafting from Sweden: 'The performance of a work at a place of business for a comparatively large closed group of people shall be considered a public performance' (Dale 1977, p 2). It would be interesting to hear non-lawyers discussing whether a hotel room hired by a firm for its staff party is a 'place of business' or whether 43 party-goers consisting of the firm's staff with a few relatives and friends is 'a comparatively large closed group'. Only a judge's discretion could give the answer, and in court there could be fevered argument on practically every word of the provision.

What are the essential features of civil-law drafting? Dale's book does not give a clear answer, perhaps because the concept is not as definite as is sometimes thought. One element is the background presence of a general code: 'Codification, willy nilly, involves — nay, is — the continental style' (*ibid* p 334). Such a code is not of course present in British law. Another element, leading from the first, is the tendency to state a principle:

The continental lawmakers, influenced by their heritage of codes, think out their laws in terms of principle, or at least of broad intention, and express the principle or intention in the legislation. This is the primary duty of the legislator — to make his general will clear (*ibid* p 332).

The contrasting English practice was described by Professor Gower in relation to the Companies Act 1948:

One of the reasons for the complication and difficulty of the . . . Act is its lack of completeness. No one by reading it could glean any real understanding of Company Law. Nowhere are the fundamental principles enunciated. Exceptions are laid down to rules which are never stated . . . (Gower 1960).

The truth is that the pragmatic British are chary of statements of principle. They distrust them because they almost invariably have to be qualified by exceptions and conditions to fit them for real life. What is the use of a principle that cannot stand on its own?

In any case, continental drafting is far from consisting entirely of statements of principle. Many of its manifestations are as lengthy and complex as anything issuing from the Parliamentary Counsel Office. Nor are they likely to be as thoroughly thought out and self-consistent. British lawyers are becoming more familiar with the continental style through reading directives and other products of the European Commission (described in chapter 5). This tends to lead to greater respect for our own drafters. The Law Commission found, for example, that a proposed directive on the law relating to commercial agents suffered from the following defects:

(1) It laid down rules without specifying what consequences flowed from their breach.
(2) It used a number of different words to express the same idea.
(3) It used the same word to express a number of different ideas.
(4) It tended to make the same point twice, once positively and once negatively.
(5) Statements of principle were followed by non-exhaustive, ill-chosen and misleading lists of illustrations.
(6) Particular instances were given of a general principle which was nowhere stated.
(7) It used a technique of descriptive drafting which did not exhaust all the possibilities.

The Law Commission felt that these defects and others meant

that the text was badly drafted, unclear, ambiguous and internally inconsistent. Their conclusion was that 'the directive in its present form is quite unworkable' (Law Com No 84, pp 11–12).

Perhaps the most telling argument in favour of common-law drafting is its greater degree of democratic control. In his 1973 study of American malpractices, *How the Government Breaks the Law*, JK Lieberman argued that public bureaucracies were given too much legislative power. This was done by over-use of what in this book we call the broad term (see chapter 16). Lieberman cited phrases like 'immoral behaviour', 'public nuisance' and 'disloyalty to the state' as being particularly corrupting of the public service.

The Australian criminologist John Braithwaite argued that much 'white-collar crime' is caused by people abusing a position of power, and that to reduce opportunities for bribery or other corruption discretion should be confined within narrow limits (Braithwaite 1979, chap 10). Even without contemplating the commission of criminal offences such as bribery (which do nevertheless occur), one can see that to vest decision making in a non-elected judge or official by bestowing wide discretionary powers on him is undemocratic. This is a vice of much human rights legislation.

I suggest that the key to the controversy between upholders of common-law and civil-law drafting is to be found in the following passage from Sir William Dale's book: '. . . one may say on behalf of the draftsmen that, when once one understands a United Kingdom Act, one can usually ascertain the answer to one's question. But what time, toil and trouble may be needed to get to the bottom of the Act!' (Dale 1977, p 82). It is to save such time, toil and trouble that one looks to adequate processing of the legislative text.

Standardisation

Drafting technique, like any other, is always capable of minor improvements here and there. The only improvement of major significance I envisage however is in the use of standardisation. Far too much unnecessary confusion is caused by the tendency of drafters to say the same thing (or virtually the same thing) in different ways. This is no fault of theirs. The drafter of a particular Bill (usually wanted in a hurry) drafts the common type of provision in his own words for the simple reason that standardisation clauses simply do not exist. They ought to be brought into existence and updated as necessary by some body charged with that function. In England it would no doubt be the Law Commission, in default of there being a body whose only task is to look after the statute law. Statute law cannot serve the community effectively if it is no one's job to look after it. For over a century that function has nominally been performed in Britain by the Statute Law Committee, which I once described in a newspaper article (accurately if disrespectfully) as an august body that meets once a year and consists of people whose job it is to do something else. This criticism has recently been supported by Lord Justice Ralph Gibson (see Zellick 1988(2), p 53). In what follows I refer to the body whose function it is to look after statute law (whatever it may be called in a particular country) as the keeper of the statute book.

I suggest then that the keeper of the statute book should produce standardised clauses wherever it is possible to do so. These could either be embodied in the Interpretation Act, to be attracted automatically by use of the term defined, or in the form of model clauses, to be inserted bodily in each Bill making use of them. They would be most effective if they were not simply definitions but were thoroughly worked out and comprehensive statements of the relevant portion of law. On this limited scale codification is practicable. Take as an example the question, so often needing to be determined, of whether a new statutory offence creates absolute liability or requires *mens rea*. There should be model clauses available which set out in a codified form the full consequences of each alternative so that all the drafters of the new offence need do is 'plug in' to one or other model clause. Indeed it might be advantageous to have several alternative clauses available, giving progressively stricter offences.

The scope for comprehensive model clauses in modern legislation is enormous. An Act imposes obligations, which immediately raises questions about the consequences of a breach of the obligation. Is it a criminal offence, and if so of what type? Does it give rise to civil liability, and if so what remedies are available? Can duties imposed on ministers or officials be enforced, and if so how? If the Act sets up a new tribunal to hear complaints of breach of duty what are its powers and procedure? If the duty of policing the Act is given to an inspectorate what are its powers? Can it use force to enter premises? Must information it acquires be kept confidential? And so on. There is no need to work these things out afresh every time a new Act is drafted. Standardisation would save time in drafting and shorten Bills. It would simplify the law and help the citizen to find out what his rights and duties are.

Standardisation is an area where cooperation between Commonwealth countries would be fruitful. Model clauses on topics like strict liability or powers of entry could be drawn up in uniform terms applicable to any common law country.

A Statute Law Institute?

In default of the production of model clauses by an official keeper of the statute book, the job could be done by an unofficial body. Here the history of the American Law Institute is relevant. In 1923 a meeting attended by judges and representatives of the American Bar Association resolved:

That we approve the formation of the American Law Institute, the object of which shall be to promote the clarification and simplification of the law and its better adaptation to social needs, to secure the better administration of justice, and to encourage and carry on scholarly and scientific legal work (Lewis 1945).

The great success of the restatements, codes and model laws produced by the Institute has fully justified this joint initiative by the American bench and bar. A non-official body of this kind has greater freedom than a state organism like our Law Commission, but can possess no less authority. It may prepare codes for enactment by the state, or merely promulgate restatements and model provisions for the service of the profession (including law publishers). Either way lawyers are contributing in a professional way to the efficiency of their operations, rather than depending altogether on the state.

There is today general dissatisfaction with the administration of justice. The feeling of dissatisfaction is not confined to that radical section of the community which would overthrow existing social, economic and political institutions. If it were, we as lawyers could afford to ignore it. But the opinion that the law is unnecessarily uncertain and complex, that many of its rules do not work well in practice, and that its administration often results not in justice, but in injustice, is general among all classes and among persons of widely divergent political and social opinions. It is unnecessary to emphasise here the danger from this general dissatisfaction. It breeds disrespect for the law, and disrespect for law is the cornerstone of revolution . . . (1 *American Law Institute Proceedings* (1923 1).

This might be said in Britain today, as well as having been said in Washington 70 years ago. The professional people whose utterance it was added that they intended to tackle the problem with 'a consciousness of the obligation which *rests upon the profession* to take informed action to better existing conditions' (*ibid*; emphasis added). Why should the legal profession in Britain today feel any less obligated in this respect than did the American legal profession of 70 years ago?

The drafting parameters

The more important statutory texts become law by the method described above as *full parliamentary validation*. The text is prepared by the drafter for consideration by legislators, who may amend it. But it also has to be in a form suitable for subsequent operation as law. The same text must serve two distinct purposes. Each purpose requires the text to possess certain characteristics, sometimes conflicting. These requirements may be called the drafting parameters. They control the form of the text. If they are not known and understood by the reader he can scarcely be expected fully to understand the text. The typical characteristics of the text cannot be recognised and allowed for. Furthermore, text processing and the need for it cannot be grasped, and the development and improvement of processing methods is likely to suffer neglect.

The drafting parameters give rise to the special skills and techniques of the legislative drafter. The parameters operate, with varying degrees of intensity, on every drafting assignment. Some are more important than others.

The parameters can be divided into two groups, broadly corresponding to the two purposes mentioned above. The first group, which may be called *preparational*, is concerned with the procedures which prepare the way for the text to emerge as part of the law. The second group, which may be called *operational*, is concerned with the subsequent working of the text as law. The groups are made up as follows:

Preparational drafting parameters	*Operational drafting parameters*
Procedural legitimacy	Legal effectiveness
Timeliness	Certainty
Comprehensibility	Comprehensibility
Debatability	Legal compatibility
Acceptability	
Brevity	

It will be noticed that comprehensibility appears in both groups. As will appear, it does not operate in quite the same way for each.

Preparational parameters

These govern the drafter's task in preparing successive drafts of the text to satisfy the ministers and officials who are his clients, and subsequently in steering the resulting Bill and any amendments to it through Parliament. In other words, they relate to what happens between the inception of the project and the signifying of assent to the Bill. (By contrast the operational parameters, which the drafter must also bear in mind from the inception of the project, relate to what happens or may happen once the Bill becomes law.)

Procedural legitimacy   As part of his function of drafting the text, the drafter is responsible for ensuring that the text (whether of the Bill itself or amendments to it) complies with the procedural requirements laid down by Parliament. Before the Bill is introduced, the drafter must satisfy the requirements of government procedure for example (in Britain) by submitting the text to the Law Officers (who supervise the drafter) and later to the Legislation Committee of the Cabinet (who under current practice must approve the text before publication). Earlier still, the drafter will have had to obtain approval of his text at each stage from ministers and civil servants in the department promoting the Bill and in other departments affected by it. From the earliest moment in the drafting process there are various procedures which must be complied with.

These procedures have an effect on the text. In the pre-parliamentary stage the drafter may (sometimes against his better judgment) be required to alter his text to meet or forestall objections by ministers and civil servants. After introduction of the Bill further such objections may be raised (particularly in relation to the drafting of proposed amendments), and in addition objections from opposition members and government backbenchers are likely. It seems best in this analysis to separate the effect such objections have on the text from the effect exerted by procedural requirements affecting legitimacy. The former are considered later in discussing the parameter of *acceptability*.

The legitimacy parameter is mainly related to rules of parliamentary procedure. If the drafter omits a step in the pre-parliamentary procedure laid down by the government this will not invalidate his Bill. It may however cause difficulty or delay, and is to be avoided. In this sense therefore it may be said to affect legitimacy. The drafter fails in his job if he does not take all the steps he is expected to take. They involve time and trouble, and may leave him insufficient opportunity to attend adequately to the other parameters.

Parliamentary procedure affects the text in a number of ways. In Britain it entirely governs the form of the Bill and of the accompanying explanatory and financial memorandum. It decrees that the Bill must begin with a long title and be composed of one or more clauses. It allows a preamble and Schedules, but no other type of formulation. It requires amendments to be in a certain form, and lays down the various stages through which the Bill must pass. On financial aspects it requires certain resolutions to be drafted and passed. It governs timetable or guillotine motions and the closure of debate. The drafter must ensure that all these complex rules of order are complied with or he risks involving the government in embarrassment and delay. In extreme cases a defective Bill, amendment or motion may have to be withdrawn.

Timeliness This parameter is mainly constituted by the government's timetable for legislation. At the beginning of each session in Britain (usually in November), the Queen's Speech sets out the principal Bills which the government intend to introduce during the session. It does not specify the order in which they will be introduced, or the projected dates. Behind the scenes however, the Future Legislation Committee of the Cabinet will have laid its plans long before the Queen's Speech is delivered. Modern governments almost invariably find themselves with inadequate parliamentary time for all the measures they wish to see passed into law. This means that departments with Bills in the programme are expected to conform meticulously to the timetable, and the drafter must follow suit. The timetable will allow for the fact that lengthy or contentious Bills must be ready for introduction early in the session, since otherwise they may fail to pass through the necessary stages before the session ends. This raises particular difficulty at the beginning of a new Parliament, especially where there is a change of government. There are few acceptable Bills in the pipeline, yet the new government is anxious to put before Parliament the measures for which the voters are taken to have given it a mandate.

Another case where the drafter finds himself the victim of a tight timetable is the emergency Bill, suddenly required to meet some unforeseen national or international development. On the other hand, an unexpected general election may give the drafter a breathing space since all current Bills fall on a dissolution of Parliament.

The Renton Committee reported that drafters were the first to recognise that time pressures may affect the quality of their output. They quoted Sir Anthony Stainton: 'By the time instructions are received, there may not be much room for the draftsman to take decisions which will make for simplicity or clarity . . . The pressure to get things done is usually great' (Renton 1975, para 8.3). This is strikingly illustrated in a story told by Sir John Fiennes:

There was one occasion, on a Financial Bill, when I sat down on a Sunday at home and rewrote a whole Part of a Finance Bill. It went to the printer on Monday night, and the text was handed in at teatime on Tuesday. The Revenue never saw the final version of that until the Bill was published (Renton 1975, para 7.12).

The drafter is expected to be timely at all stages of the preparation and enactment of a Bill, but the shoe tends to pinch most as the date fixed for publication draws near. As Sir Noël Hutton has said:

Under any system of programming, the date of introduction will eventually become more important than the precise content of the Bill when introduced and the process of drafting will have to be continued after introduction by means of government amendments moved in Parliament. This is not the best method of constructing a Bill, and it adds fuel to the complaint that Parliament is given no sufficient chance to consider the legislation placed before it . . . (Hutton 1967, p 294).

Another aspect of the importance of the date of publication is that once the wording of the Bill is public property it is much more difficult to alter it. Not only does valuable parliamentary time have to be taken in debating amendments, but the constraints of the rules of procedure inhibit the drafter. The Bill is in the possession of Parliament and even though a major change may be required, the drafter will not be able to recast his draft as he could freely do before it had seen the light of day. He must content himself with the minimum of alteration, to the prejudice very often of the finished product. There is moreover the risk that defects in the Bill as published will be damaging to the government.

These factors explain why time pressure is most powerful immediately before introduction of the Bill. In most cases the time allowed is inadequate, and drafting of the Bill perforce continues in Parliament. The majority of amendments made to Bills would have been incorporated in the Bill as first published if sufficient time had been allowed. The remainder are in response to public pressure, and here again sufficient time for their preparation is rarely available.

The drafter will protest at the insufficiency of time allowed him. He will point out that compliance with the drafting parameters requires the necessary time, or the product will suffer. He will be heard, but it will make little difference. In the end he will comply with the government's timetable, doing the best he can. It is what he is paid for. His only consolation may be to reflect on Sir Noël Hutton's remark that time can be the friend of drafters 'for they are always striving after the perfection which . . . is usually in fact unattainable; and the last bell, even if it comes too soon, does at least release them from that vain endeavour' (Hutton 1961, p 19).

Comprehensibility The government will incur criticism in Parliament if the Bill is not comprehensible to members, and so the drafter strives to make it so. Until recently, Bill drafting in Britain was governed by the 'four corners' doctrine, expressed by Lord Thring as follows: 'It is not fair to a legislative assembly that they should, as a general rule, have to look beyond the four corners of the Bill in order to comprehend its meaning' (Thring 1902, p 8). The Renton Report contains the following passage:

How far Members of Parliament are able to understand the general purpose of many Bills without reference to other documents we could not discover, but one of our witnesses, Mr Francis Bennion, has expressed the view that: 'if Members were asked whether as a contribution to clarity they would be prepared to give up the four corners doctrine, provided adequate alternative means of providing information were designed, my own feeling is that they would readily accept'.

If this is so, it would make it easier to amend existing enactments by the textual amendment method (Renton 1975, para 7.15).

The four corners doctrine required the drafter to make the text of his Bill self-explanatory. An unfortunate consequence was that Bills amending existing legislation were almost invariably expressed in indirect or non-textual form, because textual amendments require accompanying explanatory material in order to be comprehensible. Since the report of the Renton Committee condemning non-textual amendment, and the commencement of publication of the offical revised edition *Statutes in Force* (the method of publication of which necessitates use of the textual amendment system), the four corners doctrine has happily lost much of its effectiveness. We discuss this aspect more fully in chapter 14.

Comprehensibility in its preparational aspect fights with several of the other drafting parameters. This is partly because the composition of the parliamentary audience differs markedly from the general run of statute users. Most statute users are lawyers. Where they are not lawyers they are public officials or members of professions (such as accountants or architects) whose work brings them into frequent contact with enacted law. Most MPs on the other hand are neither lawyers nor familiar with law; they are politicians. The task of making legislative proposals understood by non-lawyer politicians while securing their legal effectiveness is one of the most formidable faced by the parliamentary drafter. When the other parameters are brought into consideration also (as they must be) the drafting problems can become considerable.

Debatability If a Bill is to serve its parliamentary function, it must be so framed as to allow the main points of policy to be debated. If they are buried in confused verbiage, it becomes more difficult for members to perceive what they are and deploy argument. The main policy debate takes place on second reading, where it is conducted on broad principles. This is followed by the committee stage, where a different position arises. Here it is possible to propose textual amendments to the Bill, and debate whether they should be made. The rules of order require these amendments to make grammatical sense, and fit into the structure of the Bill. If the structure is excessively complex, backbench members will have difficulty in achieving this. In evidence to the Select Committee on Procedure, I suggested that a better method would be to allow members to put down simple amendments merely raising the issue of policy. If accepted, these would be followed at the next stage by (undebatable) technical amendments giving effect to them (see Bennion 1978(2)).

It should be added that the debatability parameter sometimes operates the opposite way. A government may wish its Bill to be drawn so as to stifle debate or render amendment difficult. This occurs with highly controversial measures. Even a non-controversial Bill may contain passages which the government prefer to gloss over, for fear of trouble in the House. Parliamentary storms can suddenly spring up over relatively trivial points and the drafter needs to be constantly on guard. One device for restricting amendment is to draw the long title tightly (see p 42).

Debatability also concerns the order of clauses. Normally each clause is debated in the order in which it occurs in the Bill (though a procedural motion may provide otherwise). It is common for more time to be spent on the first few clauses of a controversial Bill than on all the rest put together, particularly where a guillotine motion is put in operation. With a controversial or 'prestige' Bill it may be important to the smooth passage of the Bill, or the kudos accruing to the government from it, to begin with the right topic. In reporting parliamentary proceedings, the media give most prominence to the opening exchanges on a Bill. The parameter of *debatability* is summarised in the following statement by Sir John Fiennes to the Renton Committee (Renton 1975, para 7.9):

One of the jobs of the draftsman is to present changes in the law to Parliament in a debatable form . . . You have to arrange a Bill, be it a new Bill or an amending Bill, in a form in which it is capable of rational debate in the House all through its stages; if possible so that the main debates occur at the right places, mopping up the subsidiary debates which will therefore not occur. If you have the subsidiary debates first they will probably blow up into the main debates, and you will then have the main debates again in their proper places afterwards.

Sir Courtenay Ilbert has written to similar effect (see Ilbert 1901, pp 241-3).

Acceptability   In framing his text, the drafter must do his best to ensure that the wording chosen is acceptable to those involved in the legislative process. Even though the policy of the Bill may be unacceptable to political opponents, the wording must be such as to minimise objection from them.

This factor applies from the start of drafting, when the audience to be satisfied consists of administrators and legal advisers within the sponsoring department. Later, government ministers may be shown the text. Before publication in Britain it has to be approved by the Law Officers and the Legislation Committee of the Cabinet. Then it runs the gauntlet of scrutiny by MPs, political and professional commentators, and by representatives of vested interests. The drafter has to keep a low profile and offer the smallest possible target.

This means that provocative language must as far as possible be avoided. The red-blooded terms of political controversy are toned down. The prose style is flat. This sometimes disappoints MPs who have campaigned for a controversial measure, and would like to see it finally enacted in ringing tones. (Such disappointment was expressed, for example, over the Sex Discrimination Act in 1975.) But it is safer so. Supporters of the Bill will not carry their disappointment into action against it; opponents must not be armed gratuitously.

Also to be reckoned with is the intense conservatism of legislators. Occasionally the drafter has an opportunity to add new meanings, or even new words, to the language. For example I did this with 'custodian' and 'custodianship' in the Children Act 1975. Once I attempted to introduce a shortened spelling of 'programme' elsewhere than in the computer field. However my use of 'program' to describe a plan of official action was rejected by the Lord Chancellor in Legislation Committee. Typically, there was no attempt at reasoned argument or discussion. On another occasion I ran into trouble by

laying down a test of whether the landlord had 'tried his best' to
let office property. This seemed better modern style than the well-
worn phrase 'used his best endeavours'. The meaning is exactly
the same, and greater precision is not attainable. In the House of
Commons Gordon Oakes described the phrase as 'amateurish', while
Denis Howell thought it a 'headmaster's phrase' and demanded that
'better phraseology' be provided in the House of Lords ((1974) 867
HC Deb cols 1545, 1551, 1573; for a comment see Renton 1975,
para 11.3). I stood firm against this, and the phrase remained (see
General Rate Act 1967, s 17A).

A good draft requires consistency of style, which can only be
achieved if it is composed throughout by the same hand. This fact
has led to the development of the current practice under which
not only the Bill itself but virtually all amendments made to it are
drafted by Parliamentary counsel. Modern Parliamentary counsel
fight to uphold this position. Lord Thring, the first head of the
Parliamentary Counsel Office, described how Mr Gladstone
understood and revised every word of a Bill, and even settled the
marginal notes (Thring 1902, p 6). That does not happen today,
though Lord Duncan-Sandys came near it during his tenure of
ministerial office in the 1950s. If any part of the draft is not acceptable,
the drafter himself alters it. It follows that in self-protection he
will leave himself open to as few demands for change as his experience
and foresight permit.

Brevity For 100 years or more—in fact since British MPs adopted
the practice of close scrutiny and lengthy debate of Bills—drafters
have been encouraged to make their Bills as brief as possible. In
particular, the number of clauses is kept down. This is because
MPs have the right to debate each clause if they wish, preparatory
to the putting of the motion that the clause stand as part of the
Bill.

In general, it must be true that the lengthier a text is, the lengthier
will be the time taken in its detailed examination. Modern
governments always have insufficient parliamentary time at their
disposal (or think they have), so the pressure on the drafter to shorten
his Bill is strong. Nor is this the only factor conducing to brevity.
Given equal quality, it takes more effort to produce a long Bill
than a short one. Drafters are usually hard-pressed, and are not
looking for work. The same applies to those instructing them. Again,
MPs would rather study a brief text than a lengthy one. They are
apt to complain if confronted with too many bulky Bills. Printing
resources are always at full stretch. Each Bill has to be reprinted
several times as it goes through Parliament, so as to incorporate
amendments made. Proof reading (which is done by the drafter
as well as the printer) becomes increasingly onerous with bulk.

All these factors conduce to brevity and that requires (or is thought

to require) compression of language. This is one of the principal
sources of obscurity. It particularly applies where the statutory
language has to be understood by lay people, such as juries. The
difficulties over certain provisions of the Theft Act 1968, are a case
in point. If drafters of criminal statutes did not feel compelled to
cram a wide variety of factual situations within one formula, but
were free to create separate offences for each type of situation, there
would be less confusion. We return to this point in chapter 14.

Besides leading to compression of language, the *brevity* parameter
induces the drafter to use the technique of *ellipsis* (discussed at length
in chapter 15). It also requires employment of the *broad term* (see
chapter 16).

Operational parameters

Having completed our consideration of the *preparational* parameters
which govern the drafting of the Bill in relation to what happens
between the inception of the project and the signifying of assent
to the Bill, we turn to the other group of parameters. As stated
above, these *operational* parameters govern the drafting of the Bill
in relation to things which happen or may happen once the Bill
becomes law.

The first group of parameters is thus concerned with the
government's desire to change the law, and Parliament's
consideration of its proposals for doing so. The second is concerned
with the functioning of the new Act as part of the statute book.
The only connection between the two is that everyone involved in
the preparational stage must have regard to how the proposed
measure will work as enacted law. Yet the same text has to serve
both purposes. As the Renton Committee said: 'The draftsman must
therefore carry out his work with one eye to the drafting of proposals
that will commend themselves to the favour of a critical legislature,
and the other to the eventual product as it will appear in the hands
of the user' (Renton 1975, para 7.9). Unfortunately British drafters,
and those influenced by them, have tended to acquire Cyclopean
tendencies. (Cyclops, it will be remembered, belonged to a race
of one-eyed giants who forged thunderbolts for Zeus.)

Legal effectiveness   Whether or not he is otherwise Cyclopean, the
drafter must always put in the forefront of his mind the need for
legal effectiveness. He must ensure, so far as he is able that the
text of his Bill is apt to carry out the intentions of the government
in promoting the legislation. If the resulting Act comes before a
court, the aim is that the court shall interpret it in the desired way.
If possible the court must be left no opportunity or pretext for
deciding it in any other way. Similarly with other functionaries,
such as tribunals or officials, whose duty it may be to apply the
new law. This parameter extends as far as firm government intention

itself extends. That intention cannot extend to unforeseeable contingencies, and even on questions which can be foreseen the government may leave the decision to others, or to itself on a future occasion. The first occurs for example where the Act authorises the making of a judicial order 'if the court thinks just'. The second occurs where a government official is given a discretion. The exercise of either type of delegated power is an example of dynamic processing, examined at length in Part IV.

Crucial to legal effectiveness is the drafter's knowledge and correct use of that part of the *corpus juris* which governs the construction of statutes, namely the Interpretation Act and the technique of interpretation. But he must also know and understand the area of law within which he is operating. (For examples of error in this respect see pp 262–263).

Certainty It is usually (but not invariably) desired that the text should be open to one construction only, that is, that its meaning should be certain. It is arguable that this should be treated as an aspect of the *legal effectiveness* parameter discussed above, but conceptually it is slightly different and so is accorded separate treatment. The justification for this separation is illustrated by the occasional case where the Government *intend* the text to be ambiguous. For example, clauses of international treaties are sometimes deliberately drawn so as to be capable of interpretation in each of the varying ways favoured by the respective high contracting parties. If such a treaty is to be given the effect of law by an Act of Parliament, the drafter of the Act will perceive that legal effectiveness is at odds with certainty and be forced to sacrifice the latter. Intentional uncertainty is discussed in chapter 17.

Comprehensibility Except in the rare case of intentional uncertainty, both legal effectiveness and certainty are aided by *comprehensibility*. We discussed above the problem of making a Bill comprehensible to MPs. They need to see as easily as possible what the proposals will amount to. Most lack legal training so cannot be expected to understand proposals purely framed as legal instruments. Nor can such instruments be understood even by lawyers without reference to other materials. Yet legislators, being hard pressed for time, are reluctant to look at other materials in addition to the Bill they are considering.

It is a paradox, if a necessary one, that the people concerned with approving legislation are mostly ill-equipped by training and experience to understand it. The paradox places the drafter in an impossible position. It is impossible because he just cannot satisfy both audiences. On this dilemma I put forward the following view at the Ottawa Symposium in 1971:

We in England have never been able to get away from the idea that the language which is destined to form part of the law of the land must also be framed so as to be comprehensible and palatable to laymen in Parliament. This is an inherent contradication; indeed an absurdity, from which flow many of our troubles. I would venture to suggest that it should be a prime axiom of legislation that, unless there are overriding reasons to the contrary, language which is destined to form part of the law should be framed solely with that end in view. In other words, it should be worded in the most effective way possible to secure that it fits properly into the structure of the statute book (Bennion 1971(2), p 143).

I am glad to say that the Renton Committee accepted this 'prime axiom' (see Renton 1975, para 10.3).

Although the comprehensibility parameter in its operational aspect requires the Bill to be drafted so that it can be understood when it becomes law, this is often hard to achieve. While legal effectiveness and certainty are aided by comprehensibility the reverse rarely applies. To be sure that an enactment will have the desired effect it is usually necessary to enter into specific detail which is often difficult for the reader to follow. This problem is at the root of the controversy between common-law and civil-law drafting discussed above (pp 23–26). It leads to the need for processing by text manipulation (chapter 23).

Comprehensibility, in both its preparational and operational aspects, involves the drafter in problems for which his training as a lawyer may not have fitted him (and in Britain he receives no other training). The skills of a creative writer are needed, with the ability to overcome so far as practicable the limitations of language as a means of communicating ideas. Communication theory and linguistics are two related studies, while devices such as algorithms and flow-charts can sometimes be usefully employed. Occasionally arithmetic, geometry or algebra may find a place (but is it fair to expect users of Acts of Parliament to understand algebra?—the drafter of para 24 of Sched 6 to the Finance Act 1965 evidently thought so). Since the object of statute law is to communicate Parliament's wishes to those bound by them, the question of comprehensibility is crucial; though it has received little study.

Legal compatibility   The final drafting parameter concerns the way the Bill, after assent, will fit into the *corpus juris*. Here the British drafter possesses a heady power. The sovereignty of Parliament ensures that its latest word overrides all previous enactments and rules of law, apart from the new restrictions under the Treaty of Rome (see chapter 5). There is thus no technical necessity for dovetailing into existing law; overriding is just as effective. In former times this led to each Act being treated as a separate entity. An occasional 'notwithstanding anything in any other Act' or 'all enactments to the contrary shall cease to have effect' was a sufficient (though not strictly necessary) gesture towards the existence of earlier contrary legislation.

Things have improved. Even in Britain, the most backward of major Commonwealth countries in this respect, the drafter acknowledges it as his duty to seek out, and repeal or modify expressly, inconsistent provisions. His task is greatly hampered by the chaotic state of the statute book, the lack of arrangement under titles, and delays in printing updated official texts. Until very recently, British drafters were also hindered by lack of access to computerised research and retrieval systems.

Compatibility includes the element of comity. Subject to changes in linguistic usage, the same thing ought to be said in the same way throughout the statute book. Contrary to most people's belief however, there are no books of precedents in the Parliamentary Counsel Office in Whitehall. Drafters vary in their willingness to spend time hunting for models in earlier legislation. They are discouraged by the knowledge that if they carry out this search it will throw up a variety of examples, not one of which may appear any better than the others. The result is predictable. Inconsistent terminology has produced flaws comparable to those of European directives. The position is particularly bad in the tax field.

While statute law is in such a chaotic state, the parameter of compatibility, though it normally places certain demands on the drafter, can if necessary be largely ignored. It would be otherwise if we had a more orderly system, but there is a strange reluctance even among reformers to press for this. The Renton Committee thought consolidation of the statute book on a one Act–one subject basis not possible (despite the fact that it has been done in all other major Commonwealth countries). 'It is not reasonable' they said, 'to expect the law on a given subject to be set forth completely in a self-contained Act of Parliament . . .' (Renton 1975, para 14.7). In fact it is both reasonable and feasible, provided there is adequate cross-referencing.

Conflicting parameters

It is obvious that situations will frequently arise where not all these nine parameters (one, *comprehensibility*, being found in both groups) can be complied with. *Procedural legitimacy* may conflict with *comprehensibility* or (though rarely) with *timeliness*. *Legal effectiveness* may preclude *brevity* and reduce *acceptability*. Comprehensibility as a preparational parameter may be inconsistent with *legal compatibility*. And so on.

Legal effectiveness conflicts with *comprehensibility* where (as frequently happens) the drafter is uncertain of the precise situations his wording must cover. To be on the safe side he then devises a wide formula, which may lack identifying features. Typically, the drafter has a particular situation in mind but fears to commit himself by describing it. He knows from experience that if he links his wording to this specific situation it may prove too narrow. Similar cases (that he cannot at present think of) will come along, and not be within the words. His provision will then be *narrower than the object* (see p 264 below).

Since the drafting parameters conflict in these ways, it is obvious that there must be an order of priority. The order is fixed by the government rather than Parliament. In practice it is usually fixed by the drafter, acting as the government's servant. From his experience the drafter is able to judge what answers ministers would give if there were time and opportunity to question them on their wishes as to priority.

The three most important parameters are not usually in conflict with each other. They place demands on the text which cannot be gainsaid. Two are preparational: *procedural legitimacy* and *timeliness.* The third, *legal effectiveness,* is operational. In describing these as the chief parameters I am not making a value judgment, but merely seeking to reflect political realities. Many who are not politicians or civil servants will think that for the health of society, other parameters, such as those of *comprehensibility* or *legal compatibility,* should be accorded greater importance. The relationship of these two parameters to the remainder lies at the heart of the problem of statute law obscurity and its solution.

Statutory instruments

As to the application of the parameters to the drafting of statutory instruments see chapter 4 (p 57).

Chapter Three

The Arrangement of an Act of Parliament

No one should expect to understand a provision of any Act of Parliament without thorough knowledge of the *form* of an Act. The long-standing failure to include statute law in their training syllabus has had unfortunate results in the way lawyers (including judges) handle statutes and determine their meaning. Since almost every legal point is now affected by statute law, the need for such training is obvious (it is spelt out in Bennion 1982(1) and (2)). This need was recognised by the Council of Legal Education, who in 1982 introduced for Bar students at the Inns of Court School of Law a preliminary course in statute law (conducted by the present author). As yet the authorities of the solicitors' branch of the profession have not followed suit.

The arrangement of the text of an Act of Parliament reflects its validating procedure. We take as our model current public general Acts (as opposed to local or private Acts) of the United Kingdom Parliament. Acts passed by the parliaments of other Commonwealth countries display similar features. (For a historical survey of the distinction between public general Acts and local or private Acts see Holdsworth 1924 XI, pp 287–303 and 324–364.) To provide concrete examples I use in this discussion and subsequently the Consumer Credit Act 1974, an Act I drafted myself and later expounded in two textbooks (*Consumer Credit Control* (1976 and updating releases) and *The Consumer Credit Act Manual* (3rd edn 1986), both published by Longman).

Preliminary material

Starting at the beginning of an Act, we find the year and chapter number. Thus the Consumer Credit Act is headed '1974 CHAPTER 39'. Acts were formerly regarded as chapters of the part of the statute book passed in a particular parliamentary session (usually running from November to July). Since the enactment of the Acts of Parliament Numbering and Citation Act 1962, chapter numbers have been assigned instead by reference to the calendar year. The first Act to receive royal assent after 31 December is numbered chapter

1, and so on to the end of the year. An Act may be cited either by its year and chapter number or by its short title.

Next comes the *long title*. The drafter is apt to regard the long title of his Bill rather differently from the way a user regards the long title of the subsequent Act (though on royal assent the one becomes the other). The drafter is concerned to comply with parliamentary rules of order under which the long title must be wide enough to embrace the contents of the Bill. At the same time he may be anxious to keep the long title as *narrow* as possible. This is because it is often politically desirable to restrict the range of amendments that can be moved. Under the doctrine of *scope* prevailing in the British House of Commons an amendment is out of order if beyond the scope of the Bill. While the long title does not entirely determine the scope, it influences the judgment of House officials in advising the Speaker on whether proposed amendments are in order.

So for the drafter the long title is a procedural device. For the practitioner, who knows little if anything of parliamentary procedure, the long title is what it appears to be: a description of the Act's contents and an aid to its construction. The dangers of one party not bearing the other's viewpoint in mind are obvious. For example the inexpert may go astray if they do not know that parliamentary rules require the long title to be amended where the Bill is altered so as to go beyond it.

The long title of the Consumer Credit Act 1974 runs:

An Act to establish for the protection of consumers a new system, administered by the Director General of Fair Trading, of licensing and other control of traders concerned with the provision of credit, or the supply of goods on hire or hire-purchase, and their transactions, in place of the present enactments regulating moneylenders, pawnbrokers and hire-purchase traders and their transactions; and for related matters.

Note at the end the sweeping-up words 'and for related matters'.

The long title of an Act is immediately followed by a date in square brackets. This is the date of passing of the Act, that is the signifying of *royal assent*. In Britain it has not been signified by the Sovereign in person since 1854 (though it has elsewhere in the Commonwealth). The procedure is now governed by the Royal Assent Act 1967, replacing the Royal Assent by Commission Act 1541. The form and manner customary before 1967 is however preserved by the Act (for details see Bennion 1984(1), pp 106–123). Royal assent cures procedural defects. The United Kingdom is not subject to procedural restrictions imposed by a written constitution, breach of which may invalidate legislation (see *Bribery Commission* v *Ranasinghe* [1965] AC 172). This has important consequences, which are not always fully understood by judges interpreting legislation. The Act in the form to which royal assent is signified is in its entirety the product of Parliament. That applies to such matters as headings, marginal notes and punctuation as much as to the substantive text. We return to this point below (p 51).

Next comes the *preamble*, where used. This is often confused with the long title. Even judges are not immune from error. In *Ward v Holman* [1964] 2 QB 580, Lord Parker CJ referred to the long title of an Act as the 'preamble'. Goff LJ did the same thing in *Re Coventry decd* [1980] Ch 461, 484. In fact, however, there is a clear distinction between preamble and long title. The preamble begins 'WHEREAS' and continues with an explanation as to why it is expedient to pass the Bill. It was often used in former times to explain to MPs the reasons and objects of the legislation. Its place is now partly taken by the explanatory memorandum which is affixed to the front of a Bill on introduction. The advantage of this is that it does not form part of the Bill and therefore no possibility can arise of inconsistency between the objects stated in the preamble and the provisions of the Bill.

Modern public Acts usually do without preambles, but they are still obligatory in an Act originating as a private Bill. I last used a preamble when drafting the Performers' Protection Act 1963. It reads:

WHEREAS, with a view to the ratification by Her Majesty of the International Convention for the Protection of Performers, Producers of Phonograms and Broadcasting Organisations entered into at Rome on 26th October 1961, it is expedient to amend and supplement the Dramatic and Musical Performers' Protection Act 1958 (in this Act referred to as 'the principal Act').

Sometimes a preamble consists of more than one paragraph. The preamble to the Parliament Act 1911, contained a second paragraph which still mocks the frailty of human intentions:

AND WHEREAS it is intended to substitute for the House of Lords as it at present exists a Second Chamber constituted on a popular instead of hereditary basis, but such substitution cannot be immediately brought into operation:

Eighty years later, the substitution is no more likely to be 'immediately brought into operation'!

Next the *enacting formula* is set out. In Britain this normally reads:

BE IT ENACTED by the Queen's most Excellent Majesty, by and with the advice and consent of the Lords Spiritual and Temporal, and Commons, in this present Parliament assembled, and by the authority of the same, as follows:

Where a preamble is used these words are preceded by 'Now Therefore'. The formula is different in the case of financial Bills for aids and supplies. These are known as 'Most Gracious Sovereign' Bills from the opening words of the enacting formula. Also different is the enacting formula for Bills passed without the consent of the peers under the Parliament Act 1911 (see s 4 of that Act). Formerly an enacting formula preceded each provision of an Act, but Lord Brougham's Act of 1850 abolished the need for this (see now Interpretation Act 1978, s 1).

Division into sections

The preliminaries over, we come to the body of the Act. This consists of *sections*. The practice of arranging an Act in this way was introduced by Lord Brougham's Act of 1850, which said that every Act containing more than one enactment should be divided up into sections. Where a section contains distinct propositions the modern practice is further to divide it into *subsections*. Every section has a *marginal note* indicating its content, but marginal notes are not affixed to subsections.

Each section should deal with one topic. Sir Courtenay Ilbert advised drafters: 'If the marginal note cannot be made short without being vague, or distinctive without being long, the presumption is that more clauses than one are required' (Ilbert 1901, p 246). An exception arises where for political reasons the number of clauses must be kept down. Only if the Act is later consolidated with others (see chapter 6) will there be an opportunity to divide up the over-long clauses. It is likely not to be taken.

The Consumer Credit Act 1974, contains 193 sections. Since it is a typical modern regulatory Act it is of interest to note its employment of subsections, as follows:

	No of sections
Not divided into subsections	37
Divided into 2 subsections	39
Divided into 3 subsections	27
Divided into 4 subsections	26
Divided into 5 subsections	25
Divided into 6 subsections	15
Divided into 7 subsections	12
Divided into 8 subsections	8
Divided into 9 subsections	3
Divided into 10 subsections	0
Divided into 11 subsections	1

When it is realised that over 80 per cent of the sections are divided into subsections it becomes apparent that the lack of marginal notes to subsections is a serious handicap to comprehension.

Each section or, where there is division into subsections, each subsection, normally consists of one sentence only — however long it may be. Defending this practice before a Select Committee of the House of Commons in 1971, Sir John Fiennes, then head of the Parliamentary Counsel Office, said:

Each subsection must be, up to a point, self-contained, or else the reader must be warned that it is not self-contained. This is a reason why, when you start breaking up the longer sentences, you very often double the overall length, because you have to put into each separate short sentence express words to indicate its link with the rest . . . You cannot have a discursive paragraph of the sort one puts into a letter, where each sentence supports the one before and the one after, and rely on people to read the whole thing and spell the meaning out from the overall effect. (Select Committee 1971, p 201. For my not very successful attempt to counter this see *ibid* pp 224–5.)

The very long sentences of modern British statute law have a history going back to the origins of voluminous parliamentary legislation. Maitland pointed out that the mass of eighteenth century statute law is enormous, and bears 'a wonderfully empirical, partial and minutely particularising character' rarely rising to the dignity of a general proposition. Parliament was endeavouring to govern the nation directly, without the aid of the permanent civil servants of today. Lengthy statutes did much of that work of detail which would now be delegated to ministers and other public authorities. 'Moreover,' adds Maitland, 'extreme and verbose particularity was required in statutes, for judges were loath to admit that the common law was capable of amendment.' Judges sought to protect it 'by a niggardly exposition of every legislating word' (Maitland 1911, p 605). Judges have long since dropped this attitude but the legacy remains: indeed Maitland himself approved of it, criticising the fact that in his own day too many statutes had been passed 'whose brevity was purchased by disgraceful obscurity' (*ibid* p 606).

A legislative sentence can be divided up as indicated by the following simplified example:

Case	— Where a person is in charge of a vehicle
Condition	— if so required by a constable
Subject	— that person
Declaration	— shall produce his licence
Exception	— unless he is exempt from holding a licence

Note that the exception, which may be expressed as a proviso, is really a modification of the Case. The latter could be rewritten: 'Where a person who is not exempt from holding a licence is in charge of a vehicle'. This is all right when the exception can be briefly expressed. In other cases it is better stated separately, either as a proviso (beginning 'Provided that . . . ') or as a separate sub-section. Note also that the Declaration is the only element which is invariably present. It appears by itself in a declaratory provision making clear the existing law (see further p 223 below).

Where the sentence exceeds a certain length the modern practice is to aid comprehension by using indented paragraphing. As a brief example of a section we may take the following from the Consumer Credit Act 1974:

Conduct of business.	**26.** Regulations may be made as to the conduct by a licensee of his business, and may in particular specify —

(a) the books and other records to be kept by him, and

(b) the information to be furnished by him to persons with whom he does business, and the way it is to be furnished.

The reader may wonder why the section does not say by whom the regulations are to be made. The answer is to be found in the *interpretation section* (s 189), which says that 'regulations' means regulations made by the Secretary of State.

Definition sections are very frequent in modern Acts. Apart from explaining the meaning of terms used, they shorten the Act by enabling repetition to be avoided. Sometimes they are inappropriately worded. Amusement was caused by the definition of 'short lease' as meaning 'a lease which is not a long lease' (Income Tax Act 1952, s 172(1)), though the definition was perfectly sensible because 'long lease' was fully defined elsewhere. A choice example is to be found in the Darlington Improvement Act 1872: ' "new building" means any building pulled or burnt down to or within ten feet from the surface of the adjoining ground'. Definitions are either comprehensive (using 'means') or enlarging (using 'includes'). As to the difference see *Earl of Normanton* v *Giles* [1980] 1 WLR 28, 31. Sometimes, on the elephant principle, a well understood term is not defined even where, being a technical term of art, it strictly needs a definition. An example is 'magistrates' court'. It receives a fairly elaborate definition in s 148 of the Magistrates' Courts Act 1980, which is expressed to be for the purposes of that Act only. Nevertheless it is frequently used in other Acts without definition.

Statutory definitions are further discussed below (pp 131–135).

Short and collective titles

A modern Act sets out the short title by which it may be referred to. Where there are two or more Acts with similar short titles the practice is also to bestow a collective title. For example s 5(1) of the Performers' Protection Act 1963 reads: '(1) This Act may be cited as the Performers' Protection Act 1963, and the principal Act and this Act may be cited together as the Performers' Protection Acts 1958 and 1963.' The short title should really be short. The following example from Africa is not recommended: 'This Act may be cited as "The Law for the people who do not pay their taxes before the end of the year for which it (*sic*) is due, 1910" ' (Cited Alison Russell 1938, p 33).

Expenditure clauses

These are required purely for the purposes of House of Commons
procedural rules, but there is nothing on the face of the Act to
indicate this. In the Consumer Credit Act 1974, s 190 is the
expenditure clause. It is too long to reproduce here but its gist
is that there shall be defrayed out of money provided by Parliament
all expenses incurred by Ministers under the Act, and that licensing
fees received by the Director General of Fair Trading shall be paid
into the Consolidated Fund. These are the usual provisions.

An expenditure clause is only needed where the Bill is introduced
in the House of Commons. The clause is printed in italics to indicate
that notionally the Bill contains no expenditure provisions (the
italicised words being treated as not present). The Bill can therefore
proceed to second reading without infringing the House rule that
financial supply can be debated only in committee. An expenditure
clause should not be included in a Bill introduced in the Lords,
though sometimes this rule is overlooked. It is not even needed
when the Lords Bill reaches the Commons, because so-called
privilege amendments are first made by the Lords.

It follows that an expenditure clause has no legislative effect, and
should not be reproduced when the Act is consolidated. This rule
too is often disregarded (see for example the Wages Councils Act
1979, s 30). The Renton Committee recommended that the practice
of italicising expenditure clauses should be abolished (Renton 1975,
para 18.22). This would require an amendment to House of Commons
practice however, and there would then be no point in having an
expenditure clause anyway. It is not needed to satisfy the procedural
requirement that new heads of public expenditure require legislative
sanction because the general provisions of the Bill do this. The only
possible exception is where there is already power to incur the
expenditure, and the sole purpose of the Bill is to satisfy the
procedural requirement. Apart from declaratory provisions, this is
the one case where an Act of Parliament does not change the law
(Hutton 1961, p 20).

Repeals

Where the Act replaces a number of existing enactments the practice
is to effect the consequential repeals by means of a columnar repeals
Schedule introduced by one of the supplemental sections found at
the end of the Act. If a repeal is important enough to be drawn
to the attention of Parliament the British practice is to effect it
in the body of the Bill by saying that the enactment in question
shall 'cease to have effect' and then insert it also in the repeals
Schedule. This habit of repealing an enactment twice over has led
judges ignorant of statute law into trouble (see *Commissioner of Police
of the Metropolis* v *Simeon* [1982] 3 WLR 289). It can create ambiguity

where the drafter fails to ensure that the effect of the two repeals is identical. For an example see the Criminal Law Act 1977, s 56(2) which, in repealing certain provisions relating to coroners, includes a saving not reproduced in the repeals Schedule to that Act (Sched 13).

This leads us to the rule in *A-G v Lamplough* (1878) 3 Ex D 214, and very deep waters indeed. The principle of textual amendment requires one to be able to treat the amended text as definitive and forget about repealed parts of it. But will *Lamplough* let us do this? The point is dealt with below (p 330).

Extent

Where a British Act contains no extent clause it is taken (unless there is some indication to the contrary) to operate throughout the United Kingdom (ie England, Scotland, Wales and Northern Ireland) but not beyond. It does not therefore extend to the Channel Islands or the Isle of Man, nor to any other British possession. It follows that there is no need to say, as for example s 193(2) of the Consumer Credit Act 1974 does, 'This Act extends to Northern Ireland'. However, by a convention designed to aid the legal officials of that province (who tend to be somewhat fewer in numbers than the workload requires) the words are inserted where appropriate.

Evidence to the Renton Committee complained that the fact that the full extent of an Act may not be specified (because to do so is legally unnecessary) is a source of obscurity. For example, an Act carrying no express statement of its extent may in fact extend only to England and Wales because it consists solely of amendments to Acts which themselves extend only to England and Wales. The Committee recommended that extent clauses should ordinarily be included whether necessary or not (Renton 1975, paras 6.11 and 18.14). Like most Renton recommendations, this has been ignored by the Parliamentary Counsel Office (for Lord Renton's complaints about the ignoring of his Committee's report see Statute Law Society, 1979, pp 2–8). The reason is no doubt that it tends to increase a busy drafter's workload.

Commencement and transitional provisions

Until 1793 the rule was that all Acts passed in a parliamentary session were deemed to have come into force on the first day of the session unless the contrary was stated in a particular Act. Reciting that this retrospectivity produced 'great and manifest injustice', the Acts of Parliament (Commencement) Act 1793 (which is still in force) required the Clerk of the Parliaments to endorse in English on every Act the date of royal assent. As mentioned above (p 42) it is to be placed 'immediately after the title' (nowadays usually called the long title) and is to be the date of commencement 'where no other commencement shall be therein provided' (see now Interpretation Act 1978, s 4).

Frequently nowadays another commencement *is* therein provided, either by specifying a date or dates or giving a minister power to make one or more commencement orders. It is felt that people should if possible be given time to prepare for the coming into force of an enactment which affects their conduct and affairs. Furthermore modern regulatory Acts require time for the erection of necessary administrative machinery. Often they are skeleton structures, requiring to be fleshed out by ministerial regulations and orders. It is the wise modern practice to conduct extensive consultations with the trade and other interests concerned before making these. All this induces delay, as the example of the Consumer Credit Act 1974 illustrates. Section 192(2) of the Act provided for the making of commencement orders bringing the operative provisions of the Act into force. The complication of the position is indicated by the fact that in my book *Consumer Credit Control* a table included as an outline guide to the commencement situation of the various provisions of the Act occupies no less than 11 pages. The final commencement order was made only in 1989, 15 years after the Act was passed!

Complaints are frequently made about the difficulty caused to practitioners by complications over the commencement of statutory provisions. One difficulty is the tracking down of commencement orders. Her Majesty's Stationery Office now publishes these in a separate series with its own numbering (preceded by the letter C), but they are often complicated by the inclusion of transitional provisions. It may be necessary, both in the Act itself and in commencement orders, to include detailed directions bridging the transition between the periods before a provision first becomes operative and the time when it is fully in force. In an attempt to assist in this problem I devised a special procedure for the Consumer Credit Act 1974. The commencement and transitional provisions are set out in a Schedule (Sched 3), of which the following paragraph is a brief sample:

Credit reference agencies
48.   Sections 157 and 158 do not apply to a request received before the day appointed for the purposes of this paragraph.

Section 192(2) requires every commencement order to include a provision amending Sched 3 so as to insert an express reference to the day appointed. Accordingly this paragraph has been amended to read: 'Sections 157 and 158 do not apply to a request received before 16th May 1977'. Sometimes the position is more complicated than this. A provision may be brought into force on different dates for different purposes, for example. Whatever is done, Sched 3 must be amended accordingly so that it gives a complete picture. The result is that a practitioner who consults an updated reprint of

Sched 3 has no need to bother with the commencement orders. (See further p 328 below.)

Before ending this account of the *sections* of an Act reference should be made to *recitals*. Occasionally these are placed at the beginning of an individual section and serve a purpose similar to that of the preamble to an Act. Modern examples are: Government of India Act 1935, s 47; Public Works Loans Act 1947, ss 3 and 4; Superannuation (Miscellaneous Provisions) Act 1948, s 13. Sometimes a mere subsection has a recital — see Income Tax Act 1952, s 444(3).

Parts and headings

In a major Act the practice is to group sections together to form *Parts*. Thus in the Consumer Credit Act 1974, the 193 sections are distributed among 11 parts each with a descriptive heading. Part III, consisting of 22 sections, is headed 'Licensing of Credit and Hire Businesses'. In his book *Legislative Drafting: A New Approach*, Sir William Dale welcomed the innovation by which in the Consumer Credit Act 1974, there is printed, at the top of the margin on each page, the title of the Part (Dale 1977, p 272). Like the innovative commencement provision it has not since been followed however.

Where an Act is not large enough to justify division into Parts each fasciculus of clauses may for convenience be given a cross-heading. This is also done within Parts. For example in Part III of the Consumer Credit Act 1974, the first six clauses have the cross-heading 'Licensing principles'. As with marginal notes, cross-headings are not subject to amendment in the Westminster Parliament. If any alteration is necessary it is made informally on the advice of the drafter.

Schedules

Finally in this description of how the text of an Act is laid out we come to *Schedules*. It is a common practice to relegate matters of detail to a Schedule placed at the end of the Act. The Schedule is introduced by appropriate words in one of the sections. For example, Sched 1 to the Consumer Credit Act 1974, groups together all the new criminal offences created by the Act. It is introduced by s 167(1), which begins: 'An offence under a provision of this Act specified in column 1 of Schedule 1 is triable in the mode or modes indicated in column 3 . . . '. Normally in British Acts the practice is to qualify every reference such as 'Schedule 1' by adding 'to this Act' or similar words. I find this repetitious and irritating, so the Consumer Credit Act 1974 includes in s 189(7) a general provision making this qualification once and for all. In most Commonwealth countries such a general provision is included in the Interpretation Act (eg Interpretation Act (Northern Ireland) 1954, s 11(6); Interpretation Act 1967–68 (Canada), s 33(2) and (3)). In the new British Interpretation Act, passed in 1978, the opportunity to incorporate this useful feature was neglected.

Schedules are usually equipped with titles in the form of an opening heading. If not tabular in form they normally consist of *paragraphs*. These are like sections in that they may if long be subdivided. The subdivisions are known as *subparagraphs*. Neither paragraphs nor subparagraphs have marginal notes. Like the sections of an Act, the paragraphs of a Schedule may be grouped into Parts or under cross-headings. It is sometimes said that the headings in a Schedule have more authenticity than those between sections because the adducing words bring in the entire Schedule. The sections are 'stood part' of the Bill individually in the form of clauses. The better view is that such distinctions are unsound. The entire Act receives royal assent, and no one outside Parliament has the right to challenge any part of it. Indeed to do so is to contravene a fundamental provision of the Bill of Rights (1688), namely that proceedings in Parliament 'ought not to be impeached or questioned in any court or place' outside it. Sir William Dale says that 'Excessive scheduling is a besetting fault in United Kingdom drafting' (Dale 1977, p 59). The Renton Committee takes the opposite view, endorsing the Law Society's submission that all detailed provisions should be relegated to Schedules (Renton 1975, para 11.25).

A special type of Schedule is that known as a Keeling Schedule, after a Member of Parliament of that name. It was first used in 1938. The purpose is to help MPs understand a Bill which makes textual amendments in an enactment. The Keeling Schedule sets out the wording of the enactment, indicating by bold type the changes proposed. For lengthy examples see Town and Country Planning Act 1947, Sched 11 and Cinematograph Films Act 1948, Sched 2. The words adducing the Schedule say that in accordance with amendments made earlier in the Bill the enactment in question shall have effect as set out in the Keeling Schedule. This has the unfortunate result that a device intended merely for the enlightenment of MPs remains in the Bill as enacted (though in printing the Bill as an Act the passages in bold type are reset in ordinary type). Awkward results have been known to follow. If you further amend the enactment on a later occasion must you also amend the Keeling Schedule? Suppose an error in transcription is made when writing out the Keeling Schedule — which version then constitutes the law? This actually happened with the Cinematograph Films Act 1948. Indeed *two* errors were made, one of which seriously affected the meaning. Further objections to the Keeling Schedule are that it cannot reflect non-textual modifications made by the Bill containing it (eg by s 9(2) and (3) of the Cinematograph Films Act 1948) and that it uselessly clutters up the statute book. The same purpose, without these drawbacks, is served by the textual memorandum (see my evidence on this to the Renton Committee, reprinted in Bennion 1979(4), pp 43–4 and 74–9). The Renton Committee accepted the value of a textual memorandum (Renton 1975, para 20.2(45)).

Punctuation

Finally a word should be said about *punctuation* in Acts. In *Craies on Statute Law* it is said that 'punctuation forms no part of any Act' (Craies 1971, p 198). This cannot be accepted. It was true only of private Acts up to 1960. Modern drafters of public general Acts take great care with punctuation, and it undoubtedly forms part of the Act as inscribed in the royal assent copy and thereafter published by authority (note that the Interpretation Act 1978, s 19 requires citation of one Act by another to be read as referring to it *as printed by authority*).

Nor can the historical justification for the statement in *Craies* (namely that on the Parliament Roll there is no punctuation) be supported, even in the case of older Acts. As Mellinkoff has shown, this is a mere canard: 'English statutes have been punctuated from the earliest days' (Mellinkoff 1963, pp 157–170). Usually worthy of high respect, Lord Reid must be disregarded when he says in *IRC v Hinchy* [1960] AC 748: 'Even if punctuation in more modern Acts can be looked at (which is very doubtful), I do not think one can have any regard to punctuation in older Acts'. I am afraid this is just one more judicial pronouncement based on inadequate knowledge of the nature of Acts of Parliament. The truth is that punctuation in an act should be regarded the way it is in any other text, as an aid to understanding. Drafters are taught that it is bad workmanship to make your meaning depend on a comma or a bracket — or any other punctuation mark. Punctuation is to facilitate comprehension not alter meaning.

For further details as to the arrangement of an Act, and its significance in interpretation, see the discussion of the functional construction rule at pp 119–131 below.

Chapter Four

Statutory Instruments

The last chapter began with the statement that no one should expect to understand a provision of any Act of Parliament without thorough knowledge of the *form* of an Act. In chapter 2 a similar remark was made about the parameters which govern drafting. Now we complete the picture by describing briefly the main type of delegated legislation, the statutory instrument. The object will then be accomplished of giving the reader a sufficient understanding of the nature of the *basic texts,* preparatory to going on to deal with their promulgation, interpretation and processing. The special attributes of European Community texts are described in the next chapter. (For fuller accounts of delegated legislation sees Miers and Page 1982, Chapter 6 and Bennion 1984 (1); pp 131-158.)

What are statutory instruments?

The definition of the term statutory instrument is contained in s 1 of the Statutory Instruments Act 1946. Orders in Council made under statutory authority are automatically comprised in the term, but the inclusion of other instruments depends on the wording of the Act under which they are made.

Pre-1948 empowering Acts

If the empowering Act was passed on or before 31 December 1947, the position largely turns on the Rules Publication Act 1893 (a measure replaced by the Statutory Instruments Act 1946). The 1893 Act was the first to regularise and control the system of delegated legislation in Britain. It coined the phrase 'statutory rules', and defined it to cover delegated legislation made by what it called 'rule-making authorities'. Any document by which such a power is exercised after 31 December 1947 is now known as a statutory instrument, provided it is of a legislative and not an executive character. (For the difficulties involved in drawing this distinction see Bennion 1962, pp 262-269).

Post-1947 empowering Acts

Section 1 (1) of the 1946 Act provides that where by any Act passed after 31 December 1947 a power is conferred on a Minister or government department to make, confirm or approve orders, rules, regulations or other subordinate legislation, and the power is stated by the empowering Act to be 'exercisable by statutory instrument', then any document by which the power is exercised is to be known as a statutory instrument.

Statutory instuments are required by the 1946 Act to be published by Her Majesty's Stationery Office in a numbered series. The numbering begins afresh at the commencement of each calendar year.

The text of a statutory instrument

A statutory instrument is an extension of the Act under which it is made. It is to be construed as one with the Act, and expressions used in it have, unless the contrary intention appears, the same meaning as they bear in the Act (Interpretation Act 1978, s 11).

It is reasonable to ask why, if this is so, the instrument is made separately and not incorporated into the Act. Would it not be more satisfactory to have the material set forth in a single unified text, rather than split between the Act and one or more statutory instruments? The answer is yes, but two points have to be made. First, relevant material may under our system be spread between two or more *Acts*, never mind statutory instruments. Second, there are compelling reasons why it may be necessary to produce statutory instruments separate from the parent Act.

The need for statutory instruments

Statutory instruments enable the final detail of a regulatory scheme to be separated from the main legislation requiring parliamentary scrutiny. Since they do not need to go through the full process of parliamentary validation, statutory instruments provide a quick and flexible method of statutory control. They can be easily altered to meet contingencies. This usually applies whether or not Parliament is in session. In the case of commencement orders the Act, or the part of it in question, can be brought into force at a convenient time when all necessary preparations have been completed. If an instrument proves defective, or a new situation arises, an amending instrument can be rapidly produced.

Parliament retains control of statutory instruments in various ways. At the beginning of each session it appoints (in Britain) a Joint Select Committee to scrutinise all new instruments and report on any which need to be drawn to attention, for example because they

constitute an unusual or unexpected use of the power. The use made
by a minister of such powers is subject to questioning and debate
in Parliament in all cases. Where however a power is of unusual
importance, say because it enables a tax to be imposed or an Act
to be amended, Parliament may word the power so that it requires
a draft of the instrument to be approved by each House before
the instrument can come into force. A less stringent control is to
make the instrument subject to annulment by Parliament. These
methods are respectively known as affirmative resolution procedure
and negative resolution procedure. The former requires the
government whips to keep the House. Under the latter it is the
government's opponents who must persuade sufficient members to
attend the debate and vote in their favour.

The arrangement of a statutory instrument

A statutory instrument may be an Order in Council or other order,
or it may consist of regulations or rules. These are the principal
types, though others are possible (for example a scheme or warrant).
The name depends on the wording of the empowering Act. The
drafter of this will have selected the term which seems most
appropriate, though there are no fixed principles. An Order in
Council can be made only at an actual meeting of the Privy Council
attended by Her Majesty or a Counsellor of State. This procedure
is reserved for statutory instruments which are of constitutional
importance or otherwise deal with matters of weight. The term 'order'
is used for instruments embodying executive acts, such as the
bringing of an Act into operation, the making of an appointment,
or the disapplying of an Act in certain cases. Many orders nevertheless
have legislative effect. The term 'regulations' is generally used for
provisions which have a continuing regulatory effect, but procedural
instructions relating to a court, company or other body are called
'rules'.

In describing the arrangement of a statutory instrument, we first
deal with the introductory matter, and the explanatory notes, which
are common to all types of instrument, and then go on to describe
the body of the instrument.

Introductory matter

Under the heading STATUTORY INSTRUMENTS printed
between parallel lines there appears first the number of the
instrument, then an indication of the subject matter, then the title.
This is followed by the date of making, and any other relevant dates.
Here is an example:

1980 No 54
CONSUMER CREDIT

The Consumer Credit (Advertisements) Regulations 1980

Made	*17th January 1980*
Laid before Parliament	*29th January 1980*
Coming into Operation	*6th October 1980*

After this comes a recital naming the person making the instrument and the powers under which it is made. To safeguard against accidental omission of a relevant power, the recital of powers ends with sweeping up words in an ancient formula. Thus the opening given above continues as follows (after setting out the arrangement of regulations):

The Secretary of State, in exercise of powers conferred on him by sections 44, 151(1) and 182(2) and (3) of the Consumer Credit Act 1974 and of all other powers enabling him in that behalf, hereby makes the following Regulations:—

Then follows the body of the instrument, ending with the signature and description of the minister making it. A government department must not issue a statutory instrument unless the minister responsible for the department has personally approved it, or it conforms to his known views or is of secondary importance. It is a rule of constitutional practice that a minister cannot be expected to give his personal attention to matters of secondary importance arising in the ordinary course of administration (*Local Government Board* v *Arlidge* [1915] AC 120).

Explanatory note

After the conclusion of the instrument there is printed an explanatory note, stated to be 'not part of' the instrument. The practice of including these notes dates from 1943, though it was done in individual cases much earlier. The practice was regularised by the House of Commons in June 1939 by a ruling which stated that the memorandum must represent the facts, must be essentially of an uncontroversial and explanatory nature, and must be not predjudice readers in favour of the instrument.

Body of the instrument

This follows a form very similar to that described in the previous chapter in relation to Acts. There can be the same allocation of subsidiary matter to Schedules, and the same division into Parts. The only significant difference is that instead of being called sections the main divisions are named according to the type of instrument. In an order they are called articles. If the instrument consists of a set of regulations or rules each division is a regulation or rule accordingly. In all cases, subdivisions are called paragraphs. The divisions do not have marginal notes in the same way as Acts. Instead, they have headnotes. By contrast with Acts, formal provisions (such as those giving the title of the instrument or containing definitions) are placed at the beginning.

Prerogative instruments

Instruments made under the Royal prerogative are not within the category of statutory instruments. They are a form of primary legislation, though of little importance now. Usually they take the form of Orders in Council. For an example see the Territorial Waters Order in Council 1964, discussed in *Post Office v Estuary Radio Ltd* [1968] 2 QB 740.

Drafting

In Britain, nearly all statutory instruments and prerogative instruments are drafted by lawyers employed in the government department responsible for the instrument or (where this does not have its own legal branch) in the office of the Treasury Solicitor. Only instruments of exceptional importance or difficulty are drafted in the Parliamentary Counsel Office.

This division of labour constitutes a basic weakness in the system. As we have seen, the parent Act and its statutory instruments form one unit of law. They should hang together coherently and consistently. Yet, the person who drafts the Act normally has nothing to do with the instruments made under it. He is not even called on to advise. Furthermore the instruments are not even drafted in the same office as the Act. The Parliamentary Counsel Office has existed for more than a century and developed its own doctrines and approach. These are not known to the departmental lawyers, who receive no training as drafters. The risks of going astray are obvious. The Canadian draftsman Mel Hoyt agreed that all legislative drafting should be done in one office: see Bennion 1980(7).

Drafting parameters

Since statutory instruments cannot be amended in Parliament, and are rarely debated, the drafting parameters described in chapter 2 have a restricted application. *Debatability* is of little relevance. *Procedural legitimacy* imposes fewer demands, though the new factor of compliance with the *ultra vires* doctrine emerges. Care must be taken to ensure that the terms of the instrument are within the powers conferred by the parent Act (as amplified by the Interpretation Act). *Timeliness* too is less demanding, since the making of subordinate legislation is not constricted by the limits of the parliamentary session. *Acceptability* is not a potent factor. Parliament has already approved the principle of the legislation, and will not scrutinise statutory instruments in detail. The instrument must be acceptable to the Joint Committee however (see p 54). The only relevance of *brevity* lies in the need to avoid unnecessary strain on the resources of the administering department and the outside interests affected.

When it comes to the operational parameters, we see that all these apply to statutory instruments as they apply to Acts. Only the greater ease of amendment when things go wrong makes them less constricting on the drafter of the former.

Chapter Five

Legislation of the European · Communities

Since 1972 there has been added to the basic legislative texts applying in the United Kingdom a further category. In addition to Acts of Parliament and statutory instruments, we now have Community legislation. As respects accessibility and comprehensibility it is a complicating factor of major proportions.

The status of Community legislation

There are two ways of regarding the status of Community legislation in United Kingdom law. One is to treat it as incorporated in that law solely by virtue of s 2(1) of the European Communities Act 1972. The other is to regard it as essentially emanating from an independent source of law having power by treaty to legislate for the United Kingdom. The position is an indeterminate one. Nobody supposes that the political organisation of Europe will remain as it is now. Either Britain is in transition to a European federation (in which legislative powers will be allocated by a new federal constitution) or it is in a temporary alliance. For the practical purpose of considering legislative texts and their processing it seems best to base our approach on the 1972 Act, taking care to respect the political realities so far as relevant.

The 1972 Act

The long title of the European Communities Act 1972 is of studied vagueness: 'to make provision in connection with the enlargement of the European Communities to include the United Kingdom . . .'. Section 1 defines 'the Communities' as meaning the European Economic Community (EEC), the European Coal and Steel Community (ECSC) and the European Atomic Energy Community (Euratom). As subsequently amended, it defines 'the Treaties' as meaning the Treaties establishing these three Communities, together with the 1965 Treaty establishing a single Council and a single Commission for the Communities. Also included in the amended definition are the United Kingdom accession treaties and various ancillary treaties, agreements and protocols, including those providing for the accession of Spain and Portugal in 1985 and the relevant provisions of the single European Act of 1986.

Section 2(1) runs to a mere eight lines. Yet by it was incorporated into our system a vast mass of law estimated to exceed ten million instruments, many unpublished. In determining what these instruments consist of, and the categories into which they are to be divided, it is necessary to study s 2(1) with care. Accordingly its main provisions are given below not as printed in the Act but broken up into clauses in the way used by the Composite Restatement method described in chapter 23.

European Communties Act 1972, section 2(1)

(1) All such rights, powers, liabilities, obligations and restrictions from time to time created or arising by or under the Treaties *and*

(2) all such remedies and procedures from time to time provided for by or under the Treaties

(3) as in accordance with the Treaties are without further enactment to be given legal effect or used in the United Kingdom

(4) shall be recognised and available in law, and be enforced, allowed and followed accordingly.

Even when it is broken up in this way, we are left to struggle with the typical compressed language of common law drafting. In view of the importance of s 2(1) it is worth attempting to decompress it without altering the basic language. The resulting repetitiveness is a small price to pay for greater clarity.

RIGHTS AND POWERS

(i) All such rights and powers from time to time created or arising by or under the Treaties

(ii) as in accordance with the Treaties are without further enactment to be given legal effect in the United Kingdom

(iii) shall be recognised in law, and enforced accordingly.

LIABILITIES, OBLIGATIONS AND RESTRICTIONS

(iv) All such liabilities, obligations and restrictions from time to time created or arising by or under the Treaties

(v) as in accordance with the Treaties are without further enactment to be given legal effect in the United Kingdom

(vi) shall be recognised in law, and enforced accordingly.

REMEDIES

(vii) All such remedies from time to time created by or arising under the Treaties

(viii) as in accordance with the Treaties are without further enactment to be given legal effect in the United Kingdom

(ix)   shall be available in law, and allowed accordingly.

PROCEDURES

(x)   All such procedures from time to time provided for by or under the Treaties

(xi)   as in accordance with the Treaties are without further enactment to be used in the United Kingdom

(xii)   shall be recognised in law, and followed accordingly.

When s 2(1) is broken up in this way we see clearly that it is a strange way of importing foreign instruments into British statute law. Article 189 of the EEC Treaty requires the Council and the Commission to make regulations. It continues: 'A regulation shall have general application. It shall be binding *in its entirety* and directly applicable in all Member States' (emphasis added). But s 2(1) does not say that such regulations shall be part of British law, in their entirety or otherwise. If a regulation creates a right, the right is to be recognised and enforced in the United Kingdom. Similarly if it imposes a liability, or gives a remedy, or lays down a procedure. But is it certain that a regulation must do these things, and only these things? As often happens, decompression of a compressed text reveals that the drafting is misconceived. Section 2(1) is now taken to mean not what it actually says, but what it would mean if worded as follows: 'The Treaties, and all such instruments as are without further enactment to be given under the Treaties the force of law in the United Kingdom, shall have effect as law accordingly.' Lord Denning went to this extent in *Re Westinghouse Uranium Contract* [1978] AC 547, 564 when he said that s 2(1) had the effect of incorporating the Treaties and all provisions made under them 'lock, stock and barrel' into British law. This was in line with his statement in *Application des Gaz* v *Falks Veritas* [1974] Ch 381, 396, that arts 85 and 86 of the EEC Treaty 'are part of our law'. Lord Diplock has also said that art 85 'forms part of the law of England' (*Re Westinghouse Uranium Contract* [1978] AC 547, 636).

There has grown up under the Treaties a body of law usually referred to (together with the Treaties) as Community law. The guardian and enunciator of this law is the Court of Justice set up by the Treaties (referred to in the European Communities Act 1972, as the European Court). Section 3(1) of the Act firmly states that as far as Britain is concerned Community law is to be taken as being whatever the European Court says it is. This is in line with art 164 of the EEC Treaty which, as interpreted by the European Court, places upon that Court the duty of ensuring that, in the interpretation and application of the Treaty, Community law is observed.

The combined effect of ss 2(1) and 3(1) is therefore to make Community law (as expounded by the European Court) part of British law. Moreover Community law overrides inconsistent British law, whether made before or after the accession of the United Kingdom (1 January 1973). Section 2(4) of the Act states that existing and future British enactments are to be construed and have effect subject to Community law. (The problems of interpretation to which this may give rise are discussed in chapter 9.)

It seems right to regard Community law as a type of statute law. Yet not only is it a type new to British jurisprudence, but it falls to be interpreted and applied along different lines. This means that from the point of view of the processing of British-type statute law, a main concern of this book, Community law is irrelevant. The principles of processing applicable to British type law do not apply to Community law, which is a product of Continental jurisprudence. The differences are twofold. First, under the Continental system regard is not paid to the literal meaning of the text if it conflicts with the underlying purpose or intention. Second, the absence of the doctrine of *stare decisis* means that judicial processing (in the sense of filling in and elaborating the textual meaning) does not occur. The court superimposes its view on the text, but that view does not form a binding precedent. It merely serves as guidance.

The concept of processing involves a textual approach to statute law. It is based on the idea that statute users can normally rely on literal meaning, as filled in and elaborated where appropriate by reported decisions and other forms of processing. This approach is not possible with Community law, and yet in Britain we now have a legal regime where the two systems co-exist. In these circumstances we can do little more here than describe what the relevant Community texts are. Their method of publication is described in chapter 7 and their interpretation briefly discussed at the end of chapter 8.

The European texts

The following texts are it seems to be treated as effectively incorporated into the body of United Kingdom statute law. Each type is briefly discussed below.

1   The texts of the Treaties themselves.
2   The texts of *regulations* made under the Treaties by the Council or Commission.
3   The texts of *directives* issued by the Council or Commission.
4   The texts of *decisions* taken by the Council or Commission.

Article 189 of the EEC Treaty also authorises the Council and the Commission to make *recommendations* and deliver *opinions*. Since however it goes on to state that these shall have no binding force they do not form part of the law.

The Treaties

Although the Treaties may be said to form part of the Community law imported into British law, not all their provisions have direct effect. This is because their wording is inapt for this. As Lord Denning has put it, an article of a Treaty can only have direct if it is 'sufficiently clear, precise and unconditional as not to require any further measure of implementation' (*Shields* v *E Coomes (Holdings) Ltd* [1978] 1 WLR 1408, 1414). This is the result of rulings by the European Court which, as stated above, has the final say on these matters.

In applying this principle the European Court has defined the literal meaning of the Treaties to an extent far beyond what an English court would have dreamed of doing. Many articles clearly contemplate, for example, that the rights they require will be conferred only by the detailed legislation of member states. Thus art 119 of the EEC Treaty says: 'Each Member State shall . . . ensure . . . that men and women shall receive equal pay for equal work'. This contemplates the passing of legislation. But the European Court has held, in this and similar cases, that individuals can obtain the right in question from their own courts even where the state has failed to pass the legislation or has framed it inadequately. (See the examples cited by Lord Denning, *ibid.*)

One consequence of this is that the careful provisions of Acts such as the Equal Pay Act 1970 and the Sex Discrimination Act 1975 are disrupted. The jurisdiction of courts and tribunals to entertain cases of sex discrimination must be treated as widened to include situations which art 119 covers but the Acts do not. The remedies provided by the Acts have to be widened to correspond. Unless Parliament steps in to amend the Acts, this widening has to be done by the courts themselves. We have the strange spectacle of English courts deliberately setting out to amend an Act of Parliament!

The direct effect of Treaty provisions means that we have entered a period when British courts, acting under the guidance of the European Court, have the task of converting vague statements into practical law. This is an openly legislative function, going far beyond the usual type of judical processing.

Regulations

A regulation of the Council or the Commission (for the EEC or Euratom) is arranged in the following way. First comes the number (regulations are not given a title), then the date and subject matter. For example:

COUNCIL REGULATION (EEC) NO 222/77
of 13 December 1976
on Community transit

Then follows a preamble, sometimes running to considerable length. This first recites the matters to which the Council or Commission has 'had regard'. It continues with one or more recitals each beginning 'Whereas'. These contain the justification for the regulation.

The body of a regulation consists of *articles*. These are numbered, but have no descriptive sidenote or heading. When sufficiently numerous, they are grouped under *Titles*. These do have headings. The subdivisions of an article are known as *paragraphs*. At the end of the regulation there may be an *annex*.

The numbering system applied to regulations has varied. From 1958 to 1967, regulations were numbered in two separate sequences: one for the EEC and the other for Euratom. From 1968, both types have been numbered in a single sequence. Numbering was continuous throughout the first five years, but from 1963 each sequence has recommenced at No 1 with the beginning of a calendar year.

Directives

Article 189 of the EEC Treaty requires the Council and the Commission to issue directives. It goes on: 'A directive shall be binding, as to the result to be achieved, upon each Member State to which it is addressed, but shall leave to the national authorities the choice of form and methods.' (Similar provision is contained in art 14 of the ECSC Treaty and art 124 of the Euratom Treaty, but in each case the term used is 'recommendation'.) Although it is clear from the wording of the Treaties that directives were not intended to have direct effect as law, that is not how the European Court has construed the Treaty provisions. It has treated directives as directly binding; as Lawrence Collins put it in his excellent book *European Community Law in the United Kingdom*, by a line of reasoning which starts by asking whether there is any reason why they should not be given this effect! (Collins 1980, p 56).

The fact is that the European Court regards it as its duty to build up the force and extent of Community law regardless of the literal meaning of Treaty provisions. The approach is illustrated by the case of *Van Duyn* v *Home Office* (1975) 1 CMLR 1, which concerned a Council directive as to the movement and residence of foreign nationals in member states. Did it confer on individuals rights enforceable in the courts of a member state? The United Kingdom argued that it did not. Since the language of art 189 distinguishes carefully between the effect of regulations and directives, the Council must be taken to rely on that distinction when deciding to issue a directive rather than a regulation. Such Anglo-Saxon reasoning did not appeal to the European Court.

The form of a directive is similar to that of a regulation. There is the same voluminous preamble (that in the Commission directive on elimination of customs duties dated 22 December 1969 for example contained no fewer than 18 recitals), and the nomenclature is similar. An illustration of how unsuitable the drafting can be for direct operation as law was given in chapter 2 (p 25).

There is no separate numbering system for directives. Since 1968 all directives and decisions of the three Communities have been lumped together with recommendations, opinions and financial regulations in a single sequence. The numbers recommence at No 1 at the beginning of the calendar year. The number is preceded by the year and followed by the name of the Community, eg Dir 72/182/Euratom. The pre-1968 system is too complex to be given here.

Decisions

The Treaties contain numerous provisions empowering the Council and the Commission to issue decisions on member states or individuals. By the same dubious reasoning as it has applied to directives, the European Court has enabled such decisions to have direct effect as law. Thus, even though a decision is directed to a member state, individuals can take advantage of it. Since there is no requirement to publish decisions, the consequences for the rule of law are serious.

As with directives, the form of decisions closely follows that of regulations. The policy adopted by the European Court robs these differences in nomenclature of any real meaning.

Statutory instruments implementing Community law

In addition to Community legislation having direct effect, there is in force in Britain a large body of statute law made under s 2(2) of the European Communities Act 1972. This authorises the making of statutory instruments for the purpose of implementing any Community obligations of the United Kingdom. The power does not allow sub-delegation nor does it extend to the imposing of taxation or the making of instruments having retrospective effect. It does not of course permit the overriding of Community law.

Statutory instruments made under s 2(2) are no different in juridical status from statutory instruments made under a provision of any other Act of Parliament. Indeed such other provisions have been frequently used for the same purpose as s 2(2).

Chapter Six

Statute Consolidation and Revision

The British have never adopted for themselves the idea of a scientific statute book, by which I mean one kept up to date and arranged under Titles on a one Act-one subject basis. We have not changed from the system under which Acts are produced as required, with the subject matter of each being determined by the political and administrative convenience of the moment. Yet strangely a far superior system was imposed by Britain on the territories which formed part of the British Empire. The independent countries of the Commonwealth who inherited and developed this system, are the beneficiaries today.

As an example of the Colonial system, we may take the West African colony of the Gold Coast (now Ghana). British rule dated from 1827. The first collected edition of legislative texts was published in one volume in 1860. Thereafter, until British rule ended a century later, no fewer than nine collected and revised editions were promulgated. The practice was to enact in advance of each edition a Revised Edition of the Laws Ordinance. This authorised the editor (usually a retired judge or law officer) to combine texts into unified Titles, omit spent matter, and carry out other improvements. On being approved by the Governor, the new edition became 'the sole and only proper Statute Book'. (For details see Bennion 1962, pp 284–291.)

Instead of this admirable practice, we have had in Britain an erratic system of bringing forward ad hoc consolidation and statute law revision Bills. The subject is complex, and can be dealt with here only in outline. We begin with a brief historical survey.

History of consolidation in Britain

To have a single topic dealt with by numerous texts, passed at different times and not designed to interlock, is a system so obviously inconvenient that we are not surprised to find that constant complaints have been made about it. These date from the beginning of the system. As early as 1549 the House of Commons proposed that the statute laws should be digested into one body under Titles and heads, and put into good Latin. In 1550 Edward VI desired that 'the superfluous and tedious statutes were brought into one sum together, and made plain and short'. Neither of these was done.

One of the earliest consolidation Acts was the Statute of Labourers 1562. Lord Keeper Bacon then drew up a scheme: 'First, where many laws be made for one thing, the same are to be reduced and established into one law, and the former to be abrogated'. It was not adopted. In 1609 James I complained of 'divers cross and cuffing statutes'. The following year a Commission was set up. It made some proposals for repeals and changes, but nothing substantial emerged. Nor did anything happen when in 1616 Bacon, now Attorney–General, made further proposals for improving the statute book.

In the Cromwellian period a committee was appointed to consider how the statutes 'may be reduced into a compendious way and exact method for the more base and clear understanding of the people', but its labours bore little fruit. In 1796 a House of Commons committee presented a report dealing with consolidation and the problem of obsolete statutes. It condemned the practice of legislating in one Act on a variety of subjects, citing as an example 20 Geo 2 c 42. Sections 1, 2 and 4 dealt with the window tax, while s 3 contained a general provision that Acts mentioning England should also extend to Wales and Berwick-on-Tweed. Section 3 remained in force until repealed by the Interpretation Act 1978.

In 1816 both Houses of Parliament passed resolutions that an eminent lawyer with 20 clerks under him be commissioned to make a digest of the statutes, which was declared 'very expedient'. The resolutions were ignored, but from time to time certain topics were consolidated in part, for example anti-slavery law and customs duties. In 1826 Sir Robert Peel presided over the consolidation of criminal statutes of widespread importance, including those relating to malicious damage and larceny.

The modern era began with the appointment of a Royal Commission in 1835. This had the duty of preparing a criminal law consolidation and reporting on how far it might be convenient to consolidate the other branches of law. The Commission sat for 12 years and produced eight reports. Not one Act was passed as a result of its labours. A further Commission was appointed in 1845 but was equally ineffective. The Statute Law Board was briefly set up in 1853. It disagreed, and was abolished. The following year a prestigious Statute Law Commission was established. It presented four reports, the last of which stated that the whole of the existing statute law might be usefully consolidated into three or four hundred statutes. It optimistically added that if 10 or 12 drafters were employed the work could be done in two years. None of the consolidation Bills prepared by this Commission was passed.

Matters then improved. In 1861 seven important criminal law consolidation Bills were passed. In 1868 the present Statute Law Committee, still today responsible for the quality of our statute law, was set up. The following year saw the establishment of the Parliamentary Counsel Office, while in 1875 a Select Committee of the House of Commons recommended that 'the work of consolidation should be carried on upon a regular system, and by skilled hands, acting under the authority of some permanent government force . . . '.

No such government force was forthcoming, but the Statute Law Committee persevered. It worked out a systematic long-term programme of consolidation. In the 30 years from 1870 to 1900, 101 consolidation Bills were prepared, though only 49 became law. This was due to poor liaison with the relevant government departments and lack of parliamentary time. By 1894 the convention had become established that consolidation Bills recommended by the Joint Select Committee of both Houses should pass without debate. The Joint Committee pronounced itself free to make 'such alterations only as are required for uniformity of expression and adaptation to existing law and practice'. This proved too wide for Parliament to accept however, and the pace of consolidation slowed.

The Statute Law Committee lost interest in consolidation, and the initiative passed to those government departments who were concerned to have their legislation consolidated. Between 1900 and 1934 a further 60 consolidation Acts were passed. In 1937 a sub-committee of the Statute Law Committee was appointed to consider 'the priority according to which consolidation should be undertaken'. It compiled a list of 41 subjects, many of which have still not been consolidated. In 1947 Sir Granville Ram procured the setting up of a consolidation department within the Parliamentary Counsel Office. An Act of 1965 passed the function to the Law Commission, where it rests today.

The pace of consolidation altered very little in the 100 years following the report of the 1875 Select Committee. The third edition of *Statutes Revised*, published in 1948, contained only 166 consolidation Acts out of a total of 4,065 Acts (6,549 pages out of 26,089). From 1949 to 1965 the average number of consolidation pages in the annual volume of statutes was 361 (out of 1,204). From 1965 (when the Law Commission assumed its duties) to 1,972 the average was 512 pages (out of 1,927). Thus during the first Law Commission period the consolidation share of total output dropped from 30 per cent to 24 per cent (Bennion 1979(4), p 45). Updating these figures, we find that from 1973 to 1978 the average of consolidation pages annually was 444 out of 1,965 (or 23 per cent). From 1979 to 1981 the annual average rose to 755 out of 2,193 (or 34 per cent). From 1982 to 1986 it was 830 out of 2,476 (or again around 34 per cent). It seems therefore that the Law Commission have settled down to an average of about one-third of consolidation Act pages out of a total of Acts tending to increase year by year.

I sought unsuccessfully to persuade the Renton Committee that

a Statute Law Commission should be set up to act as keeper of
the statute book, with functions including consolidation (Bennion
1979(4), pp 46–51 and 82–96). However, a recent Chairman of The
Law Commission, Lord Justice Gibson, has expressed support for
this idea (Zellick 1988, p 53). For a fuller account of the history
of consolidation see Simon and Webb 1975.

The modern technique of consolidation

Consolidation can be looked on as a form of processing. It takes
the texts of various Acts of Parliament and, without altering the
essential wording, combines them into a coherent whole. But we
do not regard that as processing within our definition of the term.
The consolidation Act is itself a legislative text. It has gone through
the procedures which bestow validation as law. It replaces, in the
corpus juris, the texts it embodies.

Nevertheless, consolidation performs certain functions which we
do ascribe to processing. It materially assists the process of *text-
collation*. A typical consolidation Act may embody the texts of a
dozen or more previous Acts. Under the former British practice
of indirect amendment (which one hopes is now obsolete) these
texts would all have been disparate. That is, no one of them would
have been drafted so as to fit textually with another. In these
circumstances consolidation is a great benefit, even though it tells
only part of the story. Under our system Acts are never consolidated
with statutory instruments.

One of the bugbears of consolidation has lain in the fact that
legislative texts are frequently defective. As we shall see spelt out
in detail in chapter 19, drafters often err. Their errors give rise
to doubt, and in former times it was necessary to 'consolidate the
doubt'. If the consolidating drafter sought to resolve the doubt,
he was liable to be accused by MPs of indulging in 'draftsman's
legislation'. The danger then was that his Bill would not be allowed
to pass without debate, and consequent consumption of government
time.

Sir Granville Ram was the first to do something about this. He
procured the passing of the Consolidation of Enactments (Procedure)
Act 1949, described by its long title as being 'to facilitate the
preparation of Bills for the purpose of consolidating the enactments
relating to any subject'. The Act enables corrections and minor
improvements to be made in existing law, provided the Joint Select
Committee approve them and do not consider them of such
importance that they ought to be separately enacted. The term
'corrections and minor improvements' is defined as:

. . . amendments of which the effect is confined to resolving ambiguities,
removing doubts, bringing obsolete provisions into conformity with modern
practice, or removing unnecessary provisions or anomalies which are not

of substantial importance, and amendments designed to facilitate improvement in the form or manner in which the law is stated . . .

The Law Commission introduced a further refinement to enable consolidation Bills to embody improvements going beyond the scope of what is permitted by the 1949 Act. If in connection with such a Bill they submit a report recommending amendments of the existing law, the Joint Committee consider the report and give their views to Parliament. It is now the practice to include in such a report amendments which could have been made under the 1949 Act, since it is pointless to use both procedures on the same Bill.

Where the amendments required are too substantial even for this Law Commission procedure to be employed, the practice is to set up an ad hoc expert committee. The Highways Act 1959 was produced in this way (the law not having been tidied up since the passing of the Highway Act 1835). The long title describes it as an Act 'to consolidate with amendments certain enactments relating to highways . . . ' In 1980 highway law again fell to be consolidated, but this time it was found sufficient to use the Law Commission procedure. (The Commission's report is set out in Law Com No 100 (Cmnd 7828).)

We see that there are thus four kinds of consolidation Bills:

1 Straight consolidation.
2 Consolidation with amendments under the 1949 Act.
3 Consolidation with Law Commission amendments.
4 Consolidation with amendments proposed by an *ad hoc* committee.

Only the first three types go before the Joint Select Committee of both Houses. The Bill is introduced in the House of Lords, and given a formal second reading. After being reported on by the Joint Committee it proceeds through the normal stages of a Bill in each House. Bills in the first two categories are not subject to amendment. Bills in the fourth category may be introduced in either House, and go through normal procedure. Although there is nothing to prevent members from putting down amendments to Bills in the third and fourth categories, it is expected that they will not use this opportunity to attempt substantial changes in the law. Otherwise the special virtue of a consolidation Bill, namely that it does not take up government time, would be lost. To facilitate this, Bills in the fourth category may be sent first to an *ad hoc* Joint Select Committee. This happened with Bills for the Local Government Act 1933, the Public Health Act 1936, the Customs and Excise Act 1952 and the Highways Act 1959.

Subject matter of consolidation Acts

It might be thought obvious that a consolidation Act should exhaustively set forth a distinct segment of statute law. If we cannot have an orderly statute book under Titles, at least let us have consolidated law on clearly defined topics. This reasoning has not always been followed however. The Housing Act 1957 consolidated the enactments relating to housing, except certain financial ones. These were consolidated separately as the Housing (Financial Provisions) Act 1958. Similarly, the Hire-Purchase Act 1964 consolidated all the hire-purchase law except that relating to advertisements. This was consolidated separately in the Advertisements (Hire-Purchase) Act 1967. In 1979 the enactments relating to customs and excise duties were consolidated. The previous consolidations of these provisions followed the natural course and combined them in one Act (see the Customs Consolidation Act 1876 and the Customs and Excise Act 1952). In 1979 however the provisions were consolidated in no less than seven Acts!

There are two reasons for this apparently wayward behaviour on the part of the authorities; one practical and the other theoretical. The practical reason relates to shortage of manpower. Consolidation Bills are drafted by Parliamentary Counsel on temporary secondment to the Law Commission. In giving oral evidence to the Renton Committee, I was asked what were the principal limitations on consolidation. My reply was:

First of all there is the shortage of draftsmen. Under the system of referential amendment, consolidation of the amended and amending Acts together is often extremely difficult. It requires what in my paper I call conflation, which is a useful word to describe the perplexing mental process of working out the effects of cumulative statutes piled one upon the other. This is what the consolidating draftsman has to do whenever he is faced with a referential amendment of an Act to be consolidated. If he were only concerned with textual amendments, the consolidation could be done by an assistant, I mention that because it does add to the length of time taken for consolidation; although nothing can be done about that in the case of existing Acts. The shortage of draftsmen is quite remarkable. It is highlighted by the fact that the Law Commission in their first annual report, when they were reporting the staff they had in 1965, said that there were four draftsmen on their staff of 35, and they also made the remark that 'in due course it will clearly be necessary to increase their number'. Yet in their latest annual report you find the number of draftsmen is still four, though the total staff has increased to 47. That is why we have no dramatic increase in consolidation. That is the main obstacle. Secondly, and also very important, is the shortage of staff in the Departments who operate the Acts to be consolidated. I had experience of that myself, because I did a housing consolidation which ought to have been before Parliament now, and when the first draft of the Bill, which was about 330 clauses, had been completed, the onus was then on the Department of the Environment to comment on it and say where it did not agree with what they thought the Bill should say. But owing to under-staffing in the legal department of the DOE we had no way at all of making progress, because the staff were tied up with the current Housing Bill, and it meant the consolidation was put aside. I have made a suggestion in my written evidence to deal with that, which is that there could be attached to every major department a legal officer whose sole function it is to deal with statute law consolidation and other matters of that kind (Bennion 1979(4), p 73).

The Renton Committee accepted all except the last item of this evidence (see Renton 1975, paras 14.15 to 14.20). They did not support the idea of having departmental officers with law reform duties.

Shortage of manpower leads to the philosophy that consolidation had better be done piecemeal as opportunity offers. Otherwise it may not get done at all. It is believed, no doubt rightly, that consolidation of even part of a subject does represent some improvement.

The theoretical reason for breaking up consolidation units in the manner used for the customs and excise legislation in 1979 was set out in the Renton Report. The Committee dismissed the plea for consolidation on a one Act-one subject basis put forward by the Statute Law Society and other witnesses. 'The proposal is, in our view, based on the erroneous assumption that every statute can be completely intelligible as an isolated enactment without reference to the provisions of any other statute' (Renton 1975, para 14.7). Their view as to what the proposal was based on was in fact mistaken. No one with any knowledge of the subject would suppose that titles could stand entirely on their own. But they would produce the inestimable advantage of organising each body of law as a coherent whole, with a unified system of internal numbering and cross-reference. Practitioners would know just where to look for what they wanted, as users of that invaluable work *Halsbury's Statutes* quickly learn which title to consult.

The Renton Committee argued that customs and excise enactments should be split up because 'the person who is interested in duties on hydro-carbon oil will not want to pay for, and wade through, an enormous Act containing the whole of the customs and excise legislation . . . What such a person wants is the needle without the haystack' (*ibid*). That is what we all want of course, but we are not always looking for the same needle. The person whose only legislative interest throughout life is in hydro-carbon oil duties is likely to consult a guide put out by his trade association rather than the text of an Act of Parliament.

We may take it that the Hydro-carbon Oil Duties Act 1979, owes to the Renton Committee's philosophy its existence as one of the seven Acts into which the customs and excise legislation was then divided. Yet for the meaning of no less than 16 of the expressions used in that Act, the reader is expressly referred to one or other of the remaining six Acts! So the Renton Committee's mythical needle hunter, who economised by purchasing only the one Act, would find himself cheated. Even though dealing with a non-debatable consolidation Bill, the drafter could not bring himself to incur the repetition needed to make each Act truly independent. He thus neatly proved the Renton Committee wrong — along with every one else who resists the obviously desirable reform of a one Act–one subject statute book.

Recent practice has turned away from the Renton recommendations. For example the 1985 consolidation of the Companies Acts was, following consultation with users, carried out in the form of a single Act of 747 sections and 25 Schedules rather than a number of separate Acts.

By a useful recent reform, consolidation Acts as officially published incorporate a Table of Derivations showing the derivation of each enactment comprised in the consolidation Act. Official annual volumes of Acts also include, for each consolidation Act included in the volume, a Table of Destinations. This operates in the reverse way, listing the enactments consolidated and showing where each is to be found in the consolidation Act.

Preserving integrity

It is important that once the drafter has gone to the trouble of producing a consolidation Act its textual integrity should be preserved. This is done by drafting future amendments, as and when they come to be required, in the form of textual and not indirect amendments. This enables the amended Act to be reprinted as one text.

Unfortunately, British drafters have paid scant respect to the integrity of statutory texts. With remarkable perverseness (since it is obviously untrue), the Renton Committee found that using the textual amendment method would not lengthen the interval between consolidations of a topic such as income tax. They did however add:

Nevertheless, it remains in our view a matter for regret that the integrity of [recent tax consolidations] has not been preserved, as far as possible, by casting subsequent legislation on the subjects with which they deal in the form of textual amendments . . . (Renton 1975, para 17.32).

Statute law revision

The Renton Report states that the still current series of Statute Law Revision Acts began in 1861 (Renton 1975, para 2.11). In fact this is a mistake: the first such Act was 19 and 20 Vict c 64, passed in 1856. It repealed 120 obsolete statutes. The Law Commission, charged by its constituting Act of 1965 with 'the elimination of anomalies, the repeal of obsolete and unnecessary enactments and generally the simplification and modernisation of the law' now superintends the function of preparing these Acts (see Simon and Webb 1975).

Codification

This adds to the stock of legislative texts by converting judge-made law into statute law. Since codification reduces the area of their authority, judges have not unnaturally opposed it. Apart from the successful codifications by Sir Mackenzie Chalmers of rules relating to sale of goods, partnership, bills of exchange and marine insurance, little of note has been achieved in Britain.

Codification is included among the functions conferred on the Law Commission, but it has not yet succeeded in placing a codification Act on the statute book. The Commission began immediately with proposals for codification of the law of contract, intending that the codified rules 'will later take their place in a Commercial Code or, ultimately, in a Code of Obligations' (First Annual Report, para 31). Work was also begun on a codification of the law of landlord and tenant (*ibid*, para 67).

These plans proved too ambitious. Experience in working on the latter code, for example, convinced the Law Commission that 'the task of preparing a complete code of the basic law of landlord and tenant is immense and cannot be completed for a long time unless resources are devoted to it on a scale which is at present impossible' (Law Com no 92, para 2.34). One formidable obstacle to codification is that even if the necessary Bills could be produced, parliamentary time would be difficult to find. The Bills would be fully amendable, and there are few votes in law reform of this kind. Nevertheless the Law Commission set up in 1981 a small group of academics 'to study and draft the principles upon which the General Part of a criminal code should be based' (Law Com No 119, para 2.35). For a discussion of the method which should be used in a codification of criminal law see Bennion 1986(3).

So far as a code does not alter the law, it is clear that it is equivalent to a declaratory Act. There is however lack of agreement on the degree of detail that justifies use of the term codification. Ilbert defined a code as 'an orderly and authoritative statement of the *leading* rules of law on a given subject' (Ilbert 1901, p 128; emphasis added). Chalmers, the leading English codifier, did not apply this restrictive qualification. Acting on the advice of Lord Herschell LC, he drafted the Sale of Goods Act 1893, so as 'to reproduce as exactly as possible the existing law'. In this he followed the principle employed for his highly successful Bills of Exchange Act 1882. Chalmers clearly felt that a code should be a *full* statement of the law, and not depend on extensive litigation to clarify its details. Legislation, as he pointed out, is cheaper than litigation (Chalmers 1894, p viii).

David Dudley Field, founder of the American codification

movement, also favoured a comprehensive code rather than one limited to Ilbert's 'leading rules'. When it was objected that a code would never be truly comprehensive because it could not deal with matters that had not yet come before the courts, Field retorted: 'Because we cannot provide for all cases, should be thought a poor reason for not providing for as many as possible. To render the existing law as accessible, and as intelligible, as we can is a rational object, though we cannot foresee what ought to be the law in cases yet unknown'.

Field went on to specify the true object of a code as being: 'To cast aside known rules which are obsolete, to correct those which are burdensome, or unsuitable to present circumstances, to reject anomalous or ill-considered cases, to bring the different branches into a more perfect order and agreement . . . ' (Field and Bradford 1865, p 110).

This had certainly been Bentham's view. He held that it could not be otherwise than expedient to narrow the occasion for judicial interpretation '. . . by transforming the rule of conduct from Common Law into Statute Law; that is, as I might say, into Law from no-law: to mark out the line of the subject's conduct by visible directions, instead of abandoning him in the wilds of perpetual conjecture' (Bentham 1775, p 104).

A code does not always obviate conjecture. The Bill for the Marine Insurance Act 1906, was vetted by an expert Committee which disagreed on certain points. As Lord Porter later said, these points 'were dealt with in vague terms in the hope that they would work out all right in practice, and in the knowledge that some day the Courts might make them clear' (Porter 1940, p 2).

Mill confirmed that Bentham was insistent that a code should be comprehensive. Bentham, he said:

. . . demonstrated the necessity and practicability of codification, or the conversion of all law into a written and systematically arranged code: not like the Code Napoleon, a code without a single definition, requiring a constant reference to anterior precedent for the meaning of its technical terms; but one containing within itself all that is necessary for its own interpretation . . . (Mills 1838, p 110).

Pace Sir Courtenay Ilbert, the consensus of opinion on both sides of the Atlantic is that a code should be comprehensive, and should modify existing law where thought desirable. The following definition is offered:

A code, as respects a particular area of law, is a comprehensive statute which reproduces systematically, with or without modification, the current principles, rules and other provisions of that area of law, whether they derive from common law, statute, or any other source. (See further Bennion 1986(3).)

The classic statement of how a codified provision should be

interpreted was given by Lord Herschell, the Lord Chancellor to whose reforming zeal the great English codes drafted by Chalmers are mainly due:

I think the proper course is, in the first instance, to examine the language of the statute, and to ask what is its natural meaning, uninfluenced by any considerations derived from the previous state of the law, and not to start with enquiring how the law previously stood, and then, assuming that it was intended to leave it unaltered, to see if the words of the enactment will bear an interpretation in conformity with this view. If . . . treated in this fashion it appears to me that its utility will be almost entirely destroyed and the very object with which it was enacted will be frustrated. The purpose of such a statute surely was that on any point specifically dealt with by it, the law should be ascertained by interpreting the language used instead of, as before, by roaming over a vast number of authorities . . . (*Bank of England* v *Vagliano* [1891] AC 107, 144).

An advantage of codification which is not always appreciated is that it impresses foreign lawyers who are used to codes in their own jurisdiction. The Foreign Judgments (Reciprocal Enforcement) Act 1933, was based on the report of the Greer Committee ((1932) Cmd 4213). This identified as a mischief requiring statutory remedy the fact that foreign courts were reluctant to enforce English judgments because they were not convinced that English courts would enforce foreign judgments. They enforced them under common law rules which, in the words of Lord Diplock, 'foreign courts suspected of being indefinite and discretionary as compared with written law embodied in a code or statute' (*Black-Clawson* v *Papierwerke* [1975] AC 591, 639).

Codification is more practicable on a smaller scale. Where there is need to reform a limited area of law, the opportunity may be taken to codify it at the same time. Having so far failed to realise their more ambitious aims, the Law Commission are proceeding where appropriate in this more modest fashion. Unfortunately they appear to have adopted the Ilbertian view of codification.

When in 1980 the Law Commission reported on reform of the criminal law of attempt, for example, they announced that their proposals, which included a draft Bill, codified this offence (Law Com No 102, p 87). The gist of the offence was however stated in a mere eight lines (see now the Criminal Attempts Act 1981, s 1). While the Law Commission report, which runs to more than 100 pages, deals fully and clearly with the many points that have caused difficulty in this field, the codified provisions in what is now the Act fail to mention most of them. The formulation, in other words, follows the compressed style characteristic of common law drafting (for the drawbacks of this compression see pp 217–223 below). When I ventured to raise this objection with the Commissioner responsible he replied that in the view of the Law Commission a radical change in drafting style could be contemplated only in the context of a complete Criminal Code (for a full account see Bennion 1980(9) and 1981(1); as to the desirability of codification whenever a common law rule is fundamentally altered by statute see Bennion 1980(10)).

Chapter Seven

Official Publication of Statutory Texts

The state has an obvious duty to promulgate its laws. In this chapter we briefly trace the history of this in Britain, and then go on to describe the present system (including that relating to Community law). We are concerned only with the basic texts. Publication of indexes and other aids is part of the story of *processing*, and is dealt with in chapter 23.

Historical

In early times, as we have seen (p 16), there was no official system of publishing Acts of Parliament. Indeed it was not until the close of the Middle Ages that it became possible to distinguish statutes from other forms of law. From the end of the fifteenth century, unofficial printed collections began to appear. As Sir William Holdsworth has said:

Lawyers were dependent for their knowledge of the contents of the Statute Book upon judicial dicta, books of authority and the work of private persons ... In the absence of official publications, the learning of the bar and the enterprise of the law publisher employed upon the Statute Book and the reports, have exercised a very real censorship upon the sources of English law (Holdsworth 1924, II, p 427).

The earliest and most authoritative of the printed texts of public Acts are found in the series known as *Sessional Volumes of Statutes*, which go back to 1483 and were printed until 1793 in Gothic 'black-letter' type. (Since 1940 the volumes have been published by Her Majesty's Stationery Office (HMSO) on an annual basis, rather than one tied to parliamentary sessions.) In 1796 it was ordered that the printed statutes should be distributed throughout the realm as speedily as possible after enactment.

The first official collection of statutes was published by the Record Commission in the early nineteenth century under the title *Statutes of the Realm*. The first edition of *Statutes Revised*, consisting of 18 volumes, was completed in 1885. The second edition was published by instalments between 1888 and 1929. It amounted to 24 volumes. Sir Granville Ram, who superintended the preparation of the third edition, was determined that it should all appear at the same time. He achieved this aim, and the 32 volumes were published together in 1950. They are likely to be the final edition of this particular series.

Statutory instruments   Annual editions of what were then called Statutory Rules and Orders began to be published officially in 1891. Since 1948 these annual editions have continued under the title *Statutory Instruments.* The instruments in force at the end of 1948 were published in a collected edition of 25 volumes under the title *Statutory Rules and Orders and Statutory Instruments Revised to December 31, 1948.*

Present position

Acts of Parliament   As they are passed, these are published singly by HMSO. As mentioned above, the Acts (in the form in which they are passed) are also published in annual volumes.

Where authorised by a 'printing clause' in an Act which has been amended, the Act is thereafter published in the amended form. This may involve constant reprinting (see, eg the House of Commons Disqualification Act 1975, where the printing clause is s 5(2)). Printing clauses are disliked by drafters as they are held to lead to deceptive versions of Acts. The purist prefers his Act to appear as it was when originally enacted. It is contended that a reprint of the Act as amended makes it look as if amendments subsequently made were speaking from the date of first enactment. (In fact this need not be so if suitable annotations are included.) A list of current Acts with printing clauses is given under the entry ACT OF PARLIAMENT in the *Index to the Statutes* (see p 326 below).

Single copies of past Acts, where not available from HMSO, can be obtained from the Record Office, House of Lords. This applies to all Acts passed after 1497. The Acts can also be personally inspected at the Record Office.

A new official collected edition of public Acts, begun in 1972, was completed in 1981. It is called *Statutes in Force.* The Acts are arranged under 131 Titles and printed as currently amended. Each Act forms a separate booklet, a number of detachable booklets being held together in each volume. The plan is that 'heavily-amended' Acts are reprinted in amended form, the new booklet being substituted for the old. The snag is that almost every Act, within a year or two after its passing, becomes *lightly* amended. The system guarantees that users will have few Acts in up-to-date form, though an annual supplement specifying amendments is issued.

Statutory instruments   All instruments of general effect, and the more important local instruments, are published by HMSO as they are

made. The position as to annual volumes and the 1948 collected
edition has been described (p 79).

Commonwealth legislation   As described above (p 66), the rest of
the Commonwealth enjoys a superior system. In Canada for example
the latest revision (the sixth since Confederation) dates from 1985.
(For an account of this, see *Revised Statutes of Canada* 1985,
Appendices, p v. For the titles under which it is arranged see *Revised
Statutes of Canada* 1985, Vol I, pp iii–ix). Delegated legislation in
Canada was last consolidated in 1978. (For an account, see
Consolidated Regulations of Canada 1978, Table of Contents and
Schedule, p 5.) The history of the statute law revision system in
Canada is admirably described in *Private Law in Canada* by Clarence
Smith and Kerby.

Community law   The Treaties have been published by HMSO, and
also by the Commission itself. Regulations, and some other
instruments, are published in the 'L' (Legislation) series of the
Official Journal of the European Communities, which usually appears
daily. Copies and collected editions are sold by HMSO, and
subscriptions are arranged by the Office for Official Publications
of the European Communities in Luxembourg.

Statutory Publications Office   This government office, now located
at 28 Broadway, London SW1, is responsible under the Statute Law
Committee for a number of publications relating to statute law.
These include *Statutes in Force*, the annual volumes of statutory
instruments, and various tables and indexes relating to legislation
(described in chapter 23). It is typical of the haphazard British way
that no one organisation is responsible for all aspects of statutory
publication. Until 1886, the Queen's Printer of Acts of Parliament
had the monopoly of the publication of Acts, and did not serve
merely as an agent of the Crown. Since that year, HMSO has been
the publisher of Acts. The Controller of that Office is now by letters
patent known as the Queen's Printer. Such antique arrangements
are not easily rationalised.

Part II

Statutory Interpretation

Chapter Eight

The Technique of Statutory Interpretation

This introductory chapter to Part II aims to describe the common-law technique of statutory interpretation. Before we get started, a fundamental question should be addressed. Why is such a technique necessary?

On the continent of Europe, which follows the civil law, this necessity is not felt. There the words of legislation are considered approximate. They do not have to mean what they say, even if what they say is clear. They are a mere starting point for flights by the judges. The function of the legislator is to sketch out some ideas. Filling them in, refining them, and shaping them for real life is the job of the judge and administrator. Their literal meaning is not decisive, and therefore time need not be wasted in attempting to formulate interpretative techniques.

Countries which have inherited the common law system see things differently. Despite the fact that it was their judges who created the common law, they now prefer to be ruled by a democratic legislature. Its members are people they voted for. Its Acts are passed after full debate, carried out in public. Almost every word in every Act is weighed and argued over through successive legislative stages. So it matters how these Acts are interpreted by the courts.

It follows that in common-law systems there is a technique of statutory interpretation, though admittedly it is little understood. Indeed many people, including most judges and advocates, do not wholeheartedly accept that the technique exists, let alone attempt to practise it. This is scarcely their fault, since usually they have not been taught it. Indeed up until now, the technique can hardly be said to have been worked out. The function of this Part, which is based on the more detailed treatment in the author's book *Statutory Interpretation* (Butterworths 1984, Supplement 1989), is to present the working out of such a technique.

With the advance of the European Community, it may be thought a little late in the day to present such a thesis as this. Better late than never. There is still time for people to reflect on how, and by whom, they wish to be governed.

To construe or interpret?

We began with a trivial argument: Is there any material distinction between construction and interpretation? The answer is no. The terms are interchangeable, though it is more natural to speak of interpreting a word or phrase and construing an extended passage. Bentham said: 'People in general when they speak of a Law and a Statute are apt to mean the same thing by the one as by the other. So are they when they speak of construing and interpreting' (Bentham 1775, p 9).

Interpretation perhaps connotes, more than construction does, the idea of determining the *legal* meaning of an enactment. Construction is more concerned with extracting the *grammatical* meaning, which may not be the same. This important distinction is discussed below (see pp 87–91)

The enactment as the unit of enquiry

The concept of the *enactment* is central to statutory interpretation.

Nature of an enactment

An enactment is a *proposition* expressed in an Act or other legislative text. The effect of the proposition is that, when facts fall within an indicated area (the factual outline), then specified legal consequences (the legal thrust) ensue. Difficulties about meaning are usually centred on one proposition only, though the full meaning of a legislative provision often cannot be gained without considering numerous aspects of the legal system.

An enactment consists of express words, though it is likely to have implied meanings as well. While a single word may come under examination as the root of an ambiguity or other obscurity, a word in itself can have little significance. Every word needs a verbal context to raise any question of its meaning. The enactment provides this.

Usually an enactment consists of either of the whole or part of a single sentence. One sentence may thus contain two or more enactments. On the other hand a single legislative proposition may fall to be collected from two or more sentences, whether consecutive or not. The provision in the Interpretation Act 1889, s 35(1) that 'any enactment may be cited by reference to the section or subsection of the Act in which the enactment is contained' (not reproduced in the Interpretation Act 1978) is itself an example of an enactment.

The unit of enquiry is an enactment whose legal meaning in relation to a particular factual situation falls to be determined. Where the combined effect of two or more enactments is in question, each in turn is treated as a unit of enquiry, their combined legal effect then falling to be determined. To discover which are the relevant enactments, it is necessary to frame the question of law at issue in the particular case. The significant legislative words then have to be isolated.

For this purpose the statute user must develop a technique of skimming through a legislative provision and mentally picking out the portions that matter in the case before him. If his mind can learn to blot out the irrelevant words, the remainder will often read continuously and make sense on their own. Thus in *Riley* v *A-G of Jamaica* [1983] 1 AC 719, 730 Lord Scarman cited an enactment in a form he described as 'trimmed of words inessential for present purposes'. Isolating the relevant enactment in this way often calls for use of the technique of selective comminution, described below (p 235).

How the enactment is drawn

In ascertaining the legal meaning of an enactment it is necessary to determine whether the drafting is precise or imprecise. Modern British Acts are produced by *precision drafting*, where (although there are occasional lapses) the drafter aims to use language accurately and consistently, and moreover is allowed to draft any amendments made to the Act during its parliamentary progress. Older Acts are frequently the subject of *disorganised composition*. Here the text may be the product of many hands and the language is often confused and inconsistent. Delegated legislation may be drafted with less precision than Acts. The technique of interpretation applied to any enactment can only be as precise and exacting as the method of drafting permits.

It is to be presumed, unless the contrary appears, that the enactment was competently drafted, so that the accepted principles of grammar, syntax and punctuation, and other literary canons, are taken to have been observed and the drafter is presumed to have executed his task with due knowledge of the relevant law (*Spillers Ltd* v *Cardiff Assessment Committee* [1931] 2 KB 21, 43; *New Plymouth Borough Council* v *Taranack Electric Power Board* [1933] AC 680, 682). This principle is expressed in the maxim *omnia praesumuntur rite et solemniter esse acta* (all things are presumed to be correctly and solemnly done).

The factual outline

An enactment lays down a legal rule in terms showing that the rule is triggered by the existence of certain facts. The enactment indicates these facts in outline form (the factual outline). All sets of facts that fall within the outline thus trigger the legal thrust of the enactment, unless by an authoritative decision (known as dynamic processing) the court modifies, or has previously modified, the literal meaning of the factual outline in order to carry out what it considers the true intention of Parliament.

Where the court finds it necessary to narrow the factual outline because its literal meaning goes wider than Parliament's intention, the court indicates what the narrower outline is. Alternatively, the statutory factual outline may be thought to need clarification by the court. Either way, the court processes the enactment by laying down a sub-rule from which can be drawn a description of the narrower or more precise range of facts that will in future cases trigger the operation of the enactment. Often the factual outline will show that both physical and mental facts have to be present. In criminal law the terms *actus reus* and *mens rea* are traditionally used, though they have been frowned on by the House of Lords (*R v Miller* [1983] 2 AC 161, 174).

We may take as an example of a factual outline the Criminal Damage Act 1971, s 1(1), which specifies several offences. A selective comminution of one of these reads: 'A person who without lawful excuse damages any property belonging to another, being reckless as to whether any such property would be damaged, shall be guilty of an offence.'

Here the factual outline can be set out as follows:

1   The *subject* is any person with criminal capacity, the last three words being implied by virtue of the presumption that relevant legal rules are intended to be attracted (see pp 178–181 below).
2   The *actus reus* is without lawful excuse damaging any property belonging to another.
3   The *mens rea* is being reckless as to whether any such property would be damaged.

The factual outline of a legal rule may contain alternatives, in the sense that the same legal thrust applies in two or more factual situations. Lord Diplock gave the example of buggery at common law 'which could be committed with a man *or* a woman *or* an animal' (*R v Courtie* [1984] 2 WLR 330, 335). The statutory factual outline is often too wide for juridical purposes. Grammatically it includes, or may be thought to include, some factual situations which are, and others which are not, intended to trigger the operation of the enactment. Alternatively, the statutory factual outline may be thought to need clarification, for example, by the finding of implications as to mental states. In either case it is for the court to determine the sub-rules which lay down the boundary or clarify the provision.

In a particular case the *relevant* factual outline indentifies the situations which, in relation to the legal rule or sub-rule in question, are material on the actual facts. For example, if a man charged with murder claimed to be absolved because what he admittedly maliciously killed was a person born an idiot, any enquiry as to the law would be concerned only with whether the crime of murder extends to the killing with malice aforethought of persons who are congenital idiots.

It is the function of a court accurately to identify this area of relevance. The basis of the doctrine of precedent is that like cases must be decided alike. This requires a correct identification of the factual outline that triggers the statutory rule on actual facts such as are before the court. In his book *Precedent in English Law*, Sir Rupert Cross insisted that under the doctrine of precedent, judgments must be read in the light of the facts of the cases in which they are delivered (Cross 1977, p 42). The principle is the same whether the case is decided under a rule of common law or statute law.

Judicial statements of principle must be related to the facts of the instant case, but the juristic function of the court is to *generalize* those facts. The *ratio decidendi* of a case involves postulating a general factual outline. This is part of the rule laid down or followed by the case, since a legal rule imports a factual situation to which it applies. If the facts of a later case fit within this outline but demand amendment of the legal thrust of the rule, the outline is too broadly stated. If on the other hand the facts of a later case do not fit into the outline, but elict the same legal response, the outline is too narrow.

The legal thrust of an enactment

The legal thrust is the effect in law produced by the enactment where the facts of the instant case fall within the factual outline. Problems of statutory interpretation concern either the exact nature of the factual outline, or the exact nature of the legal thrust, or both. Respectively, these turn on *when* the enactment operates and *how* it operates. In criminal law the legal thrust of an enactment is usually expressed by saying that where the factual outline is satisfied the person in question is guilty of an offence. The legal consequences of this by way of punishment and so forth may be spelt out or left to the general law.

The legal thrust of a non-criminal enactment may be more complex, and thus give rise to more difficult questions of statutory interpretation. For an illustration we may take *Inland Revenue Commissioners* v *Hinchy* [1960] AC 748. This turned on the meaning of a phrase in the Income Tax Act 1952, s 25(3) which expressed the legal thrust of the provision. Lord Reid said (p 766):

I can now state what I understand to be the rival contentions as to the meaning of section 25(3). The appellants contend that 'treble the tax which he ought to be charged under this Act' means treble his whole liability to income tax for the year in question . . . It is not so easy to state the contrary contention briefly and accurately.

Legal meaning and grammatical meaning of an enactment

The interpreter's duty is to arrive at the *legal* meaning of the enactment, which is not necessarily the same as its grammatical (or literal) meaning. There is a clear conceptual difference between grammatical meaning apart from legal considerations and the overall meaning taking those considerations into account. While it may sometimes be difficult to draw in practice, this distinction is basic in statutory interpretation.

The legal meaning of an enactment must be arrived at in accordance with the rules, principles, presumptions and canons which govern statutory interpretation (in this book referred to as the interpretative criteria or guides to legislative intention). They are described in the four following chapters.

By applying the relevant interpretative criteria to the facts of the instant case, certain interpretative *factors* will emerge. These may pull different ways. For example the desirability of applying the clear grammatical meaning may conflict with the fact that in the instant case this would not remedy the mischief that Parliament clearly intended to deal with. In such cases a balancing operation is called for. In a particular case the legal meaning of an enactment will usually be found to correspond to the grammatical meaning. If this were never so, the system would collapse. If it were always so, there would be no need for books on statutory interpretation. Where it is not so, the enactment is being given a *strained* construction.

Real doubt as to legal meaning

There may be doubt as to whether the legal meaning does or does not correspond to the grammatical meaning. There may even be doubt as to what is the grammatical meaning, for language is always prone to ambiguity.

The law will pay regard to such doubt only if it is *real*. If, on an informed interpretation, there is no real doubt that a particular meaning of an enactment is to be applied, that is to be taken as its legal meaning. If there is real doubt, it is to be resolved by applying the interpretative criteria. For this purpose a doubt is 'real' only where it is substantial, and not merely conjectural or fanciful. As Lord Cave LC said, no form of words has ever yet been framed with regard to which some ingenious counsel could not suggest a difficulty (*Pratt* v *South Eastern Railway* [1897] 1 QB 718, 721). Judges thus need to be on guard against the plausible advocate. They also need to guard against being too clever themselves. Lord Diplock pointed out that where the meaning of the statutory words is plain 'it is not for the judges to invent fancied ambiguities' (*Duport Steels* v *Sirs* [1980] 1 WLR 142, 157). The main causes of doubt, or doubt-factors, are examined in Part III.

Nature of the grammatical meaning

The grammatical (or literal) meaning of an enactment is its linguistic meaning taken in isolation. This is the meaning it bears when, as a piece of English prose, it is construed according to the rules and usages of grammar, syntax and punctuation, and the accepted linguistic canons of construction applicable to prose generally. There are often difficulties in arriving at the grammatical meaning, even before legal questions are considered. Pollock CB said: 'grammatical and philological disputes (in fact all that belongs to the history of language) are as obscure and lead to as many doubts and contentions as any question of law' (*Waugh* v *Middleton* (1853) 8 Ex 352, 356).

Ambiguity

Though judges sometimes use it in a wider sense, the term 'ambiguity' should be reserved for cases where there is more than one meaning that is grammatically apt. The drafter has produced, whether deliberately or inadvertently, a text which from the grammatical viewpoint is capable, on the facts of the instant case, of bearing either of the opposing constructions put forward by the parties. It may be a *semantic ambiguity* (caused by the fact that one word can in itself have several meanings), a *syntactic ambiguity* (arising from the grammatical relationship of words as they are chosen and arranged by the drafter), or a *contextual ambiguity* (where there is conflict between the enactment and its internal or external context).

Another subdivision is between *general ambiguity*, where the enactment is ambiguous quite apart from any particular set of facts, and *relative ambiguity*, where it is ambiguous only in relation to certain facts.

An example of general ambiguity came before the Court of Appeal in *Leung* v *Garbett* [1980] 1 WLR 1189. This concerned provisions relating to arbitration in the County Courts Act 1959, s 92(1), which said the judge 'may, with the consent of the parties, revoke the reference [to arbitration] or order another reference to be made.' Did the qualifying phrase 'with the consent of the parties' govern both limbs or only the first? It may be thought there is no ambiguity at all, and that the structure and punctuation of the sentence indicate that the qualifying phrase applied to both limbs. Yet the Court of Appeal held otherwise. As an example of relative ambiguity we may take the Finance Act 1975, Sched 5, para 3(1), of which Viscount Dilhourne LC said: I do not think the words 'interest in possession in settled property' are equally open to divers meanings. It is the determination of the application of those words to particular circumstances which give rise to difficulty.' (*Pearson* v *IRC* [1981] AC 753, 771.)

Semantic obscurity and the 'corrected version'

Where, either generally or in relation to the facts of the instant case, the wording of the enactment is disorganised, garbled or otherwise semantically *obscure*, the interpreter must go through a two-stage operation. It is first necessary to determine what was the intended grammatical formulation. The version of the enactment thus arrived at may be referred to as 'the corrected version'. The interpretative criteria are then applied to the corrected version as if it had been the actual wording of the enactment.

As our first example we may take the House of Commons Disqualification Act 1975, s 10(2), which says that the enactments 'specified in Schedule 4 to this Act' are repealed. The Act contains no Sched 4. It does however have Sched 3, which is headed 'Repeals'. Other internal evidence confirms that Sched 3 is the one intended. The court will apply a corrected version referring to the enactments 'specified in Schedule 3'.

With some garbled texts, like that in the previous example, it is quite obvious what the corrected version should be. In other cases it may be less clear, and the court must do the best it can. The considerations involved may be complex.

It is a well-known fact that in a trial on indictment the accused pleads either guilty or not guilty. If he pleads guilty there is no verdict because he is not put in charge of the jury. So an enactment worded as if there were *always* a verdict in a trial on indictment is bound to be obscure. This was the case with the Criminal Appeal Act 1907, s 4(3), which said:

On an appeal against sentence the Court of Criminal Appeal shall, if they think that a different sentence should have passed, quash the sentence passed at the trial, and pass such other sentence warranted in law *by the verdict*. . . as they think ought to have been passed.

In *R* v *Ettridge* [1909] 2 KB 24, 28 the court hearing an appeal against sentence by a prisoner who had pleaded guilty rectified s 4(3) by deleting the words 'by the verdict'. The court claimed the right to 'reject words, transpose them, or even imply words, if this be necessary to give effect to the intention and meaning of the Legislature'. (For further examples of garbled texts see pp 256-263).

Literal or strained construction?

Where the grammatical meaning of an enactment is clear, to apply that meaning is to give it a literal construction. Where on the other hand the grammatical meaning is obscure, giving the enactment a literal construction involves applying the grammatical meaning of the corrected version. If (in either case) a literal construction does not correspond to the legislative intention it becomes necessary instead to apply a *strained* construction in order to arrive at the legal meaning of the enactment.

Where the enactment, or (in the case of grammatical obscurity) its corrected version, is not ambigious the question for the interpreter therefore is: shall it be given a literal or strained construction in arriving at the legal meaning? Where the enactment is ambiguous the questions are first, which of the ambiguous meanings is more appropriate in arriving at a literal construction, and second, should it in any case be given some other (strained) meaning? As Mackinnon LJ said in *Sutherland Publishing Co* v *Caxton Publishing Co* [1938] Ch 174, 201: 'When the purpose of an enactment is clear, it is often legitimate, because it is necessary, to put a strained interpretation upon some words which have been inadvertently used . . . '

In the later case of *Jones* v *DPP* [1962] AC 635, 668 Lord Reid appeared to contradict this by saying: 'It is a cardinal principle applicable to all kinds of statutes that you may not for any reason attach to a statutory provision a meaning which the words of the provision cannot reasonably bear . . . '. In this conflict Lord Reid must be adjudged wrong and Mackinnon LJ right. There are very many decided cases where courts have attached meanings to enactments which in a grammactical sense they cannot reasonably bear. Sometimes the arguments against a literal construction are so compelling that even though the words are not, withing the rules of language, capable of another meaning they must be given one. To assert, in the face of the innumerable cases where judges have applied a strained construction, that there is no power to do so is to infringe the *principium contradictionis*, or logical principle of contradiction.

In former times the practice of giving a strained meaning to statutes was known as 'equitable construction'. This term had no more than an oblique reference to the technical doctrines of equity, but mainly indicated a free or liberal construction.

Since, in the light of the interpretative criteria which apply to a particular enactment, its legal meaning may be held to correspond either to the grammatical meaning or to a strained meaning, it follows that the legal meaning of a particular verbal formula may differ according to its statutory context *Customs and Excise Comrs* v *Cure & Deeley Ltd* [1962] 1 QB 340, 367). Automatic literalism is rejected in modern statutory interpretation. Legislative intention is always the ultimate guide to legal meaning, and this varies from Act to Act.

Filling in textual detail by implications

Parliament is presumed to intend that the literal meaning of the express word of an enactment is to be treated as elaborated by taking into account all implications which, in accordance with the recognised guides to legislative intention, it is proper to treat the legislator as having intended. Accordingly, in determining which of the opposing constructions of an enactment to apply in the factual situation of the instant case, the court seeks to identify the one that embodies the elaborations intended by the legislator.

Implications arise either because they are directly suggested by the words expressed or because they are indirectly suggested by rules or principles of law not disapplied by the words expressed. In ordinary speech it is a recognised method to say expressly no more than is required to make the meaning clear (the obvious implications remaining unexpressed). The drafter of legislation, striving to be as brief as possible and use ordinary language, adopts the same method. The distinguished American drafter Reed Dickinson observed, 'It is sometimes said that a draftsman should leave nothing to implication. This is nonsense. No communication can operate without leaving part of the total communication to implication.' (Dickerson 1981, p 133.)

An implication cannot properly be found which goes against an express statement: *expressum facit cessare tacitum* (statement ends implication). So it is not permissible to find an implied meaning where this contradicts the grammatical meaning. Where the court holds that the legal meaning of an enactment contradicts the grammatical meaning, it is not finding an implication but applying a strained construction.

So far as implications are relevant in the case before it, the court treats the enactment as if it were worded accordingly. As Coleridge J said in *Gwynne* v *Burnell* (1840) 7 Cl & F 572, 606: 'If . . . the proposed addition is already necessarily contained, although not expressed, in the statute, it is of course not the less cogent because not expressed.'

Parliament acknowledges its reliance on implications by occasionally including in its Acts an express statement that a particular implication is not to be taken as intended (see for example the Administration of Justice Act 1960, s 12(4)).

The device of leaving unsaid some portion of what the drafter means is known as ellipsis. It is discussed at length in chapter 15.

Must an implication be 'necessary'?

The question of whether an implication should be found within the express words of an enactment depends on whether it is proper, having regard to the accepted guides to legislative intention, to find the implication; and not on whether the implication is 'necessary'.

It is sometimes suggested by judges that only necessary implications may legitimately be drawn from the wording of Acts (see, eg *Salomon* v *Salomon* [1897] AC 22, 38). This is too narrow. The necessity referred to could only be *logical* necessity, but requirements of logic are not the only criteria in determining the legal meaning of a text. While the implications intended are a matter of inference, it is often psychological rather than logical inference that is involved.

The principle was accurately stated by Willes J when he said that the legal meaning of an enactment includes 'what is necessarily or properly implied' by the language used (*Chorlton* v *Lings* (1868) LR 4 CP 374, 387).

Must an implication be 'obvious'?

Another way the rule is sometimes put by judges is that the implication must be 'clear' or 'obvious'. Thus in *Temple* v *Mitchell* (1956) SC 267, 272 Lord Justice-Clerk Thomson said: 'There is no express provision, and I cannot discover any clear implication'.

This is also open to objection. Courts of construction are not usually troubled with a 'clear' provision. On the contrary they exist to give judgment where the law is not clear but doubtful. There is likely to be a fine balance to be struck where one side claims that a particular implication arises and their opponents deny it.

Implications affecting related law

The fact that Parliament has by an enactment declared its express intention in one area of law may carry an implication that it intends corresponding changes in related areas of law, or in relevant legal policy.

The courts accept that where a legislative innovation is based on a point of principle, the effect of receiving it into the body of the law may be to treat the principle in question as thereafter embodied in general legal policy. Thus Acts such as the Race Relations Act 1976, the Sex Discrimination Act 1975 and the Equal Pay Act 1970 are taken to indicate that it has become the general policy of the law to counter the relevant types of injurious personal discrimination whenever opportunity offers. Lord Morris of Borth-y-Gest said:

... by enacting the Race Relations Acts 1965 and 1968 Parliament introduced into the law of England a new guiding principle of fundamental and far-reaching importance. It is one that affects and must influence action and behaviour in this country within a wide-ranging sweep of human activities and personal relationships. (*Charter* v *Race Relations Board* [1973] AC 868, 889. *Cf* the remarks by Lord Denning MR on the effect of the European Communities Act 1972 in *Re Westinghouse Uranium Contract* [1978] AC 547, 546.)

On questions of personal morality the courts tend not to follow Parliament's lead (eg *R* v *City of London Coroner, ex parte Barber* [1975] Crim LR 515 (eg decriminalisation of suicide) *Knuller* v *DPP* [1973] AC 435 (decriminalisation of homosexual practices)).

The enactment and the facts

The court is not required to determine the meaning of an enactment in the abstract, but only when applied to the relevant facts of the case before it. The question for the court is whether or not these facts fall within the legal outline laid down by the enactment, and if so what the legal trust of the enactment is.

Because the court exercises the judicial power of the state, it has a two-fold function. First it is required to decide the *lis*, that is the dispute between the parties who are before it in the instant case. Secondly it has the duty, so that justice according to law may be seen to be done and the law in question may be known, of indicating the legal principle held to be determinative of the *lis*.

That an enactment may have fundamentally different meanings in relation to different facts was recognised by Lord Brightman in a dictum on the Statutes of Limitation: 'A limitation Act may. . . be procedural in the context of one set of facts, but substantive in the context of a different set of facts.' (*Yew Bon Tew* v *Kenderaan Bas Mara* [1983] AC 553, 563).

So the practical question for the court is not what does this enactment mean in the abstract, but what does it mean *on these facts?* The point was concisely put by Lord Somervell of Harrow:

A question of construction arises when one side submits that a particular provision of an Act covers the facts of the case and the other side submits that it does not. Or it may be agreed it applies, but the difference arises as to its application. (*A-G* v *Prince Ernest Augustus of Hanover* [1957] AC 436, 473.)

Relevant and irrelevant facts

As we have seen, the operation of the enactment is triggered by a particular factual situation comprised in the factual outline. This statutory description must be 'tranferred' to the material facts of the instant case or, as it were, fitted over them to see if it corresponds. Here it is important to grasp exactly which facts are relevant. It is necessary to separate material from immaterial facts.

Many of the actual facts of a case are irrelevant. The name of a party is irrelevant (unless a question of identity is in issue). The particular moment when an incident happened is irrelevant (unless time is of the essence), and so on. It requires skill to determine, in relation to the triggering of a particular enactment, which actual fact is a relevant fact. While a fact may be relevant, it may still be necessary to strip it of its inessential features in order to arrive at its juristic significance. This is particularly true where the decision on that fact later comes to be treated as a precedent. Where the enactment is very simple, the facts which trigger it can be stated very simply. Caution is always necessary however.

The Murder (Abolition of Death Penalty) Act 1965, s 1 says 'No person shall suffer death for murder.' The statutory factual outline might be stated as 'a conviction of murder'. This would not be strictly accurate however, since the enactment does not apply to convictions anywhere in the world. After referring to the extent provision in the 1965 Act, namely s 3(3), we arrive at the following as the statutory factual outline: 'a conviction of murder by a court in Great Britain, or by a court-martial in Northern Ireland.'

Where a court articulates the meaning of an enactment but describes the generalised facts in terms that are too wide, its decision, to the extent that it is expressed too widely, will be of merely persuasive authority. A court decision can be a binding precedent only in relation to similar facts, that is facts that do not *materially* differ from those of the instant case. In a particular case a fact is not necessarily relevant merely because it is within the statutory factual outline. The total factual outline usually has only a partial application.

Section 9 (drink driving) of the Road Traffic Act 1972, says that in certain circumstances a person may be 'required' to provide a specimen for a laboratory test, and that if without reasonable excuse he refuses, he commits an offence. In *Hier* v *Read* [1977] Crim LR 483 the defendant D, having been required to provide a specimen, was first asked to sign a consent form. He refused to sign the form without reading it first, but the opportunity to do this was refused by the police. *Held* a requirement to provide a specimen after signing a consent form which one is not allowed to read is not a 'requirement' within the meaning of the Act. Accordingly no offence was committed.

This case called for a careful assessment of just what the factual outline was. It was important to avoid confusion of thought. For example it might have been said that the behaviour of the police in refusing to allow D to read the consent form furnished him with a 'reasonable excuse' as contemplated by s 9. This would have been faulty reasoning, because that stage was never reached. On the facts, there had not been any valid 'requirement'. A full statement of the factual outline of what is a 'requirement' within the Road Traffic Act 1972, s 9 would run to many pages. All that was needed here was a statement dealing solely with cases where the defendant is asked to sign a consent form which he is not allowed to read. Once it is clear that, whatever the full factual outline may be, the instant case is outside it the matter is concluded.

Proof of facts

Usually a case contains a mass of facts. Most of these are irrelevant to the legal issues involved. The art of the advocate is to analyse the facts and present them in a way which strips them of irrelevant detail. If any are in dispute the analysis can initially be presented in the alternative. When the court determines the disputed facts the advocate may, if the determination is made by a judge or other legally-qualified functionary, have an opportunity of crystallising his legal argument by reference to the facts as so found.

Matters of fact and degree

Where facts are ascertained, the question of whether they fit the factual outline and so trigger the legal thrust of the enactment may not have an obvious answer. It is then what is called a matter of fact and degree. Such matters depend on the view taken by the fact-finding tribunal. If the tribunal has directed itself properly in law and reached its decision in good faith, the decision is beyond challenge.

A matter of fact and degree marks the limit of statutory interpretation. After the relevant law has been ascertained correctly, it becomes a question for the judgment of the magistrate, jury, official, or other fact-finding tribunal to determine whether the matter is within or outside the factual outline laid down by the enactment.

As Woolf J said on the question of whether certain persons were members of a 'household' within the meaning of the Family Income Supplements Act 1970, s 1(1) *England* v *Secretary of State for Social Services* [1982] 3 FLR 222, 224), there are three possibilities:

1 The only decision the tribunal of fact can, as a matter of law, come to is that the persons concerned *are* members of the household.

2 The only decision the tribunal of fact can, as a matter of law, come to is that the persons concerned *are not* members of the household

3 It is proper to regard the persons concernced as being or not being members of the household, depending on 'the view which the fact-finding tribunal takes of all the circumstances as a matter of fact and degree'.

Difficulties over matters of fact and degree usually arise in connection with *broad terms*, which are fully discussed in chapter 16 of this book.

The opposing constructions of the enactment

The usual circumstance in which a doubtful enactment falls to be construed is where the respective parties each contend for a different meaning of the enactment in its application to the facts of the instant case. These may be referred to as the opposing constructions. The enactment may be ambiguous in all cases, or only on certain facts. An example of the former is the Rent Act 1968, s 18, of which Lord Wilberforce remarked 'the section is certainly one which admits, almost invites, opposing constructions' (*Maunsell* v *Olins* [1974] 3 WLR 835, 840).

Where the enactment is grammatically ambiguous, the opposing constructions put forward are likely to be alternative meanings each of which is grammatically possible. Where on the other hand the enactment is grammatically capable of one meaning only, the opposing constructions are likely to contrast the grammatical (or literal) meaning with a strained construction.

In some cases one of the opposing constructions may be said to present a wide and the other a narrow meaning of the enactment. This is a convenient usage, but requires care. It is necessary to remember that one is speaking of a wider or narrower construction of the enactment forming the unit of enquiry, and not necessarily of the Act as a whole. An enactment which is the unit of enquiry may be a proviso cutting down the effect of a substantive provision. A wider construction of the proviso then amounts to a narrower construction of the substantive provision.

In other cases there may be no sense in which a construction is wider or narrower. For example an enactment may bear on the question whether a person who undoubtedly needs a licence for some activity needs one type of licence (say a category A licence) or another (category B). If the legal meaning of the enactment is uncertain, the opposing constructions on the facts of the instant case will respectively be that it requires a category A licence or requires a category B licence.

The art of determining precisely which is the most helpful yet plausible construction to advance to the court is an important forensic accomplishment. Reed Dickerson said, 'A knack for detecting the two (or more) meanings which are being confused in a disputed verbal question is of more service in reasoning than the most thorough knowledge of the moods and figures and syllogism.' (Dickerson 1981, p 63)

Where the parties advance opposing constructions of the enactment the court may reject both of them and apply its own version. Or it may insist on applying the unvarnished words, which amounts to holding that there is no 'real doubt' over the meaning.

An enactment regulating taxis made it an offence for an unlicensed cab to display a notice which 'may suggest' that the vehicle is being used for hire. In *Green* v *Turkington* [1975] Crim LR 242, which concerned a notice displayed in an unlicensed cab, the opposing constructions for 'may suggest' put forward in the magistrates' court were (1) 'is reasonably likely to suggest' and (2) 'might possibly suggest'. The Divisional Court rejected both constructions, holding that on the facts opposing constructions were not needed. There could be no doubt that the notice in question fell within the wording of the enactment as it stood.

Legislative intention as the paramount criterion

As we have seen, an enactment has the legal meaning taken to be intended by the legislator. In other words the legal meaning corresponds to what is considered to be the legislative intention.

As Lord Radcliffe said in *A-G for Canada* v *Hallett & Carey Ltd* [1952] AC 427, 449:

There are many so-called rules of construction that courts of law have resorted to in their interpretation of statutes but the paramount rule remains that every statute is to be expounded according to its manifest and expressed intention.

This is a general rule for the construction of written instruments, and is not confined to legislation. Halsbury's *Laws of England* (4th edn, vol 36, para 578) says: 'The object of all interpretation of a written instrument is to discover the intention of the author as expressed in the instrument.'

Statutory interpretation is concerned with written texts, in which an intention is taken to be embodied, and by which that intention is communicated to those it affects. This idea that a society should govern itself by verbal formulas, frozen in the day of their originators yet continuing to rule, is a remarkable one. It is pregnant with unreality, yet can scarcely be improved upon. Those concerned with working out its effect have an important role, in which sincerity must be uppermost. An Act is a statement by the democratic Parliament. What the interpreter is required to do is give just effect to that statement.

Lord Halsbury LC summed up the historical principle in *Eastman Photographic Materials Co Ltd* v *Comptroller-General of Patents, Designs and Trade-Marks* [1898] AC 571, 575:

Turner LJ in *Hawkins* v *Gathercole* and adding his own high authority to that of the judges in *Stradling* v *Morgan*, after enforcing the proposition that the intention of the Legislature must be regarded, quotes at length the judgment in that case: that the judges have collected the intention 'sometimes by considering the cause and necessity of making the Act . . . sometimes by foreign circumstances' (thereby meaning extraneous circumstances), 'so that they have been guided by the intent of the Legislature, which they have always taken according to the necessity of the matter, and according to that which is consonant to reason and good discretion'. And he adds: 'We have therefore to consider not merely the words of this Act of Parliament, but the intent of the Legislature, to be collected from the cause and necessity of the Act being made, from a comparison of its several parts, and from foreign (meaning extraneous) circumstances so far as they can justly be considered to throw light upon the subject'.

In former times Acts commonly referred to 'the true intent and meaning' of an Act (see eg 2 Geo 3 c 19 (1762) s 4). In our own day Lord Lane CJ has said that when *interpreting* an Act the court must be careful not to *misinterpret* Parliament's intention (*A-G's Reference (No 1 of 1981)* [1982] QB 848, 856).

Many commentators have mistakenly written off the concept of legislative intention as unreal. Max Radin called it 'a transparent and absurd fiction' (Radin 1930, p 881). The least reflection, he said, makes clear that the lawmaker 'does not exist' (*ibid*, p 870). If the lawmaker does not exist, what human mind first thinks of and then validates the legislative text? It is not made into law otherwise than through the agency of the human mind. We have not yet reached the point of having our laws made by a computer. Under our present system Acts are produced, down to the last word and comma, by people. The lawmaker may be difficult to identify, but it is absurd to say that the lawmaker does not exist. As Dickerson argues, legislative intent is ultimately rooted in individual intents (Dickerson 1981, p 51). These go right down to the democratic roots, as C K Allen grasped when he said that laws are not solely the creation of individuals who happen to compose the legislative body: 'Legislators, at least in democratic countries, are still representative enough to be unable to flout with impunity the main currents of contemporary opinion.' (*Law in the Making* (4th edn, 1946, p 388).

Allen might have added that on the contrary legislators *reflect* such currents. The idea that there is no true intention behind an Act of Parliament is anti-democratic. An Act is usually the product of much debate and compromise, both public and private. The intention that emerges as the result of these forces is not to be dismissed as in any sense illusory. Such dismissal marks a failure to grasp the true nature of legislation. The judges know this well enough; and would not dream of treating a legislative text as having no genuine intendent. As said by Lord Simon of Glaisdale: 'In essence drafting, enactment and interpretation are integral parts of the process of translating the volition of the electorate into rules which will bind themselves.' (*Black-Clawson* v *Papierwerke* [1975] AC 591, 651.)

The guides to legislative intention

The guides to legislative intention, or interpretative criteria, consist of various rules, principles, presumptions and linguistic canons applied at common law or laid down by statute for assisting in statutory interpretation. These can be broadly distinguished as follows:

1 A rule of construction is of binding force, but in cases of real doubt rarely yields a conclusive answer.
2 A principle embodies the policy of the law, and is mainly persuasive.
3 A presumption is based on the nature of legislation, and affords a *prima facie* indication of the legislator's intention.
4 A linguistic canon of construction reflects the nature or use of language and reasoning generally, and is not specially referable to legislation.

The guides to legislative intention are peculiar in that, while most general legal rules or principles directly govern the actions of the subject, these directly govern the actions of the court. There is however an indirect effect on the subject. Since the court is obliged to apply an enactment in accordance with the interpretative criteria, persons governed by the enactment are well advised to read it in that light. The law in its practical application is not what an Act says but what a court says the Act means.

The way the interpretative criteria operate can be shown schematically as follows:

A question of the legal meaning of enactment E arises. Opposing constructions are put forward by the respective parties in relation to the facts of the instant case. The plaintiff puts forward construction P and the defendant construction D.

In the light of the facts of the instant case and the guides to legislative intention, constructions P and D are considered in turn by the court. On examining construction P the court finds some of the interpretative criteria produce factors that tell in its favour. The plaintiff might call them positive factors. Other criteria produce factors (negative factors) that tell against construction P. The court repeats the process with construction D, and then assesses whether on balance P or D comes out as more likely to embody the legislator's intention.

A variety of interpretative criteria are likely to be relevant, but to simplify the example suppose there are only two: the primacy of the grammatical meaning and the desirability of purposive construction. In relation to construction P, a postive factor is that it corresponds to the grammatical meaning while a negative factor is that it does not carry out the purpose of the enactment. In relation to construction D, a positive factor is that it does carry out the purpose of the enactment while a negative factor is that it is a strained construction. The court weighs the factors, and gives its decision.

Obviously this brief analysis does not necessarily correspond to the steps actually taken in court. In practice the intellectual processes and interchanges usually occur in a less formal way. The persons involved are, after all, experts engaging in a familiar routine. But formal analysis must be attempted if we are to believe that the law of statutory interpretation has progressed beyond what it was in the fourteenth century, when:

. . . the courts themselves had no ordered ideas on the subject and were apt to regard each case on its merits without reference to any other case— still less to any general canons of interpretation—and trust implicity in the light of nature and the inspiration of the moment. (Plucknett 1980, p 9.)

Applying the guides to legislative intention

As we have seen, where on an informed construction there is no real doubt, the plain meaning is to be applied. We now examine the practical way of arriving at the legal meaning of the enactment where there is real doubt.

First the cause of the doubt must be ascertained. The doubt is then resolved by assembling the relevant guides to legislative intention, or interpretative criteria. From them the interpreter extracts, in the light of the facts of the instant case and the wording of the enactment which forms the unit of enquiry, the interpretative *factors* that govern the case. Where the relevant factors point in different directions, the interpreter embarks on the operation of *weighing* them. The factors that weigh heaviest dictate the result.

Ascertaining the cause of the doubt

As explained above, the categories where there is real doubt about the legal meaning of an enactment in relation to particular facts can be reduced to two: grammatical ambiguity and the possible need for a strained construction. Semantic obscurity may also cause doubt, but as has been explained this is a defect of a different nature. It is a corruption of the text which, when resolved by producing the 'corrected version', still leaves the possibility of ambiguity or the need for a strained construction.

A particular factor may both cause the doubt and give the means to resolve it. If a literal construction would produce gravely adverse consequences, for example the endangering of national security, this will raise doubt as to whether it could really have been Parliament's intention that the court should apply the grammatical meaning. At the same time the presumption that Parliament does not intend to endanger national security will assist in the working out of the appropriate strained construction.

The doubt-factors arising in statutory interpretation are discussed at length in Part III of this book.

Nature of an interpretative factor

The term 'interpretative factor' denotes a specific legal consideration which derives from the way a general interpretative criterion applies (a) to the text of the enactment under enquiry and (b) to the facts of the instant case (and to other factual situations within the relevant factual outline). The factor serves as a guide to the construction of the enactment in its application to those facts. As respects either of the opposing constructions of the enactment, an interpretative factor may be either positive (tending in favour of that construction) or negative (tending away from it).

There are many different criteria which may be relevant in deciding

which of the opposing constructions of a doubtful enactment the
court should adopt. The principle to be followed was stated by Lord
Reid in *Maunsell* v *Olins* [1974] 3 WLR 835, 837:

> Then rules of construction are relied on. They are not rules in the ordinary
> sense of having some binding force. They are our servants not our masters.
> They are aids to construction, presumptions or pointers. Not infrequently
> one 'rule' points in one direction, another in a different direction. In each
> case we must look at all relevant circumstances, and decide as a matter
> of judgment what weight to attach to any particular 'rule'.

When Lord Reid put the word rule in quotation marks here he
meant to acknowledge that many of the interpretative criteria are
not true rules. Some can be formulated as such. Others, as we have
seen, are more accurately described as principles, presumptions or
canons.

Weighing the interpretative factors

There are no fixed priorities as between various factors, since so
much depends on the wording of the enactment and the particular
facts. For example, in some cases the adverse consequences of a
particular construction may be very likely to arise whereas in others
they may be unlikely.

Injustice will usually weigh heavily, as will the grammatical
meaning of the enactment. Mere inconvenience will usually get a
low rating, as Lord Wilberforce indicated in *Tuck* v *National Freight
Corporation* [1979] 1 WLR 137, 41 when he said: 'It would require
a high degree of inconvenience to deter me from what seemed to
me, on the language, the true meaning'. On the other hand in an
old Irish case the court declined to allow duty evaders to rely on
the privilege against self-incrimination because 'so much public
inconvenience would result from a contrary decision' (*A-G* v *Conroy*
(1838) 2 Jo Ex Ir 791, 792).

The judge may feel confident in his decision or agonise over it.
In a borderline case he may find it very difficult to make up his
mind. It is notorious that different judicial minds may, and frequently
do, conscientiously arrive at differential readings (as to these see
pp 316–320 below).

Great difficulty may arise where different values are truly
incommensurable, for example, those respectively attached to
property and human life. How do you equate personal freedom and
public inconvenience? In the end judges can find no better words
to use than 'instinct' or 'feel'.

The wording of an enactment may indicate that the legislature
has determined the relative weights which are to be given to certain
factors, or at least wished to give guidance on the matter. In such
a case the court must conform to the legislative intention thus
signified.

The weight given by the courts to a particular interpretative criterion may change from time to time. For example, the presumption that an enactment is to be given its grammatical (or literal) meaning has varied in weight over the years. At its height in the middle of the nineteenth century, it has declined somewhat recently. All legal doctrines are subject to this kind of temporal variation, a fact to be borne in mind when considering, in the light of the binding or persuasive authority of relevant precedents, the weight to be attached in the instant case to a factor derived from the criterion of legal policy.

Community law

The detailed principles we have been discussing have little reference to Community law. The failure of Britain to enter the Common Market at the outset meant the loss of any slim chance there might have been that British type statute law would prevail in the Community. It is the continental principles of drafting and interpretation that apply there, and French law has a dominating influence. As Daniel Pépy, formerly a member of the Conseil d'Etat has said: *'Aucune régle de principe n'existe en France pour l'interpretation des textes de loi et decret . . . '* (Pépy 1971, p 108). Grammatical rules and principles are of course followed, but there is nothing akin to the British interpretative criteria.

As we have seen, Community legislation provides one important interpretative tool by its use of preambles. These are indeed obligatory, by virtue of art 190 of the EEC Treaty. Since the European Court concentrates on the purpose rather than the text of the legislation, the preamble furnishes valuable help in interpretation.

Another difference is that Community law is a unique, self-contained body of law. Our rules of interpretation partly derive from the fact that historically statute law in Britain has been an intruder in the domain of common law. The use of external aids is also historically different. The European judge is imbued by training and experience with the spirit of the *code civil*. He is accustomed to consult *travaux préparatoires*, and does not find that they unduly delay proceedings. He, and the advocates with whom he works, know from long experience how to extract the contribution these materials have to make without damage to the fabric of justice.

In *R* v *Henn* [1980] 2 WLR 597, the House of Lords stressed the danger that lay ahead if our judges sought to apply their own rules of interpretation to Community law. Lord Diplock pointed out (p 636) that: 'The European Court, in contrast to English courts, applies teleological rather than historical methods to the interpretation of the treaties and other Community legislation.'

Chapter Nine

Guides to Legislative Intention I: Rules of Construction

As we saw in the previous chapter, the law lays down various guides to legislative intention, or interpretative criteria. Now examining these more closely we see that they can be identified as consisting of the following: six common law *rules*, a varying number of *rules* laid down by statute, eight *principles* derived from legal policy, ten *presumptions* as to legislative intention, and a collection of linguistic *canons* of construction which are applicable to the deciphering of language generally. These criteria are described in detail in this and the next three chapters.

The six common law rules of statutory interpretation are:

1 the basic rule,
2 the informed interpretation rule (recognising that the interpreter needs to be well informed on all relevant aspects),
3 the plain meaning rule,
4 the effectiveness rule (*ut res magis valeat quam pereat*),
5 the commonsense construction rule, and
6 the functional construction rule (concerning the function of different elements in an enactment, such as long title and sidenotes).

In addition there are various statutory rules, usually laid down for the purpose of shortening the verbiage used in legislation.

Basic rule of statutory interpretation

The basic rule of statutory interpretation is that it is taken to be the legislator's intention that the enactment shall be construed in accordance with the guides laid down by law; and that where in a particular case these do not yield a plain answer but point in different directions the problem shall be resolved by a balancing exercise, that is by weighing and balancing the factors they produce.

For at least the past half century the teaching of this subject has been bedevilled by the false notion that statutory interpretation is governed by a mere three 'rules' and that the court selects which 'rule' it prefers and then applies it in order to reach a result. The error perhaps originated in an article published in 1938 by J Willis, a Canadian academic. After warning his readers that it is a mistake to suppose that there is only one rule of statutory interpretation because 'there are three—the literal, golden and mischief rules', Willis went on to say that a court invokes 'whichever of the rules produces a result which satisfies its sense of justice in the case before it' (Willis 1938, p 16). Academics are still producing textbooks which suggest that the matter is dealt with by these three simple 'rules' (see eg Zander (1989) pp 90–114). However, as demonstrated at length in my 1984 textbook *Statutory Interpretation*, and more briefly in this part of the present book, the truth is far more complex.

Willis, and those who have followed him, are wrong in two ways. First, there are not just three guides to interpretation but a considerable number. Second, the court does not 'select' one of the guides and then apply it to the exclusion of the others. The court takes (or should take) an overall view, weighs all the relevant factors, and arrives at a balanced conclusion. What is here called the basic rule of statutory interpretation sets out this truth. It is a *rule* because it is the duty of the interpreter to apply it in every case. (Thus Cotton LJ said in *Ralph* v *Carrick* (1879) 11 Ch D 873, 878 that judges 'are bound to have regard to any rules of construction which have been established by the Courts'.) It is the basic rule because it embraces all the guides to legislative intention that exist to be employed as and when relevant.

Informed interpretation rule

Next it is a rule of law, which may be called the informed interpretation rule, that the interpreter is to infer that the legislator, when settling the wording of an enactment, intended it to be given a fully informed, rather than a purely literal, interpretation (though the two usually produce the same result). Accordingly, the court does not decide whether or not any real doubt exists as to the meaning of a disputed enactment (and if so how to resolve it) until it has first discerned and considered, in the light of the guides to legislative intention, the overall context of the enactment, including all such matters as may illumine the text and make clear the meaning intended by the legislator in the factual situation of the instant case.

This rule is a necessary one, for if the drafter had to frame the enactment in terms suitable for a reader ignorant both of past and contemporary facts and legal principles (and in particular the principles of statutory interpretation), he would need to use far more words than is practicable in order to convey the legal meaning intended.

In interpreting an enactment, a two-stage approach is necessary. It is not simply a matter of deciding what doubtful words mean. It must first be decided, on an informed basis, whether or not there *is* a real doubt about the legal meaning of the enactment. If there is, the interpreter moves on to the second stage of resolving the doubt. (The experienced interpreter combines the stages, but notionally they are separate.) As Lord Upjohn said: 'you must look at all the admissible surrounding circumstances before starting to construe the Act' (*R* v *Schildkamp* [1971] AC 1, 23).

The interpreter of an enactment needs to be someone who is, or is advised by, a person with legal knowledge. This is because an Act is a legal instrument. It forms part of the body of law, and necessarily partakes of the character of law. It cannot therefore be reliably understood by a lay person. Moreover the meaning of the enactment which is needed by any person required to comply with the Act is its *legal* meaning.

The informed interpretation rule is to be applied no matter how plain the statutory words may seem at first glance. Indeed the plainer they seem, the more the interpreter needs to be on guard. A first glance is not a fully-informed glance. Without exception, statutory words require careful assessment of themselves and their context if they are to be construed correctly. A danger of the first glance approach lies in what is called *impression*. When the human mind comes into contact with a verbal proposition an impression of meaning may immediately form, which can be difficult to dislodge. Judges often say that the matter before them is 'one of impression' but it is important that the impression should not be allowed to form before all surrounding circumstances concerning the enactment in question have been grasped.

The informed interpretation rule thus requires that, in the construction of an enactment, attention should be paid to the entire content of the Act containing the enactment. It should also be paid to relevant aspects of: (1) the state of the law before the Act was passed, (2) the history of the enacting of the Act, and (3) the events which have occurred in relation to the Act subsequent to its passing. These may be described collectively as the legislative history of the enactment, and respectively as the pre-enacting, enacting, and post-enacting history.

Another aspect of the need for an informed interpretation relates to the factual situation in the case before the court. In order to determine the legal meaning of an enactment as it applies in a particular case it is necessary to know the relevant facts of the case and relate them to the factual outline laid down by the enactment. It is by reference to these that the parties submit to the court their opposing constructions of an enactment whose meaning is disputed.

For the purpose of applying the informed interpretation rule, the context of an enactment thus comprises, in addition to the other provisions of the Act containing it, the legislative history of that Act, the provisions of other Acts *in pari materia*, and all facts constituting or concerning the subject-matter of the Act. Viscount Simonds said in *A-G* v *Prince Ernest Augustus of Hanover* [1957] AC 436, 463:

... it must often be difficult to say that any terms are clear and unambiguous until they have been read in their context ... the elementary rule must be observed that no one should profess to understand any part of a statute ... before he has read the whole of it. Until he has done so he is not entitled to say that it or any part of it is clear and unambiguous.

The surrounding facts are also important to the understanding, and therefore correct interpretation, of an Act. For example why does s 1(3)(a) of the Factories Act 1961 (a consolidation Act) require the inside walls of factories to be washed every *14 months*? An annual spring cleaning one could understand, but why this odd period? Sir Harold Kent, who drafted the original provision in the Factories Act 1937, gives the answer: factory spring cleaning takes place at Easter, and Easter is a movable feast (Kent 1979, p 88).

In determining whether consideration should be given to any item of legislative history or other informative material, and if so what weight should be given to it, regard is to be had (a) to the desirability of persons being able to rely on the ordinary meaning conveyed by the text of the enactment, taking into account its context in the Act or other instrument and the legislative intention; and (b) to the need to avoid prolonging legal or other proceedings without compensating advantage. (This statement of the law is taken from s 15AB(3) of an Australian statute, the Acts Interpretation Act 1901 as amended by the Acts Interpretation Amendment Act 1984, s 7. In turn s 15AB was derived from clause 5(3) of the draft Bill proposed in the present book (see p 344 below).)

The informed interpretation rule does not go so far as to permit the court to take into account material which is not generally available. As Lord Reid said in *Black-Clawson* v *Papierwerke* [1975] AC 591, 614: 'An Act is addressed to all the lieges and it would seem wrong to take into account anything that was not public knowledge at the time'. Nevertheless the mind of the interpreter can never be too well stocked. A conscientious judge, like a conscientious legislator or drafter, keeps himself fully informed about what is going on in the world.

Legislative history

An enactment does not stand alone. It is part of the Act containing it. The Act in its turn is part of the total mass of legislation loosely referred to as the statute book, which is itself part of the whole *corpus juris*. The enactment must therefore be construed in the light of its overall context. Subject to certain restrictive rules (for example that restraining reference to *Hansard*), a court considering an enactment is master of its own procedure (*R* v *Board of Visitors of Wormwood Scrubs Prison, ex parte Anderson* [1985] QB 251). It therefore has the power, indeed the duty, to consider such aspects of the legislative history of the enactment as may be necessary to arrive at its legal meaning, and must give them their proper weight. For a correct understanding of an item of *delegated* legislation, it is necessary not only to consider the wording of the enabling Act, but also the legislative history of that Act (*Crompton* v *General Medical Council* [1981] 1 WLR 1435, 1437).

Pre-enacting history

The interpreter cannot judge soundly what mischief an enactment is intended to remedy unless he knows the previous state of the law, the defects found to exist in that law, and the facts that caused the legislator to pass the Act in question. The first book on statutory interpretation in England, written in the sixteenth century, said that interpreters who disregard the pre-enacting history are much deceived 'for they shall neither know the statute nor expound it well, but shall as it were follow their noses and grope at it in the dark' (cited Plucknett 1944, p 245).

Under the doctrine of judicial notice, the court is taken to know the relevant law prevailing within its jurisdiction. This applies both to past and present law. Accordingly there can be no restriction on the sources available to the court for reminding itself as to the content of past and present law (*Black-Clawson International Ltd* v *Papierwerke Waldhof-Aschaffenberg AG* [1975] AC 591, 637).

Where a subject has been dealt with by a developing series of Acts, the courts often find it necessary, in construing the latest Act, to trace the course of this development. By seeing what changes have been made in the relevant provision, and why, the court can better assess its current legal meaning (eg *R* v *Governor of Holloway Prison, ex parte Jennings* [1982] 3 WLR 450, 458).

Where an Act uses a term with a previous legal history it may be inferred that Parliament intended to use it in the sense given by the earlier history, and again the court is entitled to inform itself about this (eg *Welham* v *DPP* [1961] AC 103, 123). Lord Reid said: 'Where Parliament has continued to use words of which the meaning has been settled by decisions of the court, it is to be presumed that Parliament intends the words to continue to have that meaning' (*Truman Hanbury Buxton & Co Ltd* v *Kerslake* [1955] AC 337, 361).

If two Acts are *in pari materia*, it is assumed that uniformity of language and meaning was intended. This attracts the considerations arising from the linguistic canon of construction that an Act is to be construed as a whole. Such Acts 'are to be taken together as forming one system, and as interpreting and enforcing each other' (*Palmer's Case* (1785) 1 Burr 445, 447). This has even been applied to repealed Acts within a group (*Ex parte Copeland* (1852) 22 LJ Bank 17, 21). The following are *in pari materia*:

1 Acts which have been given a collective title.
2 Acts which are required to be construed as one.

3 Acts having short titles that are identical (apart from the calendar year).
4 Other Acts which deal with the same subject matter on the same lines (here it must be remembered that the Latin word *par* or *paris* means equal, and not merely similar). Such Acts are sometimes loosely described as forming a code.

Consolidation

Consolidation brings together different Acts which are *in pari materia*, so the relevant pre-enacting history is that of the consolidation Act's component enactments. This fights against the presumption that such an Act is prima facie to be construed in the same way as any other Act. If any real doubt as to its meaning arises, the following rules apply:

1 Unless the contrary intention appears, an Act stated in its long title to be a consolidation Act is presumed not to be intended to change the law (*Gilbert* v *Gilbert and Boucher* [1928] 1, 8; *R* v *Governor of Brixton Prison, ex parte De Demko* [1959] 1 QB 268, 280–1; *Atkinson* v *US Government* [1971] AC 197).
2 In so far as the Act constitutes straight consolidation, its words are to be construed exactly as if they remained in the earlier Act. Re-enactment in the form of straight consolidation makes no difference to legal meaning. It does not import parliamentary approval of judicial decisions on the enactments consolidated, because Parliament has not had those decisions in mind. Not even the drafter will have had them in mind. He will not have taken time to look them up, because his concern is simply to reproduce accurately the statutory wording.
3 In so far as the Act constitutes consolidation with amendments, its words are to be construed as if they were contained in an ordinary amending Act.

Straight consolidation consists of reproduction of the original wording without significant change; consolidation with amendments is any other consolidation (see p 70 above). For examples of consolidation Acts where there was real doubt and the earlier law was looked at, see *Mitchell* v *Simpson* (1890) 25 QBD 183, 188; *Smith* v *Baker* [1891] AC 325, 349; *IRC* v *Hinchy* [1960] AC 748, 768; *Barentz* v *Whiting* [1965] 1 WLR 433.

A common type of consolidation with amendments arises where a consolidation Act incorporates either corrections and minor improvements made under the Consolidation of Enactments (Procedure) Act 1949, or (as is more common in recent legislation) 'lawyer's law' amendments proposed by the Law Commission. In such cases the court may look at any official memorandum published in connection with an Act (*Atkinson* v *United States of America Government* [1971] AC 197).

Where, without any express indication that an amendment is intended, a consolidation Act reproduces the previous wording in *altered* form the court must construe it as it stands. It is not permissible, just because the Act is described as a consolidation Act, to treat it as if it reproduced the original wording (*Pocock* v *Steel* [1985] 1 WLR 229, 233). In *Re a solicitor* [1961] Ch 491 the court applied this rule where the Solicitors Act 1843, s 41, providing that *application* for a costs order could not be made after one year, had been consolidated in the Solicitors Act 1932, s 66(2) to the effect that *the order* must be made within one year. A change in meaning should not be effected in a provision purporting to be straight consolidation, since this amounts to a fraud on Parliament. For an example see Bennion 1986(4) (omission of 'any' from Companies Act 1985, s 196(2)).

Codification

Codification consists in the useful reduction of scattered enactments and judgments on a particular topic to coherent expression within a single formulation. It may therefore condense into one Act rules both of common law and statute. The codifying Act may also embrace custom, prerogative, and practice. In *Mutual Shipping Corporation of New York* v *Bayshore Shipping Co of Monrovia* [1985] 1 WLR 625, 640 Sir Roger Ormrod remarked that codification of what had previously been no more than usage 'converts a practice into a discretion and subtly changes its complexion'.

A codifying Act is prima facie to be construed in the same way as any other Act. If however any real doubt as to its meaning arises, the following rules apply:

1 Unless the contrary intention appears, an Act stated in its long title to be a codifying Act is presumed not to be intended to change the law.
2 In so far as the Act constitutes codification (with or without amendment) of common law rules or judicial sub-rules, reports of the relevant decisions may be referred to but only if this is really necessary.
3 In so far as the Act constitutes consolidation of previous enactments (with or without amendment), the rules stated above in relation to consolidation Acts apply.

These are aspects of the plain meaning rule discussed below. They accord with the classic principle laid down by Lord Herschell LC in *Bank of England* v *Vagliano* [1891] AC 107, 144 (see p 76 above).

For a case where there was real doubt, and the previous law was looked at, see *Yorkshire Insurance Co Ltd* v *Nisbet Shipping Co* [1962] 2 QB 330.

Enacting history

The enacting history of an Act is the surrounding corpus of public knowledge relative to its introduction into Parliament as a Bill, and subsequent progress through, and ultimate passing by, Parliament. In particular it is the extrinsic material assumed to be within the contemplation of Parliament when it passed the act, which may or may not be expressly mentioned therein (*Salomon* v *Commrs of Customs and Excise* [1967] 2 QB 116). Judicial notice is to be taken of such facts 'as must be assumed to have been within the contemplation of the legislature when the Acts in question were passed' (*Govindan Sellappah Nayar Kodakan Pillai* v *Punchi Banda Mundanayake* [1953] AC 514, 528). The court may permit counsel to cite any item of enacting history in support of his construction of the enactment where the purpose is to show that his construction is not contrary to that item (*Cozens* v *North Devon Hospital Management Committee*; *Hunter* v *Turners (Soham) Ltd* [1966] 2 QB 318, 321; *Beswick* v *Beswick* [1968] AC 58, 105).

In considering whether to admit an item of enacting history, the court needs to bear in mind that it is unlikely to be proper to take the item at face value. Material should not be used in the interpretation of the enactment without correct evaluation of its nature and significance. This may in some cases greatly prolong the court proceedings if the item is admitted. Justice Frankfurter accurately summed up the constraining factors: 'Spurious use of legislative history must not swallow the legislation so as to give point to the quip that only when legislative history is doubtful do you go to the statute.' (Frankfurter 1947, p 234.)

Although the court has power to inspect whatever enacting history it thinks fit, it will be governed by the submissions of the counsel on either side, at least where they are in agreement. (See *M/S Aswan Engineering Establishment Co* v *Lupdine Ltd* [1987] 1 WLR 1, 14).

A court, after admitting an item of legislative history, often finds that it carries the matter no further. The question of marginal utility arises here, since admitting the item inevitably adds to trial costs. In an Australian case the judge commented:

I have necessarily ventured far into the use of legislative history only, in the outcome, to discover that it leads to no conclusion different from that which would have followed from a disregard of anything extrinsic to the words of the legislation itself. (*Dugan* v *Mirror Newspapers Ltd* (1979) 142 CLR 583, 599.)

Committee reports may be referred to as useful sources of enacting history. (*Black-Clawson International Ltd* v *Papierwerke Waldhof-Aschaffenberg AG* [1975] AC 591, 647; see also *Fothergill* v *Monarch Airlines Ltd* [1981] AC 251.)

In *Eastman Photographic Materials Co Ltd* v *Comptroller-General of Patents* [1898] AC 571 the House of Lords considered the meaning of a provision of the Patents, Designs and Trade Marks Act 1888 based on the report of a departmental commission. Lord Halsbury LC said (p 573): '. . . I think no more accurate source of information as to what was the evil or defect which the Act of Parliament now under construction was intended to remedy could be imagined than the report of that commission.'

In *Assam Railways and Trading Co Ltd* v *IRC* [1935] AC 445, 458, Lord Wright stressed that Lord Halsbury here approved the citation of the commission's report 'not directly to ascertain the intention of the words used in the Act' but merely 'to show what were the surrounding circumstances'.

In *R* v *Allen (Christopher)* [1985] AC 1029, 1035 Lord Hailsham of St Marylebone LC said that the present practice is for courts to look at committee reports 'for the purpose of defining the mischief of the Act but not to construe it'. However in *British Leyland Motor Corporation Ltd* v *Armstrong Patents Co Ltd* [1986] AC 577 the House of Lords allowed detailed argument relating to the Gregory Report (Report of the Copyright Committee (1952) Cmd 8662), upon which the Copyright Act 1956 was based. The argument was permitted to go beyond merely ascertaining the mischief, and touched on the intended legal effect of certain of the Act's provisions.

Bills are often preceded by government white papers and similar memoranda. Resort may be had to these in interpretation of the ensuing Act. Thus the House of Lords in *Duke* v *GEC Reliance Ltd* [1988] 2 WLR 359 referred to the 1974 government White Paper *Equality for Women* (Cmnd 5724) as a guide to Parliament's intention in enacting provisions of the Sex Discrimination Act 1975. Lord Templeman said (pp 368–369):

If the government had intended to sweep away the widespread practice of differential retirement ages, the 1974 White Paper would not have given a contrary assurance and if Parliament had intended to outlaw differential retirement ages, s 6(4) of the Sex Discrimination Act 1975 would have been very differently worded in order to make clear the profound change which Parliament contemplated.

In *Pickstone* v *Freemans plc* [1989] AC 66, 27 Lord Oliver said that though an explanatory note attached to regulations is not part of the regulations it 'is of use in identifying the mischief which the regulations were attempting to remedy'.

Hansard reports, and other reports of parliamentary proceedings on the Bill which became the Act in question, are of obvious relevance to its meaning. They are of doubtful reliability and limited availability however. The Canadian jurist JA Corry suggested that 'to appeal from the carefully pondered terms of the statute to the hurly-burly of Parliamentary debate is more like appealing from Philip sober to Philip drunk' (Corry 1954, p 632). The American realist Charles P Curtis described the court which unrestrainedly pursues enacting history as 'fumbling about in the ashcans of the legislative process

for the shoddiest unenacted expressions of intention' (Curtis 1949).
A further objection is that once legislators realised that their
statements might influence judicial interpretation they would
inevitably insert in them passages designed only for this purpose.
Thus would be perverted, not only the judicial technique of
interpretation, but the very legislative process itself.

Out of considerations of comity, that is the courtesy and respect
that ought to prevail between two prime organs of state the legislature
and the judiciary, and because such materials are essentially
unreliable and pursuit of them involves an expenditure of time and
effort that can only add to costs, *Hansard* and other parliamentary
materials such as amendment papers and explanatory memoranda
are not in general admissible for purposes of statutory interpretation.
In 1982 Lord Diplock said:

> There are a series of rulings by this House, unbroken for a hundred years,
> and most recently affirmed emphatically and unanimously in *Davis* v *Johnson*
> [1979] AC 264, that recourse to reports of proceedings in either House
> of Parliament during the passage of the Bill that on a signification of royal
> assent became the Act of Parliament which falls to be construed is not
> permissible as an aid to its construction. (*Hadmor Productions Ltd* v *Hamilton*
> [1983] 1 AC 191, 232.)

Nevertheless the court retains a residuary right to admit
parliamentary materials where, in rare cases, the need to carry out
the legislator's intention appears so to require. Courts must be in
charge of their own procedure, and it is ultimately for the court
with the duty of interpreting a particular enactment to decide what
items of enacting history it will permit counsel to cite, having regard
to the various relevant considerations (including the need not to
protract the proceedings without commensurate benefit). The
numerous precedents for citation of parliamentary material cancel
out dicta saying it can *never* be done. In *Pierce* v *Bemis* [1986] QB
384, 392 for example Sheen J allowed counsel to cite, and himself
cited in his judgment, extensive details as to the parliamentary
proceedings on the Bill which became the Merchant Shipping Act
1906, including details as to how the clause that became the Merchant
Shipping Act 1906, s 72 was added to the Bill during its passage
through the House of Commons.

The House of Lords has justified reference to *Hansard* in the
case of an amendment to an Act made by regulations which, though
subject to parliamentary approval, could not be amended by
Parliament (*Pickstone* v *Freemans plc* [1989] AC 66.)

A treaty (a term which may be used to cover any type of
international agreement) is not self-executing in English law
(*Fothergill* v *Monarch Airlines Ltd* [1981] AC 251). The enacting
history of an Act to implement an international treaty includes the
terms of the treaty, its preparatory work or *travaux preparatoires*
(*Porter* v *Freudenberg* [1915] 1 KB 857, 876; *Post Office* v *Estuary*

Radio Ltd [1968] 2 QB 740, 761; *Fothergill v Monarch Airlines Ltd* [1981] AC 251), the decisions on it of foreign courts, known as *la jurisprudence*, and the views on it of foreign jurists, known as *la doctrine*.

A treaty may have three different kinds of status, considered as a source of law.

1 An Act may embody, whether or not in the same words, provisions having the effect of the treaty. This may be referred to as direct enactment of the treaty.
2 An Act may say that the treaty is itself to have effect as law, leaving the treaty's provisions to apply with or without modification. This may be referred to as indirect enactment of the treaty.
3 The treaty may be left simply as an international obligation, being referred to in the interpretation of a relevant enactment only so far as called for by the presumption that Parliament intends to comply with public international law.

The interpretation of a treaty imported into municipal law by indirect enactment was described by Lord Wilberforce as being 'unconstrained by technical rules of English law, or by English legal precedent, but [conducted] on broad principles of general acceptation' (*Buchanan (James) & Co Ltd v Babco Forwarding and Shipping (UK) Ltd* [1978] AC 141, 152). This echoes the dictum of Lord Widgery CJ that the words 'are to be given their general meaning, general to lawyer and layman alike . . . the meaning of the diplomat rather than the lawyer' (*R v Governor of Pentonville Prison, ex parte Ecke* [1974] Crim LR 102). Dicta suggesting that the court is entitled to consult a relevant treaty only where the enactment is ambiguous (see, *Ellerman Lines Ltd v Murray* [1931] AC 126; *IRC v Collco Dealings Ltd* [1962] AC 1; *Warwick Film Productions Ltd v Eisinger* [1969] 1 Ch 508) can no longer be relied on. The true rule is that in this area, as in others, the court is to arrive at an informed interpretation. The Vienna Convention on the Law of Treaties (Treaty Series No 58 (1980); Cmnd 7964) contains provisions governing the interpretation of treaties (the details are set out in Bennion 1984(1), pp 539–540).

Post-enacting history

It may be thought that nothing that happens after an Act is passed can affect the legislative intention at the time it was passed. This overlooks two factors: (1) in the period immediately following its enactment, the history of how an enactment is understood forms part of the *contemporanea expositio*, and may be held to throw light on the legislative intention; (2) the later history may, under the doctrine that an Act is always speaking, indicate how the enactment is regarded in the light of developments from time to time.

Contemporary exposition of an Act (*contemporanea expositio*) helps
to show what people thought the Act meant in the period immediately
after it was passed. Official statements on its meaning are particularly
important here, since the working of almost every Act is supervised,
and most were originally promoted, by a government department
which may be assumed to know what the legislative intention was.
Official statements by the government department administering
an Act, or by any other authority concerned with the Act, may
be taken into account as persuasive authority on the meaning of
its provisions (*Wicks* v *Firth (Inspector of Taxes)* [1983] 2 AC 214).

In *Hanning* v *Maitland (No 2)* [1970] 1 QB 580 the Court of
Appeal admitted statistics showing that, whereas £40,000 a year
was being appropriated by Parliament towards the expenses under
a legal aid enactment, only about £300 a year was actually being
expended. This followed an earlier restrictive court ruling on the
operation of the enactment, and suggested that the ruling did not
conform to Parliament's intention.

One element in the post-enacting history of an Act is delegated
legislation made under the Act. This may be taken into account
as persuasive authority on the meaning of the Act's provisions (*Britt*
v *Buckinghamshire County Council* [1964] 1 QB 77; *Leung* v *Garbett*
[1980] 1 WLR 1189; *R* v *Uxbridge JJ, ex parte Commissioner of
Police of the Metropolis* [1981] QB 829).

In *Jackson* v *Hall* [1980] AC 854, 884 Viscount Dilhorne rejected
the submission that the contents of a form produced pursuant to
rules made by the Agricultural Land Tribunals (Succession to
Agricultural Tenancies) Order 1976 could be relied on as an aid
to the construction of the Agriculture (Miscellaneous Provisions)
Act 1976. Yet in *British Amusement Catering Trades Association* v
Westminster City Council [1988] 2 WLR 485 the House of Lords
declined to take this as authority for the general proposition that
subordinate legislation can never be used as an aid to statutory
interpretation, citing *Hanlon* v *The Law Society* [1981] AC 124. They
held that the meaning of the term 'cinematograph exhibition' as
defined in the Cinematograph (Amendment) Act 1982, s 1(3) should
be arrived at by reference to the Cinematograph (Safety) Regulations
1955.

Where a later Act is *in pari materia* with an earlier Act, provisions
of the later Act may be used to aid the construction of the earlier
Act. In determining whether the later provision *alters* the legal
meaning of the earlier, the test as always is whether or not Parliament
intended to effect such an alteration (*Casanova* v *R* (1866) LR 1
QB 444, 457). Such an intention is more readily gathered where
the Acts are expressly required to be construed as one, since this
is a positive indication that Parliament has given its mind to the
question.

Where a term is used without definition in one Act, but is defined
in another Act which is *in pari materia* with the first Act, the definition

may be treated as applicable to the use of the term in the first Act. This may be done even where the definition is contained in a later Act. Thus in *Wood* v *Commissioner of Police of the Metropolis* [1986] 1 WLR 796 the Divisional Court construed the undefined term 'offensive weapon' in the Vagrancy Act 1824, s 4, in the light of the definition of that term laid down for different though related purposes by the Prevention of Crime Act 1953, s 1(4).

Where Parliament passes an Act which on one (but not the other) of two disputed views of the existing law is unnecessary, this suggests that the other view is correct. Thus in *Murphy* v *Duke* [1985] QB 905 it was held that since the meaning of the House to House Collections Act 1939 which was applied in *Emanuel* v *Smith* [1968] 2 All ER 529, would render the Trading Representations (Disabled Persons) Act 1958 unnecessary the latter case must be held to have been decided *per incuriam*. (This sensible view was dissented from on doubtful grounds in *Cooper* v *Coles* [1987] QB 230.)

Where it is clear that an enactment proceeds upon a mistaken view of earlier law, the question may arise of whether this effects a change in that law (apart from any amendment directly made by the enactment). Here it is necessary to remember that, except when legislating, Parliament has no power authoritatively to interpret the law. That function belongs to the judiciary alone. When legislating, Parliament may, with binding effect, *declare* what the law is to be considered to be or have been. But a declaratory enactment must be intended as such. A mere inference that Parliament has mistaken the nature or effect of some legal rule does not in itself amount to a declaration that the rule is other than what it is (*Dore* v *Gray* (1788) 2 TR 358, 365; *IRC* v *Dowdall, O'Mahoney & Co Ltd* [1952] AC 401, 417, 421; *IRC* v *Butterley & Co Ltd* [1955] 2 WLR 785, 807–808). However the view taken by Parliament as to the legal meaning of a doubtful enactment may be treated as of persuasive, though not binding, authority (*Cape Brandy Syndicate* v *IRC* [1921] 2 KB 403, 414; *Camille & Henry Dreyfus Foundation Inc* v *IRC* [1954] Ch 672, 690).

The court will not only be guided by later Acts, but by later delegated legislation which is *in pari materia* with the enactment being construed. (*R* v *Newcastle-upon-Tyne Justices, ex parte Skinner* [1987] 1 WLR 312.)

Under the doctrine of precedent or *stare decisis* dynamic processing of an enactment by the court produces sub-rules which are of either binding or persuasive authority in relation to the future construction of the enactment. Where Parliament subsequently indicates that it adopts any such sub-rule, the status of the sub-rule becomes equivalent to that of legislation. If Parliament has a subsequent opportunity to alter the effect of a decision on the legal meaning of an enactment, but refrains from doing so, the implication may be that Parliament approves of that decision and adopts it (eg *Denman* v *Essex Area Health Authority* [1984] 3 WLR 73). This is an aspect of what may be called *tacit legislation*.

The House of Lords held in *Otter* v *Norman* [1988] 3 WLR 321 that the provision of one meal only a day, namely continental breakfast, amounted to 'board'. In so holding it was influenced by the fact that Parliament had impliedly adopted a similar ruling on the meaning of this term laid down by the Court of Appeal in *Wilkes* v *Goodwin* [1923] 2 KB 86.

The court may treat as of persuasive authority in the construction of an enactment the view of an official committee reporting on the meaning of the enactment (eg *Mohammed-Holgate* v *Duke* [1984] QB 209).

Plain meaning rule

Where the meaning is plain it must be followed, but for this purpose a meaning is 'plain' only where no relevant interpretative criterion points away from it. It is thus a rule of law (which may be called the plain meaning rule) that where, in relation to the facts of the instant case, (a) the enactment under enquiry is grammatically capable of one meaning only, and (b) on an informed interpretation of that enactment the interpretative criteria raise no real doubt as to whether that grammatical meaning is the one intended by the legislator, the legal meaning of the enactment corresponds to that grammatical meaning and is to be applied accordingly. As it is put in Halsbury's *Laws of England*:

If there is nothing to modify, nothing to alter, nothing to qualify the language which a statute contains, the words and sentences must be construed in their ordinary and natural meaning. (4th edn, Vol 36 para 585.)

The plain meaning rule determines the operation of nearly every enactment, simply because nearly every enactment has a straightforward and clear meaning with no counter-indications.

Rule where meaning not 'plain'

Where on the facts of the instant case the enactment is grammatically ambiguous, the legal meaning is determined by weighing the interpretative factors in the manner explained in the previous chapter. Where the enactment is semantically obscure, the interpreter first arrives at the 'corrected version' (see pp 89–90 above). This is then treated as if it were the actual text, of which the meaning may be either 'plain' or not. In other words the plain meaning rule either will or will not apply to the corrected version.

Effectiveness rule (*ut res magis valeat quam pereat*)

It is a rule of law that the legislator intends the interpreter of an enactment to observe the maxim *ut res magis valeat quam pereat* (it is better for a thing to have effect than to be made void). He must thus construe the enactment in such a way as to implement, rather than defeat, the legislative purpose. As Dr Lushington put it in *The Beta* (1865) 3 Moo PCC NS 23, 25:

> . . . if very serious consequences to the beneficial and reasonable operation of the Act necessarily follow from one construction, I apprehend that, unless the words imperatively require it, it is the duty of the court to prefer such a construction that *res majis* [*sic*] *valeat, quam pereat*.

The rule requires inconsistencies within an Act to be reconciled. Blackstone said: 'One part of the statute must be so construed by another, that the whole may, if possible, stand: *ut res magis valeat quam pereat,* (Blackstone 1765, i 64). It also means that, if the obvious intention of the enactment gives rise to difficulties in implementation, the court must do its best to find ways of resolving these.

An important application of the rule is that an Act is taken to give the courts such jurisdiction and powers as are necessary for its implementation, even though not expressly conferred (eg *Buckley* v *Law Society (No 2)* [1984] 1 WLR 1101).

Commonsense construction rule

It is a rule of law (which may be called the commonsense construction rule) that when considering, in relation to the facts of the instant case, which of the opposing constructions of the enactment would give effect to the legislative intention, the court should presume that the legislator intended common sense to be used. Thus Lord Lane CJ said when construing an enactment: 'We are dealing with the real world and not some fanciful world' (*Gaimster* v *Marlow* [1984] QB 218, 225).

Many judicial dicta say that common sense, or good sense, or native wit, or the reason of the case, are expected by Parliament to be applied in the interpretation of its laws (see eg *Barnes* v *Jarvis* [1953] 1 WLR 649, 652). Indeed common sense is a quality frequently called for in law generally (eg *R* v *Rennie* [1982] 1 WLR 64).

It follows that when a particular matter is not expressly dealt with in the enactment this may simply be because the drafter thought it went without saying as a matter of common sense (eg *Re Green's Will Trusts* [1985] 3 All ER 455; *R* v *Orpin* [1975] QB 283). Where the court fails to employ common sense it may be right to conclude that the decision is arrived at *per incuriam* and should, when opportunity offers, be overruled (as happened in *R* v *Pigg* [1982] 1 WLR 762).

Greater includes less   The requirement that common sense shall be used in interpretation brings in such principles as that the greater includes the less, which the law recognises in many contexts in accordance with the maxim *omne majus continet in se minus* (eg *R* v *Cousins* [1982] QB 526). Common sense may not provide an answer where the elements are incommensurable. Thus one cannot measure whether an *actual* minor assault is 'greater' or 'less' than a *threat* to carry out a major assault (eg the Australian case of *Rosza* v *Samuels* [1969] SASR 205).

The concept that the greater includes the less is akin to the reverse concept that it is common sense to assume that an Act remedying a lesser mischief is also intended to remedy a greater mischief of the same class (eg *Quiltotex Co Ltd* v *Minister of Housing and Local Government* [1966] 1 QB 704, 712).

Separate ingredients   Where the enactment uses a phrase mentioning two or more ingredients, it is common sense to conclude that if the ingredients are each present separately the description is met. Caution is needed however where the phrase has a special meaning amounting to more than the sum of its parts. This arose in *Leech Leisure Ltd* v *Hotel and Catering Industry Training Board* (1984) *The Times*, 18 January), which concerned the Industrial Training Levy (Hotel and Catering) Order 1981, art 3. This imposes a levy on businesses providing 'board and lodging' for guests or lodgers. It was argued that a self-catering establishment which provided lodging, and also operated a cafe in which cooked meals and snacks could be consumed, was liable to the levy. *Held* the phrase 'board and lodging' is a composite one, and it is not satisfied where lodging is provided and, as an independent activity, food is also made available.

Formal ambiguity   Formal or syntactical ambiguity can sometimes be resolved by the use of common sense. In *The Complete Plain Words*, a manual written to improve the use of language by civil servants, Sir Ernest Gowers cited as an example of formal ambiguity an instruction contained in a child care handbook: 'If the baby does not thrive on raw milk, boil it' (Gowers 1973, p 191). The way the instruction is worded raises a theoretical doubt which common sense is enough to resolve. The same is true of a government regulation cited by Gowers: 'No child shall be employed on any weekday when the school is not open for a longer period than four hours.' (ibid, p 163).

Interpretation by non-lawyers   In the rare cases where an enactment is to be applied by non-lawyers such as juries and lay magistrates it is particularly important that room should be found for a commonsense approach (eg *R* v *Boyesen* [1982] AC 768).

Functional construction rule

The various components of an Act or statutory instrument have been described in chapters 3 and 4. It is a rule of law (which may be called the functional construction rule) that in construing an enactment the significance to be attached to each type of component of the Act or other instrument containing it must be assessed in conformity with its legislative function and juridical nature as a component of that type.

Knowledge of the relevant parliamentary procedure (including royal assent procedure) will assist the interpreter to give correct weight to each component of an Act, judged as an aid to construction. Some components, although part of the Act, carry little if any weight for this purpose: they are intended as nothing more than quick guides to content. Other components (for example the long title) owe their presence in the Act wholly or mainly to the procedural rules applicable to parliamentary Bills, and are to be regarded in that light.

Are there 'second class' components?

Any suggestion that certain components of an Act are to be treated, for reasons connected with their parliamentary nature or history, as not being part of the Act is unsound and contrary to principle. As Scrutton LJ said in relation to the short title:

. . . I do not understand on what principle of construction I am not to look at the words of the Act itself to help me understand its scope in order to interpret the words Parliament has used in the circumstances in which they were legislating. (In *re the Vexatious Actions Act 1886*—In *re Bernard Boaler* [1915] 1 KB 21, 40).

To suppose, as some judges have done, that the components of a Bill which are subject to printing corrections by parliamentary clerks (such as punctuation, sidenotes and headings) cannot be looked at in interpretation of the ensuing Act is to treat them as in some way 'unreliable'. Dicta to this effect in cases such as *R* v *Schildkamp* [1971] AC 1 ignore two major considerations. One is that the entire product is put out by Parliament as its Act and the courts have no authority to question this (Bill of Rights 1688, art 9) and the other is that by virtue of the Interpretation Act 1978, s 19(1) a reference to an Act is a reference to it *as officially published* and this includes all components. Such dicta transgress the principle of law expressed in the maxim *omnia praesumuntur rite et solemniter esse acta donec probetur in contrarium* (all things are presumed to be rightly and duly performed unless the contrary is proved). They are also open to objection as introducing an unjustified distinction between the interpretation of Acts and that of statutory instruments. A statutory instrument is not subject to the making of printing corrections by parliamentary clerks. The headings, marginal notes and punctuation of a statutory instrument must necessarily therefore be treated as being as much part of the instrument as any other component. To avoid an unjustified distinction (never drawn in practice), the same must be taken to be true of an Act. In their 1969 report on statutory interpretation, the Law Commissions said 'it seems clear that the courts when dealing with [delegated] legislation apply the same general common law principles of interpretation which they apply to statutes' (*The Interpretation of Statutes* (Law Com No 21), para 77).

Components used in different ways

Apart from the distinctions between components which have been mentioned so far, there is another type of distinction to be drawn. A component of one kind, for example a section of an Act, may be used in different ways and thus have different functions. Thus a section or similar item may be one of the substantive provisions of the Act, or it may be purely concerned with the machinery of bringing the Act into operation. Difficulty is caused by the fact that under our system provisions of the latter type (known as commencement and transitional provisons) are not clearly differentiated in the arrangement of the Act.

That internal distinctions of this kind may be relevant in interpretation is illustrated by the following dictum of Nourse J in relation to the Development Land Tax Act 1976, s 45(4) and (8):

One thing which is clear about sub-ss (4) and (8) is that the former is a permanent provision and the latter is a transitional one. On a superficial level I can see the attractions of the argument which appealed to the Special Commissioners. But I think it would be very dangerous, in trying to get to the effect of the permanent provision, to attach too much weight to the particular wording of the transitional one. (*IRC* v *Metrolands (Property Finance) Ltd* [1981] 1 WLR 637, 649.)

Categories of components

For purposes of interpretation the components of an Act may be classified as operative components, amendable descriptive components, and unamendable descriptive components.

Operative components

The operative components of an Act or statutory instrument are those that constitute the legislator's pronouncements of law, or in other words consist of *enactments*. In an Act they consist of *sections* and *Schedules*, either of which may incorporate a *proviso* or a *saving*. They carry the direct message of the legislator, forming the Act's 'cutting edge' (*Spencer* v *Metropolitan Board of Works* (1882) 22 Ch D 142, 162). All other components serve as commentaries on the operative components, of greater or lesser utility in interpretation depending on their function.

Sections   Each section is deemed to be a substantive enactment, without the need for enacting words other than the Act's initial enacting formula (Interpretation Act 1978, s 1). To aid the reader, the modern drafter makes use of paragraphing in his undivided section, or in his subsection. The provision remains a single sentence, but is printed with indentations and paragraph numbers so as to bring out the sense and aid cross-referencing. Judges take notice of the paragraphing as a guide to what are intended to be the units of sense (eg *The Eastman Photographic Materials Co Ltd* v *The Comptroller-General of Patents, Designs and Trade-Marks* [1898] AC 571, 579, 584; *Nugent-Head* v *Jacob (Inspector of Taxes)* [1948] AC 321, 329). Drafters take great care to design a section so that it deals with a single point. Under the present system of precision drafting, the way the sections are organised and arranged is a useful guide to legislative intention.

Schedules   The Schedule is an extension of the section which induces it, and is to be read in the light of the wording of that section. Material is put into a Schedule because it is too lengthy or detailed to be conveniently accommodated within the section, or because it forms a separate document (such as a treaty). If by mischance the inducing words were omitted, the Schedule would still form part of the Act if that was the apparent intention. A note of the section or sections in which the inducing words appear is given in the margin at the head of the Schedule. Sometimes an error is made in citing the relevant section or sections (eg the heading to the Crown Proceedings Act 1947, Sched 1, which omits a reference to s 13 of the Act). Such an error does not affect the validity of the Schedule.

Whether material is put in a section or in a Schedule is usually a mere matter of convenience. Little significance should therefore be attached to it. As Brett LJ said in *A-G* v *Lamplough* (1878) 3 Ex D 214, 229: 'A schedule in an Act is a mere question of drafting, a mere question of words. The schedule is as much a part of the statute, and is as much an enactment, as any other part.'

Since an Act is to be read as a whole, a Schedule does not have 'second-class' status as compared to a section. In *IRC* v *Gittus* [1920] 1 KB 563, 576 Lord Sterndale MR gave the following guidance on conflicts between a Schedule and the inducing section:

If the Act says that the Schedule is to be used for a certain purpose and the heading of the part of the Schedule in question shows that it is prima facie at any rate devoted to that purpose, then you must read the Act and the Schedule as though the Schedule were operating for that purpose, and if you can satisfy the language of the section without extending it beyond that purpose you ought to do it.

But if in spite of that you find in the language of the Schedule words and terms that go clearly outside that purpose, then you must give effect to them and you must not consider them as limited by the heading of that part of the Schedule or by the purpose mentioned in the Act for which the Schedule is prima facie to be used. You cannot refuse to give effect to clear words simply because prima facie they seem to be limited by the heading of the Schedule and the definition of the purpose of the Schedule contained in the Act.

For a case where ambiguous words in a Schedule were construed by reference to a heading see *Qualter, Hall & Co Ltd* v *Board of Trade* [1962] Ch 273.

The proviso A proviso is a formula beginning 'Provided that . . .' which is placed at the end of a section or subsection of an Act, or of a paragraph or sub-paragraph of a Schedule, and the intention of which is to narrow the effect of the preceding words. It enables a general statement to be made as a clear proposition, any necessary qualifications being kept out of it and relegated to the proviso.

As Mervyn Davies J said in *Re Memco Engineering Ltd* [1986] Ch 86, 98 'a proviso is usually construed as operating to qualify that which precedes it'. In *Mullins* v *Treasurer of Surrey* (1880) 5 QBD 170, 173 Lush J said: 'When one finds a proviso to a section, the natural presumption is that, but for the proviso, the enacting part of the section would have included the subject-matter of the proviso'. While the substance of this dictum is undoubtedly correct, the treatment of the proviso as qualitatively different from the rest of the section is not. The entire section, including the proviso, is an operative component of the Act (*Gubay* v *Kington (Inspector of Taxes)* [1984] 1 WLR 163).

Judges used to cast doubt on the value of a proviso in throwing light on the meaning of the words qualified by it. This was because provisos, like savings, were often put down as amendments to Bills by their opponents, and accepted to allay usually groundless fears. This still happens in the case of private Bills; but is no longer true of public general Acts.

In the case of precision drafting, the proviso is to be taken as limited in its operation to the section or other provision it qualifies (*Leah* v *Two Worlds Publishing Co* [1951] Ch 393, 398); *Lloyds and Scottish Finance Ltd* v *Modern Cars & Caravans (Kingston) Ltd* [1966] 1 QB 764, 780–781). Where however the Act is the subject of disorganised composition, what is in form a proviso may in fact be an independent substantive provision (*Rhondda UDC* v *Taff Vale Railway* [1909] AC 253, 258; *Eastbourne Corpn* v *Fortes Ltd* [1959] 2 QB 92, 107. The proviso is then said not to be a 'true' proviso (*Commissioner of Stamp Duties* v *Atwill* [1973] AC 558, 561).

A reference to a section includes any proviso to the section, since the proviso forms part of the section. Thus the repeal of the section also repeals the proviso (*Horsnail* v *Bruce* (1873) LR 8 CP 378, 385; cf *Piper* v *Harvey* [1958] 1 QB 439, where the proviso extended beyond the repealed enactment). In accordance with principle, the repeal may be effected by implication.

Savings   A saving is a provision the intention of which is to narrow the effect of the enactment to which it refers so as to preserve some existing legal rule or right from its operation. A saving thus resembles a proviso, except that it has no particular form. Furthermore it relates to an existing legal rule or right, whereas a proviso is usually concerned with limiting the new provision made by the section to which it is attached. A saving often begins with the words 'Nothing in this [Act] [section] [etc] shall . . .'.

Very often a saving is unnecessary, but is put in *ex abundanti cautela* to quieten doubts (*Ealing London Borough Council* v *Race Relations Board* [1972] AC 342, 363). There is an example of this in the Welsh Language Act 1967, which deals with the use of Welsh in legal proceedings and matters. Its final provision is s 5(3), which reads: 'Nothing in this Act shall prejudice the use of Welsh in any case in which it is lawful apart from this Act'. An important example of a saving is the Interpretation Act 1978, s 16, relating to the effect of repeals.

A saving is taken not to be intended to confer any right which did not exist already (*Alton Woods' Case* (1600) 1 Co Rep 40b; *Arnold* v *Gravesend Corpn* (1856) 2 K & J 574, 591; *Butcher* v *Henderson* (1868) LR 3 QB 335; *R* v *Pirehill North JJ* (1884) 14 QBD 13, 19). An unsatisfactory feature of savings, and a reason why drafters resist the addition of unnecessary savings, is that they may throw doubt on matters which it is intended to preserve, but which are not mentioned in the saving (eg *Re Williams, Jones* v *Williams* (1887) 36 Ch D 573). This is an aspect of the application of the *expressio unius* principle (see pp 201–203 below).

Amendable descriptive components

An amendable descriptive component of an Act is one that (a) in some way describes the whole or some part of the Act, and (b) was subject to amendment (as opposed to a mere printing correction) when the Bill for the Act was going through Parliament. The following are amendable descriptive components: long title, preamble, purpose clause, recital, short title, example.

Long title   The long title of an Act (formerly and more correctly called the title) appears at the beginning of the Act. As it is really no more than a remnant from the Bill which on royal assent became the Act, its true function pertains to the Bill rather than the Act.

It sets out in general terms the purposes of the Bill, and under the rules of parliamentary procedure should cover everything in the Bill. If the Bill is amended so as to go wider than the long title, the long title is required to be amended to correspond. Although thus being of a procedural nature, the long title is nevertheless regarded by the courts as a guide to legislative intention.

The long title begins with the words 'An Act to . . .'. Being drafted to comply with parliamentary procedural rules, it is not designed as a guide to the contents of the Act. It is a parliamentary device, whose purpose is in relation to the Bill and its parliamentary progress. Under parliamentary rules, a Bill of which notice of presentation has been given is deemed to exist as a Bill even though it consists of nothing else but the long title. Once the Bill has received royal assent, the long title is therefore vestigial.

The long title is undoubtedly part of the Act, though its value in interpretation has often been exaggerated by judges (eg *Fielding* v *Morley Corpn* [1899] 1 Ch 1, 3, 4; *Suffolk County Council* v *Mason* [1979] AC 705; *Gold Star Publications Ltd* v *DPP* [1981] 1 WLR 732). The courts have been inconsistent on the question of whether the effect of operative provisions should be treated as cut down by the long title. This is to be expected, since the weight of other relevant interpretative factors is bound to vary. Thus in *Watkinson* v *Hollington* [1944] KB 16 the Court of Appeal resorted to the long title to cut down the plain literal meaning of the phrase 'the levying of distress' in the Courts (Emergency Powers) Act 1943, s 1(2) and exclude from it the impounding of trespassing cattle by the ancient remedy of levying distress *damage feasant*. This was because the consequence of applying the literal meaning of s 1(2) would have been unfortunate. On the other hand, in *In the Estate of Groos* [1904] P 269 the court declined to limit the application of the Wills Act 1861, s 3 to British subjects merely because of the reference to them in the long title (see also, to like effect, *Ward* v *Holman* [1964] 2 QB 580).

We may summarise by saying that the long title is an unreliable guide in interpretation, but should not be ignored. It may arouse doubt where it appears to conflict with the operative parts of the Act; and this doubt should then be resolved by a balancing exercise in the usual way. It is not right to say with Slade LJ in *Manuel* v *A-G* [1982] 3 WLR 821, 846 that the court is not entitled to look at the long title unless the operative provisions are ambiguous, because this strikes at the basis of the informed interpretation rule. Lord Simon of Glaisdale said:

In these days, when the long title can be amended in both Houses, I can see no reason for having recourse to it only in case of an ambiguity— it is the plainest of all guides to the general objectives of a statute. But it will not always help as to particular provisions.' (*Black-Clawson*

International Ltd v *Papierwerke Waldhof-Aschaffenberg AG* [1975] AC 591, 647).

Preamble   The courts are reluctant to allow a preamble to override inconsistent operative provisions. Thus it was laid down by the House of Lords in *A-G* v *Prince Ernest Augustus of Hanover* [1957] AC 436 that the preamble should not be allowed to contradict plain words in the body of an Act. The recital of facts in the preamble to an Act does not amount to conclusive proof that the facts are true; but constitutes prima facie evidence of them (*R* v *Sutton* (1816) 4 M & S 532; *A-G* v *Foundling Hospital* [1914] 2 Ch 154; *Dawson* v *Commonwealth of Australia* (1946) 73 CLR 157, 175). Further evidence is then admissible (*DFC of T (NSW)* v *W R Moran Pty Ltd* (1939) 61 CLR 735).

Since the preamble may be a guide to the legal meaning of an enactment, it is unsafe to construe the enactment without reference to the preamble; indeed to do so contravenes the informed interpretation rule. The repeal of a preamble by a Statute Law Revision Act does not affect the meaning of the Act (*Powell* v *Kempton Park Racecourse Co Ltd* [1899] AC 143).

Purpose clauses   A purpose clause, which is an optional component of an Act, is an express statement of the legislative intention. When present, it is included in the body of the Act. It may apply to the whole or a part of the Act. An example is the Income and Corporation Taxes Act 1970, s 488(1): 'This section is enacted to prevent the avoidance of tax by persons concerned with land or the development of land.'

Drafters tend to dislike the purpose clause, taking the view that often the aims of legislation cannot usefully or safely be summarised or condensed by such means. A political purpose clause is no more than a manifesto, which may obscure what is otherwise precise and exact. Moreover detailed amendments made to a Bill after introduction may not merely falsify the purpose clause but even render it impracticable to retain any broad description of the purpose. The drafter's view is that his Act should be allowed to speak for itself. (See Renton 1975, para 11.7.)

Recitals   A recital has the same function as a preamble, but is confined to a single section or other textual unit. It is so called because it recites some relevant matter, often the state of facts that constitutes the mischief the provision is designed to remedy. There may be recitals in this sense within a preamble. Or indeed they may occur anywhere else in an Act. The specialised use of the term however confines it to a statement beginning 'Whereas . . .' which forms the prefix to a distinct enactment. For example the Statute Law (Repeals) Act 1975, s 1(3) begins: 'Whereas this Act repeals so much of section 16(4) of the Marriage Act 1949 as requires a surrogate to have given security by his bond . . .' and then goes on to release surrogates from their bonds.

A recital in a private Act is strong but not conclusive evidence of the truth of what is recited (*Wyld* v *Silver* [1963] 1 QB 169, 187; *Neaverson* v *Peterborough Rural Council* [1901] 1 Ch 22).

Short title   When using the short title as a guide to legislative intention, it must be remembered that its function is simply to provide a brief label by which the Act may be referred to. As Scrutton LJ said: '. . . the short title being a label, accuracy may be sacrificed to brevity' (*In re the Vexatious Actions Act 1886–in re Bernard Boaler* [1915] 1 KB 21, 40). This does not mean that such limited help as it can give must be rejected, and judges not infrequently mention the short title as being at least confirmatory of one of the opposing constructions (eg *Lonrho Ltd* v *Shell Petroleum Co Ltd* [1982] AC 173, 187).

Examples   Where an Act includes examples of its operation, these are to be treated as detailed indications of how Parliament intended the enactment to operate in practice (*Amin* v *Entry Clearance Officer, Bombay* [1983] 2 AC 818). If however an example contradicts the clear meaning of the enactment the latter is accorded preference, it being assumed in the absence of indication to the contrary that the framer of the example was in error. Acts containing examples include the Occupiers Liability Act 1953, s 2(3) and (4), the Race Relations Act 1968, s 2(2), the Sex Discrimination Act 1975, s 29(2), and the Consumer Credit Act 1974, s 188 and Sched 2.

Unamendable descriptive components

An unamendable descriptive component of an Act is one which describes the whole or some part of the Act, and is not subject to any amendment (as opposed to a mere printing correction) when the Bill for the Act is going through Parliament. It is part of the Act, and may be used in interpretation so far as, having regard to its function, it is capable of providing a reliable guide. The following are unamendable descriptive components: chapter number, date of passing, enacting formula, heading, sidenote or marginal note, punctuation, format.

Chapter number   The only significance of the chapter number for statutory interpretation is in determining which of two Acts receiving royal assent on the same date are to be treated as first in time. Thus where two Acts passed on the same day are inconsistent, the chapter numbers indicate which of them, being deemed the later, is to prevail. Where two or more Acts receive assent by the same letters patent, chapter numbers are allocated according to the order in which the short titles are set out in the schedule to the letters patent. Accordingly where Acts are shown as receiving royal assent on the same day, the chapter number shows the deemed order of passing.

The chapter number for a public general Act is in large arabic figures. It is in small roman for local Acts (including Provisional Order Confirmation Acts), and small *italicised* arabic for personal Acts (if printed). This is important because the type face of the chapter number is the only thing that tells the reader which sort of Act he is looking at, or is being referred to.

Date of passing   The passing of the Act and the receiving of royal assent amount to the same thing (*R* v *Smith* [1910] 1 KB 17). The significance of the date of passing is therefore that, unless the contrary intention appears, it is also the date of commencement.

Headings   A heading within an Act, whether contained in the body of the Act or a Schedule, is part of the Act. It may be considered in construing any provision of the Act, provided due account is taken of the fact that its function is merely to serve as a brief, and therefore often inaccurate, guide to the material to which it is attached. In accordance with the informed interpretation rule modern judges consider it not only their right but their duty to take account of headings (eg *Dixon* v *British Broadcasting Corpn* [1979] QB 546; *Customs and Excise Commrs* v *Mechanical Services (Trailer Engineers) Ltd* [1979] 1 WLR 305; *Lloyds Bank Ltd* v *Secretary of State for Employment* [1979] 1 WLR 498; *Re Phelps (decd)* [1980] Ch 275).

Where a heading differs from the material it describes, this puts the court on enquiry. However it is most unlikely to be right to allow the plain literal meaning of the words to be overridden purely by reason of a heading (*Fitzgerald* v *Hall Russell & Co Ltd* [1970] AC 984, 1000; *Pilkington Bros Ltd* v *IRC* [1982] 1 WLR 136, 145). However where general words are preceded by a heading indicating a narrower scope it has been held to be legitimate to treat the general words as cut down by the heading (*Inglis* v *Robertson and Baxter* [1898] AC 616).

Sidenotes   A sidenote or marginal note to a section is part of the Act. It may be considered in construing the section or any other provision of the Act, provided due account is taken of the fact that its function is merely to serve as a brief, and therefore necessarily inaccurate, guide to the content of the section (*R* v *Schildkamp* [1971] AC 1, 10). For example the Bail Act 1976, s 6 makes it an offence if a person who has been released on bail in criminal proceedings fails without reasonable cause to surrender to custody. The sidenote reads: 'Offence of *absconding* by person released on bail' (emphasis added). Absconding is not the only possible reason for failing to surrender to bail. Does the sidenote restrict the width of the section? The answer returned in *R* v *Harbax Singh* [1979] QB 319 was no.

Thring said that the sidenotes, when read together in the arrangement of sections at the beginning of the Act, 'should have such a consecutive meaning as will give a tolerably accurate idea of the contents of the Act' (Thring 1902, p 60). This is an aim drafters pursue, so that the arrangement of sections (or collection of sidenotes) gives a helpful indication of the scope and intention of the Act.

Format   The layout or format is part of the Act. It may be considered in construing any provision of the Act, provided due account is taken of the fact that it is designed merely for ease of reference. Megarry V-C said extra-judicially that 'arrangement may be of the highest importance in suggesting one interpretation and concealing another' ((1959) 75 LQR 31). For example it is the modern practice to break a long section or subsection into paragraphs. Where a provision consists of several numbered paragraphs with the word 'or' before the last paragraph only, that word is taken to be implied before the previous paragraphs after the first (R E Megarry (1959) 75 LQR 29; *Phillips* v *Price* [1958] 3 WLR 616).

The following statement of the reasons for dividing an Act into parts was given by Holroyd J in the Australian case of *Re The Commercial Bank of Australia Ltd* (1893) 19 VLR 333, 375:

When an Act is divided and cut into parts or heads, *prima facie* it is, we think, to be presumed that those heads were intended to indicate a certain group of clauses as relating to a particular object . . . The object is prima facie to enable everybody who reads to discriminate as to what clauses relate to such and such a subject matter. It must be perfectly clear that a clause introduced into a part of an Act relating to one subject matter is meant to relate to other subject matters in another part of the Act before we can hold that it does so.

In *Chalmers* v *Thompson* (1913) 30 WN (NSW) 162 the court considered a section of the Children's Protection Act (a consolidation Act). The section, relating to ill-treatment of children, appeared in a Part headed 'Adoption of Children'. The question was whether a child's natural father could be convicted of contravening the section. The court held that he could, reaching this result by consulting the preconsolidation version, which was not divided into parts.

If material is put into the form of a *footnote* it is still fully a part of the Act, and must be construed accordingly (*Erven Warnink BV* v *Townend & Sons (Hull) Ltd* [1982] 3 All ER 312, 316). For other cases where the court was guided in its construction of an enactment by its typography and layout see *Piper* v *Harvey* [1958] 1 QB 439; *In re Allsop* [1914] 1 Ch 1; *Dormer* v *Newcastle-on-Tyne Corp* [1940] 2 KB 204.

Punctuation   Since fashions in punctuation change, an Act should be construed with regard to the fashion prevailing when it was passed. The Australian case of *Moore* v *Hubbard* [1935] VLR 93 concerned the construction of an enactment making it an offence to deface 'any house or building or any wall fence lamp post or gate'. The defendant had defaced a post carrying electric lines. He was convicted on the ground that the word 'post' stood by itself, and appealed. *Held* The enactment, having been passed in the days when it was not customary to use hyphens in legislation, should be read as if it was written 'any house or building, or any wall, fence, lamp-post, or gate'.

Incorporation by reference

It is a common device of drafters to incorporate earlier statutory provisions by reference, rather than setting out similar provisions in full. This device saves space, and also attracts the case law and other learning attached to the earlier provisions. Its main advantage is a parliamentary one however, since it shortens Bills and cuts down the area for debate. The functional construction rule applies to incorporation by reference, since the provisions incorporated are in a sense components of the Act or other instrument into which they are incorporated.

Where two Acts are required by a provision in the later Act to be construed as one, every enactment in the two Acts is to be construed as if contained in a single Act, except in so far as the context indicates that the later Act was intended to modify the earlier Act. The like principle applies where more than two Acts are to be construed as one, or where a part only of an Act is to be construed as one with other enactments (*Canada Southern Railway Company* v *International Bridge Company* (1883) 8 App Cas 723, 727; *Hart* v *Hudson Bros Ltd* [1928] 2 KB 629; *Phillips* v *Parnaby* [1934] 2 KB 299). Construction as one often causes difficulty to the interpreter. This is because it is a 'blind' form of drafting, far inferior to textual amendment. Mackinnon LJ, a member of the committee whose proposals led to the Arbitration Act 1934, recorded how the drafter of the Act came to see him about the rejection of the committee's recommendation that there should be no legislation by reference in the Act:

I declined to take any interest in it: I reminded him of our request, but 'Here', I said, 'is the detestable thing—legislation by reference of the worst sort'. By way of defence he said what we had proposed was impossible. A Bill so drafted would be intelligible to any MP of the meanest parts; he could debate every section of it, and move endless amendments. (MacKinnon 1942, p 14).

An enactment sometimes incorporates into the Act a whole body of law as it existed at a given time. This may include the practice prevailing at that time, as well as the substantive law then operative. The provisions thus incorporated may not otherwise continue in force. This form of legislation by reference may be called *archival drafting* because it requires persons applying the Act, after a considerable period has elapsed since the relevant date, to engage in historical research in order to find out what the law thus imported amounts to. The effect of archival drafting is to 'freeze' the body of law, so far as thus imported, in the form it was in on the relevant date. Subject to any amendments subsequently made for the purposes of the applying Act, the body of law is to be interpreted for those purposes at any subsequent time, unless the contrary intention appears, as if it had remained unaltered since that date. Thus the Representation of the People Act 1983, s 5(1) says that residence is to be determined 'in accordance with the general principles formerly applied'.

Rules laid down by statute (statutory definitions)

For the purposes of shortening language, and avoiding repetition, Parliament often finds it convenient to lay down limited rules of interpretation by statute. Whether or not framed as such, these are usually in essence *definitions* of some word or phrase, which must then be understood in the stipulated sense. Wherever the defined term appears, the text must be read as if the full definition were substituted for it (*Thomas* v *Marshall* [1953] AC 543, 556; *Suffolk County Council* v *Mason* [1979] AC 709, 713).

Statutory definitions may be general, or restricted to the appearance of the defined term in the defining Act. Whether it is so stated or not, the definition does not apply if the contrary intention appears from an Act in which the defined term is used, since the legislator is always free to disapply a definition whether expressly or by implication (*Jobbins* v *Middlesex County Council* [1949] 1 KB 142, 160; *Parkes* v *Secretary of State for the Environment* [1978] 1 WLR 1308). A contrary legislative intention displacing a statutory rule of construction relating to a particular term may be manifested by the enactment which uses the term spelling out, in a way different to the statutory rule, how the term is to be construed (*Austin Rover Group* v *Crouch Butler Savage Associates* [1986] 1 WLR 1102).

A term may be defined differently in different Acts, according to the purpose of the Act (eg *Earl of Normanton* v *Giles* [1980] 1 WLR 28, which was concerned with varying definitions of 'livestock'). It is even possible for a term to have different meanings within the same Act (eg the Protection of Birds Act 1954, s 14(1), which gives 'wild bird' one meaning in ss 5, 10 and 12 of the Act and a different meaning elsewhere in the Act). This produces obvious risk of confusion.

The wording of a definition may in relation to certain uses of the defined term produce a meaning that is unexpected or unlikely. This does not require the meaning to be rejected if the wording of the definition is clear. It does however suggest caution, and such cases have attracted judicial censure (eg *Lindsay* v *Cundy* (1876) 1 QBD 348, 358; *Bradley* v *Baylis* (1881) 8 QBD 195, 210, 230; *R* v *Commissioners under the Boilers Explosion Act 1882* [1891] 1 QB 703, 716). The Factories Act 1961, s 175 was unexpectedly held to require a film studio to be treated as a 'factory' since articles (namely films) were made there (*Dunsby* v *British Broadcasting Corporation* (1983) *The Times*, 25 July; cf *Savoy Hotel Co* v *London County Council* [1900] 1 QB 665, 669, where the Savoy Hotel was treated as a 'shop').

It is a drafting error (less frequent now than formerly) to incorporate a substantive enactment in a definition (eg *Wakefield Board of Health* v *West Riding & Grimsby Railway Company* (1865) LR 1 QB 84). A definition is not expected to have operative effect as an independent enactment. If it is worded in that way, the courts will tend to construe it restrictively and confine it to the proper function of a definition.

Sometimes a drafter causes confusion by defining an established term in a misleading way. For example the Parliament Act 1911, s 1(2) gives 'Money Bill' a meaning slightly different from that borne by the term in parliamentary usage. Erskine May comments:

. . . the number of bills which are money bills in both senses of the term is sufficiently large to create the mistaken belief that the term has only one meaning. As the framers of the Parliament Act did not realise the inconvenience of using an established term in a new and partly different sense, the resulting ambiguity must be frankly recognised. (May 1976, p 810).

Sometimes a term is given a definition which is omitted in later legislation within the same field. Here it is assumed, unless the contrary intention appears, that the definition is intended to continue to apply (eg *Newbury District Council* v *Secretary of State for the Environment* [1981] AC 578, 596).

Statutory definitions, which may be simple or complex, can be divided into the following six types: clarifying, labelling, referential, exclusionary, enlarging, and comprehensive—some of these overlap:

Clarifying definition   This clarifies the meaning of a common word or phrase, by stating expressly that as used in the Act it does or does not include specified matters. The purpose is to avoid doubt. As Viscount Dilhorne said: 'It is a familiar device of a draftsman to state expressly that certain matters are to be treated as coming within a definition to avoid argument on whether they [do] or not' (*IRC* v *Parker* [1966] AC 141, 161). A term may have a fairly certain meaning, yet give rise to uneasiness by the drafter about leaving it to stand without comment. The remedy is to specify the main ingredients, and rely for any others on the potency of the term itself. This greatly reduces the danger area. The formula is 'T means A, B, C or D, or any other manifestation of T'. An example is the following definition contained in the Supreme Court Act 1981, s 72(5): '"intellectual property" means any patent, trade mark, copyright, registered design, technical or commercial information or other intellectual property'.

Labelling definition   This uses a term as a label denoting a concept which can then be referred to merely by use of the label. Instead of the drafter having to keep repeating the description of the concept, the label alone can be used. In its simplest form a labelling definition may be very brief. Thus the Courts Act 1971, s 57(1) stated that in the Act 'the Judicature Act 1925' meant the Supreme Court of Judicature Act 1925. This enabled a commonly used abbreviated short title to be employed throughout the Act. A common device is for an amending Act to use the label 'the principal Act' to described the Act it is amending.

A labelling definition may be in indirect form. Thus the Employment Protection (Consolidation) Act 1978, s 58(5) states: 'Any reason by virtue of which a dismissal is to be regarded as unfair in consequence of subsection (1) or (3) is in this Part referred to as an inadmissible reason'.

In selecting a label the drafter must bear in mind that words have their own potency. Whatever meaning may be expressly attached to a term, the dictionary or legal meaning exercises some sway over the way the definition will be understood by the court. As Richard Robinson said: 'it is not possible to cancel the ingrained emotion of a word merely by an announcement' (Robinson 1952, p 77). An example related to dictionary meaning arose in *Eastleigh BC* v *Betts* [1982] 2 AC 613, 628, where the definition said that a person is to be taken to have, or not to have, a 'local connection' with a place by reference to stated concepts such as normal residence, employment, and family connections. The House of Lords treated the stated concepts not in their ordinary sense but as coloured by the overall idea of 'local connection'. An example related to legal meaning is furnished by *McCollom* v *Wrightson* [1968] AC 522, where the House of Lords considered the apparently comprehensive definition of 'gaming' in the Betting, Gaming and Lotteries Act 1963 s 55(1) and held that the common law meaning of 'gaming' must be taken to apply so as to cut down the width of the statutory definition.

Referential definition   This attracts a meaning already established in law, whether by statute or otherwise. Thus the Charities Act 1960, s 45(1) says that in the Act 'ecclesiastical charity' has the same meaning as in the Local Government Act 1894. The method carries a danger. Suppose the Act referred to is amended or repealed? Here the principle is clear. Unless the amending or repealing Act contains an indication to the contrary, the amendment or repeal does not affect the meaning of the referential definition.

Exclusionary definition   This expressly deprives the term of a meaning it would or might otherwise be taken to have. Such a definition tends to mislead however if a wide term is artificially cut down by an unexpected extent. Thus the long title of the Animal Boarding Establishments Act 1963 says it is 'An Act to regulate the keeping of boarding establishments for animals'. All the way through, the Act refers to 'animals'. Only when the reader gets to the definition section at the end is he informed that the term 'animal' means cats and dogs only.

The short title of an Act may warn the reader, and so justify a definition of this kind. Thus a definition of 'suspected' as 'suspected of being diseased' could be criticised if it were not contained in a measure called the Diseases of Animals Act 1950 (see s 84(4)).

Enlarging definition   This adds a meaning that otherwise would or might not be included in the term. The formula is 'T includes X', which is taken to signify 'T means a combination of the ordinary meaning of T plus the ordinary meaning of X'. In other words the mention of X does not affect the application of the enactment to T in its ordinary meaning (*Nutter* v *Accrington Local Board* (1878) 4 QBD 375, 384; *Deeble* v *Robinson* [1954] 1 QB 77, 81–2; *Ex parte Ferguson* (1871) LR 6 QB 280, 291). The Income and Corporation Taxes Act 1970, s 454(3) begins: 'In this Chapter, "settlement" includes any disposition, trust, covenant, agreement or arrangement . . .'. In *Thomas* v *Marshall* [1953] AC 543, 556 Lord Morton, considering an earlier version of this definition in the Income Tax Act 1952, s 42, said: 'the object of the subsection is, surely, to make it plain that . . . the word "settlement" is to be enlarged to include other transactions which would not be regarded as "settlements" within the meaning which that word ordinarily bears'.

An enlarging definition may not fall to be applied to its full literal extent. Thus in a later case the House of Lords held the definition considered in the previous example to be restricted by implication to 'settlements' (in the enlarged sense) which contain an element of bounty (*IRC* v *Plummer* [1980] AC 896).

An enlarging definition may make the term include a division or section of the matter in question (eg the Employment Protection (Consolidation) Act 1978, s 58(6)); *Bradley* v *Baylis* (1881) 8 QBD 210, 230).

Where an enactment contains an enlarging definition of a term, words used in connection with the term in its normal meaning are by implication required to be modified as necessary.

Comprehensive definition   This provides a full statement of the meaning of the term, specifying everything that is to be taken as included in it. Thus the Charities Act 1960, s 46 says: '"charitable purposes" means purposes which are exclusively charitable according to the law of England and Wales'. This comprehensively describes the concept in question. It is also an example of a referential definition, since it draws on the legal meaning of 'charity'.

Interpretation Act 1978

The general Interpretation Act currently in force is the Interpretation Act 1978. This replaced the Interpretation Act 1889, which in turn replaced the first Interpretation Act, known as Lord Brougham's Act 1850.

The basic idea of an Interpretation Act is indicated by the long title to Lord Brougham's Act: 'An Act for shortening the Language used in Acts of Parliament'. An Interpretation Act is thus essentially a collection of labelling definitions.

Every interpreter needs to bear in mind the provisions of the Interpretation Act 1978, which are constantly overlooked in practice.

For a list of terms defined generally by Act see the title 'Act of Parliament' in the official publication *Index to the Statutes*.

Chapter Ten

Guides to Legislative Intention II: Principles Derived from Legal Policy

The present chapter deals with the eight principles derived from legal policy. These are:

1 law should serve the public interest
2 law should be just
3 persons should not be penalised under a doubtful law
4 'adverse' law should not operate retrospectively
5 law should be predictable
6 law should be coherent and self-consistent
7 law should not be subject to casual change
8 municipal law should conform to public international law.

Some of these principles overlap. For example the principle against doubtful penalisation and the principle against retrospectivity are both manifestations of the wider principle that law should be just. It is however convenient to treat them separately because of their individual importance.

Nature of legal policy

A principle of statutory interpretation derives from the wider policy of the law, which is in turn based on what is called public policy. The interpreting court is required to presume, unless the contrary intention appears, that the legislator intended to conform to this. Thus in *Re Royse (decd)* [1985] Ch 22, 27 Ackner LJ said of the principle that a person should not benefit from his own wrong that the Inheritance (Provision for Family and Dependants) Act 1975 'must be taken to have been passed against the background of this well-accepted principle of public policy'.

A principle of statutory interpretation can thus be described as a principle of legal policy formulated as a guide to legislative intention. Here it is necessary to remember the juridical distinction between principles and rules. A rule binds, but a principle guides: *principiorum non est ratio*. As we saw in the previous chapter, if an enactment incorporates a rule it makes that rule binding in discerning the purposes of the Act. But if it attracts a principle it leaves scope for flexible application.

General principles of law and public policy underlie and support the specific rules laid down by the body of legislation. If it were not so the latter would be merely arbitrary. Even where a rule does appear arbitrary (for example that one must drive on the left), there is likely to be a non-arbitrary principle underlying it (road safety is desirable). However that sort of principle is an element of social policy. While it may point to the mischief and remedy of a particular enactment, and assist in purposive construction, it is not the kind of principle this chapter is concerned with.

What we are now considering is the body of general principle built up by the judiciary over the centuries, and referred to as legal policy. It is also referred to as public policy; but it is the judges' view of public policy, and confined to justiciable issues. Public policy in this sense has been judicially described as 'a very unruly horse' (*Richardson* v *Mellish* (1824) 2 Bing 252), and is not a concept that admits of precise definition. Nevertheless it is clear that it exists, and necessarily has a powerful influence on the interpretation of statutes.

Legal policy, equivalent to what the Germans call *Reschtspolitik*, consists of the collection of principles the judges consider it their duty to uphold. It is directed always to the wellbeing of the community, and is by no means confined to statute law. Thus without reference to any statute it was said by the court in *R* v *Higgins* (1801) 2 East 5 that all such acts and attempts as tend to the prejudice of the community are indictable. The framing of legal policy goes to the root of the judicial function as understood in Britain. The judges do not exactly invent legal policy: it evolves through the cases. Yet the function is an important creative one, even in relation to statutes. Friedmann remarked, that in his auxiliary function as interpreter of statutes, 'the task of the judge is to leave policy to the elected organs of democracy and to interpret such policy intelligently' (Friedmann 1949, p 315).

The constituent elements of legal policy are drawn from many sources. These include parliamentary enactments, past judgments, ideas of natural law, the writings of domestic jurists, and comparative jurisprudence. The sources are not all legal however. Religious, philosophical and economic doctrine enters in. Political reality flavours the mixture. International obligations are not forgotten. Common sense and savoir faire bind the whole together.

The underlying basis of legal policy is the welfare of the inhabitants: *Salus populi est suprema lex* (13 Co Inst 139). It follows that in the formation of legal policy public opinion plays its part, and should never be far from the judge's mind (eg *Foley* v *Foley* [1981] Fam 160, 167 where on a claim for maintenance by a divorced wife, Eveleigh LJ said 'public opinion would readily recognise a stronger claim founded on years of marriage than on years of cohabitation').

Neither principles of law nor those of wider public policy are static. In their judgments, the courts reflect developments in these principles. In their Acts, legislators do likewise. There is an interaction between the two. As Lord Sumner said:

The fact that opinion grounded on experience has moved one way does not in law preclude the possibility of its moving on fresh experience in the other; nor does it bind succeeding generations, when conditions have again changed. (*Bowman* v *Secular Society Ltd* [1917] AC 406, 467.)

However the court ought not to enunciate a new head of public policy in an area where Parliament has demonstrated its willingness to intervene when considered necessary (*Re Brightlife Ltd* [1987] 2 WLR 197). For the concept of public policy in the European Community see *R* v *Bouchereau* [1978] QB 732.

Principle that law should serve the public interest

It is the basic principle of legal policy that law should serve the public interest. The court, when considering, in relation to the facts of the instant case, which of the opposing constructions of the enactment would give effect to the legislative intention, should presume that the legislator intended to observe this principle. It should therefore strive to avoid adopting a construction which is in any way adverse to the public interest. All enactments are presumed to be for the public benefit, there being no sound method of distinguishing between them in this regard. This means that the court must always assume that it is in the public interest to give effect to the true intention of the legislator, even though it may disagree with that intention. Every legal system must concern itself primarily with the public interest. Hence the numerous Latin maxims beginning with the phrase *interest reipublicae* (it concerns the state).

One of these maxims, *interest reipublicae ut sit finis litium*, is of frequent application, though modern judges often prefer not to use the Latin form. In *R* v *Pinfold* [1988] 2 WLR 635 the Court of Appeal, Criminal Division, construed the Criminal Appeal Act 1968, ss 1(1) and 2(1) (which confer a right of appeal in cases of conviction on indictment) by applying the maxim. The convict had already instituted one (unsuccessful) appeal, and now sought to lodge a second appeal on the ground of new evidence. Delivering the judgment of the court Lord Lane CJ did not cite the maxim directly, but nevertheless relied on it. Dismissing the application he said ' . . . one must read those provisions against the background of the fact that it is in the interests of the public in general that there should be a limit or a finality of legal proceedings, sometimes put in a Latin maxim, but that is what it means in English'. On the application of this maxim see also *Buckbod Investments Ltd* v *Nana-Otchere* [1985] 1 WLR 342 (reluctance of courts to allow appeal to be withdrawn rather than dismissed); *G* v *G* [1985] 1 WLR 647, 652 (maxim applies strongly in child custody cases, since children are disturbed by prolonged uncertainty).

A proper balance needs to be struck between individual and community rights. Nor is this an even balance, since our present and inherited law constantly takes the view that *jura publica anteferenda privatis* (public rights are to be preferred to private). Lord Denning quoted the statement by Lord Reid in *A-G v Times Newspapers Ltd* [1974] AC 273, 296 that 'there must be a balancing of relevant considerations', then added his own rider: 'The most weighty consideration is the public interest' (*Wallersteiner v Moir* [1974] 1 WLR 991, 1005). Too great an emphasis on the principle against doubtful penalisation can harm the public interest, for the public suffers if dangerous criminals escape on a technicality, or taxes are improperly evaded. In time of war or other national emergency the need to curtail some human rights is greater, as the case of *Liversidge v Anderson* [1942] AC 206 illustrated. Different aspects of the public interest may conflict. In the case of public interest immunity, for instance, 'the balance . . . has to be struck between the public interest in the proper functioning of the public service (ie the executive arm of government) and the public interest in the administration of justice' (*Burmah Oil Co Ltd v Bank of England (A-G intervening)* [1980] AC 1090, *per* Lord Scarman at p 1145.

Construction in bonam partem In pursuance of the principle that law should serve the public interest the courts have evolved the technique of construction *in bonam partem*. This ensures that, if a statutory benefit is given on a specified condition being satisfied, the court presumes that Parliament intended the benefit to operate only where the required act is performed in a *lawful* manner. Thus where an Act gave efficacy to a fine levied on land, it was held to refer only to a fine lawfully levied (Co Litt s 728). A more recent example concerned the construction of the Town and Country Planning Act 1947, s 12(5), which said that, in respect of land which on the appointed day was unoccupied, planning permission was not required 'in respect of the use of the land for the purpose for which it was last used'. In *Glamorgan County Council v Carter* [1963] 1 WLR 1 the last use of the land had contravened a local Act, so the court held that s 12(5) did not apply. For other examples see *Gridlow-Jackson v Middlegate Properties Ltd* [1974] QB 361 (the 'letting value' of a property, within the meaning of the Leasehold Reform Act 1967, s 4(1), could not exceed the statutory standard rent); *Harris v Amery* (1865) LR 1 CP 148 (voting qualification based on interest in land: actual interest illegal); *Hipperson v Electoral Registration Officer for the Distict of Newbury* [1985] QB 1060 (residential qualification for the franchise did not by implication require the residence to be lawful, though it did require that it should not be in breach of a court order).

Equally a person does not forfeit a statutory right because he has abstained from acting illegally, as by becoming intentionally homeless to avoid remaining as a trespasser (*R v Portsmouth City*

Council, ex parte Knight (1983) *The Times,* 18 July) or to avoid infringing immigration laws (*R* v *Hillingdon London Borough Council, ex parte Wilson* (1983) *The Times*).

Construction *in bonam partem* applies where a disability is removed conditionally, since the removal of a disability ranks as a benefit (eg *Adlam* v *The Law Society* [1968] 1 WLR 6, where 'in continuous practice as a solicitor' in the Solicitors Act 1957, s 41(1) was read as 'in continuous *lawful* practice').

Principle that law should be just

It is a principle of legal policy that law should be just, and that court decisions should further the ends of justice. The court, when considering, in relation to the facts of the instant case, which of the opposing constructions of the enactment would give effect to the legislative intention, should presume that the legislator intended to observe this principle. It should therefore strive to avoid adopting a construction that leads to injustice.

Parliament is presumed to intend to act justly and reasonably (*IRC* v *Hinchy* [1960] AC 748, 768), and for this purpose justice includes social justice (*Williams & Glyn's Bank Ltd* v *Boland* [1981] AC 487, 510). Here courts rely on 'impression and instinctive judgment as to what is fair and just' (*Home Office* v *Dorset Yacht Co Ltd* [1970] AC 1004, 1054). Thus in *De Vesci (Evelyn Viscountess)* v *O'Connell* [1908] AC 298, 310 Lord Macnaghten said: 'The process vulgarly described as robbing Peter to pay Paul is not a principle of equity, nor is it, I think, likely to be attributed to the Legislature even in an Irish Land Act.'

In *Coutts & Co* v *IRC* [1953] AC 267, 281, where the Crown demanded estate duty of £60,000 although by reason of the death of a trust beneficiary the income of another beneficiary was increased by a mere £1,976 per annum, Lord Reid said:

In general if it is alleged that a statutory provision brings about a result which is so startling, one looks for some other possible meaning of the statute which will avoid such a result, because there is some presumption that Parliament does not intend its legislation to produce highly inequitable results.

It sometimes happens that injustice to someone will arise whichever way the decision goes. Here the court carries out a balancing exercise, as in *Pickett* v *British Rail Engineering Ltd* [1980] AC 136. The case concerned damages recoverable by a deceased's estate under the Law Reform (Miscellaneous Provisions) Act 1934, and Lord Wilberforce said that there might in some cases be duplication of recovery. He went on (p 151):

To that extent injustice may be caused to the wrongdoer. But if there is a choice between taking a view of the law which mitigates a clear and recognised injustice in cases of normal occurrence, at the cost of the possibility in fewer cases of excess payments being made, or leaving the law as it is, I think our duty is clear. We should carry the judicial process of seeking a just principle as far as we can, confident that a wise legislator will correct resultant anomalies.

The courts nowadays frequently use the concept of *fairness* as the standard of just treatment (eg *Cardshops Ltd* v *John Lewis Properties Ltd* [1983] QB 161). This is sometimes referred to as the 'aequum et bonum', after the maxim *aequum et bonum est lex legum* (that which is equitable and good is the law of laws).

Discretionary powers

The principle that law should be just means that Parliament is taken to intend, when conferring a discretionary power, that it is to be exercised justly. Thus in *R* v *Tower Hamlets London Borough Council, ex parte Chetnik Developments Ltd* [1988] 2 WLR 654 the House of Lords laid down the principle that where an apparently unfettered discretion is conferred by statute on a public authority it is to be inferred that Parliament intended the discretion to be exercised in the same high-principled way as is expected by the court of its own officers.

Principle against doubtful penalisation

A person is not to be put in peril upon an ambiguity. As an aspect of the principle that law should be just, legal policy requires that a person should not be penalised except under clear law, which may be called the principle against doubtful penalisation. The court, when considering, in relation to the facts of the instant case, which of the opposing constructions of the enactment would give effect to the legislative intention, should presume that the legislator intended to observe this principle. It should therefore strive to avoid adopting a construction that penalises a person where the legislator's intention to do so is doubtful, or penalises him in a way or to an extent which was not made clear in the enactment.

For this purpose a law that inflicts hardship or deprivation of any kind is treated as penal. There are degress of penalisation, but the concept of detriment inflicted through the state's coercive power pervades them all. Accordingly this principle is not concerned with any technical rules as to what is or is not a penal enactment. The substance is what matters. Whenever it can be argued that an enactment has a meaning requiring infliction of a detriment of any kind, the principle against doubtful penalisation comes into play. If the detriment is minor, the principle will carry little weight. If the detriment is severe, the principle will be correspondingly powerful. However it operates, the principle states that persons should not be subjected by law to any sort of detriment unless this is imposed by clear words. As Brett J said in *Dickenson* v *Fletcher* (1873) LR 9 CP 1, 7:

Those who contend that a penalty may be inflicted must show that the words of the Act distinctly enact that it shall be incurred under the present circumstances. They must fail if the words are merely equally capable of a construction that would, and one that would not, inflict the penalty.

Deprivation without compensation

An obvious detriment is to take away rights without commensurate compensation. The common law has always frowned on this. Brett MR said: It is a proper rule of construction not to construe an Act of Parliament as interfering with or injuring persons' rights without compensation unless one is obliged so to construe it.' (*A-G* v *Horner* (1884) 14 QBD 245, 257; approved *Consett Iron Co* v *Clavering* [1935] 2 KB 42, 58; *Bond* v *Nottingham Corpn* [1940] Ch 429, 435.)

The same applies where rights, though not taken away, are restricted (*London and North-Western Railway Co* v *Evans* [1893] 1 Ch 16, 27; *Mayor etc of Yarmouth* v *Simmons* (1879) 10 Ch D 518, 527). It applies both to the rights of an individual and those possessed by the public at large (*Forbes* v *Ecclesiastical Commissioners* (1872) LR 15 Eq 51, 53; *R* v *Strachan* (1872) LR 7 QB 463, 465).

Where a statutory procedure exists for taking away rights with compensation, the court will resist the argument that some other procedure can legitimately be used for doing the same thing without compensation (*Hartnell* v *Minister of Housing* [1965] AC 1134; *Hall* v *Shoreham-by-Sea UDC* [1964] 1 WLR 240).

Common law rights   The principle against doubtful penalisation applies to the taking away of what is given at common law: 'Plain words are necessary to establish an intention to interfere with . . . common law rights' (*Deeble* v *Robinson* [1954] 1 QB 77, 81).

Detailed statutory codes   Where Parliament finds it necessary to lay down a detailed system of regulation in some area of the national life the courts recognise that it may then be impossible to avoid inflicting detriments which, taken in isolation, are unjustified. The presumption against doubtful penalisation is therefore applied less rigorously in such cases (*Young* v *Secretary of State for the Environment* [1983] 2 AC 662, 671).

Standard of proof   Where an enactment would inflict a serious detriment on a person if certain facts were established then, even though the case is not a criminal cause or matter, the criminal standard of proof will be required to establish those facts (eg *R* v *Milk Marketing Board, ex parte Austin* (1983) *The Times* 21 March).

Types of detriment

We now consider in detail the various types of detriment to which the principle against doubtful penalisation applies. It is convenient to do this in conjunction with references to relevant provisions of the European Convention on Human Rights, since our courts are required by treaty to have regard to these.

First we look at impairment of human life or health. Then follow various kinds of interference, namely with freedom of the person, family rights, religion, free asssembly and association, and free speech. Next come detriment to property and other economic interests, detriment to status or reputation, and infringement of privacy. We conclude with impairment of rights in relation to law and legal proceedings, and with other infringement of a person's rights as a citizen. Criminal sanctions, with which the principle against doubtful penalisation is chiefly identified, appear in several of these categories. Capital and corporal punishment fall within the first. Imprisonment curtails freedom of the person and interferes with family rights. A fine is an economic detriment. All convictions impose a stigma, and therefore affect status or reputation.

Impairment of human life or health The leading aspect of the principle against doubtful penalisation is that by the exercise of state power the life or health of a person should not be taken away, impaired or endangered, except under clear authority of law. An exception as to preservation of human life is imported whenever necessary into a penal enactment. Even where the exception is not stated expressly, the probability that it is to be taken as implied necessarily raises doubt as to the application of the enactment, and thus the principle against doubtful penalisation applies. As was said long ago by an advocate in *Reniger* v *Fogossa* (1550) 1 Plowd 1, 13:

When laws or statutes are made, yet there are certain things which are exempted and excepted out of the provision of the same by the law of reason, although they are not expressly excepted. As the breaking of prison is felony in the prisoner himself by the Statute de Frangentibus Prisonam: yet if the prison be on fire, and they who are in break the prison to save their lives, this shall be excused by the law of reason, and yet the words of the statute are against it.

Similarly in *R* v *Rose* (1847) 2 Cox CC 329 an enactment penalising 'revolt in a ship' was held subject to an implied exception where revolt was justified to prevent the master from unlawfully killing persons on board.

When in a poor law case it was objected that the law gave an alien no claim to subsistence, Lord Ellenborough CJ said:

> . . . the law of humanity, which is anterior to all positive laws, obliges us to afford them relief, to save them from starving; and [the poor laws] were only passed to fix the obligation more certainly, and point out distinctly in what manner it should be borne. (*R* v *Inhabitants of Eastbourne* (1803) 4 East 103, 106.)

The law requires convincing justification before it permits any physical interference, under alleged statutory powers, with a person's body (eg *W* v *W* (1963) [1964] P 67); *Aspinall* v *Sterling Mansell Ltd* [1981] 2 All ER 866; *Prescott* v *Bulldog Tools Ltd* [1981] 3 All ER 869). The court will be reluctant to arrive at a meaning which would hinder self-help by a person whose health is endangered (eg *R* v *Dunbar* [1981] 1 WLR 1536).

Article 2 of the European Convention on Human Rights requires everyone's right to life to be protected by law, and states that no one shall be deprived of his life intentionally save in the execution of a court sentence following conviction for a crime for which the law imposes the death penalty. Exceptions cover self-defence, lawful arrest, and action taken to quell riot or insurrection. Article 3 of the Convention follows the Bill of Rights (1688) in prohibiting torture, and 'inhuman or degrading treatment or punishment'.

Physical restraint of the person   One aspect of the principle against doubtful penalisation is that by the exercise of state power the physical liberty of a person should not be interfered with except under clear authority of law. Freedom from unwarranted restraint of the person has always been a keystone of English law, and continues to be recognised by Parliament (eg the Supreme Court Act 1981, s 18(*h*)(i)). If follows that an enactment is not held to impair this without clear words. As Goff LJ said in *Collins* v *Wilcock* [1984] 1 WLR 1172, 1177, where a conviction for assaulting a police officer who took hold of the defendant's arm was quashed: 'the fundamental principle, plain and incontestable, is that every person's body is inviolate'.

Article 4 of the European Convention on Human Rights states that no one shall be held in slavery or servitude, or be required to perform forced or compulsory labour. Exceptions cover lawful imprisonment, military service, work to meet an emergency threatening the life or well-being of the community, and 'normal civic obligations'. Article 5 of the Convention states that everyone has the right to liberty and security of person, and that no one shall be deprived of his liberty except in one of a number of specified cases. These cover lawful imprisonment, care of minors, and detention of lunatics, alcoholics, drug addicts, vagrants, and persons with infectious diseases. Protocol 4 to the Convention forbids imprisonment merely on the ground of inability to fulfil a contractual obligation. It also states that, subject to obvious exceptions, everyone lawfully within the territory of the state shall have the right to liberty of movement (including freedom to choose his residence), and freedom to leave the state.

Interference with family rights One aspect of the principle against doubtful penalisation is that by the exercise of state power the family arrangements of a person should not be interfered with, nor his relationships with family members impaired, except under clear authority of law.

English law has always concerned itself with the protection of the home. Unless the contrary intention appears, an enactment by implication imports the principle *domus sua cuique est tutissimum refugium*, which may be freely translated as 'a man's home is his castle'. An interpretation that would make a person homeless is adopted with reluctance (eg *Annicola Investments Ltd* v *Minister of Housing and Local Government* [1968] 1 QB 631, 644).

In considering the enactments relating to child care, Lord Scarman said:

The policy of the legislation emerges clearly from a study of its provisions. The encouragement and support of family life are basic. The local authority are given duties and powers primarily to help, not to supplant, parents. A child is not to be removed from his home or family against the will of his parent save by the order of a court, where the parent will have an opportunity to be heard before the order is made. Respect for parental rights and duties is, however, balanced against the need to protect children from neglect, ill-treatment, abandonment and danger, for the welfare of the child is paramount. (*London Borough of Lewisham* v *Lewisham Juvenile Court JJ* [1980] AC 273, 307.)

The courts lean in favour of the transmission of an intestate's estate to members of his family, rather than that it should pass to the state as *bona vacantia* (eg *Re Lockwood, Atherton* v *Brooke* [1958] Ch 231).

Article 8 of the European Convention on Human Rights states that everyone has the right to respect for his family life and his home, with exceptions for national security, public safety, economic well-being of the state, prevention of crime or disorder, protection of health or morals, and the freedom of others. Article 12 of the Convention says that men and women of marriageable age have the right to marry and to found a family. Protocol 1 states that no person shall be denied the right to education, and adds that the state shall respect the right of parents to ensure that education is in conformity with their own 'religious and philosophical convictions'.

Interference with religious freedom Another aspect of the principle against doubtful penalisation is that by the exercise of state power the religious freedom of a person should not be interfered with, except under clear authority of law.

English law is still predisposed to the Christian religion, particularly that form of it which is established by law (or in other words Anglicanism). However Parliament has discarded most of the former laws, such as the Corporation and Test Acts, which caused discrimination against persons of other faiths or none. The House of Lords dismissed as 'mere rhetoric' Hale's statement that Christianity is 'parcel of the laws of England' (*Bowman* v *Secular Society Ltd* [1917] AC 406, 458). Yet the House of Lords has recently enforced, after an interval of more than half a century, the ancient offence of blasphemous libel as a safeguard solely of Christian believers (*R* v *Lemon* [1979] AC 617). The previous recorded conviction for this offence was *R* v *Gott* (1922) 16 Cr App R 87.

Article 9 of the European Convention on Human Rights states that, within obvious limitations, everyone has the right to freedom of thought, conscience and religion. This is stated to include freedom to change one's religion or belief, and freedom (either alone or in community with others, and either in public or private) to manifest one's religion or belief in worship, teaching, practice and observance. Lord Scarman has said that by necessary implication art 9 'imposes a duty on all of us to refrain from insulting or outraging the religious feelings of others' (*R* v *Lemon* [1979] AC 617, 665).

Interference with free assembly and association   The principle against doubtful penalisation requires that by the exercise of state power the freedom of a person to assemble and associate freely with others should not be interfered with, except under clear authority of law.

Thus in *Beatty* v *Gillbanks* (1882) 9 QBD 308, 313, where local Salvation Army leaders were convicted of unlawful assembly for organising revival meetings and marches which would have been entirely peaceful if a hostile group had not sought to break them up by force, Field J said:

As far as these appellants are concerned there was nothing in their conduct when they were assembled together which was either tumultuous or against the peace. But it is said, that the conduct pursued by them on this occasion was such, as on several previous occasions, had produced riots and disturbances of the peace and terror to the inhabitants . . . Now I entirely concede that everyone must be taken to intend the natural consequences of his own acts . . . the finding of the justices amounts to this, that a man may be convicted for doing a lawful act if he knows that his doing it may cause another to do an unlawful act. There is no authority for such a proposition . . .

Article 11 of the European Convention on Human Rights states that everyone has the right to freedom of peaceful assembly and to freedom of association with others, including the right to form and to join trade unions for the protection of his interests. There are exceptions for members of the armed forces, police and state administration, and the other usual qualifications.

Interference with free speech   One aspect of the principle against doubtful penalisation is that by the exercise of state power a person's freedom of speech should not be interfered with, except under clear authority of law. Lord Mansfield said: 'The liberty of the press consists in printing without any previous licence, subject to the consequences of law' (*R v Dean of St Asaph (1784) 3 TR 428 (note);* see also *R v Cobbett* (1804) 29 St Tr 1). Scarman LJ, in remarks concerning the Administration of Justice Act 1960, s 12(4), referred to 'the law's basic concern to protect freedom of speech and individual liberty' (*Re F (a minor) (publication of information)* [1977] Fam 58, 99). The dictum was approved by Lord Edmund-Davies on appeal (see [1979] AC 440, 465).

In *Re X (a minor)* [1975] Fam 47 it was sought to prohibit the publication of discreditable details about a deceased person on the gound that this might harm his infant child if the child became aware of them. *Held* the public interest in free speech outweighed the possible harm to the child, and the injunction would be refused.

Article 10 of the European Convention on Human Rights says that everyone has the right to freedom of expression. This includes freedom to hold opinions and receive and impart information and ideas without interference by public authority, and regardless of frontiers. Licensing of broadcasting and cinemas is allowed, but not licensing of the press. Other restrictions such as 'are necessary in a democratic society' are allowed. Article 6 of the Convention permits restrictions on the reporting of criminal trials.

Detriment to property and other economic interests   The principle against doubtful penalisation requires that by the exercise of state power the property or other economic intersts of a person should not be taken away, impaired or endangered, except under clear authority of law.

It was said by Pratt CJ in the great case against general warrants, *Entick v Carrington* (1765) 19 St Tr 1030, 1060 that: 'The great end for which men entered into society was to secure their property. That right is preserved sacred and incommunicable in all instances where it has not been abridged by some public law for the good of the whole'

Blackstone said that the right of property is an absolute right, inherent in every Englishman: 'which consists in the free use, enjoyment, and disposal of all his acquisitions, without any control or diminution, save only by the laws of the land'. He added that the laws of England are therefore 'extremely watchful in ascertaining and protecting this right' (Blackstone 1765, i 109). It follows that whenever an enactment is alleged to authorise interference with property the court will apply the principle against doubtful penalisation. The interference may take many forms. All kinds of taxation involve detriment to property rights. So do many criminal and other penalties, such as fines, compensation orders and costs orders. Compulsory purchase, trade regulation and restrictions, import controls, forced redistribution on divorce or death, and maintenance orders are further categories. It must be stressed however that, as so often in statutory interpretation, there are other criteria operating *in favour* of all these and the result must be a balancing exercise.

Perhaps the most severe interference with property rights is expropriation. Buckley LJ said that:

. . . in an Act such as the Leasehold Reform Act 1967, which, although it is not a confiscatory Act is certainly a disproprietory Act, if there is any doubt as to the way in which language should be construed, it should be construed in favour of the party who is to be dispropriated rather than otherwise. (*Methuen-Campbell* v *Walters* [1979] QB 525, 542).

Property rights include the right of a person who is sui juris to manage and control his own property. Nourse J referred to 'the general principle in our law that the rights of a person whom it regards as having the status to deal with them on his own behalf will not . . . be overridden' (*Re Savoy Hotel Ltd* [1981] Ch 351, 365).

The tendency is for the conferring of property rights to be by common law, and for their abridgement to be by statute. The courts, having created the common law, are jealous of attempts to deprive the citizen of its benefits (eg *Turton* v *Turnbull* [1934] 2 KB 197, 199; *Newtons of Wembley Ltd* v *Williams* [1965] 1 QB 560, 574). Where property rights given at common law are curtailed by statute, the statutory conditions must be strictly complied with. Thus Davies LJ said of the Landlord and Tenant Act 1954: 'The statute, as we all know, is an invasion of the landlord's right, for perfectly proper and sound reasons; but it must be construed strictly in accordance with its terms' (*Stile Hall Properties Ltd* v *Gooch* [1980] 1 WLR 62, 65).

On taxation the modern attitude of the courts is that the revenue from taxation is essential to the running of the state, and that the duty of the judiciary is to aid its collection while remaining fair to the subject, eg *IRC* v *Berrill* [1981] 1 WLR 1449 (construction rejected which would have made it impossible for Inland Revenue to raise an assessment).

Protocol 1 to the European Convention on Human Rights says that every natural or legal person is entitled to the peaceful enjoyment of his possessions. No one is to be deprived of his possessions except in the public interest and by due process of law.

Detriment to status or reputation   Under the principle against doubtful penalisation it is accepted that by the exercise of state power the status or reputation of a person should not be impaired or endangered, except under clear authority of law. Therefore the more a particular construction is likely to damage a person's reputation, the stricter the interpretation a court is likely to give.

The court accepts that any conviction of a criminal offence imparts a stigma, even though an absolute discharge is given. Thus in *DPP for Northern Ireland* v *Lynch* [1975] AC 653, 707 Lord Edmund-Davies spoke of 'the obloquy involved in the mere fact of conviction'. If an offence carries a heavy penalty, the stigma will be correspondingly greater (*Sweet* v *Parsley* [1970] AC 132, 149). This is an important consideration in determining whether Parliament intended to require *mens rea*.

The European Convention on Human Rights does not reproduce the provision in the Universal Declaration of Human Rights 1948 stating that no one shall be subjected to 'attacks upon his honour and reputation' (art 12). However art 10 of the European Convention, in conferring the right of free speech, does include an exception 'for the protection of the reputation or rights of others'.

Infringement of privacy   One aspect of the principle against doubtful penalisation is that by the exercise of state power the privacy of a person should not be infringed, except under clear authority of law. An important element in the law's protection of privacy springs from the principle that a man's home is his castle, discussed above (p 145). Even outside the home, the courts tend to require clear words to authorise an invasion of privacy. For example it was held that a predecessor of the Licensing Act 1964, s 186, which says that a constable 'may at any time enter licensed premises . . . for the purpose of preventing or detecting the commission of any offence', must be treated as subject to the implied limitation that it did not authorise a constable to enter unless he had some reasonable ground for suspecting a breach of the law (*Duncan* v *Dowding* [1897] 1 QB 575).

There is no principle in English law by which documents are protected from discovery by reason of confidentiality alone. This does not mean that, in deciding whether to order discovery under statutory powers, an authority is intended to ignore the question of confidentiality. It is to be taken into account along with other factors (*Science Research Council* v *Nasse* [1980] AC 1028, 1065). Article 8 of the European Convention on Human Rights states that everyone has the right to respect for his private life and his correspondence, with exceptions for national security, public safety, economic well-being of the state, prevention of crime or disorder, protection of health or morals, and the freedom of others.

Impairment of rights in relation to law and legal proceedings   One aspect of the principle against doubtful penalisation is that by the exercise of state power the rights of a person in relation to law and legal proceedings should not be removed or impaired, except under clear authority of law. The rule of law requires that the law should apply equally, and that all should be equal before it (*Richards* v *McBride* (1881) 51 LJMC 15, at p 16). It also requires that all penalties be inflicted by due process of law, which in turn demands that there should be no unauthorised interference with that process. In general, no citizen should without clear authority be 'shut out from the seat of justice' (*Aspinall* v *Sterling Mansell Ltd* [1981] 3 All ER 866, 867). This applies even to a convicted prisoner (*Raymond* v *Honey* [1983] AC 1, 12). These principles are embedded in various ancient constitutional enactments. Thus a chapter of Magna Carta enshrines the Crown's promise that a man shall not be condemned 'but by lawful judgment of his peers, or by the law of the land'. It goes on: 'we will sell to no man, we will not deny or defer to any man either justice or right' (25 Edw 1 (1297) c 29). The statute 28 Edw 3 c 3 (1354) enacts that 'no man of what estate or condition that he be, shall be put out of land or tenement, nor taken, nor imprisoned, nor disinherited, nor put to death, without being brought to answer by due process of law'. The Bill of Rights (1688) forbids excessive bail, excessive fines, and cruel and unusual punishments; and requires jurors to be duly empannelled and returned. Alleged deprivation of the common law right to trial by jury will be strictly construed (*Looker* v *Halcomb* (1827) 4 Bing 183, 188).

The right to bring, defend and conduct legal proceedings without unwarranted interference is a basic right of citizenship (*In re the Vexatious Actions Act 1896—in re Bernard Boaler* [1915] 1 KB 21, 34-5). While the court has control, subject to legal rules, of its own procedure, this does not authorise any ruling which abridges the basic right. In the case of a defendant, the right covers 'the right to defend himself in the litigation as he and his advisers think fit [and] choose the witnesses that he will call' (*Starr* v *National Coal Board* [1977] 1 WLR 63, 71).

The removal of legal remedies is strictly construed (*Boulting* v *Association of Cinematograph, Television and Allied Technicians* [1963] 2 QB 606), as are provisions allowing technical defences (*Sanders* v *Scott* [1961] 2 QB 326). It is presumed that a party is not to be deprived of his right of appeal (*Mackey* v *Monks* [1918] AC 59, 91). A litigant who has obtained a judgment is by law entitled not to be deprived of that judgment without 'very solid grounds' (*Brown* v *Dean* [1910] AC 373, 374. An important aspect of rights in relation to law is the right not to have legal burdens thrust upon one. It is a detriment to be obliged to carry out statutory duties against one's will, or to incur the risk of being the subject of legal proceedings. This is so even though no economic loss is involved. (*R* v *Loxdale* (1758) 1 Burr 445; *R* v *Cousins* (1864) 33 LJMC 87; *Finch* v *Bannister* [1908] 2 KB 441; *Gaby* v *Palmer* (1916) 85 LJKB 1240, 1244.)

Articles 5 and 6 of the European Convention on Human Rights give elaborate protection for rights in legal proceedings. This covers safeguards in case of arrest, the presumption of innocence, the right to a fair trial, the right of cross-examination, the publicity of proceedings, and other matters.

Other interference with rights as a citizen   In addition to the rights previously referred to, the principle against doubtful penalisation requires that by the exercise of state power no other right of a person as a citizen should be interfered with except under clear authority of law. The policy of the law is to protect the rights enjoyed by a person as a citizen. In a notable dissenting judgment, Earl Warren CJ said: 'Citizenship *is* man's basic right for it is nothing less than the right to have rights. Remove this priceless possession and there remains a stateless person, disgraced and degraded in the eyes of his countrymen'. (*Perez* v *Brownell* (1958) 356 US 64.)

Thus because of the importance attached to *voting rights* the courts tend to give a strict construction to any enactment curtailing the franchise (*Randolph* v *Milman* (1868) LR 4 CP 107; *Piercy* v *Maclean* (1870) LR 5 CP 252, 261 *Hipperson* v *Electoral Registration Officer for the Distinct of Newbury* [1985] QB 1060, 1067).

Protocol 1 to the European Convention on Human Rights requires the holding of free elections at reasonable intervals by secret ballot, under conditions which ensure the free expression of the opinions of the people in the choice of the legislature. Protocol 4 requires that no one shall be expelled, by means either of an individual or of a collective measure, from the territory of the state of which he is a national. It also says that no one shall be deprived of the right to enter the territory of the state of which he is a national.

Principle against retrospectivity

As a further aspect of the principle that law should be just, legal policy requires that, except in relation to procedural matters, changes in the law should not take effect retrospectively. The court, when considering, in relation to the facts of the instant case, which of the opposing constructions of the enactment would give effect to the legislative intention, should presume that the legislator intended to observe this principle.

A person is presumed to know the law, and is required to obey the law. It follows that he should be able to trust the law. Having fulfilled his duty to know the law, he should then be able to act on his knowledge with confidence. The rule of law means nothing else. It follows that to alter the law retrospectively, at least where that is to the disadvantage of the subject, is a betrayal of what law stands for. Parliament is presumed not to intend such betrayal. As Willes J said, retrospective legislation is:

. . . contrary to the general principle that legislation by which the conduct of mankind is to be regulated ought, when introduced for the first time, to deal with future acts, and ought not to change the character of past transactions carried on upon the faith of the then existing law (*Phillips v Eyre* (1870) LR 6 QB 1, 23).

Thus in the absence of a clear indication in an amending enactment the substantive rights of the parties to any civil legal proceedings fall to be determined by the law as it existed when the action commenced (*Re Royse (decd)* [1985] Ch 22, 29).

Degrees of retrospectivity   Where, on a weighing of the factors, it seems that *some* retrospective effect was intended, the general presumption against retrospectivity indicates that this should be kept to as narrow a compass as will accord with the legislative intention (*Lauri* v *Renad* [1892] 3 Ch 402, 421; *Skinner* v *Cooper* [1979] 1 WLR 666).

Procedural changes   Rules of legal procedure are taken to be intended to facilitate the proper settlement of civil or, as the case may be, criminal disputes. Changes in such rules are assumed to be for the better. They are also assumed to be neutral as between the parties, merely holding the ring. Accordingly the principle against retrospectivity does not apply to them, since they are supposed not to possess any penal character (*Yew Bon Tew* v *Kenderaan Bas Maria* [1983] 1 AC 553). Indeed if they have any substantial penal effect they cannot be merely procedural.

Pending actions   Where an amending enactment is intended to be retrospective it will apply to pending actions, including appeals from decisions taken before the passing of the amending Act (*Hewitt* v *Lewis* [1986] 1 WLR 444).

Penalties for offences   It has been held that an enactment fixing the penalty, or maximum penalty, for an offence is merely procedural for the purpose of determining retrospectivity (*DPP* v *Lamb* [1941] 2 KB 89; *Buckman* v *Button* [1943] KB 405; *R* v *Oliver* [1944] KB 68). This seems wrong in principle, as well as conflicting with our international obligations under the European Convention on Human Rights. Article 7 of this says: 'Nor shall a heavier penalty be imposed than the one that was applicable at the time the criminal offence was committed'. In *R* v *Deery* [1977] Crim LR 550 the Northern Ireland Court of Criminal Appeal declined to follow the English authorities mentioned above. In *R* v *Penwith JJ, ex parte Hay* (1979) 1 Cr App R (S) 265 it was said by the Divisional Court that, where the maximum penalty for an offence is increased, this should not be applied to offences committed before the increase unless there is a clear legislative intention to this effect (see also commentary on *R* v *Craig* [1982] Crim LR 132 at [1982] Crim LR 191–2).

European Convention on Human Rights

Article 7 of the European Convention on Human Rights states that no one shall be held guilty of any criminal offence on account of any act or omission which did not constitute a criminal offence under national or international law at the time when it was committed. As mentioned above, where the act or omission did constitute an offence when committed, no penalty is to be imposed which is heavier than the one applicable at that time. Article 7 is expressed not to prejudice the trial and punishment of any person for any act or omission which, at the time it was committed, was criminal according to 'the general principles of law recognised by civilised nations'.

The principle laid down by art 7 is common to all the legal orders of the member states. It is among the general principles of law whose observance is ensured by the European Court (*R v Kirk (Kent) (No 63/83)* [1985] 1 All ER 453, 462).

Principle that law should be predictable

It is a principle of legal policy that law should be certain, and therefore predictable. The court, when considering, in relation to the facts of the instant case, which of the opposing constructions of the enactment would give effect to the legislative intention, should presume that the legislator intended to observe this principle. It should therefore strive to reach a construction which was reasonably foreseeable by the parties concerned. As Lord Diplock said: 'Unless men know what the rule of conduct is they cannot regulate their actions to conform to it. It fails in its primary function as a rule.' (Diplock 1965, p 16).

This follows a maxim cited by Coke (4 Inst 246): *misera est servitus, ubi jus est vagum aut incertum* (obedience is a hardship where the law is vague or uncertain).

The classic modern statement of the need for predictability is that of Lord Diplock in *Black-Clawson International Ltd* v *Papierwerke Waldhof-Aschaffenberg AG* [1975] AC 591, 638:

The acceptance of the rule of law as a constitutional principle requires that a citizen, before committing himself to any course of action, should be able to know in advance what are the legal consequences that will flow from it. Where those consequences are regulated by a statute the source of that knowledge is what the statute says. In construing it the court must give effect to what the words of the statute would be reasonably understood to mean by those whose conduct it regulates.

One advantage of predictability is that it encourages the settlement of disputes without recourse to litigation. And where litigation has been embarked upon, predictability helps to promote settlements without pursuing the litigation to the bitter end.

It is the policy of the law to promote settlement of disputes.

Thus Lord Diplock, in referring to a judicial guideline as to the rate of interest to be adopted in relation to damages awards, said its purpose lay 'in promoting predictability and so facilitating settlements' (*Wright* v *British Railways Board* [1983] 2 AC 773, 785).

Principle that law should be coherent and self-consistent

It is a principle of legal policy that law should be coherent and self-consistent. The court, when considering, in relation to the facts of the instant case, which of the opposing constructions of the enactment would give effect to the legislative intention, should presume that the legislator intended to observe this principle. The court should therefore strive to avoid adopting a construction which involves accepting that on the point in question the law lacks coherence or is inconsistent.

Consistency within the system of laws is an obvious benefit, as recognised by the maxim *lex beneficialis rei consimili remedium praestat* (a beneficial law affords a remedy for cases which are on the same footing) (2 Co Inst 689). It is encouraged by our legal system, under which until recently judges were all drawn from the practising Bar. One of the grounds on which Blackstone praised the old system of travelling assize judges was the resulting consistency in the law:

These justices, though . . . varied and shifted at every assizes, are all sworn to the same laws, have had the same education, have pursued the same studies, converse and consult together, communicate their decisions and resolution . . . And hence their administration of justice and conduct of trials are consonant and uniform; whereby . . . confusion and contrariety are avoided . . . (Blackstone 1765, iii 354).

The dangers where a court cuts accross established legal categories and procedures were spelt out by Lord Dilhorne in *Imperial Tobacco Ltd* v *A-G* [1981] AC 718, 741, a case where it was sought to obtain a civil law declaration on whether particular conduct constituted a criminal offence. In *Vestey* v *IRC* [1980] AC 1148 the House of Lords justified its departure from a previous decision of the House on the ground that it could now see what Lord Edmund-Davies called (p 1196) the 'startling and unacceptable' consequences of that decision when applied to circumstances never contemplated by the House when reaching it. Again, where a literal construction of the phrase 'a matter relating to trial on indictment' in the Supreme Court Act 1981, s 29(3) would mean that no appeal lay from certain Crown Court decisions, the House of Lords applied a narrow meaning of the phrase (*Re Smalley* [1985] AC 622, 636).

The integrity of legal doctrines should be safeguarded when courts construe legislation. Thus in *Mutual Shipping Corporation York* v *Bayshore Shipping Co of Monrovia* [1985] 1 WLR 625 it was held that the wide descretion given by the literal meaning of the Arbitration Act 1950, s 22 was subject to severe implied restrictions so as to preserve the finality of arbitration awards.

Principle that law should not be subject to casual change

It is a principle of legal policy that law should be altered deliberately rather than casually, and that Parliament should not be assumed to change either common law or statute law by a side-wind, but only by measured and considered provisions. In the case of common law, or Acts embodying common law, the principle is somewhat stronger than in other cases. It is also stronger the more fundamental the change is. As Lord Devlin said: 'It is a well-established principle of construction that a statute is not to be taken as effecting a fundamental alteration in the general law unless it uses words that point unmistakably to that conclusion.' (*National Assistance Board* v *Wilkinson* [1952] 2 QB 648, 661.)

There are many examples of the application of this principle. Thus the House of Lords refused to place on the Law of Property Act 1925, s 56 a construction which would overturn the doctrine of privity of contract (*Beswick* v *Beswick* [1968] AC 58). Similarly the Court of Appeal preserved the equity doctrine of mortgages in construing s 86(2) of that Act (*Grangeside Properties Ltd* v *Collingwoods Securities Ltd* [1964] 1 WLR 139).

In *Leach* v *R* [1912] AC 305 the House of Lords refused, in the absence of clear words, to acknowledge a departure from the principle that a wife cannot be compelled to testify against her husband. Lord Atkinson said (p 311) the principle 'is deep seated in the common law of this country, and I think if it is to be overturned it must be overturned by a clear, definite and positive enactment'.

In *Re Seaford* [1968] p 53, 68 the Court of Appeal refused to hold that the doctrine of relation back of a judicial decision to the beginning of the day on which it was pronounced 'was, as a result of the Supreme Court of Judicature Act 1873 made applicable, as it were by a side-wind , in matrimonial proceedings'. In *R* v *Owens* (1859) 28 LJQB 316 the court held that an Act allowing a mayor to stand as a councillor did not enable him to act as returning officer at an election for which he was a candidate since it would not be legitimate to infer from the language used that the legislature had intended to repeal by a side-wind the principle that a man shall not be a judge in his own cause.

Courts prefer to treat an Act as regulating rather than replacing a common law rule (*Lee* v *Walker* [1985] QB 1191, which concerned the power to suspend committal orders in contempt proceedings). Alteration of the common law is presumed not to be intended unless this is made clear (eg *Basildon District Council* v *Lesser (JE) (Properties) Ltd* [1985] QB 839, 849: 'it would be surprising if Parliament when limiting the effect of contributory negligence in tort [in the Law Reform (Contributory Negligence) Act 1945] introduced it into contract)'.

Principle that municipal law should conform to public international law

It is a principle of legal policy that the municipal law should conform to public international law. The court, when considering, in relation to the facts of the instant case, which of the opposing constructions of the enactment would give effect to the legislative intention, should presume that the legislator intended to observe this principle.

Public international law is what used to be called the law of nations, or *jus gentium*. A rule of public international law which is incorporated by a decision of a competent court then becomes part of the municipal law (*Thai-Europe Tapioca Service Ltd* v *Govt of Pakistan* [1975] 1 WLR 1485, 1495. Or, under the principle known as *adoption*, a rule of international law may be incorporated into municipal law by custom or statute. It is an important principle of public policy to respect the comity of nations, and obey treaties which are binding under public international law. Thus Diplock LJ said:

> . . . there is a prima facie presumption that Parliament does not intend to act in breach of [public] international law, including therein specific treaty obligations; and if one of the meanings that can reasonably be attributed to the legislation is consonant with the treaty obligations and another or others are not, the meaning which is so consonant is to be preferred. (*Salomon* v *Commrs of Customs and Excise* [1967] 2 QB 116. 143).

European Convention   The European Convention on Human Rights (Cmnd 8969) entered into force on 3 September 1953. To date it has been ratified by 22 nations, including the United Kingdom. For these it imposes the usual obligations and rights under a treaty in public international law. The machinery for enforcement of these consists of the European Commission of Human Rights and the European Court of Human Rights, both of which operate at Strasbourg. The United Kingdom has accepted the right of individual petition to the Commission, but has not made the Convention part of its municipal law.

It follows that the Convention does not directly govern the exercise of powers conferred by or under an Act (*R* v *Secretary of State for the Home Department, ex parte Fernandes* (1980) *The Times* 21 November; *R* v *Secretary of State for the Home Department, ex parte Kirkwood* [1984] 1 WLR 913). However it is presumed that Parliament, when it passes an Act, intends it to be construed in conformity with the Convention, unless the contrary intention appears.

Judicial notice   Judicial notice is taken of rules and principles of public international law, even when not embodied in municipal law (*Re Queensland Mercantile and Agency Ltd* [1892] 1 Ch 219, 226). This also applies to treaties made by the British Crown. As Scarman

LJ said in *Pan-American World Ariways Inc* v *Department of Trade* [1976] 1 Lloyd's Rep 257, 261 (emphasis added):

If statutory words have to be construed or a legal principle formulated in an area of the law where Her Majesty has accepted international obligations, our courts—*who, of course, take notice of the acts of Her Majesty done in the exercise of her sovereign power*—will have regard to the convention as part of the full content or background of the law. Such a convention, especially a multilateral one, should then be considered by the Courts even though no statute expressly or impliedly incorporates it into our law.

Citation of treaties   The existence of the principle under discussion means that the court is obliged to consider any relevant rule of public international law, and permit the citation of any relevant treaty. For this reason it seems that Lord Parker CJ was mistaken when in *Urey* v *Lummis* [1962] 1 WLR 826, 832 he said it was not for the court to consider whether the United Kingdom had implemented the international Agreement regarding the status of forces of parties to the North Atlantic Treaty.

Uniform statutes   An act passed to give effect to an international agreement will be construed in the light of meanings attached to the agreement in other contracting states, so as to promote uniformity (*Stag Line Ltd* v *Foscolo Mango & Co Ltd* [1932] AC 328, 350; *Riverstone Meat Co* v *Lancashire Shipping Co* [1961] AC 807, 8690. See further F A Man 'The Interpretation of Uniform Statues' (1946) 62 LQR 278; 'Uniform Statutes in English Law' (1983) 99 LQR 376.

Chapter Eleven

Guides to Legislative Intention III: Presumptions Derived from the Nature of Legislation

The present chapter deals with the ten presumptions derived from the nature of legislation, which are that:

1 the text is the primary indication of intended meaning
2 the text is *prima facie* to be given a literal construction
3 the court is to apply the remedy provided for the 'mischief'
4 an enactment is to be given a purposive construction
5 regard is to be had to the consequences of a particular construction
6 an 'absurd' result is not intended
7 errors in the legislation are to be rectified
8 evasion of the legislation is not to be allowed
9 the legislation is intended to be construed by the light of ancillary rules of law and legal maxims
10 an updating construction is to be applied wherever requisite.

Nature of legislative presumptions A presumption affords guidance, arising from the nature of legislation in a parliamentary democracy, as to the legislator's *prima facie* intention regarding the working of the enactment. It looks in particular to the effective implementation of what the legislator has enacted.

Presumption that text to be primary indication of intention

In construing an enactment, the text of the enactment, in its setting within the Act or instrument containing it, is to be regarded as the pre-eminent indication of the legislator's intention. British courts, towards the end of the twentieth century, regard the text of Acts of the United Kingdom Parliament with great respect. When called upon to construe an Act, the court takes its primary duty as being to look at the text and say what, in itself, it means: 'The safer and more correct course of dealing with a question of construction is to take the words themselves and arrive if possible at their meaning without, in the first instance, reference to cases' (*Barrell* v *Fordree* [1932] AC 676, 682).

The text is the starting point, and the centre of the interpreter's attention from then on. It is the text, after all, that is being interpreted. In the next chapter we consider the purely linguistic canons of construction that assist in this. Meanwhile we turn to one consequence of the present presumption: the respect paid to the literal meaning.

Presumption that enactment to be given its literal meaning

Prima facie, the meaning of an enactment intended by the legislator (in other words its legal meaning) is taken to be the literal meaning. As explained above (pp 87–91), the 'literal meaning' corresponds to the grammatical meaning where this is straightforward. If however the grammatical meaning, when applied to the facts of the instant case, is ambiguous, then any of the possible grammatical meanings may be described as the literal meaning. If the grammatical meaning is garbled or otherwise semantically obscure, then the grammatical meaning likely to have been intended (or any one of them in the case of ambiguity) is taken as the literal meaning.

The point here is that the literal meaning is one arrived at from the wording of the enactment alone, without consideration of other interpretative criteria. When account is taken of such other criteria it may be found necessary to depart from the literal meaning and adopt a strained construction. The initial presumption is however in favour of the literal meaning (*Caledonian Railway Co* v *North British Railway Co* (1881) 6 App Cas 114, 121; *Capper* v *Baldwin* [1965] 2 QB 53, 61). In general, the weight to be attached to the literal meaning is far greater than applies to any other interpretative criterion, though with older Acts it tends to be less. As Lord Bridge said of an Act of 1847, it is 'legitimate to take account, when construing old statutes, of the prevailing style and standards of draftsmanship' (*Wills* v *Bowley* [1983] 1 AC 57, 104).

Presumption that court to apply remedy provided for the mischief

Parliament intends that an enactment shall remedy a particular mischief. It therefore intends the court, in construing the enactment, so to apply the remedy provided by it as to suppress that mischief. Except in the case of purely declaratory provisions, virtually the only reason for passing an Act is to change the law. So the reason for an Act's passing must lie in some defect in the law. If the law were not defective, Parliament would not need or want to change it. That defect is the 'mischief' to which the Act is directed.

Social or legal mischief

Since all an Act can do is change the law, the immediate mischief must be some defect in the law. However the overall mischief may be a social mischief coupled with this legal mischief. As society changes, what are thought of as social mischiefs continually emerge. Whether or not they are really so may be disputable. But it is true that only a static society concentrates on removing purely legal mischiefs.

A social mischief is a factual situation, or mischief 'on the ground', that is causing concern to the society (such as an increase in mugging, or a decline in the birthrate). While a mischief on the ground may correspond to a defect in the law, this is not necessarily so. An increase in mugging may arise because the law is inadequate. Or it may arise because an adequate law is inadequately enforced. A decline in the birthrate may lie beyond the reach of law.

An example of a *social* mischief is given in the preamble to the statute 4 Hen 7 c 19 (1488):

Great inconveniences daily doth increase by desolation and pulling down and wilfull waste of houses and Towns within [the king's realm], and laying to pasture lands which customarily have been used in tillage, whereby idleness—ground and beginning of all mischiefs—daily doth increase . . . to the subversion of the policy and good rule of this land.

A purely *legal* mischief was remedied by the statute 2 & 3 Edw 6 c 24 (1548). So refined had the common law rules of criminal venue become that, where a person was fatally wounded in one county but expired in the next, the assailant could be indicted in neither.

The Water Act 1973 introduced a new system, to be financed by water rates, for the management of the nation's water resources. The Act was silent on the important question of who was to be liable to pay these rates (*Daymond* v *South West Water Authority* [1976] AC 609). This 'mischief of omission', as Lord Scarman called it in *South West Water Authority* v *Rumble's* [1985] AC 609, 618, was remedied by the Water Charges Act 1976, s 2.

Party-political mischiefs

In modern times there has arisen a new class of legislation. No longer is Parliament largely concerned with repelling the nation's enemies, keeping the Queen's peace, financing the administration, and holding the ring between citizens. The legislature becomes an engine of social change. It regulates the national economy. It takes on the management and control of great industries. The subject matter of its Acts enters the realm of argument and opinion, party politics, economic theory, religious or sociological controversy, class warfare, and other matters as to which there is no consensus.

How is the interpreter to regard legislation of this type? The answer is clear. A court of construction is bound to ignore the fact that what to the majority in one Parliament seemed a defect in the existing law may appear the reverse to their successors of a different political hue. Until the successors get round to repealing an Act with which they disagree, it stands as the will of the Parliament that made it. The same applies where a decisive change has occurred in the views of a political party since the Act's passing (eg *R* v *Secretary of State for the Environment, ex parte Greater London Council* (1983) *The Times,* 2 December).

It is important not to let confusion creep in by treating the mischief as somehow altered by later events. These may indeed require to be taken into account, but not as altering or glossing the historical facts which occasioned the passing of the Act.

Heydon's Case

In medieval times the country was largely governed by common law. Then, as social progress set in, there arose many varieties of social mischief. These exposed legal mischiefs, which marred the common law and required correction by Parliament. Arguments began to arise among common lawyers as to the attitude the judges administering the common law should adopt towards legislative interventions. The judges, having framed 'our lady the common law', were not disposed to acknowledge flaws in their creation. The question became pressing, and at the instance of the king was considered by the Barons of the Exchequer in *Heydon's Case* (1584) 3 Co Rep 7a. They passed the following resolution (I have modified the wording slightly to assist reference and improve clarity):

That for the sure and true interpretation of all statutes in general (be they penal or beneficial, restrictive or enlarging of the common law), four things are to be discerned and considered:

(1) what was the common law before the making of the Act;
(2) what was the mischief and defect for which the common law did not provide;
(3) what remedy the Parliament hath resolved and appointed to cure the disease of the commonwealth; and
(4) the true reason of the remedy,

and then the office of all the judges is always to make such construction as shall:

(a) suppress the mischief and advance the remedy, and
(b) suppress subtle inventions and evasions for the continuance of the mischief *pro privato commodo* (for private benefit), and
(c) add force and life to the cure and remedy according to the true intent of the makers of the Act *pro bono publico* (for the public good).

This resolution, which forms the basis of the so-called 'mischief rule' of statutory interpretation, has been approved in many cases down to the present day (eg *Salkeld* v *Johnson* (1848) 2 Ex 256, 272; *Blackwell* v *England* (1857) 8 El & Bl Rep 541; *River Wear Commissioners* v *Adamson* (1877) 2 App Cas 743, 764; *Re Mayfair*

Property Co, Bartlett v Mayfair Property Co [1898] 2 Ch 28, 35; *Ealing LBC v Race Relations Board* [1972] AC 342, 368).

Dangers in relying on the mischief

It does not necessarily follow that legislation enacted to deal with a mischief (a) was intended to deal with the whole of it (eg *Hussain v Hussain* [1982] 3 WLR 679), or (b) was not intended to deal with other things also (see *Central Asbestos Co Ltd v Dodd* [1973] AC 518; *Maunsell v Olins* [1974] 3 WLR 835, 842). As Viscount Simonds LC said: 'Parliament may well intend the remedy to extend beyond the immediate mischief' (*A-G v Prince Ernest Augustus of Hanover* [1957] AC 436, 462).

Furthermore common sense may indicate that the ambit of the mischief is narrower than the literal meaning of the remedial enactment, as occurred in the Australian case of *Ingham v Hie Lie* (1912) 15 CLR 267. A Chinese laundryman was charged under an Act whose purpose was to limit the hours of work of Chinese in factories, laundries etc so as to protect other industries. The defendant, who had been found *ironing his own shirt*, was held not guilty of an offence that on a literal interpretation of the Act it had created.

Unknown mischief

Particularly with older Acts, it may not be possible for the court to find out what the mischief was. It must then do the best it can with the Act as it stands (eg *Nugent-Head v Jacob (Inspector of Taxes)* [1948] AC 321, 327).

Remedy provided for the mischief

The remedy provided by an Act for a mischief takes the form of an amendment of the existing law. It is to be presumed that Parliament, having identified the mischief with which it proposes to deal, intends the remedy to operate in a way which may reasonably be expected to cure the mischief. At its simplest, the remedy for the mischief may consist of removing the obnoxious legal provision and not replacing it by anything. This often happens with a party-political Act when the opposition gets into power. For example the Conservative Government of 1971 disliked the Land Commission set up by an Act of its Labour predecessors. The very existence of the Commission was conceived to be a mischief, so it was abolished by the Land Commission (Dissolution) Act 1971. That simple procedure, accompanied by a few transitional provisions, constituted the 'remedy'. Another example from the same year is the Licensing (Abolition of State Management) Act 1971.

Counter-mischief

Clearly Parliament is unlikely to intend to abolish one mischief at
the cost of establishing another which is just as bad, or even worse.
Avoiding such an anomaly is an important consideration in statutory
interpretation (see p 172–3 below).

Presumption that court to apply a purposive construction

A construction that promotes the remedy Parliament has provided
to cure a particular mischief is nowadays known as a purposive
construction. Parliament is presumed to intend that in construing
an Act the court, by advancing the remedy which is indicated by
the words of the Act and the implications arising from those words,
should aim to further every aspect of the legislative purpose. A
purposive construction is one which gives effect to the legislative
purpose by either (a) following the literal meaning where that is
in accordance with that purpose, which may be called a purposive
and literal construction; or (b) applying a strained meaning where
the literal meaning is not in accordance with the purpose, which
may be called a purposive and strained construction.

When present day judges speak of a purposive construction, they
usually mean a purposive and strained construction. Thus Staughton
J referred to 'the power of the courts to disregard the literal meaning
of an Act and to give it a purposive construction' (*A-G of New
Zealand* v *Ortiz* [1982] 3 All ER 432, 442). Lord Diplock spoke
of 'competing approaches to the task of statutory construction—
the literal and the purposive approach' (*Kammins Ballrooms Co Ltd*
v *Zenith Investments (Torquay) Ltd* [1971] AC 850, 879).

Novelty of the term

The term 'purposive construction' is new, though the concept is
not. Viscount Dilhorne said that, while it is now fashionable to
talk of the purposive construction of a statute, the need for such
a construction has been recognised since the seventeenth century
(*Stock* v *Frank Jones (Tipton) Ltd* [1978] 1 WLR 231, 234). The
term's entry into fashion betokens a swing by the appellate courts
away from literal construction. Lord Diplock said in 1975:

If one looks back to the actual decisions of [the House of Lords] on questions
of statutory construction over the last 30 years one cannot fail to be struck
by the evidence of a trend away from the purely literal towards the purposive
construction of statutory provisions. (*Carter* v *Bradbeer* [1975] 1 WLR 1204,
1206–7.)

Supervening factors

As always in statutory interpretation it is necessary, when considering the possibility of applying a purposive construction, to take account of any other applicable criteria also. The overriding object is to give effect to Parliament's intention, and this is unlikely to be to achieve the immediate purpose at no matter what cost. Contrary purposes of a more general nature may supervene, as in *A-G of New Zealand* v *Ortiz* [1982] 3 WLR 570. Here it was held at first instance that the phrase 'shall be forfeited' in the New Zealand Historic Articles Act 1962, s 12(2) was ambiguous, and that a purposive construction should be applied to decide whether forfeiture was automatic or depended upon actual seizure of the historic article in question. The decision was overruled on appeal because, though right as far as it went, it failed to take into account a further (and overriding) criterion. This was the rule of international law that limits the extra-territorial effect of legislation relating to property rights.

Non-purposive-and-literal construction

In the sense used in English law, purposive construction is an almost invariable requirement. But a non-purposive construction may be necessary, because unavoidable, where there is insufficient indication of (a) what the legislative purpose is, or (b) how it is to be carried out. Thus in *IRC* v *Hinchy* [1960] AC 748, 781 Lord Keith of Avonholm declined to apply a purposive construction of an income tax enactment because, as he said, the court could not take upon itself the task of working out an assessment in a different way to that indicated on a literal construction. For a further example see *IRC* v *Ayrshire Employers Mutual Insurance Association Ltd* [1946] 1 All ER 637.

Non-purposive construction may be necessary where the court considers a predictable construction (see p 153 above) is required. Apart from these cases, it is usually only where the literal meaning is too strong to be overborne that the court will apply a non-purposive-and-literal construction (eg *Richards* v *MacBride* (1881) 8 QBD 119).

Statements of purpose

The search for the purpose of an enactment is sometimes assisted by an express statement on the lines of: 'The purpose of [this enactment] is to remedy the defect in the law consisting of [*description of the mischief*] by amending the law so as to [*description of the remedy*].' A statement of purpose (whether on these lines or not, and whether comprehensive or not) may be found either in the Act or in the judgment of a court devising the statement as an aid to construction (see *Whitley* v *Stumbles* [1930] AC 544, 547; *Haskins* v *Lewis* [1931] 2 KB 1, 14; *Dudley and District Building Society* v *Emerson* [1949] Ch 707, 715; *Wallersteiner* v *Moir* [1974] 1 WLR 991, 1032; *R* v

Marlborough Street Magistrates' Court Metropolitan Stipendiary Magistrate, ex parte Simpson (1980) 70 Cr App R 291, 293).

When found in the Act, the statement of purpose may be in the long title or preamble, or in a purpose clause or recital. A well-known example is the Fires Prevention (Metropolis) Act 1774, s 83, which is still in force. The opening recital tells us that the section was enacted 'in order to deter and hinder ill-minded persons from wilfully setting their house or houses or other buildings on fire with a view to gaining to themselves the insurance money, whereby the lives and fortunes of many families may be lost or endangered'. For modern examples see the Road Traffic Act 1960, s 73(1) and the Wildlife and Countryside Act 1981, s 39(1).

Judicial duty not to deny the statute

It is the duty of the court to accept the purpose decided on by Parliament. This applies even though the court disagrees with it. It even applies where the court considers the result unjust, provided it is satisfied that Parliament really did intend that result. As Lord Scarman said in *Duport Steels Ltd* v *Sirs* [1980] 1 WLR 142, 168:

. . . in the field of statute law the judge must be obedient to the will of Parliament as expressed in its enactments. In this field Parliament makes and unmakes the law [and] the judge's duty is to interpret and to apply the law, not to change it to meet the judge's idea of what justice requires. Interpretation does, of course, imply in the interpreter a power of choice where differing constructions are possible. But our law requires the judge to choose the construction which in his judgment best meets the legislative purpose of the enactment. If the result be unjust but inevitable, the judge may say so and invite Parliament to reconsider its provision. But he must not deny the statute.

Alteration of an Act's purpose

A later Act *in pari materia* may have the effect of altering an Act's purpose, so far as concerns matters arising after the commencement of the later Act. In *R* v *Hammersmith and Fulham LBC, ex parte Beddowes* [1987] QB 1050, 1065 Fox LJ said:

Historically, local authority housing has been rented. But a substantial inroad on that was made by Part I of the Housing Act 1980, which gave municipal tenants the right to purchase their dwellings. In the circumstances it does not seem to me that a policy which is designed to produce good accommodation for owner-occupiers is now any less within the purposes of the Housing Acts than the provision of rented housing . . .

British and European versions of purposive construction

The British doctrine of purposive construction is more literalist than the European variety, and permits a strained construction only in comparatively rare cases. Lord Denning said:

[European judges] do not go by the literal meaning of the words or by the grammatical structure of the sentence. They go by the design or purpose . . . behind it. When they come upon a situation which is *to their minds* within the spirit—but not the letter—of the legislation, they solve the problem by looking at the design and purpose of the legislature—at the effect it was sought to achieve. They then interpret the legislation so as to produce the desired effect. This means they fill in gaps, quite unashamedly, without hesitation. They ask simply: what is the sensible way of dealing with this situation so as to give effect to the presumed purpose of the legislation? *They lay down the law* accordingly. (*James Buchanan & Co Ltd v Babco Forwarding & Shipping (UK) Ltd* [1977] 2 WLR 107, 112 (emphasis added).)

Presumption that regard to be had to consequences of a construction

It is presumed to be the legislator's intention that the court, when considering, in relation to the facts of the instant case, which of the opposing constructions of the enactment corresponds to its legal meaning, should assess the likely consequences of adopting each construction, both to the parties in the case and (where similar facts arise in future cases) for the law generally. If on balance the consequences of a particular construction are more likely to be *adverse* than *beneficent* this is a factor telling against that construction.

Consequential construction is of modern adoption. The earlier attitude of the judges was expressed by Lord Abinger CB in *A-G v Lockwood* (1842) 9 M & W 378, 395:

. . . I cannot enter into a speculation of what might have been in the contemplation of the legislature, because they have not stated what they contemplated . . . The Act of Parliament practically has had, I believe, a very pernicious effect—an effect not at all contemplated—but we cannot construe the Act by that result.

The modern attitude is shown by Mustill J in *R v Committee of Lloyd's, ex parte Moran* (1983) *The Times*, 24 June: 'a statute . . . cannot be interpreted according to its literal meaning without testing that meaning against the practical outcome of giving effect to it'.

Adverse and beneficent consequences

The consequence of a particular construction may be regarded as 'adverse' if it is such that in the light of the interpretative criteria the court views it with disquiet because, for example, it frustrates the purpose of the Act, or works injustice, or is contrary to public policy, or is productive of inconvenience or hardship. Any other consequences (whether merely neutral or positively advantageous) may be called 'beneficent'. For this purpose a consequence clearly intended by Parliament is to be treated as beneficent even though the judge personally dislikes it.

Consequences for the parties and the law

In judging consequences it is important to distinguish consequences to the parties in the instant case and consequences for the law generally. It will usually be a straightforward matter to determine the effect on the court's final order of a finding in favour of one possible construction rather than another. But the court must also bear in mind that under the doctrine of precedent its decision may be of binding, or at least persuasive, authority for the future.

The court may be less unwilling to adopt an 'adverse' construction where some functionary is interposed whose discretion may be so exercised as to reduce the practical ill-effects (see, eg, *IRC* v *Hinchy* [1960] AC 748).

Judges are particularly ready to apply a strained construction on consequential grounds where this will assist the work of the courts. Thus in *R* v *Stratford-on-Avon District Council, ex parte Jackson* [1985] 1 WLR 1319 the Court of Appeal held that, although the literal meaning of RSC Ord 53, r 4 is to lay down a time limit for making substantive applications for judicial review, it should be construed instead as referring to applications for *leave* to make such substantive applications. This reading confirmed the existing practice of the courts, which is 'the only sensible course from a practical point of view' (p 772).

Consequences tending both ways

Since the consequences to be borne in mind are often of a wide variety it is not surprising that they may tend in both directions. Each of the opposing constructions may involve some adverse and some beneficent consequences. Lord Morris of Borth-y-Gest pointed this out in relation to anti-racist legislation:

In one sense there results for some people a limitation on what could be called their freedom: they may no longer treat certain people, because of their colour or race, or ethnic or national origins, less favourably than they would treat others. But in the same cause of freedom, although differently viewed, Parliament has, in statutory terms now calling for consideration, proscribed discrimination . . . (*Charter* v *Race Relations Board* [1973] AC 868, 889).

Where the result of a literal construction is sufficiently 'adverse', consequential construction usually indicates a decision requiring a strained construction of the enactment (eg *Mann* v *Malcolmson (The Beta)* (1865) 3 Moo PCC NS 23).

Presumption that 'absurd' result not intended

The court seeks to avoid a construction that produces an absurd result, since this is unlikely to have been intended by Parliament. Here the courts give a wide meaning to the concept of 'absurdity', using it to include virtually anything that appears inappropriate, unfitting or unreasonable.

In *Williams* v *Evans* (1876) 1 Ex D 277 the court had to construe the Highway Act 1835, s 78, which created an offence of furious horse riding but omitted to include this in the penalty provision. Grove J said (p 282) that unless a strained construction were applied the court would be holding that the legislature had made an 'absurd mistake'. Field J agreed, adding (p 284):

No doubt it is a maxim to be followed in the interpretation of statutes, that the ordinary grammatical construction is to be adopted; but when this leads to a manifest absurdity, a construction not strictly grammatical is allowed, if this will lead to a reasonable conclusion as to the intention of the legislature.

Six types of 'absurdity'

The six types of 'absurdity' a court seeks to avoid when construing an enactment are: (a) an unworkable or impracticable result; (b) an inconvenient result; (c) an anomalous or illogical result; (d) a futile or pointless result; (e) an artificial result; and (f) a disproportionate counter-mischief.

Unworkable or impracticable result   The court seeks to avoid a construction of an enactment that produces an unworkable or impracticable result, since this is unlikely to have been intended by Parliament. For example Lord Reid said in *Federal Steam Navigation Co* v *Department of Trade and Industry* [1974] 1 WLR 505, 509 that cases where it has properly been held that one word can be struck out of a statute and another substituted include the case where without such substitution the provision would be unworkable.

An obvious justification for strained construction arises where the literal meaning presents a logical impossibility. This arose in *Jones* v *Conway Water Supply* [1893] 2 Ch 603. The court had to construe the Public Health Act 1875, s 54, which said that where a local authority 'supply water' they have power to lay water mains (or pipes). Since the authority could not satisfy the condition of 'supplying' water unless they first had mains to carry it in, the power to lay mains was held to operate as soon as the authority had *undertaken* to supply water.

In *Wills* v *Bowley* [1983] 1 AC 57, 102 Lord Bridge said it would be 'quite ridiculous' to construe the Town Police Clauses Act 1847, s 28 in such a way as to force on a constable 'a choice between the risk of making an unlawful arrest and the risk of committing a criminal neglect of duty'. That would be 'to impale him on the horns of an impossible dilemma'. In *S J Grange Ltd* v *Customs and Excise Commissioners* [1979] 2 All ER 91, 101 Lord Denning MR said of a VAT provision in the Finance Act 1972, s 31 that a literal construction 'leads to such impracticable results that it is necessary to do a little adjustment so as to make the section workable'.

The courts are always anxious to facilitate the smooth working of legal proceedings and avoid the intention of the law being stultified. In *R* v *West Yorkshire Coroner, ex parte Smith* [1985] QB 1096 the court rejected the argument that, although a coroner clearly had a statutory power to fine for contempt, it could not be operated since no machinery had been provided for collecting such a fine. In *R* v *Sowden* [1964] 1 WLR 1454, 1458 the court gave a strained interpretation to the Poor Prisoners' Defence Act 1930, s 1(1), which entitled a person committed for trial to free legal aid for the preparation and conduct of his defence. It held that this did not give him an unrestricted right to have a solicitor at the trial, since if misused this could cause 'expense to the country, delays and abuse of the whole procedure' (cf *Amin* v *Entry Clearance Officer, Bombay* [1983] 2 AC 818, 868, where a construction was rejected which would give a right of appeal 'unworkable in practice').

Sometimes Parliament contemplates that an enactment may in some circumstances prove unworkable, and makes express provision for this (eg the Mines and Quarries Act 1954, s 157).

Inconvenient result   The court seeks to avoid a construction that causes unjustifiable inconvenience to persons who are subject to the enactment, since this is unlikely to have been intended by Parliament. Modern courts seek to cut down technicalities attendant upon a statutory procedure where these cannot be shown to be necessary to the fulfilment of the purposes of the legislation (see, eg, *Lawrence Chemical Co Ltd* v *Rubenstein* [1982] 1 WLR 284). Modern regulatory enactments bear heavily on business enterprise, and the courts are alert to avoid any inconvenience which is not essential to the operation of the Act, and which may in addition have adverse economic consequences (eg *Cutler* v *Wandsworth Stadium Ltd* [1949] AC 398, 417). The financial demands of the welfare state make modern legislation particularly coercive on the taxpayer, and again the courts are ready to ensure that, even though in the public interest proper taxes must be paid, the taxpayer is not unreasonably harassed by the tax authorities (eg *Hallamshire Industrial Finance Trust Ltd* v *IRC* [1979] 1 WLR 620; *IRC* v *Helen Slater Charitable Trust Ltd* [1982] Ch 49).

It sometimes happens that each of the constructions contended for involves some measure of inconvenience, and the court then has to balance the effect of each construction and determine which inconvenience is greater (eg *Pascoe* v *Nicholson* [1981] 1 WLR 1061; *Dillon* v *The Queen* [1982] AC 484).

Anomalous or illogical result   The court seeks to avoid a construction that creates an anomaly or otherwise produces an irrational or illogical result. Every legal system must seek to avoid unjustified differences and inconsistencies in the way it deals with similar matters, for as Lord Devlin said, 'no system of law can be workable if it has not got logic at the root of it' (*Hedley Byrne & Co Ltd* v *Heller and Partners Ltd* [1964] AC 465, 516). Consistency requires that a statutory remedy or benefit should be available, and should operate in the same way, in all cases of the same kind (eg *Davidson* v *Hill* [1901] 2 KB 606, 614). In *Gordon* v *Cradock* [1964] 1 QB 503, 506 where it was argued that the Supreme Court of Judicature (Consolidation) Act 1925, s 31(2) should be construed in a way which would mean that a plaintiff could cross-appeal only with leave while a defendant could appeal without leave, Willmer LJ said this would be 'a very strange result', and the court declined to implement it.

The converse of the principle that a statutory remedy should be available in all like cases is that a statutory duty should be imposed in all like cases (eg *Din* v *National Assistance Board* [1967] 2 QB 213; *Mills* v *Cooper* [1967] 2 QB 459; *T & E Homes Ltd* v *Robinson (Inspector of Taxes)* [1979] 1 WLR 452; *A-G's Reference (No 1 of 1981)* [1982] QB 848).

It is clearly anomalous to treat a person as being under a statutory duty where some essential factual pre-requisite that must have been in the contemplation of the legislator is missing. In the Australian case of *Turner* v *Ciappara* [1969] VR 851 the court considered the application of an enactment requiring obedience to automatic traffic signals. On the facts before the court it was shown that through mechanical failure the device was not working properly. *Held* it must be treated as implicit that obedience was required only where the apparatus was in working order.

For examples of other legal anomalies on certain constructions see *Re Lockwood decd* [1958] Ch 231 (distant relatives preferred to nearer on intestacy); *R* v *Minister of Agriculture and Fisheries, ex parte Graham* [1955] 2 QB 140, 168 (officer of sub-committee could hear representations while officer of main committee could not); *R* v *Baker* [1962] 2 QB 530 (person arrested on suspicion of offence liable to higher penalty than if he had committed the offence).

A possible anomaly carries less weight if there is interposed the discretion of some responsible person, by the sensible exercise of which the risk may be obviated (eg *Re a Debtor (No 13 of 1964), ex parte Official Receiver* [1980] 1 WLR 263). The court will pay little attention to a proclaimed anomaly if it is purely hypothetical, and unlikely to arise in practice (see, eg, *Home Office* v *Harman* [1983] AC 280). If an anomaly has remained on the statute book for a lengthy period, during which Parliament has had opportunities to rectify it but has neglected to do so, this may indicate that the anomaly is intended. Thus where an anomalous distinction between the relative powers of the High Court and the county court in relation to relief against forfeiture had existed for well over a century, the Court of Appeal declined to place any interpretative weight on the fact that it was anomalous (*Di Palma* v *Victoria Square Property Co Ltd* [1985] 3 WLR 207).

Futile or pointless result   The court seeks to avoid a construction that produces a futile or pointless result, since this is unlikely to have been intended by Parliament. Parliament does nothing in vain, a principle also expressed as *lex nil frustra facit* (the law does nothing in vain). It is an old maxim of the law that *quod vanum et inutile est, lex non requirit* (the law does not call for what is vain and useless). Lord Denning MR said: 'The law never compels a person to do that which is useless and unnecessary' (*Lickiss* v *Milestone Motor Policies at Lloyd's* [1966] 2 All ER 972, 975).

Where an enactment appears to impose a legal duty that, by reason of some other enactment or rule of law, already exists *aliunde*, the court strives to avoid pronouncing in favour of such a duplication in the law (eg *Re Ternan* (1864) 33 LJMC 201). Where the literal meaning of an enactment appears to impose some legal disability that can be avoided by a trifling rearrangement of affairs, the court will be slow to penalise a person who has inadvertently failed to make this rearrangement or could still easily do so (*Holmes* v *Bradfield RDC* [1949] 2 KB 1, 7).

The court is always averse to requiring litigants to embark on futile or unnecessary legal proceedings. This includes a stage in proceedings that could without detriment to any party be avoided. Judges are uncomfortably aware of the costs and delays involved in a legal action, and do all in their power to minimise them. Thus Lord Reid ruled against a construction of the Landlord and Tenant Act 1954, s 29(3) that for no substantial reason would require judges to scrutinise every application for a new business tenancy, and thus incur needless delay and cost (*Kammins Ballrooms Ltd* v *Zenith Investments (Torquay) Ltd* [1971] AC 850, 860).

Artificial result   The court seeks to avoid a construction that leads to an artificial result, since this is unlikely to have been intended by Parliament. Thus when in *R* v *Cash* [1985] QB 801 it was argued that the Theft Act 1968, s 22(1) required the prosecution to prove that an alleged handling was not done in the course of stealing, the Court of Appeal rejected the argument on the ground that it would require the court to engage in artificial reasoning. Lord Lane CJ said (p 806): 'We do not believe that this tortuous process, leading in some cases to such an artificial verdict could have been the intention of Parliament.

The law can deem anything to be the case, however unreal. The law brings itself into disrepute however if it dignifies with legal significance a wholly artificial hypothesis. Thus in the Scottish case of *Maclennan* v *Maclennan* (1958) SC 105 the court declined to rule that a wife's having availed herself, without the husband's knowledge or consent, of AID (artificial insemination by a donor) constituted her adultery within the meaning of that term in the relevant Scottish divorce Act. To do so, the court argued, would lead to wholly artificial results. For example if the donor had happened to die before the date of insemination, the legally-imputed adultery would be with a dead man—involving a kind of constructive necrophilia.

Artificiality need not be so extreme as this to rank as a significant factor in statutory interpretation. One area of importance here concerns corporations. Being entities purely of legal creation, these are imbued with a certain artificiality from the start. Sight must not be lost of the realities behind them. In *Re New Timbiqui Gold Mines Ltd* [1961] Ch 319 it was held that a person who purported to have become a member of a company *after it had been dissolved* could not, as a 'member' of the company, petition for its restoration to the register under the Companies Act 1948, s 353(6). Commenting that s 353(6) already involved 'some degree of make-believe', Buckley J said (p 326) that this should not be carried further than was absolutely necessary.

Whenever an Act sets up some fiction the courts are astute to limit the scope of its artificial effect, and are particularly concerned to ensure that it does not create harm in ways outside the intended purview of the Act (eg *Re Levy, Ex parte Walton* (1881) 17 Ch D 746, 756).

Avoiding a disproportionate counter-mischief   The court seeks to avoid a construction that cures the mischief the enactment was designed to remedy only at the cost of setting up a disproportionate counter-mischief, since this is unlikely to have been intended by Parliament. Where one possible construction of an enactment intended to remedy the mischief caused by the operations of unskilful river pilots would prevent there being any pilots at all for a period, Dr Lushington looked 'at the mischief which would accrue' from the latter restriction and adopted the other reading of the enactment (*Mann* v *Malcolmson (The Beta)*(1865) 3 Moo PCC NS 23, 27). Again, where one construction of an enactment meant that the defendant escaped conviction for fraud because in earlier bankruptcy proceedings he had 'disclosed' what was already known, Lord Campbell CJ rejected it as productive of 'great public mischief' outweighing the mischief at which the protective enactment was directed (*R* v *Skeen and Freeman* (1859) LJMC 91, 95).

A type of mischief which is often the subject of modern legislation is danger to the safety of industrial workers. The court will be reluctant to read an Act as requiring one danger to be obviated at the cost of creating another (eg *Jayne* v *National Coal Board* [1963] 2 All ER 220, 224). Often it is reasonable to assume that the counter-mischief that has arisen was quite unforeseen by Parliament. Enacted law suffers by comparison with unwritten law in that it involves laying down in advance an untried remedy.

As interpreters of legislation, it is the function of the courts to mitigate this defect of the legislative process so far as they properly can. Where an unforeseen counter-mischief becomes evident it may be reasonable to impute a remedial intention to Parliament. This would be an intention that, if such an untoward event should happen, the court would modify the literal meaning of the enactment so as to remedy the unexpected counter-mischief.

This is one aspect of consequential construction (see p 166 above). Similar considerations may arise where some drafting error has occurred (as to rectifying construction). A third possible cause of an unforeseen counter-mischief, or increase in an expected counter-mischief, is social or other change taking place after the passing of the Act (updating construction is discussed at p 181 below).

Presumption that drafting errors to be rectified

It is presumed that the legislator intends the court to apply a construction which rectifies any error in the drafting of the enactment, where this is required to give effect to the legislator's intention. There are occasions when, as Baron Parke said, the language of the legislature must be modified in order to avoid inconsistency with its manifest intentions (*Miller* v *Salomons* (1852) 7 Ex 475, 553). Cross held that rectification is the right word for this procedure 'because it is a word which at least implies some sort of intention on the part of Parliament with regard to the added words' (Cross 1987, p 35).

It has to be accepted that drafting errors frequently occur (for an account of the various types of drafting error see chapter 19). The promulgating of a flawed text as expressing the legislative intention raises a difficult conflict between literal and purposive construction. Judges tread a wary middle way between the extremes. The court must do the best it can to implement the intention without being unfair to those who not unreasonably looked for a predictable construction.

The cases where rectifying construction may be required can be divided into:

(a) the garbled or corrupt text
(b) errors of meaning
(c) the *casus omissum*
(d) the *casus male inclusus* and
(e) the textual conflict.

Garbled or corrupt text

A text may be garbled by the omission of necessary words, the
inclusion of unnecessary words, or the presence of mistaken words,
typographical errors or punctuation mistakes. The duty of the court
is to rectify the text so as to give it the intended meaning. This
produces what may be called the 'corrected version' of the text (see
pp 89-90 above).

If a legislative text is garbled the fact is usually obvious on the
face of it, at least when the reading is careful (eg the Salford Hundred
Court of Record (Extension of Jurisdiction) Rules 1955, r 2, which
authorises a defendant to apply to have the action transferred to
'the County Court in which he resides or carries on business').

The Queen's printer sometimes corrects merely typographical
errors. As originally promulgated the Landlord and Tenant (Rent
Control) Act 1949, s 11(5) referred to s 6 (instead of s 7) of the
Furnished Houses (Rent Control) Act 1946. This was corrected in
subsequent published copies.

In other cases Parliament itself finds it necessary to step in. In
1879 an Act was passed with the clumsy short title of the Artizans
and Labourers Dwellings Act (1868) Amendment Act 1879. The
clumsiness did not stop there. Section 22(3) of the Act required
loans under the Act to be secured by a mortgage 'in the form set
forth in the Third Schedule hereto'. There was no Third Schedule;
and nowhere in the Act was a mortgage form to be found. The
mistake was put right in the following year by an Act which apparently
had the same drafter. Its short title was the Artizans and Labourers
Dwellings Act (1868) Amendment Act (1879) Amendment Act 1880.

Sometimes the error is made in transcribing an enactment for
inclusion in a consolidation Act (eg *Re a solicitor* [1961] Ch 491
and comments thereon in *Harrison* v *Tew* [1988] 2 WLR 1, 10-
12, concerning an error in the (consolidating) Solicitors Act 1932,
s 66 repeated in the (also consolidating) Solicitors Act 1957, s 69).
Here there is an inference that the original wording should be
followed. The Law of Property Act 1922, s 125(2) empowered
trustees to appoint agents for 'executing and perfecting assurances
of property'. In the Trustee Act 1925, s 23(2) this appears as a
reference to *insurances* of property (for a judicial comment see *Green*
v *Whitehead* [1930] 1 Ch 38, 45). For another consolidation Act
case see *The Arabert* [1963] P 102.

One of the best known examples of an incomplete text is the
Statute of Frauds Amendment Act 1828 (Lord Tenterden's Act),
s 6. For the fascinatingly varied ways in which three judges attempted
to rectify the obvious omission of words in this section see *Lyde*
v *Barnard* (1836) 1 M & W 101. (For other examples of omitted
words see *Re Wainwright* (1843) 1 Ph 258; *A-G* v *Beauchamp* [1920]
1 KB 650).

Instead of intended words being omitted, unintended words may be included. The Criminal Appeal Act 1907, s 4(3) said that on an appeal against sentence the court could impose another sentence warranted in law 'by the verdict', overlooking that where the accused pleads guilty there is no verdict. In *R* v *Ettridge* [1909] 2 KB 24 the court rectified the enactment by deleting the intrusive words.

Errors of meaning

Rectification of a more substantial kind may be required where the meaning is vitiated by some error on the part of the drafter which is not apparent on the face of the text. He may have misconceived the legislative project, or based the text on a mistake of fact. Or he may have made an error in the applicable law or mishandled a legal concept. Examples of such errors, and how the courts dealt with them, are given in chapter 19.

Casus omissus

Where the literal meaning of an enactment is narrower than the object there arises what is called a *casus omissus*. Nowadays it is regarded as not in accordance with public policy for the court to allow a drafter's ineptitude to prevent the legislative intention being carried out, and so a rectifying construction may be applied (eg *R* v *Corby Juvenile Court, ex parte M* [1987] 1 WLR 55).

Another type of *casus omissus* is where an enactment requires a thing to be done which can be done in more than one way, but fails to specify which way is to be employed (eg *Re Unit 2 Windows Ltd* [1985] 1 WLR 1383).

Casus male inclusus

Again the court may apply a rectifying construction where a case obviously intended to be excluded is covered by the literal meaning (eg *Crook* v *Edmondson* [1966] 2 QB 81).

Textual conflicts

Some form of rectifying construction is obviously needed where the court is confronted with conflicting texts (see p 189 below).

Presumption that evasion not to be allowed

It is the duty of a court to further the legislator's aim of providing a remedy for the mischief against which the enactment is directed. Accordingly the court will prefer a construction which advances this object rather than one which circumvents it. When deliberately embarked on, evasion is judicially described as a fraud on the Act (*Ramsden* v *Lupton* (1873) LR 9 QB 17, 24; *Bills* v *Smith* (1865)

6 B & S 314, 319). It was so prevalent in early times that a general prohibition was entered on the Statute Roll: 'And every man . . . shall keep and observe the aforesaid ordinances and statutes . . . without addition, or fraud, by covin, evasion, art or contrivance, or by interpretation of the words' (10 Edw 3 st 3, 1336).

To prevent evasion, the court turns away from a construction that would allow the subject (a) to do what Parliament has indicated by the Act it considers mischievous (eg *R* v *Ealing London Borough Council, ex parte Sidhu* (1982) *The Times*, 16 January; or (b) to refrain from doing what Parliament has indicated it considers desirable (eg *Lambert* v *Ealing London Borough Council* [1982] 1 WLR 550).

The desire of the courts to prevent evasion of statutes is manifest in many fields (eg *Dutton* v *Atkins* (1871) LR 6 QB 373 (vaccination order could be made where parent failed to produce the child, since otherwise the parent could evade the intention of Parliament that children should be vaccinated); *London School Board* v *Wood* (1885) 15 QBD 415 (parent did not satisfy the requirement to 'cause the child to attend school' where he sent him to school without the school fees); *Patterson* v *Redpath Brothers Ltd* [1979] 1 WLR 553, 557 ('it cannot have been the intention of the legislature to allow the provisions of the regulations to be circumvented merely by packing goods into a larger receptacle'); *London Borough of Hackney* v *Ezedinma* [1981] 3 All ER 438, 442 (the term 'household' in the Housing Act 1961 must be construed widely since otherwise 'lodging houses would be taken out of the code which is applied by the Act for houses in multiple occupation').

Evasion distinguished from avoidance

It is necessary to distinguish, as respects the requirements of an enactment, between lawfully escaping those requirements by so arranging matters that they do not apply (referred to as avoidance) and unlawfully contravening or failing to comply with the requirements (referred to as evasion). As Grove J expressed it, there can be no objection to 'getting away from the remedial operation of the statute while complying with the words of the statute' (*Ramsden* v *Lupton* (1873) LR 9 QB 17, 32).

Literal compliance will not suffice where it amounts to a sham. The Theatres Act 1843 prohibited the performance of plays on a stage without a licence. It was held in *Day* v *Simpson* (1865) 34 LJMC 149 that it was an evasion of this for the actors to perform below stage, their actions being reflected by mirrors so that to the audience they appeared to be on stage.

The *Ramsay* principle, whereby the court sets its face against purely artificial tax avoidance schemes, was laid down in *W T Ramsay Ltd* v *IRC* [1982] AC 300. That it is not confined to revenue cases is shown by *Sherdley* v *Sherdley* [1986] 1 WLR 732, where the

Court of Appeal held that the principle should also be applied by the Family Division (reversed by the House of Lords on other grounds in *Sherdley* v *Sherdley* [1987] 2 WLR 1071). In *Gisborne* v *Burton* [1988] 3 WLR 921 the Court of Appeal applied the *Ramsay* principle in the case of the protection intended to be given to tenants by the Agricultural Holdings (Notices to Quit) Act 1977, s 2(1).

What must not be done directly should not be done indirectly

Where an enactment prohibits the doing of a thing, the prohibition is taken to extend to the doing of it by indirect or roundabout means, even though not expressly referred to in the enactment. Where Parliament wishes to prohibit the doing of any act, it tends to concentrate in its wording on the obvious and direct ways of doing it. Yet if the intention is to be achieved, the prohibition must be taken to extend to indirect methods of achieving the same object— even though these are not expressly mentioned (eg *Walker* v *Walker* [1983] 3 WLR 421; *Street* v *Mountford* [1985] AC 809).

Evasion by deferring liability

The court will infer an intention by Parliament to treat as evasion of an Act the deferring of liability under it in ways not envisaged by the Act. If an Act imposes a liability falling at a certain time, it is an evasion of the Act to procure a postponement of the liability by artificial means not contemplated by the Act (eg *Furniss (Inspector of Taxes)* v *Dawson* [1984] AC 474).

Evasion by repetitious acts

The court will infer an intention by Parliament that evasion of an Act should not be countenanced where the method used is constant repetition of acts which taken singly are unexceptionable, but which considered together cumulatively effect an evasion of the purpose of the Act. The Public Houses Amendment (Scotland) Act 1862 gave magistrates power to order the public houses 'in any particular locality' to close at an earlier hour than the statutory closing time. An attempt was made to use this power to close *all* public houses early by making one order after another until the whole district was covered. In *Macbeth* v *Ashley* (1874) LR 2 HL(SC) 352, 357 this was held unlawful as 'evading an Act of Parliament'.

Sometimes the monetary penalties for breach laid down by the Act are, or through inflation have become, so inadequate that they fail to deter. Here the court may resort to the use of the injunction to counter continued repetition of evasive acts. In *A-G* v *Harris* [1961] 1 QB 74 repeated breaches of a byelaw against the selling of flowers outside cemeteries were restrained by injunction, since the statutory penalties were considered by the court insufficient.

Construction which hinders legal proceedings under Act

So that the purpose of an Act may be achieved, it is necessary that any legal proceedings connected with its enforcement and administration should be facilitated and not hindered. Accordingly the courts frown on attempts to construe an enactment in such a way as to frustrate or stultify prosecutions or other legal proceedings under the Act (eg *R* v *Aubrey-Fletcher, ex parte Ross-Munro* [1968] 1 QB 620, 627; *R* v *Holt* [1981] 1 WLR 1000).

Construction which otherwise defeats legislative purpose

The principle requiring a construction against evasion is not limited to cases of deliberate or obvious evasion. It extends to any way by which an Act's integrity may be undermined, even innocently or unwittingly (eg *Stile Hall Properties Ltd* v *Gooch* [1980] 1 WLR 62).

Presumption that ancillary rules of law and legal maxims apply

Unless the contrary intention appears, an enactment by implication imports any principle or rule of law (whether statutory or non-statutory), and the principle of any legal maxim, which prevails in the territory to which the enactment extends and is relevant to its operation in that territory. An Act of Parliament is not a statement in a vacuum. Parliament intends its Act to be read and applied within the context of the existing corpus juris, or body of law. The Act relies for its effectiveness on this implied importation of surrounding legal principles and rules.

It is impossible for the drafter to restate in express terms all those ancillary legal considerations which are, or may become, necessary for the Act's working. In this respect an Act is treated in the same way as a contract. With a contract, by importing established legal principles in accordance with the maxim *quando abest provisio partis, adest provisio legis* (when provision of party is wanting, provision of law is present), the law supplies what the parties have failed to say (*Flack* v *Downing College, Cambridge* (1853) 13 CB 945, 960). An Act requires similar treatment.

This is a presumption of very great importance in statutory interpretation. Each relevant item of the existing law, so far as not altered by the Act in question (whether expressly or by implication) operates for the purposes of that Act just as if written into it. It goes without saying, in Lord Denning's homely phrase (*R* v *Secretary of State for Foreign and Commonwealth Affairs, ex parte Indian Association of Alberta* [1982] QB 892, 919).

These implied ancillary rules range from the widest principles of legal policy to narrow technical rules. They include both statutory and non-statutory principles and rules. They may be substantive or procedural. Equally they may be domestic or international, civil or criminal. All that matters is that they should have a place in the law of the territory to which the Act extends. This means that virtually the whole body of law is imported, by one enactment or another, as implied ancillary rules or maxims.

Unless the contrary intention appears As usual in statutory interpretation, this presumption applies except where the intention that it should not apply is indicated in the Act in question. It is axiomatic that in its Act Parliament can always, if it chooses, disapply any existing principle or rule. It is equally axiomatic that, unless Parliament does so, the principle or rule, being relevant, applies. Thus Lord Pearce said of a tribunal set up by Act: 'it is assumed, unless special provisions provide otherwise, that the tribunal will make its enquiry and decision according to the law of the land' (*Anisminic Ltd* v *Foreign Compensation Commission* [1969] 2 AC 147, 195). Equally Byles J said that 'it is a sound rule to construe a statute in conformity with the common law, except where or in so far as the statute is plainly intended to alter the course of the common law' (*R* v *Morris* (1867) LR 1 CCR 90, 95). See also *Lord Eldon* v *Hedley Bros* [1935] 2 KB 1, 24; *R* v *Thomas* [1950] 1 KB 26, 31.

Disapplication or modification?

Sometimes it is difficult to be sure whether or not Parliament does intend to disapply an ancillary rule. Or the problem may be whether the intention is to disapply a rule altogether or merely modify it. This can be particularly troublesome where the rule is peripheral to the subject-matter of the Act.

Rules relating to surrounding areas of criminal law (such as inchoate offences or the position of accessories) present problems with many Acts, usually because the drafter has overlooked them. Drafters framing a new criminal offence tend to have a blind spot about such matters. There is no difficulty if the new offence is worded so as not to trespass on the peripheral area: the latter's rules then come in by implication as they stand. But suppose the drafter forgets the peripheral area and words the new offence so as inadvertently to trespass on some part, but not the whole, of it?

The Misuse of Drugs Act 1971, s 4(2)(*b*) makes it an offence 'to be concerned in the production of [a controlled drug] in contravention of [s 4(1) of the Act] by another'. This looks very like a description of aiding and abetting, but is it intended to replace the whole law of aiding and abetting, or leave it standing so far as not inconsistent? This is a difficult question to answer because probably the truth is that the drafter did not think about the law of aiding and abetting, and so had no true intention in the matter (see *R* v *Farr* [1982] Crim LR 745).

Geographical extent

The presumption as stated above refers to the geographical extent of the Act because the implied ancillary rules and maxims will be those of the relevant territory. If an Act extends both to England and Scotland then, so far as the Act applies in England the implied ancillary rules will be those prevailing under English law while so far as the Act applies in Scotland they will be those of Scots law. Thus in the Scottish case of *Temple* v *Mitchell* (1956) SC 267 the court treated a difference in implied ancillary rules between England and Scotland as precluding the court from following English precedents in a Rent Act case.

Legal concepts

Use in an enactment of a concept, eg relating to age, time or status, attracts general legal rules applying to that concept. Thus the statement in the Landlord and Tenant Act 1954, s 29(3) that no application under s 24(1) of the Act shall be entertained 'unless it is made not less than two . . . months after the giving of the landlord's notice' under s 25 attracts the *corresponding date rule*, under which, if the relevant period is a specified number of months after the relevant event, the period ends on the corresponding day of the subsequent month (*Riley (E J) Investments Ltd* v *Eurostile Holdings Ltd* [1985] 1 WLR 1139).

Free-standing terms

One of the most obvious ways in which Parliament indicates its intention to attract ancillary rules is by the use of a free-standing term, that is a word or phrase which is not defined in the Act but has an independent meaning at common law or otherwise.

The Sexual Offences Act 1956, s 14(1) states that it is an offence 'for a person to make an indecent assault on a woman'. The Act contains no definition either of 'indecent' or 'assault'. Parliament is therefore taken to intend to apply the common-law meaning of these terms when taken in conjunction (*R* v *Kimber* [1983] Crim LR 630).

Ancillary maxims

Legal maxims are repositories of that wisdom the best lawyers

contribute to human welfare. While a broadly-stated maxim is likely
to have exceptions and require qualification, the law still finds a
use for this way of expressing some basic principle. Coke said: It
is holden for an inconvenience that any of the maxims of the law
should be broken . . . for that by infringing of a maxim, not only
a general prejudice to many, but in the end a public uncertainty
and confusion to all would follow.' (Co Litt 152b.) What is said
above about the implied importation of ancillary rules of law also
applies to maxims.

Development of applied rules of law

The court will not merely treat an existing rule of law as intended
to apply in the construction of an enactment, but will if necessary
go further and modify or develop the rule as it applies to that
enactment.

The House of Lords developed an applied rule in *British Leyland
Motor Corporation Ltd* v *Armstrong Patents Co Ltd* [1986] AC 577.
The plaintiffs alleged that in copying parts of their vehicles, and
marketing the copies as spare parts, the defendants were guilty of
breaches of design copyright under the Copyright Act 1956, s 3.
It was held that Parliament could not be taken to intend that the
copyright should apply so as to enable the plaintiffs to deny
purchasers of their cars the right to have them repaired by use
of spare parts, and in arriving at this result the House of Lords
applied and modified the real property principle whereby a person
is not to be permitted to derogate from his grant.

Presumption that updating construction to be applied

While it remains law, an Act is to be treated as always speaking.
In its application on any date, the language of the Act, though
necessarily embedded in its own time, is nevertheless to be construed
in accordance with the need to treat it as current law. With regard
to updating, Acts can be divided into two categories: the Act that
is intended to develop in meaning with developing circumstances
(which may be called an ongoing Act) and the Act that is intended
to be of unchanging effect (a fixed-time Act). Most Acts are of
the former kind.

The ongoing Act

It is presumed that Parliament intends the court to apply to an
ongoing Act a construction that continuously updates its wording
to allow for changes since the Act was initially framed. In particular
where, owing to developments occurring since the original passing
of an enactment, a counter-mischief comes into existence or increases,
it is presumed that Parliament intends the court so to construe the

enactment as to minimise the adverse effects of the counter-mischief. The editors of the second edition of Cross's *Statutory Interpretation* express agreement (p 49) with the present author that 'there is a general rule in favour of an "updating" or "ambulatory" approach, rather than an "historical" one'.

It was the great Victorian drafter Lord Thring who said that an Act is taken to be always speaking (Thring 1902, p 83). While it remains in force, the Act is necessarily to be treated as current law. It speaks from day to day, though always (unless textually amended) in the words of its original drafter. With this in mind, the competent drafter frames his language in terms suitable for continuing operation into the unforeseeable future. He does not conspicuously compose the Act as at the date of his draft. Rather, he aims to employ a continuous present tense. He uses, as Thring enjoined, the word 'shall' as 'an imperative only, and not as a future' (ibid).

Each generation is largely ruled by the law it inherits. Constant formal updating is not practicable, so an Act takes on a life of its own. What the original framers intended sinks gradually into history. While their language may endure as law, its current subjects are likely to find that law more and more ill-fitting if taken literally.

In construing an ongoing Act, the interpreter is to presume that Parliament intended the Act to be applied at any future time in such a way as to give effect to the true original intention. Accordingly the interpreter is to make allowances for any relevant changes that have occurred since the Act's passing in the law, social conditions, technology, the meaning of words, and other matters. That today's construction involves the supposition that Parliament was catering long ago for a state of affairs that did not then exist is no argument against that construction. Parliament, in the wording of an enactment, is expected to anticipate developments. The drafter should try to foresee the future, and allow for it so much as possible in his wording.

On one view of the definition of 'superior court' in the Contempt of Court Act 1981, s 19, it applied to a type of court that did not exist in 1981. In *Peart* v *Stewart* [1983] 2 AC 109, 117 Lord Diplock said:

I should . . . have reached the same conclusion on the construction of the definition of 'superior court' in s 19, even if it were impossible to point to any existing court which complied with the description and one were driven to the conclusion that the draftsman was making anticipatory provision for possible new courts that might be subsequently created with the status of superior courts of record.

Changes in the mischief

The mischief at which an enactment was originally directed needs to be 'discerned and considered' in order to construe the enactment correctly (see p 161 above). Difficulty can be caused by the obvious fact that while the enactment may be suffered to continue in force the social mischief, or mischief on the ground, is likely to change. If the remedial enactment is successful it will remove, or at least alleviate, the social mischief. In the early days however the court will need to help the enactment achieve its object. At best, the enactment may have only partial success. Persons wishing to continue the mischief may attempt to do so. As time goes on, various factors may cause changes in the mischief or may lead to its disappearance. It is by no means certain that the enactment will be amended or repealed at the moment the need for this arises. It may continue to have effect well after the conditions which caused it to be added to the statute book have significantly changed or even disappeared.

Towards the end of an enactment's life on the statute book, perhaps the mischief has dwindled to little or nothing. It is then not something that needs to be remedied. The enactment declines into the category of a technical or nominal law. If it is activated by a prosecution the court will react accordingly. It will criticise the bringing of the case. It will sum up against the prosecution. If the legal meaning of the enactment is doubtful, the court will give little weight to the original mischief and much weight to the principle against doubtful penalisation. It will apply an updating construction.

Changes in relevant law

After an Act is passed, later amendments of law (perhaps carried out for a quite different purpose) may mean that the legal remedy provided by the Act to deal with the original mischief has become inadequate or inappropriate. The court must then, in interpreting the Act, make allowances for the fact that the surrounding legal conditions prevailing on the date of its passing have changed. Thus in *Gissing* v *Liverpool Corporation* [1935] Ch 1 the word 'tax' in a pre-income tax enactment was held to include income tax.

Drafters of amending Acts sometimes fail to realise that changes in surrounding law call for corresponding changes in the language they choose. In *Nugent-Head* v *Jacob (Inspector of Taxes)* [1948] AC 321, 322 Viscount Simon complained that the language of the income tax enactments relating to married women had not been updated: 'the words now in operation are largely borrowed from Acts of 1803, 1805 and 1806, at which dates the effect of marriage on the property of a wife was very different from what it is today'.

When the question arises of whether an ongoing enactment covers a legal entity not known at the date it was passed, the key is whether it is of the same type or genus as things originally covered by the enactment. Where in *R* v *Manners* [1976] Crim LR 255 the question arose whether the North Thames Gas Board, set up under the Gas Act 1948, was a 'public body' within the meaning of the Prevention of Corruption Acts 1889 to 1916, it was held that it was to be answered by determining what type of body was regarded in 1916 as a 'public body'.

Where there has been a significant change in law since the enactment was framed, it is applied to the *substance* of the new law. If the original terminology referred to has been allotted a different meaning, the court will look at the substance behind the wording. The fact that the term referred to by the enactment is still in use does not mean the enactment will apply if the current use gives the term an essentially different meaning (eg *Zezza* v *Government of Italy* [1982] 2 WLR 1077.)

Also relevant are changes in judicial approach over the years. An Act might be differently construed before and after such a change. Thus Lord Diplock said in 1981 that 'Any judicial statements on matters of public law if made before 1950 are likely to be a misleading guide to what the law is today' (*IRC* v *National Federation of Self-Employed and Small Businesses Ltd* [1981] 2 WLR 722, 736).

Changes in social conditions

Where relevant social conditions have changed since the date of enactment, what was then classed as a social mischief may not be so regarded today. It is very difficult for the court to apply an enactment so as to 'remedy' what is no longer regarded as a mischief. The consequence is an interpretation that minimises the coercive effect of the enactment and gives great weight to criteria such as the principle against doubtful penalisation.

The London Hackney Carriage Act 1853, s 17 makes it an offence for a cab driver to demand *or take* more than the proper fare. The literal meaning clearly includes taking a tip, whether demanded or not. A century later, the tipping of cab drivers had become an accepted social custom. In *Bassam* v *Green* [1981] Crim LR 626 both members of the Divisional Court stated *obiter*, without giving reasons, that tipping did *not* contravene s 17.

Changes in the practices of mankind may necessitate a strained construction if the legislator's object is to be achieved (eg *Collins* v *British Airways Board* [1982] QB 734); *Marina Shipping Ltd* v *Laughton* [1982] QB 1127). Similarly the earlier processing by the court of an enactment may be disregarded if it is no longer appropriate in the light of changed conditions (eg *R* v *Bow Road JJ, ex parte Adedigba* [1968] 2 QB 572, 586).

Developments in technology

The nature of an ongoing Act requires the court to take account of changes in technology, and treat the statutory language as modified accordingly when this is needed to implement the legislative intention.

Section 3(1) of the Coroners Act 1887 (a consolidation Act) says that where a coroner is informed that the dead body of a person is lying within his jurisdiction, and certain conditions are satisfied, the coroner, whether or not the cause of death arose within his jurisdiction, shall hold an inquest. The development of refrigeration and air freight services means that bodies can now easily be brought to England from foreign parts. In 1887 this was impossible, so there was no need for the Act to state that the death must have occurred in Britain. Now that new technology makes real the possibility that a decedent whose body is in Britain died abroad, the courts have had to decide whether a territorial limitation is to be treated as implied (*R v West Yorkshire Coroner, ex parte Smith* [1982] QB 335 and [1983] QB 335).

In *Pierce v Bemis, The Lusitania* [1986] QB 384 the court considered the question whether the sunken ship *Lusitania* was 'derelict', which could scarcely have arisen before modern techniques of wreck recovery had been developed. Sheen J held (p 394) that because of changes since its passing 'it is now necessary to disregard some part of the language of [the Merchant Shipping Act 1894]'.

Changes in meaning of words

Where an expression used in an Act has changed its original meaning, the Act may have to be construed as if there were substituted for that expression a term with a modern meaning corresponding to that original meaning (*The Longford* (1889) 14 PD 34). If it seems that the meaning of an expression used in an Act may have changed materially since the Act was passed, evidence may be adduced to establish the original meaning (*London and North Eastern Rly Co v Berriman* [1946] AC 278, 312, *Hardwick Game Farm v Suffolk Agricultural and Poultry Producers Assn Ltd* [1966] 1 WLR 287).

The fixed-time Act

A fixed-time Act is one which, contrary to the usual rule, was intended to be applied in the same way whatever changes might occur after its passing. It has a once for all operation. It is to such an Act only that the much quoted words of Lord Esher apply: 'the Act must be construed as if one were interpreting it the day after it was passed' (*The Longford* (1889) 14 PD 34, 36). An obvious example is the Indemnity Act. There are various other possibilities. Thus it was held in *Lord Colchester v Kewney* (1866) LR 1 Ex 368, 380 that the Land Tax Act 1798, s 25, which exempted 'any hospital' from the land tax, was intended by Parliament to apply only to hospitals which were in existence at the time the Act was passed.

The presumption is that an Act is intended to be an ongoing Act, since this is the nature of statute law: an Act is always speaking. So there must be some reason adduced for finding it to be a fixed-time Act. One such reason is where the Act is of the nature of a *contract*. If an Act can be said to form or ratify a contract its meaning cannot properly be 'developed' in the usual way, an obvious example being an Act implementing an international convention. (The convention itself may be subject to 'development', but that is another matter.) Thus in a Canadian constitutional appeal Lord Sankey LC said:

The process of interpretation as the years go on ought not to be allowed to dim or whittle down the provisions of the original contract upon which the federation was founded, nor is it legitimate that any judicial construction of the provisions of ss 91 and 92 should impose a new and different contract upon the federating bodies. (*Re the Regulation and Control of Aeronautics in Canada* [1932] AC 54, 70.)

It was held in *A-G for Alberta* v *Huggard Assets Ltd* [1953] AC 420 that the Tenures Abolition Act 1660 was of the nature of a compact between the king and his people in England and Wales, and thus did not extend to after-acquired territories of the Crown such as those in Canada.

An obvious instance of the Act which partakes of the nature of a compact is the private Act. The courts treat this as a contract between its promoters (or that portion of the public directly interested in it) and Parliament (*Milnes* v *Mayor etc of Huddersfield* (1886) 11 App Cas 511; *Perchard* v *Heywood* (1800) 8 TR 468).

Increase in counter-mischief

Where, owing to developments occurring since the original passing of an enactment, a counter-mischief comes into existence or increases, it is presumed that Parliament intends the court so to construe the enactment as to minimise the adverse effects of the counter-mischief (eg *R* v *Wilkinson* [1980] 1 WLR 396).

Chapter Twelve

Guides to Legislative Intention IV: Linguistic Canons of Construction

The present chapter deals with the linguistic canons of construction, which reflect the nature or use of language. They are employed to arrive at the literal meaning of an enactment, and depend neither on its legislative character nor on its quality as a legal pronouncement. These canons apply in much the same way to all verbal forms, being based on the rules of grammar, syntax and punctuation and the use of language as a general medium of communication. When judges say, as they sometimes do, that the principles of statutory interpretation do not materially differ from those applicable to the interpretation of documents generally, it is these linguistic canons they have in mind.

Construction of text as a whole

The first linguistic canon is that an Act or other legislative instrument is to be read as a whole, so that an enactment within it is not treated as standing alone but is interpreted in its verbal context. As Holmes J said, 'you let whatever galvanic current may come from the rest of the instrument run through the particular sentence' (Holmes 1898–99, 417).

Coke said that it is the most natural and genuine exposition of a statute to construe one part of it by another 'for that best expresseth the meaning of the makers' (1 Co Inst 381 1b). In *South West Water Authority* v *Rumble's* [1985] AC 609, 617 Lord Scarman said of paragraphs (a) and (b) of the Water Act 1973, s 30: 'It is not . . . possible to determine their true meaning save in the context of the legislation read as a whole'.

It follows that a general term used in one provision of an Act may by implication be modified by another provision elsewhere in the Act. Thus in *Cooper* v *Motor Insurers' Bureau* [1985] QB 575 the general term 'any person' in the Road Traffic Act 1972, s 145(3)(*a*) was held to be modified by an implication rising from s 143(1) of the Act.

Certain specific rules follow from the idea that a legislative text is to be construed as a whole.

All words to be given meaning

On the presumption that Parliament does nothing in vain, the court must endeavour to give significance to every part of an enactment. It is presumed that if a word or phrase appears in the enactment, it was put there for a purpose and must not be disregarded. This applies *a fortiori* to a longer passage, such as a section or subsection. Where in *Albert* v *Lavin* [1981] 2 WLR 1070, 1083 Hodgson J said that in an enactment defining a criminal offence the word 'unlawful' was surely tautologous he was rebuked by Lawton LJ in a later case (*R* v *Kimber* [1983] 1 WLR 1118, 1122).

In *A-G's Reference (No 1 of 1975)* [1975] QB 773, 778 it was held that in the Accessories and Abettors Act 1861, s 8 the words 'aid, abet, counsel or procure' must each be taken to have a distinct meaning since otherwise Parliament would be indulging in tautology in using all four words. In *R* v *Millward* [1985] QB 519 the Court of Appeal rejected the appellant's argument that the Perjury Act 1916, s 1(1) applies only where the witness believes his false statement to be material, because this reading would render s 1(6) of the Act meaningless. In *Chaudhary* v *Chaudhary* [1984] Fam 19 it was held that the Recognition of Divorces and Legal Separations Act 1971, s 2(*a*) must have a restrictive effect, since otherwise it would have no operation.

It may happen however that no sensible meaning can be given to some statutory word or phrase. It must then be disregarded. As Brett J said in *Stone* v *Corporation of Yeovil* (1876) 1 CPD 691, 701: 'It is a canon of construction that, if it be possible, effect must be given to every word of an Act of Parliament or other document; but that, if there be a word or phrase therein to which no sensible meaning can be given, it must be eliminated'. Words may be robbed of meaning by a subsequent change in the law and the failure of the drafter of the amending Act to effect a consequential amendment (eg *R* v *Wilson (Clarence)* [1983] 3 WLR 686, 691).

Same words to be given same meaning

It is presumed that a word or phrase is not to be taken as having different meanings within the same instrument, unless this intention is made clear. Where the context shows that the term has a particular meaning in one place, it will be taken to have that meaning elsewhere. Thus Cleasby B said: 'It is a sound rule of construction to give the same meaning to the same words occurring in different parts of an Act of Parliament' (*Courtauld* v *Legn* (1869) LR 4 Ex 126, 130). Where through unskilful drafting there is doubt as to whether this was indeed Parliament's intention, much difficulty may be caused (eg *Doe d Angell* v *Angell* (1846) 9 QB 328, 355, where 'rent' was used in two different senses throughout an Act).

A word or phrase with more than one ordinary meaning is termed a homonym. It is presumed, unless the contrary intention appears, that where the legislator uses a homonym in an Act or other instrument it is intended to have the same meaning in each place. The same applies to cognate expressions such as 'married' and 'marry' (*R* v *Allen* (1872) LR 1 CCR 367, 374).

Where an artificial meaning is given to a term for a particular purpose, it will not apply to use of the term where that purpose does not operate (eg *Moir* v *Williams* [1892] 1 QB 264).

Different words to be given different meanings

It is presumed that the drafter did not indulge in elegant variation, but kept to a particular term when he wished to convey a particular meaning. Accordingly a variation in the term used is taken to denote a different meaning. Blackburn J said in *Hadley* v *Perks* (1866) LR 1 QB 444, 457:

It has been a general rule for drawing legal documents from the earliest times, one which one is taught when one first becomes a pupil to a conveyancer, never to change the form of words unless you are going to change the meaning . . .

In the same place however Blackburn J recognised the possibility of elegant variation when he said that the legislature 'to improve the graces of the style and to avoid using the same words over and over again' may employ different words without any intention to change the meaning. It can only be said that this is bad drafting. Making use of pronouns when safe, the drafter should otherwise stick to the same word. Graces of style are all very well, but in Acts of Parliament they take a far second place to certainty of meaning.

Conflicting statements within one instrument

Where two enactments within an Act or other instrument conflict, it is necessary to treat one as modifying the other. If no other method of reconciliation is possible, the court adopts the principle that the enactment nearest the end of the instrument prevails (*Wood* v *Riley* (1867) LR 3 CP 26, 27) (see further pp 275–278).

Effect of specific on general provision

Drafters who wish to make clear that a specific provision is not intended to modify the meaning of a wider general provision often preface the former with the formula 'without prejudice to the generality of [the general provision] . . . This type of formula has its dangers, since often courts find themselves mentally unable to disregard the special provision when construing the wider one (eg

R v *Akan* [1973] QB 491, followed in *R* v *Secretary of State for the Home Department, ex parte Thornton* [1987] QB 36).

Consolidation Acts

The presumption of consistent meaning is weaker with consolidation Acts, since these combine the work of different drafters executed at different times (see *IRC* v *Hinchy* [1960] AC 748, 766). This particularly applies to tax enactments. Thus ss 428 and 455 of the Income and Corporation Taxes Act 1970, reproducing provisions of the Finance Act 1938, achieve results similar to those of s 16 of the Finance Act 1973, though by a different form of words. On this Lord Templeman said in *Carver* v *Duncan (Inspector of Taxes)* [1985] AC 1082, 1125:

... the Income Tax Acts are a vast patchwork begun in the nineteenth century and doomed never to be completed. It is useless to speculate why the draftsman in 1973 used words different from those employed by the draftsman in 1938. Oversight, or some difficulty, real or imagined, may have played a part.

Meaning of ordinary words

The legal meaning of a non-technical word used in an enactment is presumed to correspond to its ordinary meaning, which has been defined as its 'proper and most known signification'. If there is more than one ordinary meaning, the most common and well-established is taken to be intended.

Lord Tenterden said words are to be applied 'as they are understood in common language' (*A-G* v *Winstanley* (1831) 2 D & C1 302, 310). Parke B spoke of adhering to 'the grammatical and ordinary sense of the words used' (*Grey* v *Pearson* (1857) 6 HL Cas 61, 106). Viscount Dilhorne LC required words to be given 'their ordinary natural meaning' (*Selvey* v *DPP* [1970] AC 304, 330). Graham J said 'words must be treated as having their ordinary English meaning as applied to the subject-matter with which they are dealing' (*Exxon Corpn* v *Exxon Insurance Consultants International Ltd* [1981] 1 WLR 624, 633). In an appeal concerning who should be treated as a 'member of the family' within the meaning of the Rent Acts, Cohen LJ said that the question the county court judge should have asked himself was: 'Would an ordinary man, addressing his mind to the question whether Mrs Wollams was a member of the family or not, have answered "Yes" or "No"?'

Several ordinary meanings

Many terms have more than one ordinary meaning. Here the starting point is the most common and well-established meaning. In *R* v

Income Tax Commissioners (1888) 22 QBD 296, 309 Fry LJ said:
'The words of a statute are to be taken in their primary, and not
in their secondary, signification'.

Composite expressions

A composite expression must be construed as a whole, but it is
incorrect to assume that the whole is necessarily the sum of its
parts. Because a certain meaning can be collected by taking each
word in turn and then combining their several meanings, it does
not follow that this is the true meaning of the whole phrase. Each
word in the phrase may modify the meaning of the others, giving
the whole its own meaning. (See *Mersey Docks and Harbour Board*
v *Henderson* (1883) 13 App C as 595, 599.)

Constructive meaning

The court will apply a statutory term in a sense wide enough to
include constructive meanings of the term. Thus in *Re Clore (decd)*
(No 3) [1985] 1 WLR 1290 it was held that the provision in the
Finance Act 1975, Sched 4, para 2(1) requiring a trustee to deliver
an account specifying certain information 'to the best of his
knowledge' extended to information contained in documents etc
within the trustee's possession or control, even though not present
to his mind.

Technical terms

If a word or phrase has a technical meaning in relation to a particular
expertise, and is used in a context dealing with that expertise, it
is to be given its technical meaning unless the contrary intention
appears.

Technical terms are not terms in ordinary use, but require
knowledge of the expertise with which they are connected in order
to be correctly understood. As Blackstone said, they must be taken
according to the acceptation of the learned in each art, trade and
science (Blackstone 1765, i 39). Lord Esher MR said, where used
in connection with a particular business, words are presumed to
be used in the sense in which they are understood in regard to
that business (*Unwin* v *Hanson* [1891] 2 QB 115, 119).

A technical expression may incorporate an ordinary word and
give it a special meaning. An obvious example is Bombay duck,
which not being duck at all but fish, would not be covered by an
enactment regulating 'duck'. Again the Excise Acts place a duty
on 'spirits' without elaborating the meaning. In *A-G* v *Bailey* (1847)
1 Ex 281 it was held that this, being a word of known import,
is used in the sense in which it is ordinarily understood. It therefore

does not cover sweet spirits of nitre, an article of commerce not ordinarily described as 'spirits'.

A technical term may have different meanings, or a wider and narrower meaning. Lord Macmillan once said that the term 'assessment' is used in the Income Tax Acts with no less than eight different meanings (*Commissioners for the General Purposes of the Income Tax Acts for the City of London* v *Gibbs* [1942] AC 402, 424). For examples of the judicial treatment of technical terms see, *Prophet* v *Platt Bros & Co Ltd* [1961] 1 WLR 1130 (fettling of metal castings); *Blankley* v *Godley* [1952] 1 All ER 436n (aircraft 'taking off'); *London and North Eastern Railway Co* v *Berriman* [1946] AC 278 (repairing of permanent way).

Technical legal terms

If a word or phrase has a technical meaning in a certain branch of law, and is used in a context dealing with that branch, it is to be given its technical legal meaning, unless the contrary intention appears. Thus in *R* v *Slator* (1881) 8 QBD 267, 272, where it was argued that the term indictment as used in the Corrupt Practices Prevention Act 1863, s 7 applied to any form of criminal proceeding, Denman J said: 'It always requires the strong compulsion of other words in an Act to induce the court to alter the well-known meaning of a legal term' (see also *Jenkins* v *Inland Revenue Commissioners* [1944] 2 All ER 491, 495; *Knocker* v *Youle* [1986] 1 WLR 934, 936).

Free-standing legal terms stand on their own feet, without need of definition. They have a meaning in law which exists for all purposes, not just for those of a particular enactment. This may be given by statute or at common law. Thus *highway* is defined at common law whereas *highway maintainable at the public expense* is defined generally by the Highways Act 1980, s 36(2).

Technical non-legal terms

If a word or phrase has a technical meaning in relation to a certain area of trade, business, technology, or other non-legal expertise, and is used in a context dealing with that expertise, it is to be given its technical meaning, unless the contrary intention appears. In *Jenner* v *Allen West & Co Ltd* [1959] 1 WLR 554 it was argued that the term 'crawling boards' in certain regulations should be given the literal meaning of plain boards over which workmen could crawl. Evidence showed however that the term had a technical meaning in the trades concerned which required cross battens to be fitted to the boards, so as to prevent men from slipping. It was held that this technical meaning should be applied.

If a word is a technical term of two or more different fields of expertise it is necessary to determine which field is intended. In

Chesterfield Tube Co Ltd v *Thomas (Valuation Officer)* [1970] 1 WLR
1483 the Court of Appeal held that the legal meaning of the technical
phrase 'generation . . . of power' in the General Rate Act 1967, Sched
3, para 1(*a*) was what the phrase meant to rating valuers not physicists.

Terms with both ordinary and technical meaning

Where an enactment uses a term which has both an ordinary and
a technical meaning, the question of which meaning the term is
intended to have is influenced by the context. If the context is
technical, the presumption is that the technical meaning of the term
is intended. Otherwise the ordinary meaning is taken as meant.

In *R* v *Commissioners under Boiler Explosions Act 1882* [1891] 1
QB 703, 716 Lord Esher MR, when considering in the light of
scientific evidence the meaning of the word 'boiler', concluded that
the Act 'was not meant to draw these scientific distinctions but
to deal with the thing in which there is steam under pressure which
is likely to explode'.

The Restriction of Offensive Weapons Act 1959, s 1(1) penalises
any person 'who manufactures, sells or *offers for sale* or hire, or
lends or hires, to any other person' any flick-knife. In *Fisher* v *Bell*
[1961] 1 QB 394 a shopkeeper was accused of offering a flick-knife
for sale by putting it in his shop window. The question was whether
'offer' was used in its popular or technical sense. Rather surprisingly
it was held to be used in its technical sense in the law of contract,
under which placing goods in a shop window does not constitute
an 'offer'.

Case law may give an ordinary word a technical meaning. As
Lord Wilberforce said in connection with 'office' as used in the
Income Tax Acts, many words of ordinary meaning acquire a
signification coloured over the years by legal construction in a
technical context such that return to the pure source of common
parlance is no longer possible (*Edwards (Inspector of Taxes)* v *Clinch*
[1981] 3 WLR 707, 710). Where a term is used which has both
an ordinary and a technical meaning it is permissible, in order to
determine which meaning was intended, to seek guidance from the
pre-enacting history. (*R* v *Nanayakkara* [1987] 1 WLR 265).

Archaisms

Sometimes, though very rarely, the legislator may use a term which
is already archaic or obsolete. It is presumed that the term is intended
to have this archaic meaning, though that does not prevent its legal
meaning in the Act from being developed by the courts in the ordinary
way (see pp 181–6 above as to updating construction).

The Civil Evidence Act 1968, s 8(2)(*b*) provides for enabling a
party to require a person to be called as a witness unless he is
'beyond the seas', a phrase which also occurs in the Criminal Evidence

Act 1965, s 1(1)(*b*). In *Rover International Ltd* v *Cannon Film Sales Ltd (No 2)* [1987] 1 WLR 1597, 1601 Harman J said of this:

> It is a phrase which seems to me to be entirely archaic today. It has splendid overtones of Elizabeth I's reign and suchlike matters but is not a matter, I would think, of current speech or even lawyers' speech . . . However Parliament in its wisdom has chosen to use that phrase and I have to wrestle with it.

Both archaic and modern meaning   Where Parliament uses a term which has an archaic meaning and also a (different) modern meaning it will be presumed, in the absence of any indication to the contrary, that the modern meaning is intended. In *R* v *Secretary of State for the Environment, ex parte Hillingdon LBC* [1986] 1 WLR 192 (affd [1986] 1 WLR 807) Woolf J held that 'committee' as used in the Local Government Act 1972, s 101(1)(*a*) was intended to have its modern meaning of a group of two or more persons, and not its obsolete meaning of a person to whom any function is committed.

Term becoming archaic   Where a term used in relation to a statutory procedure has become archaic since the statute was enacted, the procedure should if possible employ an alternative term in current use (eg *R* v *Portsmouth Coroner, ex parte Anderson* [1987] 1 WLR 1640, 1645 (meaning of 'misadventure').

Judicial notice of meaning

Judicial notice is taken of the meaning of words in Acts and delegated legislation (other than technical terms not being those of the law prevailing within the court's jurisdiction). Martin B said: 'Is not the Judge bound to know the meaning of all words in the English language?' (*Hills* v *London Gaslight Co* (1857) 27 LJ Ex 60, 63), while Pollock CB remarked that 'Judges are philologists of the highest order' (*Ex parte David* (1857) 5 W R 522, 523).

Most judges allow their putative memories to be refreshed by the citation of dictionaries and other works of reference. Lord Coleridge said of dictionaries: 'it is a well-known rule of courts of law that words should be taken to be used in their ordinary sense, and we are therefore sent for instruction to these books' (*R* v *Peters* (1886) 16 QBD 636, 641). A dictionary cited should be well known and authoritative' (*Camden (Marquess)* v *IRC* [1914] 1 KB 641, 647).

If the court is concerned with the contemporary meaning of a word at the time the Act was passed, it should consult a dictionary of that period (*Hardwick Game Farm* v *Suffolk Agricultural and Poultry Producers Association Ltd* [1966] 1 WLR 287; *R* v *Bouch* [1982] 3 WLR 673, 677).

Dictionaries can be used to arrive at the etymology of the word, which may guide the court (eg *R* v *Bates* [1952] 1 All ER 842, 845–846). If the term has been judicially defined in a relevant context, this will be treated by the court as a more reliable guide to its meaning than a dictionary is likely to provide (*Midland Railway* v *Robinson* (1889) 15 App Cas 19, 34; *Kerr* v *Kennedy* [1942] 1 KB 409, 413). This is because the term has then been 'processed' by the court, a topic discussed in Part IV below.

Evidence of meaning

Evidence may not be adduced of the meaning of terms of which the court takes judicial notice; but is admissible as respects the meaning of other terms (*Camden (Marquess)* v *IRC* [1914] 1 KB 641, 650; *R* v *Calder and Boyars Ltd* [1969] 1 QB 151; *R* v *Anderson* [1972]1 QB 304; *R* v *Stamford* [1972] 2 QB 391).

It seems that evidence should be admitted to establish whether or not a term is a technical term (*London and North Eastern Railway Company* v *Berriman* [1946] AC 278, 305). If the evidence shows it is, then the court determines whether it was intended to be understood in the technical sense.

Expert evidence of a technical matter may be admitted in order to determine whether the matter falls within a statutory term. Thus in *R* v *Skirving* [1985] QB 819 a book on cocaine was alleged to be an 'obscene article' within the meaning of the Obscene Publications Act 1959. It was held that expert evidence as to the nature and effect of cocaine was admissible, since this was not within the experience of an ordinary person.

Reference books may be consulted in lieu of evidence. Thus books by Mill and Stephen were cited in *Re Castioni* [1891] 1 QB 149 on the question of what offences are 'of a political character' within the meaning of the Extradition Act 1870, s 3(1). (See also *Bank of Toronto* v *Lambe* (1887) 12 App Cas 575, 581 (works on political economy cited as to meaning of 'direct taxation' in British North America Act 1867); *R* v *Bouch* [1983] QB 246 (*Encyclopædia Britannica* cited as to definition of 'explosive substance' in the Explosive Substances Act 1883, s 3(1)).

We now go on to consider certain specific canons of construction. Many of these are of great antiquity, as indicated by the fact that they are usually known in the form of a Latin phrase or maxim.

Noscitur a sociis

A statutory term is often coloured by its associated words. As Viscount Simonds said in *A-G* v *Prince Ernest Augustus of Hanover* [1957] AC 436, 461: 'words, and particularly general words, cannot be read in isolation; their colour and their content are derived from their context'. The Latin maxim *noscitur a sociis* (it is recognised by its associates) states this contextual principle, whereby a word or phrase is not to be construed as if it stood alone but in the light of its surroundings. While of general application and validity, the maxim has given rise to particular precepts such as the *ejusdem generis* principle and the rank principle, discussed later. The general contextual principle was well stated by Stamp J in *Bourne v Norwich Crematorium Ltd* [1967] 1 WLR 691, 696:

English words derive colour from those which surround them. Sentences are not mere collections of words to be taken out of the sentence, defined separately by reference to the dictionary or decided cases, and then put back into the sentence with the meaning which you have assigned to them as separate words . . . (See also *Peart v Stewart* [1983] AC 109, 117).

As always with an interpretative criterion, other considerations may displace the principle. For example the drafter may have specified certain terms not so as to give colour to a general phrase but to prevent any doubt as to whether they are included (*IRC v Parker* [1966] AC 141, 161). Where an enactment includes a word which in itself is neutral or colourless, the context provides the colouring agent. Walton J said that the word 'payment' 'has no one settled meaning but . . . takes its colour very much from the context in which it is found' (*Garforth (Inspector of Taxes) v Newsmith Stainless Ltd* [1979] 1 WLR 409, 412). In another case Stamp LJ said 'the words "occupation" and "occupier" are not words of art having an ascertained legal meaning applicable, or prima facie applicable, wherever you find them in a statute, but take their colour from the context' (*Lee-Verhulst (Investments) Ltd) v Harwood Trust* [1973] 1 QB 204, 217).

Ejusdem generis

The Latin words *ejusdem generis* (of the same kind or nature), have been attached to a canon of construction whereby wide words associated in the text with more limited words are taken to be restricted by implication to matters of the same limited character. The principle may apply whatever the form of the association, but the most usual form is a list or string of genus-describing terms followed by wider residuary or sweeping-up words. The canon arises from the linguistic implication by which words having literally a wide meaning (when taken in isolation) are treated as reduced in scope by the verbal context. It is an instance of ellipsis, or reliance on implication.

As Rupert Cross put it, following Lord Diplock: 'the draftsman must be taken to have inserted the general words in case something which ought to have been included among the specifically enumerated items had been omitted . . .' (Cross 1987, 133). Or, as Odgers says, it is assumed 'that the general words were only intended to guard against some accidental omission in the objects of the kind mentioned and were not intended to extend to objects of a wholly different kind' (Odgers 1987, 184). It follows that the principle is presumed to apply unless there is some contrary indication *(Tillmans & Co v SS Knutsford Ltd* [1908] 2 KB 385).

It is necessary to be able to formulate the genus; for if it cannot be formulated it does not exist. 'Unless you can find a category', said Farwell LJ, 'there is no room for the application of the *ejusdem generis* doctrine' *(ibid)*.

Judges do not always trouble to formulate the genus fully, it often being enough to indicate how it might be framed. In *Coleshill and District Investment Co Ltd* v *Minister of Housing and Local Government* [1968] 1 All ER 62, 65, where the generic string was 'building, engineering, mining', Widgery J said: 'without attempting to define the genus in detail, it seems clear to me that it is restricted to operations of the scale, complexity and difficulty which require a builder or an engineer or some mining expert'.

Nature of a 'genus'

For the *ejusdem generis* principle to apply there must be a sufficient indication of a category that can properly be described as a class or genus, even though not specified as such in the enactment. Furthermore the genus must be narrower than the literal meaning of the words it is said to regulate. The Customs Consolidation Act 1876, s 43 reads: 'The importation of arms, ammunition, gunpowder, *or any other goods* may be prohibited'. Although the italicised words are completely general, it is obvious that some limitation is intended. Otherwise why did not the drafter simply say 'The importation of any goods may be prohibited'? In *A-G* v *Brown* [1920] 1 KB 773 it was held that the *ejusdem generis* principle applied to restrict the italicised words to objects of the same nature as the substantives listed in the generic string.

The *ejusdem generis* principle has also been applied to strings of adjectives (eg *Re Stockport Ragged, Industrial & Reformatory Schools* [1898] 2 Ch 687, where the phrase in question was 'cathedral, collegiate, chapter or other schools').

The tendency of the courts is to restrict the imputed genus to an area that goes no wider than is necessary to encompass the entire generic string. Thus a string specified as 'boots, shoes, stockings and other articles' would import the genus 'footwear' rather than the wider category of 'wearing apparel' *(Magnhild (SS)* v *McIntyre Bros & Co* [1920] 2 KB 321, 331). The string 'railway, road, pipeline or other facility' imports a facility for conveying goods, and so excludes storage facilities (see the Australian case of *Canwan Coals Pty Ltd* v *FCT* (1974) 4 ALR 223).

In addition to the generic string, other parts of the context may give assistance in finding the genus. The Finance Act 1894, s 8(4) contained the string 'every trustee, guardian, committee, or other person'. It was held in *Re Latham, IRC* v *Barclays Bank Ltd* [1962] Ch 616 that the genus was persons holding property in a fiduciary capacity, but this was helped by previous mention in the subsection of persons holding beneficially.

Single genus-describing term   Despite numerous dicta to the contrary, the *ejusdem generis* principle may apply where one term only establishes the genus, though in such cases the presumption favouring the principle is weakened. Thus in *A-G* v *Seccombe* [1911] 2 KB 688 it was held that the words 'or otherwise' in the phrase 'any benefit to him by contract or otherwise' in the Customs and Inland Revenue Act 1889, s 11(1) must be construed *ejusdem generis* with 'contract'. In *Lewisham BC* v *Maloney* [1948] 1 KB 51 it was held that in the phrase 'easement, right or other privilege' the word 'right' must be construed *ejusdem generis* with 'easement'. In *Parkes* v *Secretary of State for the Environment* [1978] 1 WLR 1308 the Court of Appeal held that in the phrase 'building or other operations' in the Town and Country Planning Act 1971, s 290 the other operations must be read as akin to building.

Genus-describing terms surrounding wider word   Where a word of wider meaning is included in a string of genus-describing terms of narrower meaning, the *ejusdem generis* principle may operate to restrict the meaning of the wider word so as to keep it within the genus. The Dublin Carriages Act 1853, s 25 required a licence to be held before any person could lawfully 'use or let to hire any hackney carriage, job carriage, stage carriage, *cart*, or job horse'. In *Shaw* v *Ruddin* (1859) 9 Ir CLR 214 it was held that hackney carriage, job carriage, stage carriage and job horse were genus-describing words, the genus being conveyances used for hire. According the unrestricted word *cart* when found in their company, must be construed as limited to carts used for hire. (See also *Scales* v *Pickering* (1828) 4 Bing 448).

General words followed by narrower genus-describing terms   The *ejusdem generis* principle is presumed not to apply where apparently general words are followed by narrower words suggesting a genus more limited than the initial general words, if taken by themselves, would indicate: *Re Wellsted's Will Trusts* [1949] Ch 296, 318; *Ambatielos* v *Anton Jurgens Margarine Works* [1923] AC 175, 183; *Canadian National Railways* v *Canadian Steamship Lines Ltd* [1945] AC 204, 211; *Re Wellsteds Will Trusts* [1949] Ch 296, 305.

Exclusion of ejusdem generis principle

An intention to exclude the *ejusdem generis* principle may be shown expressly or by implication. Thus if he desires to indicate that the *ejusdem generis* principle is not to apply, the drafter may qualify the residuary or sweeping-up words by a suitable generalisation such as 'or things of whatever description' (*A-G* v *Leicester Corporation* [1910] 2 Ch 359, 369). However the word 'whatsoever' in the phrase 'or other person whatsoever' in the Sunday Observance Act 1677, was held *not* to disapply the principle (*Palmer* v *Snow* [1900] 1 QB 725). Again, the principle was applied to the phrase 'corn and grass, hops, roots, fruits, pulse' notwithstanding that the residuary words were 'or other product whatsoever' (*Clark* v *Gaskarth* (1818) 8 Taunt 431).

These examples show that the only safe drafting method is to use in relation to the residuary words explicit disapplying words. (See, eg, the Finance Act 1976, s 61(2), which speaks of benefits 'whether or not similar to any of those mentioned above in this subsection'). Another method is to include a definition of the residuary words. This will be construed on its own, without reference to the *ejusdem generis* principle (*Beswick* v *Beswick* [1968] AC 58, 87).

An implication against the application of the *ejusdem generis* principle to narrow a term arises where the term is used elsewhere in the Act in a wide sense (eg *Young* v *Grattridge* (1868) LR 4 QB 166).

The rank principle

Where a string of items of a certain rank or level is followed by general residuary words, it is presumed that the residuary words are not intended to include items of a higher rank than those specified. By specifiying only items of lower rank the impression is created that higher ranks are not intened to be covered. If they were, then their mention would be expected *a fortiori*.

Examples of the application of the rank principle include the following. In the Sunday Observance Act 1677, s 1, the string 'tradesman, artificer, workman, labourer, or other person whatsoever' was held not to include persons above the artisan class (*Gregory* v *Fearn* [1953] 1 WLR 974). The string 'copper, brass, pewter, and tin, and all other metals' in a local Act of 1825 was held not to include precious metals such as gold and silver (*Casher* v *Holmes* (1831) 2 B & Ad 592). A power given to the Barons of the Exchequer by s 26 of the Queen's Remembrancer Act 1859 to make procedural rules for their court did not extend to giving rights of appeal to higher courts (*A-G* v *Sillem* (1864) 10 HLC 704; *Hotel and Catering Industry Training Board* v *Automobile Proprietary Ltd* [1968] 1 WLR 1526).

Megarry V-C suggests that the principle may apply to exclude a judge from the provision that in Welsh legal proceedings the Welsh language may be spoken 'by any party, witness or other person who desires to use it' (Welsh Language Act 1967, s 1(1); see Megarry 1973, 169). Another modern example is the phrase 'an officer or examiner of the court or some other person' in RSC Ord 39, r 4(a). The concluding words have been held not to include judges (*Re Brickman's Settlement* [1981] 1 WLR 1560).

Tapering strings   The rank principle has been held to apply where the string was regarded as tapering down, and the item in quesiton, though not superior to items at the beginning, was superior to those listed towards the end. Thus where the string was 'horse, mare, gelding, mule, ass, ox, cow, heifer, steer, sheep or other cattle' bulls were held to be excluded since, although not superior to horses, they were regarded as superior to oxen, cows etc (*Ex parte Hill* (1827) 3 C & P 225). See also *R v Marcus* [1981] 1 WLR 774.

Necessary disapplication   The rank principle does not apply if no items are left for the residuary words to cover but those of higher rank, or as Blackstone puts it, where 'the general words would otherwise be entirely void' (Blackstone 1765, i 63). He gives as an example the provision in the Statute of Marlborough 1267 which lists essoigns 'in counties, hundreds, or in courts baron, or in other courts'. Since there were no other courts of lower or equal jurisdiction, the latter words were held to include the king's courts of record at Westminster (2 Inst 137).

Reddendo singula singulis

The *reddendo singula singulis* principle concerns the use of words distributively. Where a complex sentence has more than one subject, and more than one object, it may be the right construction to *render each to each*, by reading the provision distributively and applying each object to its appropriate subject. A similar principle applies to verbs and their subjects, and to other parts of speech. A typical application of this principle is where a testator says 'I *devise and bequeath* all my *real and personal* property to B'. The term *devise* is appropriate only to real property. The term *bequeath* is appropriate only to personal property. Accordingly, by the application of the principle *reddendo singula singulis*, the testamentary disposition is read as if it were worded 'I devise all my real property, and bequeath all my personal property, to B'.

The Immigration Act 1971, s 1 lays down general principles. It begins: 'All those who are in this Act expressed to have the right of abode in the United Kingdom shall be free to live in, and to come and go into and from, the United Kindom . . .'. The phrase 'to come and go into and from' the United Kindgom appears clumsy. Applied *reddendo singula singulis*, it is to be read as if it said 'to come into the United Knigdom and go from it'. Why did not the drafter put it in this way? No doubt because he wished to use the evocative phrase 'come and go'.

Enactments often need to be read *reddendo singula singulis*. An important modern example is the European Communities Act 1972, s 2(1) (see p 60 above). For an instructive example founded on the Local Government Act 1933, s 59(1) see *Bishop* v *Deakin* [1936] Ch 409.

Expressum facit cessare tacitum

To state a thing expressly ends the possibility that something inconsistent with it is implied in the passage in question. No inference is proper if it goes against the express words Parliament has used. 'Express enactment shuts the door to further implication' (*Whiteman* v *Sadler* [1910] AC 514, 527).

Where an enactment codifies a rule of common law, equity, custom or prerogative it is presumed to displace that rule altogether. This applies even where the term codification is not used. Accordingly the statutory formulation of the rule, whether or not it is to the like effect as the previous rule, by implicaiton disapplies any aspect of that rule not embodied in the new formulation. Note that this principle raises a purely linguistic assumption. It does not affect the possibility that on balance the interpretative factors may call for a strained construction of the enactment.

The chief application of the principle *expressum facit cessare tacitum* lies in the so-called *expressio unius* principle. This is dealt with next.

Expressio unius est exclusio alterius

The maxim *expressio unius est exclusio alterius* (to express one thing is to exclude another) is an aspect of the principle *expressum facit cessare tacitum*. Known for short as the *expressio unius* principle, it is applied where a statutory proposition might have covered a number of matters but in fact mentions only some of them. Unless these are mentioned merely as examples, or *ex abundanti cautela*, or for some other sufficient reason, the rest are taken to be excluded from the proposition.

The *expressio unius* principle is also applied where a formula which in itself may or may not include a certain class is accompanied by words of *extension* naming only some members of that class. The remaining members of the class are then taken to be excluded. Again, the principle may apply where an item is mentioned in relation to one matter but not in relation to another matter equally eligible.

Section 16 of the Licensing Act 1872, an imperfectly-drafted Act, laid down three separate offences against public order. In the statement of the first offence the word 'knowingly' was included, but it was omitted in the case of the other two. This gave rise to the logical implication that these could be committed with or without knowledge, and it was so held in *Mullins* v *Collins* (1874) LR 9 QB 292, 295. However in *Somerset* v *Wade* [1894] 1 QB 574, which concerned the contrast between 'permitting' in s 13 of the Act and 'knowingly permitting' in s 14, the decision went against the application of the *expressio unius* principle (see also *Dean* v *Wiesengrund* [1955] 2 QB 120).

Words of designation

The *expressio unius* principle applies where some only out of a possible series of substantives or other items are expressly designated. The application of the principle therefore turns on these words of designation.

The Diplomatic Privileges Act 1964 gave the force of law to certain provisions of the Vienna Convention on Diplomatic Relations 1961. These protected, in relation to a foreign mission, what were defined as the 'premises of the mission'. In *Intpro Properties (UK) Ltd* v *Sauvel* [1983] QB 1019 it was alleged that a private dwelling occupied by a financial counsellor at the French embassy in London was the subject of diplomatic immunity as being 'premises of the mission'. The definition of this phrase in art 1 of the Convention is 'the buildings or parts of buildings and the land ancillary thereto, irrespective of ownership, used for the purposes of the mission including *the residence of the head of the mission*'. It was held that the specific mention of the residence of the 'head' of the mission made it clear that the residences of other members of the mission could not form part of the premises of the mission. (See also *R* v *Caledonian Railway* (1850) 16 QB 19).

Words of extension

Where it is doubtful whether a stated term does or does not include a certain class, and words of extension are added which cover some only of the members of the class, it is implied that the remaining members of the class are excluded. The most common technique of extending the indisputable meaning of a term is by the use of an enlarging definition, that is one in the form 'A includes B' (see p 134 above). Where B does not exhaust the class of which it is a member, the remaining class members are taken to be excluded from the ambit of the enactment. The Immigration Act 1971, s 2(3) states that for the purposes of s 2(1) of the Act the word 'parent' includes the *mother* of an illegitimate child. The class to which this extension relates is the *parents* of an illegitimate child. In *R* v *Immigration Appeals Adjudicator, ex parte Crew* (1982) *The Times*, 26 November, Lord Lane CJ said: 'Under the rule *expressio unius exclusio alterius*, that express mention of the mother implies that the father is excluded'.

Words of exception

The *expressio unius* principle is often applied to words of exception. An excepting provision may except certain categories either from the Act in which the provision is contained, or from the law generally. It is presumed that these are the only exceptions of the kind intended.

The Road Traffic Regulation Act 1967, s 79 states that no statutory provision imposing a *speed limit* on motor vehicles shall apply to any vehicle on an occasion when it is being used for fire brigade, ambulance or police purposes. Speed limits are not the only statutory restrictions which might hinder such vehicles in an emergency, yet under the *expressio unius* principle these other restrictions, such as the duty to stop at a red light, would continue to apply (see *Buckoke* v *Greater London Council* [1971] 1 Ch 655).

Words providing remedies etc

Where an Act sets out specific remedies, penalties or procedures it is presumed that other remedies, penalties or procedures that might have been applicable are by implication excluded (eg *Felix* v *Shiva* [1983] QB 82 90–91; *Payne* v *Lord Harris of Greenwich* [1981] 1 WLR 754, 767).

Where other cause for the expressio unius principle

The *expressio unius* principle does not apply where it appears that there is a reason for singling out the words of designation other than an intention to exclude other terms. Thus they may be used merely as examples, or be included *ex abundanti cautela,* or for some other purpose. By the Poor Relief Act 1601, s 1 a poor-rate was imposed on occupiers of 'lands, houses, tithes and *coal* mines'. In *R* v *Inhabitants of Sedgley* (1831) 2 B & Ad 65 the argument that other mines were also intended to be rated, and that coal mines were mentioned merely as an example, was rejected (see also *C Maurice & Co Ltd* v *Minister of Labour* [1968] 1 WLR 1337, 1345; *Prestcold (Central) Ltd* v *Minister of Labour* [1969] 1 WLR 89).

As to items mentioned *ex abundanti cautela* see *McLaughlin* v *Westgarth* (1906) 75 LJPC 117, 118 (savings in private Acts); *Duke of Newcastle* v *Morris* (1870) LR 4 HL 661, 671 (peers' privilege of freedom from arrest) and the Canadian case of *Docksteader* v *Clark* (1903) 11 BCR 37. For an example of a case where there was some other reason for singling out the item in question for express mention see *Dean* v *Wiesengrund* [1955] 2 QB 120.

If an item which on the application of the *expressio unius* principle would be excluded is of a class which came into existence only after the passing of the enactment, it is probably right to disregard the principle as an aid to construction (*A-G for Northern Ireland's Reference (No 1 of 1975)* [1977] AC 105, 132).

Implication by oblique reference

Uncertainty in one part of a proposition may be resolved by implication from what is said in another part, even though that other part is not directly referring to the first part. Accordingly account is to be taken of a meaning of one provision in an Act that logically if obliquely arises from what is said elsewhere in the Act. Equally an express statement in an enactment may carry oblique implications respecting the legal meaning of other Acts, or of unenacted rules of law. It often happens that what is expressed in one place throws light on the meaning intended elsewhere. Thus doubt as to whether treason was a felony was settled by a passage in the Treason Act 1351 which, speaking of some dubious crimes, directed a reference to Parliament that it may there be adjudged 'whether they be treason, or other felony' (Blackstone 1765, iv 82).

Doubt as to whether 'interest' was confined to annual interest in the phrase 'interest, annuities or other annual payments' occurring in the Income Tax Act 1952 was set at rest by the necessary implication arising from the reference to *other* annual payments (*IRC v Frere* [1965] AC 402). An Act requiring Members of Parliament to swear 'on the true faith of a Christian' was held by necessary implication to exclude Jews from Parliament (*Miller* v *Salomons* (1853) 7 Ex 475; *Solomons* v *Miller* (1853) 8 Ex 778). When it was expressly enacted that an offence triable by magistrates might be committed within territorial waters, an implied jurisdiction to *try* that offence was held to be created (*R* v *Kent JJ, ex parte Lye* [1967] 2 QB 153, 178). The requirement in the Firearms Act 1968, s 26 that an application for a firearm certificate must be made to the chief constable for the area in which the applicant resides was held in *Burditt* v *Joslin* [1981] 3 All ER 203, where the applicant was a British army officer resident in Germany, to imply that a person who is not resident in an area which has a chief constable is not entitled to a certificate.

In making orders, following divorce, for financial provision or property adjustment, the court is required by the Matrimonial Causes Act 1973, s 25(1) 'to have regard to all the circumstances of the case'. The House of Lords held in *Jenkins* v *Livesey (formerly) Jenkins)* [1985] AC 424 that by implication this placed a duty of disclosure on the parties, and empowered the court to set aside an order obtained without due disclosure.

Implication where statutory description imperfectly met

Where the facts of the instant case substantially though not entirely correspond to a description in the relevant enactment, it is presumed that the enactment is intended to apply in the same way as it would if they did entirely correspond. Where on the other hand the statutory description is partly but not substantially met, it is presumed that the enactment is intended to apply in the same way as it would if the description were not met at all.

Where a statutory description is only partly met on the facts of the instant case, the question whether the enactment nevertheless applies is usually one of fact and degree. Necessary compression of statutory language makes it difficult for the drafter to use all the words needed to supply adequate connotation. This principle assists by providing guidance in the frequent cases where the statutory description is only partially complied with. Thus an Act prohibiting the making of 'wooden buttons' was held to be infringed by making buttons of wood notwithstanding that they had a shank of wire (*R* v *Roberts*) (1701) 1 Ld Raym 712). A car minus its engine was held to be within the statutory description 'mechanically propelled vehicle' (*Newberry* v *Simmonds* [1961] 2 QB 345). A policeman not wearing his helmet was held to be a 'constable in uniform' (*Wallwork* v *Giles* [1970] RTR 117; *Taylor* v *Baldwin* [1976] Crim LR 137).

Where on the other hand the facts do not substantially answer to the required description, the enactment does not apply. Thus a car bought for scrap, of which the engine was rusted up, the tyres were flat, and the gearbox and electrical apparatus were missing was held not to be a 'mechanically propelled vehicle' in *Smart* v *Allan* [1963] 1 QB 291, 298, where Lord Parker CJ said 'It seems to me as a matter of common sense that some limit must be put, and some stage must be reached, when one can say: "This is so immobile that it has ceased to be a mechanically propelled vehicle"'. There may be substantial correspondence with a statutory description even though on a quantitative basis the correspondence appears slight. Thus in *Hayes (Valuation Officer)* v *Lloyd* [1985] 1 WLR 714 it was held that certain agricultural land complied with the description 'land used as a racecourse' within the meaning of the General Rate Act 1967, s 26(3) even though racing took place on one day a year only. The racing took place at Easter and was attended by some 10,000 people.

Multi-purpose cases

Where a public authority reaches a decision for two purposes, only one of which is within its statutory powers, the validity of the decision depends on whether the other purpose is one of the main purposes or is merely subsidiary (eg *R* v *Inner London Education Authority, ex parte Westminster City Council* [1986] 1 WLR 28).

(Further discussion of linguistic canons of construction will be found in Part III below.)

Part III

The Need for Processing of Texts

Chapter Thirteen

Difficulties of the Statute User

In the remainder of this book we consider the processing of the text. Processing is necessary because the statutory text by itself is insufficient as a means of communication between legislator and citizen. It is not even sufficient as a means of communication between the legislator and citizen's professional adviser. It is drafted as if to stand alone, but the reader who looks at nothing else has small chance of understanding it. It is all cutting edge, doing little to reveal the purpose of that edge. Drafters learn that unnecessary words lead to trouble. Like an appendix, what is not needed to achieve legal effect can become gangrenous. Drafters' explanations give hostages to fortune. Mistakes will creep into them (since mistakes creep into everything). They cannot allow for future development. They are liable to conflict with the text itself.

For these reasons and others (such as lack of time), the drafter concentrates on the cutting edge. Explanations must be provided by other people, and in other ways. We begin this Part by considering in detail just why explanations are necessary, and in what respects. This requires us to examine the difficulties experienced by the user in attempting to rely on the legislative texts alone. First we must ask: Who is the user?

Who is the statute user?

Many people have thought (and many still think) that in a democracy the laws should be such as can be understood directly by the citizen. He cannot plead ignorance of law as an excuse for his transgression. Common fairness requires that knowledge of law should therefore be accessible. Here, as elsewhere, life defeats fairness. The truth has been expressed by a distinguished drafter, and expounder of drafting principles, Professor Driedger:

There is always the complaint that legislation is complicated. Of course it is, because life is complicated. The bulk of the legislation enacted nowadays is social, economic or financial; the laws they must express and the life situations they must regulate are in themselves complicated, and these laws cannot in any language or in any style be reduced to kindergarten level, any more than can the theory of relativity. One might as well ask why television sets are so complicated. Why do they not make television sets so everyone can understand them? Well, you can't expect to put a colour image on a screen in your living-room with a crystal set. And you can't have crystal set legislation in a television age (Driedger 1971, p 78).

In a paper written in 1966 I attempted to describe the statute user, beginning by pointing out that the legislative audience will differ according to the type of legislation. The paper continued:

In the case of administrative legislation the Act will principally be the concern of the civil servants or local government officials responsible for administering it. On the whole, judges and other lawyers will have relatively little to do with the working of this type of legislation while the general public will rely mainly on advertisments and leaflets summarising the effect of the legislation in simple language. The main legislative audience here is therefore the official who will implement the Act.

With other types of legislation judges and other lawyers will be more closely concerned. Few, if any, laymen desiring information as to their tax position, for example, will go direct to the Act. They will probably take advice from lawyers or accountants, or at least will look at a textbook. The main legislative audience here is therefore the professional one, with the courts to the forefront (Bennion 1966, p 2).

The paper went on to conclude that for practical purposes the user is principally the practising lawyer (on the bench, at the bar or in a solicitor's office), the public official, or the non-legal professional adviser (such as the accountant, planner or estate agent) whose services call for knowledge of some branch of statute law. (See also Bennion 1971 (2), pp 132-4).

Apart from adding a reference to company lawyers on the receiving end of administrative or regulatory legislation, I see no reason now to alter this description; and in this book that is what I mean by the user of legislative texts.

Text-collation

When the user seeks to discover and apply the statute law relevant to a subject area, or to a particular point, he first needs to find out which are the relevant texts and to assemble them. This is often a difficult task in itself. The user's failure to perform it correctly gives rise to *a wrong understanding of what the relevant law is*. It can be demonstrated by a simplified model. Suppose the statute law relevant to a point consists of four texts, as follows:

A — an Act of Parliament
B — another Act of Parliament
C — an order made under a power conferred by A
D — regulations made under a power conferred by B

If a user has ABCD available, he has all the statutory texts needed to work out his problem. He may not be able to construe the material properly, but at least he has it before him. Now suppose the user has done some research into what the relevant material is, but has failed to do it successfully. He comes up with the idea that the relevant texts consist only of ABD. He is under a misapprehension consisting of a wrong understanding of what the relevant law is. This may be because the system provides him with inadequate tools for finding the answer.

Now let us complicate the model slightly. Suppose there is a leading case on the meaning of A. In the language of this book the court has 'processed' A, and the result is a reported decision and set of judgments which we may call X. It is clear that the user now needs not only the statutory texts ABCD but the reported case as well. Even if his researches have produced the answer ABCD, he is still under a wrong understanding of what the relevant law is because the relevant law is ABCDX. Here the system that may have let him down is a different one. It is not the system that tells the user which statutory texts are relevant to certain subjects or points. It is the system that tells the user which reported cases have processed a particular text, and in what way.

Complicating the model still further, we may now suppose that the user's point is dealt with partly by the statutory provisions mentioned and partly by common law. Call the leading reported case at common law Z. The complete kit for the user to solve his problem is now ABCDXZ. If his researches produce only ABCDX he is once more under a wrong understanding of what the relevant law is. This time a third system may be at fault, namely that which tells people which reported cases are relevant for arriving at a rule of common law. That system is not however within the scope of this book.

The problem of text-comprehension

A further type of user's misapprehension is a *failure to understand* the statutory texts. Taking our model before its final complicating development, let us assume that the relevant material consists of ABCDX. This time our user has succeeded in his researches. He has before him the statutory texts ABCD and the reported case X. He studies this material, but either comes up with the wrong answer or retires baffled. Why?

Assuming the user has the intelligence and legal training needed, and has been able to devote sufficient time to the operation, the answer must lie in the form and arrangement of the materials and the nature of the task. If the user is concerned with the *entire* subject matter covered by ABCDX (say because he is the legal officer of a trade association concerned to draw up proposals for changing the law) his task is to work out the general effect of ABCDX. In practice he may rely on the efforts of someone else (say a textbook writer) who has already worked this out and published his conclusions. But it is unsafe to rely entirely on the labour of others. It is also unprofessional. The conscientious user wishes to work things out for himself. If he is to assume personal responsbility, in accordance with his professional duty, he should if possible arrive at his own conclusions. (On this aspect of general professional ethics see Bennion 1969, chap 7.)

What is the nature of the task of the user who is concerned to work out the overall effect of ABCDX? It is governed by the fact that he has to handle five seperate texts, which under our system are likely to be only tenuously related textually. They will not be organised as a single coherent structure. Nor is it possible that in their original form they could be, since their timing and origins are different. A and B were passed by Parliament at separate times. C was made by a Minister some time after the passing of A. D was made by another Minister some time after the passing of B. X perhaps consists of three judgments, given by a court at a time later still.

The task of a reader faced with arriving at the combined meaning of disparate texts in this way is called *conflation*. As I said in evidence to the Renton Committee, conflation of statutory material is usually difficult, sometimes extremely difficult, and occasionally impossible (Bennion 1979 (4), p 32).

Nor is conflation the only problem. Acts of Parliament start life as Bills. As we saw in chapter 2, their form is subject to parliamentary considerations irrelevant to the needs of the ultimate user. The arrangement is distorted, the text compressed, and the headings and other signposts relatively few. These considerations do not apply to statutory instruments, but their standard of drafting tends to be less expert and they can only tell part of the story—the remainder always being in the parent Act. Court judgments are different in nature to statutory texts. The two can be combined only by *codification*, a difficult process rarely achieved in Britain.

What of the user merely faced with finding in ABCDX the answer to a *specific* problem? He has first to go through the procedure outlined above in relation to the general user. If the whole of this is not needed, he must at least work out the principles governing his own particular case. Then he must apply them to the facts of the case and work out the conclusion.

When it is remembered that our model is a very simple one, the scope for failure in text-comprehension under actual working conditions is seen to be formidable. The factors causing it are examined in greater detail in the next chapter.

Doubt-resolving

Suppose the user avoids a wrong understanding of what the relevant law is, and also avoids a failure to understand the statutory texts.

He assembles all the relevant texts, and none that are irrelevant. He accomplishes the difficult task of conflating them, and correctly extracts their combined meaning. Does he then have his solution? If he has sought a general view of that area of statute law does he achieve it? If he required the answer to a specific problem has he found it?

The answer is not necessarily. This is because statute law contains areas of doubt, which can only be resolved by processing. There are various reasons for this—all inescapable, and all linked to the drafter.

The drafter cannot say everything. We saw in chapter 2 how he is under a duty to keep his text as brief as possible. Even if it were not so, he could not as a creative writer do without implication. He would be bound to assume a knowledge of the surrounding legal system (including of course the Interpretation Act). He would have to leave the obvious unsaid (though aware that what is obvious to one person is far from obvious to another). The technique of *ellipsis* is a necessary tool of any author, and the drafter brings it to his aid. We discuss it further in chapter 15.

Another source of doubt is that, just as the drafter cannot say everything, so Parliament cannot decide everything. There are points beyond which it cannot exert its will, and must leave the choice to others. The name for this process is *delegation*. We have seen how Parliament delegates its powers to ministers, to be exercised by means of statutory instruments. There are other forms of delegation. Officials may be left to work out, by the use of their discretion, the detailed operation of an enactment. Or the task may be entrusted to courts or tribunals. Either way, the drafter is likely to effect this statutory delegation by use of what we may call a *broad term*. The effecting of delegation in this way is explored in chapter 16.

Ellipsis and this form of delegation are techniques by which the drafter deliberately causes doubt or, as we may call them for convenience, *doubt-factors*. The third deliberate doubt-factor, thankfully much rarer, is *intentional obscurity*. For various reasons the legislator feels unable or unwilling to express a precise and clear meaning, and requires that the provision be 'fudged'. Where it is an operative provision, and not mere window-dressing, the drafter knows that this inevitably means that some agency, probably the court, is liable one day to be called on to give an interpretation. Intentional obscurity, which is thus a form of delegation by the legislator, is discussed in chapter 17.

A further doubt-factor, this time not deliberate, is *unforeseeable development*. A statute is to be treated as always speaking. While it remains unrepealed it remains law, day in day out. But its language belongs to the period of text-creation. Every passing year brings changes in the nuances of our language. There are developments also in inventions, and in social practices and values. Our society is always in a state of flux. These points are explored in chapter 18.

The final doubt-factor, again not deliberate, is *error*. Drafters make a great many errors, a fact which drafters (being human) are apt not to acknowledge in public. As a drafter myself I see no need for this coyness, which gets in the way of a just assessment of the workings of statute law. There is not necessarily any blame to be attributed. To err is human, and the person who never makes a mistake never makes anything. Furthermore, errors causing doubt are not always made by the drafter—another member of the team may be at fault. Even where they are made by the drafter, and he discovers them in time, he may not be allowed a *locus poenitentiae*. Still, he has an overall responsibility for the product, second only to that of Parliament itself. The concept of parliamentary infallibility was discussed in chapter 1, in a brief survey of the duplex approach to legislative meaning. The drafter's fallibility, linked to it in a way crucial to the duplex approach, is examined in detail in chapter 19.

Differential readings

Even when the statute user has successfully surmounted all the difficulties previously outlined in this chapter, a further hazard awaits him. He may have collected all the relevant texts, understood them, resolved any doubts correctly, and still fail. This is because it is possible for different minds to reach opposing views about the plain meaning of a text. One person entertains no doubt that the text has one meaning, while another person feels equally sure that it has another. The process of applying a general rule to particular facts can only end in a mental 'feeling' that one interpretation or another is 'correct'. Such feelings are justified in presentation by magnifying the supporting arguments and diminshing the others. The weight to be attached to each argument, and the offsetting weight of each counter-argument, are in every case a question that ultimately can only be subjective.

A practitioner advising a client may thus feel sure about the answer the law gives to the client's case. Yet he could be confounded if the matter came to court, for the judge may confidently find for the opposite view. Then the only hope is an appeal. This problem is further discussed in chapter 22.

Processing as a remedy

It is a principal theme of this book that problems of text-collation, text comprehension and doubt resolving fall to be dealt with by processing. *Text-collation* becomes less difficult as the number of different texts relevant to a subject is reduced by combining them into a unified whole. Consolidation and composite restatement are two methods of doing this. The subject of *text-manipulation* is explored generally in chapter 23. To the extent that texts remain separate, adequate indexing and other aids assume greater importance, and this aspect is also dealt with in chapter 23.

Text-manipulation is also an answer to failure in *text-comprehension*. The vices of statute law described in the next chapter can be alleviated, if not removed, by suitable treatment of the text— as chapter 23 again demonstrates.

The dynamic processing of *doubt factors* is carried out in various ways by government officials, by academic and professional commentators, and of course by judges. The contribution made by each is discussed in chapters 20–22.

We have reached the point where we can begin working out in detail a new approach to statute law. Already we have seen that there is more to the problem of understanding statute law than rules of 'interpretation'; important though these are. Methods of text-creation and text-validation need to be grasped. The user must tackle the problems of text collation. The subjective comprehension of the texts, quite apart from any doubts that may exist objectively, is a major topic in itself.

But the main opportunity for a new approach lies in the area of doubt-resolving. First comes diagnosis. We find the meaning unclear, and are satisified that this is not due to our own failure in text collation and text comprehension. There is an objective area of doubt. Instead of applying the rules of interpretation, or the presumptions, or any other general aids discussed in Part II, let us take a different approach. Precisely what, in the text we are examining, causes the doubt? What is its etiology, as a medical practitioner would say? Only when we understand that can we proceed further along the road to resolving it.

I have explained how in this Part the various doubt factors are examined. I conclude this summary of the difficulties of the statute user by showing the *deliberate* doubt factors in diagrammatic form (see p 216).

The circle depicts the whole area of legislative meaning and intention in a particular text. The dark areas represent those parts of the meaning and intention that are *expressed*. The white areas represent the parts that, by the technique of ellipsis are to be *implied*. The hatched area indicate parts which the drafter has not felt able to work out in detail. Instead, by the use of a *broad term*, he has left the detail to be elaborated later. The agents for this are the *processors*, whether administrative authorities (chapter 21), or the courts (chapter 21). The dotted area stands for *politic uncertainty*.

The diagram does not include the two *unintentional* doubt factors, namely the unforeseeable development and the drafting error. These superimpose confusion on the intended plan.

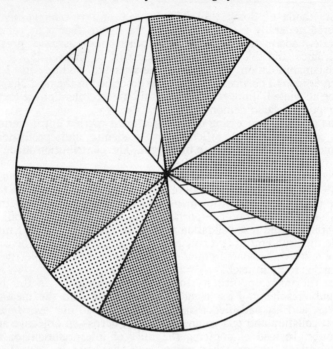

Chapter Fourteen

Vices that Block Comprehension

The methods of text-creation and text-validation employed in British type legislation produce four characteristics which can justly be described as the four vices of statute law. In the title of an article, *Our legislators are CADS* (Bennion 1976(1)), I offered a mnemonic for remembering them. The four vices are Compression, Anonymity, Distortion and Scatter.

Compression

In chapter 2 we saw how modern drafters are required to make their Bills as brief as possible. At the same time, governments and legislators in British-type systems wish to see statutes worked out in close detail. This provides the origin and justification for common-law drafting as opposed to civil-law drafting. Where both brevity and detail are demanded the only course available to the drafter is compression of language. If we add the parameters of certainty and legal effectiveness we tighten the screw further. As the Renton Committee remarked, 'a primary objective is certainty of legal effect, and the United Kingdom legislature tends to prize this objective exceptionally highly'. They added:

For these reasons statutory phrases often irritate or baffle the reader, either because they state the obvious or because the 'punch-line' is delivered with such economy that it is intelligible only to those who have the time and inclination to inform themselves of the whole context on which it operates (Renton 1975, para 7.5).

The Renton Committee received with sympathy complaints that 'skilfully compressed wording' was difficult to understand, and that it would be preferable 'to sacrifice such elegant economy of expression in order to achieve greater clarity, even at the cost of increased length' (Renton 1975, para 17.18). They cited the following example:

For the purposes of this Part of this Schedule a person over pensionable age, not being an insured person, shall be treated as an employed person if he would be an insured person were he under pensionable age and would be an employed person were he an insured person.

217

The Committee commented that 'any enactment of this type is liable to be provocative, and the more so the more skilfully it is compressed' (Renton 1975, para 6.3). However they missed a vitally important point, which is that the difficulty can be largely removed by better presentation of the same wording.

The quoted passage contains a number of defined terms. If by typographical means (say the use of italics) this fact is conveyed to the reader, and he knows where to find the definitions, his task of comprehension is eased. It is eased still further if the passage is spatially broken up into its grammatical clauses. The treatment, which may be called *comminution* (from the Latin *comminuere*, to split into smaller parts), produces the following:

(1) For the purposes of this Part of this Schedule

(2) a person OVER *pensionable age* (not being an *insured person*)

(3) shall be treated as an *employed person* if—

(4) he would be an *insured person* were he UNDER *pensionable age* AND

(5) he would be an *employed person* were he an *insured person*.

Why cannot our legislation be produced in this form? There are practical difficulties. A Bill printed like this would take up more pages, and would be more difficult to amend. It is better to administer this treatment *after* enactment, combining it with remedies for the other three vices of statute law. That is the course adopted in the Composite Restatement method (chapter 23). The above is an extreme instance of the technique of compression by use of defined terms. Its 'provocative' quality springs from the fact that to the unwary reader it appears to be nothing more than clever gibberish. Unless you realise it to be stuffed with defined terms, and you read it alongside the definitions, it *is* gibberish when considered as a sample of English prose. In truth, it is not prose at all but telegraphese.

Another form taken by the vice of compression is the covering of too many different cases by a single formula. Sometimes this grossly distorts the natural meaning of words, and inevitably leads to difficulties in interpretation. An example is the way the law deals with certain types of dishonest conduct. If dishonest trespass to the person or to goods is 'unsuccessful', so that the ingredients of the crime of theft are not present, all the law (as expressed in the Theft Acts 1968 and 1978) can do is fall back on the concept of 'attempt'. Yet from the viewpoint of common sense, many cases of dishonest trespass amount neither to theft nor attempted theft.

The House of Lords held in *Haughton* v *Smith* [1975] AC 476 that one cannot 'attempt' to do something which is in fact impossible, eg steal from an empty pocket. In *R* v *Easom* [1971] 2 QB 315 it was held that a would-be thief committed no crime when he picked up a woman's handbag from the floor in a cinema, went through it and (finding nothing he wanted) put it back intact. Both cases would have been caught by an offence of dishonest trespass on the following lines:

(1) A person commits an offence if, with intent to steal, he commits trespass to the person or trespass to goods.

(2) For the purposes of subsection (1) a person may be treated as intending to steal notwithstanding that his intent is conditional and the condition is unsatisfied.

These are examples of conceptual error, treating as 'attempts' acts which are not. Even without conceptual error, compression leads to trouble. Different cases are treated in one formula when it would be more comprehensible to present each in turn separately. The drafter, in search of brevity, uses a single statement to encompass a wide variety of circumstances. The crime of burglary furnishes an example, of heightened importance since it has to be understood by lay jurors (not to mention ill-educated members of the criminal class). The Theft Act 1968 defines burglary in a building (as opposed to a vehicle or vessel) in two brief subsections (s 9(1) and (2)). These encompass no fewer than six basic situations, but do not separate them out:

(1) A person is guilty of burglary if—

(*a*) he enters a building or part of a building as a trespasser and with intent to commit any such offence as is mentioned in subsection (2) below; or

(*b*) having entered any building or part of a building as a trespasser he steals or attempts to steal anything in the building or that part of it or inflicts or attempts to inflict on any person therein any grievous bodily harm.

(2) The offences referred to in subsection (1)(*a*) above are offences of stealing anything in the building or part of a building in question, of inflicting on any person therein any grievous bodily harm or raping any woman therein, and doing unlawful damage to the building or anything therein.

These few words encompass a number of serious criminal offences, all of great concern to the citizen. They are as follows:

(1) entry as a trespasser with intent to steal,

(2) stealing or attempting to steal *after* entry as a trespasser,

(3) entry as a trespasser with intent to inflict grievous bodily harm,

(4) inflicting or attempting to inflict grievous bodily harm *after* entry as a trespasser,

(5) entry as a trespasser with intent to rape,

(6) entry as a trespasser with intent to do unlawful damage.

A jury is likely to be faced with an indictment, and evidence, related to only one of these six situations. The jurors would obviously find life much simpler if the law they had to consider were framed only in terms of that one. In other words there should be six separate formulations of the burglary offences, instead of a drafter's omelette frying them all together in one pan.

Why did the drafter of the Theft Act 1968 not create six separate burglary offences? He would no doubt answer, somewhat impatiently, that to do so would have made his Bill six times as long, and ministers would not have stood for that. It may not be altogether a sufficient answer. Drafters could often do more in this direction if they wished to, since they have much *de facto* authority. Nor would the Theft Act 1968 really have been six times as long on this basis (though it might have been twice as long). Fortunately, by post-enactment processing, we can achieve much the same result. Unlike a real omelette, a drafter's omelette can usually be unscrambled.

Of the six offences of burglary listed above, the first and second (both concerned with stealing) are the most commonly committed. Unscrambling the omelette for the first would produce the following:

A person is guilty of burglary if he enters a building or part of a building as a trespasser with intent to steal anything therein.

This is considerably simpler than the way entry with intent to steal is scrambled together with the other five fact-situations in s 9(1) and (2) of the Theft Act 1968. Indeed it is too simple, as we can now see. It does not fit all the circumstances it was intended to catch. Also it is ambiguous in its reference to stealing 'anything therein'. (For details see Bennion 1979(3), p 1172.) Here we perceive a major drawback of compression of language. Even the drafter may fail in the task of text-comprehension, notwithstanding that it is his own text.

A drafting technique for easing compression is the *spacing-out* of provisions. This can be shown schematically as follows. It is desired to say 'X shall apply except in cases Y and Z'. To describe each of X, Y and Z requires many words, so the proposition is spaced out in the form of three provisions, as follows:

(1) X [describing it] shall apply, subject to paragraph (2).
(2) X shall not apply where [description of case Y], nor in a case falling within paragraph (3).
(3) A case falls within this paragraph if it is [description of case Z].

The advantage of this technique of spacing out is that, instead of three complicated descriptions being crammed together into one paragraph, each gets a paragraph to itself. The user does not always appreciate this advantage. Thus a practising solicitor described spacing out as 'the contradictory style beloved of draftsmen but no one else' (see Bennion 1981(6), where a full description of the above schematic treatment is given). It is true that spacing out makes for tortuous prose. Statute users need to learn the characteristics of this prose, so that they can better understand it. It is not adopted just to annoy.

Failure in text-comprehension is more likely still with another compression technique. This is the device of *applying* detailed provisions, with specified modifications, to a situation they were not drafted to cover. Returning to the Consumer Credit Act 1974, used as an example in chapter 3, we find an instance of this. Part III of the Act creates a licensing system for credit and hire businesses. It contains 22 sections, and is very detailed. When (in Part X) the Acts get round to dealing with another kind of business, to which it gives the label 'ancillary credit business', it needs to impose a licensing system on this also. To avoid setting out a further 22 sections in similar words, the Act says (in s 147) that the provisions of Part III apply to an ancillary credit business as they apply to a credit business. But it is not quite as simple as that, because the whole of Part III is not suitable as it stands. So some of its provisions are disapplied, and others are modified, for this purpose.

The device is also used as a means of extending *non-statutory* legal rules to additional cases. For example the rules relating to contempt of court were originally developed by the judges, without assistance from Parliament. Section 6(1) of the Bail Act 1976 extends the rules by making absconding from bail an offence punishable 'as if it were a criminal contempt of court'. The difficulties of interpretation that can be caused by the use of what might be termed *asifism* are illustrated by *R v Singh* [1979] QB 319. An absconder from bail was given a custodial sentence by the Crown Court. He appealed on the ground (*a*) that the judge-made rules only provided for imposing a custodial sentence where a contempt was committed *in the face of the court* and (*b*) that these words did not appear in the statutory hypothesis. The Court of Appeal held that they were implied. (As we shall see in chapter 15, this is an example of the drafter's technique of *ellipsis*.)

A case that went the other way is *Slater v Richardson and Bottoms Ltd* [1980] 1 WLR 563. To end tax dodging in the building industry by the so-called 'lump', the Finance Act 1971 requires main contractors to withhold 30 per cent of sums due to non-exempt subcontractors and pay it over to the collector of taxes. Relief may be given by the collector against inadvertent failure to comply. In *Slater*, the collector refused relief, and the contractor sought to appeal. The relevant regulations dealt with appeals by applying 'all the provisions of the Income Tax Acts regarding appeals'. Nevertheless the right to appeal was denied by the court. The Income Tax Acts deal with appeals from decisions of *inspectors*. This was a decision of a *collector*.

Asifism, or the statutory pretence that something is so when it is not, appears in a wide variety of forms. One example, contained in s 72 of the Housing Act 1980, was characterised by Lord Roskill as 'the worst piece of parliamentary drafting for 1980' (125 SJ 232). Section 72 is brief. It starts by abolishing rent tribunals. Then it says that the functions previously conferred on rent tribunals are to be carried out by rent assessment committees. Finally comes this piece of asifism: '(3) A rent assessment committee shall, when constituted to carry out functions so conferred, be known as a rent tribunal'. This is what aroused Lord Roskill's ire. It was not altogether the drafter's fault. He was instructed to do it by the department sponsoring the Bill (though he would have been wiser not to accept the instruction). The department acted with the best of motives. They thought it would be helpful to the public to retain the name rent tribunal even though the animal itself had vanished. The grin, according to respectable precedent, was to survive the Cheshire cat.

Another respectable precedent tells us that tangled webs get woven once we embark on deception. Nor is innocent, well-meaning deception immune. Are there heated arguments in pubs (or elsewhere) between citizens who are sure they have heard that rent tribunals have been abolished and other citizens who insist that they have just been up before one? If a kindly lawyer within earshot attempts an explanation will this, if understood, enhance the law's reputation or diminish it? Can it really be wise to shield the public from confusion by a pretence which confuses even learned law lords?

Because the 'application' technique provides an easy and brief way of legislating, it is frequently employed. But this is a convenience gained by the drafter and legislator at the expense of the statute user. It is a difficult mental exercise to read a text drafted for one type of case as if it were instead drafted in terms of another. The usual problems of text-comprehension are compounded. The difficulty is made worse where the reader is further instructed to bear in mind specified modifications to the text. A frequent victim of this technique has been the Scottish lawyer. Acts of the Westminster Parliament often have provisions tacked on which 'adapt' them to Scottish law. The resulting problems were thus described by the Law Society of Scotland:

Whereas an English practitioner has a clear run-through of the legislation, the Scottish practitioner has to engage in a most time-consuming and frustrating process of elimination and amendment before he can make sense of the new legislation (cited in Renton 1975, para 12.1).

Here the form of text-manipulation which can come to the rescue is a rewriting of the 'applied' provisions, incorporating the specified modifications. Thus the Land Compensation (Scotland) Act 1973 re-enacted (under the procedure applicable to consolidation) the provisions and Scottish modifications contained in the Land Compensation Act 1973. On the consolidation of any Act which uses the 'application' technique it would be possible to write out the applied provisions in full, but this is rarely done. The device of 'writing-out' forms a useful feature of the Composite Restatement method (chapter 23).

Drawing together the threads on Compression, the first of the four vices of British-type statute law, we may say that it works in two different ways. One way retains and condenses material, while the other omits it. Here it may be useful to summarise.

Retaining and condensing material

We saw above that a legislative proposition can be divided up under the headings Case, Condition, Subject, Declaration and Exception. Compression by retaining and condensing material involves dealing in a single proposition with a *number* of elements falling under one of these headings, instead of with just one. It may even extend this treatment to two or more of the headings. If we took the original example given on p 45 and applied this kind of compression to it throughout, we might get the following result:

Heading	*Elements*
Case	Where a person is in charge of a vehicle, or is driving or attempting to drive it, or is the owner of it
Condition	if so required by a constable, or a traffic warden, or anyone having reasonable cause to believe an offence is being committed
Subject	that person, or anyone authorised by him, or otherwise acting on his behalf
Declaration	shall produce his licence or (if the licence is not in his possession or custody, or he does not hold a licence) shall give his name and address
Exception	unless he is exempt from holding a licence, or is a police constable, ambulance officer or fire officer on duty.

A drafter who combined all these elements in one legislative sentence (or even in two) would furnish an example of Compression by retaining and condensing material. We have examined a real life example relating to burglary, where the draftsman combined no less than six disparate elements in his statement of the Case (p 219).

Omitting material

As we have seen, the two ways of achieving Compression by omitting relevant material from the legislative proposition are (*a*) by relegating it to a definition section and using a defined term to denote it, or (*b*) by utilising material which exists elsewhere by 'applying' it with or without modifications.

Anonymity

The second of the four vices of statute law can be dealt with more briefly. From the descriptions of Acts and statutory instruments given in chapters 3 and 4 it can be seen that few headings, sidenotes and other signposts are provided for the user. Cross-references are sometimes given, but are more often omitted. Typographical devices are not employed to pick out key phrases or defined terms.

There are sound reasons for these deficiencies. A Bill is usually heavily amended in its progress through Parliament. This amendment takes place at four or five different stages. Each time, the Bill is reprinted in updated form. The numbering of clauses, subsections etc is altered accordingly. It would add to the difficulties of the legislative process if the provisions were not largely anonymous, and numerous headings, cross-references etc had to be changed at every stage. Printing problems would multiply, and errors increase. But, it may be asked, cannot these aids be added when the Act is printed after assent? Parliament however is rightly jealous of any tinkering with its finished work. If what is produced is to carry full authority as an Act of Parliament it must be scrutinised by Parliament, and must be capable of amendment. That would lead back into the difficulties mentioned in the previous paragraph.

Mere typographical changes might avoid this objection. The Renton Committee examined the question, and the objections put forward by officials. Sir Anthony Stainton, for example, feared that special type might be a distraction to the reader (Renton 1975, para 11.18). Finally the Renton Committee recommended that the Statute Law Committee 'should consider what visual aids and pointers could be helpful in the light of available type faces, page space and technology generally' (Renton 1975, para 11.21). Nothing has come of this.

There are two practical remedies for anonymity of the type described above. One is the provision of indexes and other external aids. The other is the addition of signposting and typographical devices in reprinted versions of the text. This is a feature of Composite Restatement. Both are described in chapter 23.

Statutory anonymity has another aspect. As explained above, common law drafting eschews explanations, and concentrates on cutting edge. Furthermore the drafter may shrink from committing himself to the situation he has in mind, in case other unforeseen situations arise. So while the literal meaning of a provision may be clear, the reason why Parliament enacted it may not. Again, the remedy lies in subsequent treatment of the text.

Distortion

The third of the four vices of statute law is distortion. By this is principally meant the deformity of structure and arrangement induced by text-validation procedures. Considered as operative law, a text might be most helpfully presented in a certain way. One can envisage the possibility of its assuming an ideal form. So far as this is practicable, it is prevented by parliamentary factors.

An Act of Parliament starts life as a Bill, which is a dual-purpose text. As a vehicle for legislative proposals submitted for debate and amendment, it must comply with the parameter of *procedural legitimacy*. It must be in the form of clauses and Schedules. It must be drafted in a way to disarm political criticism and enable its crucial features to be debated in logical order. A Bill often introduces novel concepts, which have to be led up to and adequately explained. As a potential Act, it must be designed to function effectively long after its novelty has worn off and the conditions in which it was drafted and debated have passed into history. Plainly what may be desirable for a Bill may be less desirable for an Act, and vice versa. So that is one cause of distortion.

Another cause lies in the fact that when the drafter is designing his Bill he does not know what, when Parliament has finished with it, it will contain. Many Bills are heavily amended during their passage, sometimes by the insertion of wholly new material. Thus Part III of the Health and Safety at Work etc Act 1974 goes very much wider than health and safety *at work*. It is largely concerned with building regulations, which apply to buildings of every kind. Originally a separate Bill, it was tacked on to the end of this measure to get it through when it might otherwise have failed for want of parliamentary time (see Spencer 1981). As a pointer to this, the drafter had the grace to insert 'etc' in the short title to the Act.

An architect would not design a very tidy building if at each stage of its construction he were told that the client's requirements had radically changed. Even after assent this process of unforeseeable alteration continues, as one amending Act follows another.

Party-political factors can cause distortion. There have been many instances of the shape and content of a Bill being distorted purely for political motives. A classic example is the Children Bill of 1908, which was put forward by the new Liberal Government as a 'Children's Charter'. The proper method of legislating would have been to deal with the various matters involved by amendment of the separate Acts relating to each of them—for example those governing the sale of intoxicating liquor, variation of trusts, criminal procedure and public health. Instead, the whole was dressed up as something it clearly was not: a comprehensive reform of the legal position of children.

A common form of distortion dictated by political factors is the placing of the contents of a Bill in a smaller number of clauses than would be natural, simply in order to reduce the number of debates on 'Clause stand part'.

The average statute user is ignorant of all these considerations. He seeks to understand the text as it appears before him. It is a segment of enacted law, a portion of the Statute Book. Why is it not easier to follow, more logically arranged? As the Departmental Committee on Income Tax Codification (1927–1936) said: 'the more difficult and elaborate the subject, the more important are precision and orderliness in its presentation' (Cmd 5131, para 26).

Even an experienced legal civil servant, Sir William Dale, fell into the trap of overlooking the factors that cause distortion. In his book extolling civil-law drafting, *Legislative Drafting—A New Approach*, he criticised a number of modern British Acts on this score. One of them is the Consumer Credit Act 1974. As an illustration of the effect Distortion can have, it is instructive to examine Dale's comments (all made without reference to, or apparent awareness of, parliamentary factors).

He begins by saying that the long title of the Consumer Credit Act (set out on p 42 above) is 'admirable'. Then the criticisms start. 'Part I sets up the Director General of Fair Trading, and one must again protest that matters of administration are not of the first, or perhaps of any, concern to the normal enquirer' (Dale 1977, p 270). This happens not to be true, since the fact that the Act is administered by the Office of Fair Trading closely concerns almost everyone involved with it. Even if it were true, it is irrelevant. This is because the question of who was to administer the Act was of great interest to MPs. It was about the only issue which divided the Labour Party from the Conservatives (who wished to set up a new department headed by a Consumer Credit Commissioner).

Sir William's next complaint is that Part II of the Act consists wholly of definitions. He mysteriously adds 'and that Part cannot be, and probably was not meant to be, absorbed'. Part II is a good example of the effect of distortion. The statute user would find it convenient to have all definitions assembled in one place (under British practice he would look for them at the end of the Act). But the legislator, faced with proposals for wide-ranging new controls over more than half the commercial firms operating in this country, has a different priority. He first needs to settle just what activities are to be subject to the controls. Novel terms and concepts, of basic importance to the legislative scheme, must be hammered out and agreed before detailed consideration can start.

Dale regards the Act as 'an advanced case of what we may call the centrifugal style of drafting . . . The draftsman, instead of gathering his material into central propositions of maximum content, has made it fly off to the extremities, fragmented in definitions and similar ancillary clauses . . .' Dales cites s 21, which states 'a licence is required to carry on a consumer credit business or consumer hire business'. Strangely, he describes this as a proposition 'bare of any content at all' (*ibid*, pp 271-2).

The arrangement of the Consumer Credit Act 1974 is actually an orderly one, allowing for the fact that political considerations dictated the content of the first two Parts. Part III imposes the licensing system on credit and hire businesses. Then successive Parts deal in a natural order with seeking business, entry into agreements, matters arising during the currency of agreements, termination of agreements etc. Only when we come to Part X do we again see the effect of distortion. This deals with ancillary businesses, such as credit brokerage. The statute user would no doubt prefer to see them dealt with alongside credit and hire businesses, and not hived off at the end of the Act. Parliamentary considerations required however that all the details regarding the two main types of business subject to control should first be worked out and agreed. Only then was it politically convenient to turn attention to the question of how far these basic provisions needed to be modified for ancillary businesses.

If distortion causes deformity in the arrangement of an Act, the only remedy is to rearrange the Act when opportunity offers. This can be done on consolidation (chapter 6), and is a principal feature of the Composite Restatement method (chapter 23). Meanwhile, adequate indexes and other aids are of assistance.

Scatter

The last of the four vices is scatter. Instead of being dealt with in one place, the law on a topic is found in two or more different texts. We discussed in the last chapter the problems of textcollation and conflation to which this gives rise.

There are various causes of scatter, some overlapping:

(1) The absence of a Statute Book arranged under Titles on a one Act-one subject basis means that a topic may be dealt with in two or more different Acts. Sometimes the number of Acts on a particular topic is very large indeed, though things have improved in this respect with the growth of consolidation during the last century. Writing in 1876, RM Kerr, an editor of Blackstone's *Commentaries,* said of the poor law statutes:

It is impossible to give more than an outline of the laws for the relief of the poor. The statutes in force on this subject are nearly 300 in number, and to them, therefore, the editor will on no account venture to refer the reader (1 Kerr 1876, p 329).

(2) Compression by omitting material involves scatter between the text containing the 'application' provision or defined term and the text which is applied or which contains the definition, as the case may be.

(3) Indirect or non-textual amendment of Acts (see below) creates scatter between the principal Act and the amending Act or Acts.

(4) The practice of supplementing an Act by statutory instruments made under it (chapter 4) involves scatter between the parent Act and the statutory instruments.

(5) Internal scatter occurs because of the rules governing the arrangement of an Act or statutory instrument. In particular, there is scatter between the provision introducing a Schedule and the Schedule itself. Every Act must be read as a whole, and its provisions hang together. One can never be certain of the Act's effect on a particular topic without considering all its provisions.

(6) Since the Interpretation Act applies to all other Acts, and to statutory instruments, it is invariably a cause of scatter.

Scatter of the first three types can be alleviated by consolidation (chapter 6). Acts and statutory instruments are never consolidated together however. Nor can consolidation assist with internal Scatter or the problems created by the existence of an Interpretation Act. Composite Restatement can cure all types of scatter. The greater the degree of scatter, the more important it is to have adequate indexes and other aids (chapter 23).

Indirect amendment

Finally in considering the factors that impede text-comprehension, we consider a peculiarly British phenomenon. Although Britain has never possessed a Statute Book arranged under Titles on a one Act-one subject basis, its Parliament has from time to time passed Acts each of which could be regarded as the *principal Act* on the subject it deals with. Principal Acts can be identified broadly as of three types: (1) the consolidation Act; (2) the Act which embodies initial legislation on a novel topic; and (3) the Act which is a substantially-altered version of a previous principal Act. An example of the second type is the Consumer Credit Act 1974, while an example of the third is the Highways Act 1959 (p 70).

Whichever category it may fall into, a principal Act is the product of a great deal of skilled work. It tidies up the area of law with which it is concerned. Common sense would indicate that if it is later amended, the amendments should be done textually and not indirectly. That way the amended Act can be reprinted as one text. Its integrity is preserved, and the vice of scatter avoided. Instead of each statute user being required to accomplish the difficult task of *conflation*, it is done once and for all by the drafter of the amending Act. With this method, the need for consolidation is less frequent. (See further Bennion 1980(11)).

Yet the British practice has been to amend *indirectly*, and not by altering the text of the principal Act. Here is an example. The Improvement of Live Stock (Licensing of Bulls) Act 1931 imposed a licensing system for the keeping of bulls, and empowered the Minister of Agriculture to refuse a licence on certain grounds. In 1944 it was desired to extend this system to boars. Instead of amending the 1931 Act textually and altering its title accordingly, the 1944 Act extended it indirectly. Then in 1963 it was desired to broaden the grounds on which a licence could be refused. Once more the opportunity of producing a unified text was disdained. Instead, s 17 of the Agriculture (Miscellaneous Provisions) Act 1963 said:

The powers of the Minister . . . under section 2(2) of the Improvement of Livestock (Licensing of Bulls) Act 1931, or under that section as applied to pigs by s 6 of the Agriculture (Miscellaneous Provisions) Act 1944, to refuse to grant a licence to keep a bull or boar for breeding purposes shall include power to refuse to grant such a licence if he is not satisfied that the bull or boar conforms to such standard of suitability for breeding purposes as may be prescribed for bulls or boars respectively under the said Act of 1931; and different standards may be so prescribed for different classes of bulls or boars.

The result was that anyone who, not content with a textbook summary, was concerned to discover the law on licensing of bulls and boars *from the source* had to get hold of three different texts and perform the troublesome task of conflating them. Since this was the almost invariable technique by which amendments were effected, the same applied generally throughout the field of statute law. Why should this be so? Why should a system so obviously inimical to understanding of the law be officially adopted?

The answer lies in the *four-corners doctrine* (see p 32). Indirect amendment satisfies this doctrine, whereas textual amendment is often incomprehensible without some form of accompanying explanation.

The pernicious four-corners doctrine served the convenience of those who make the law at the expense of those who need to understand and apply it. The doctrine was laid to rest by the Renton Committee in these words: 'We recommend that in principle the interests of the ultimate users should always have priority over those of the legislators: a Bill, which serves a merely temporary purpose, should always be regarded primarily as a future Act, and should be drafted and arranged with this object in view' (Renton 1975, para 10.3). (For further details of the four-corners doctrine see Bennion 1979 (4) pp 36–43 and 54–60. As to the current use of textual amendment in Britain, see Bennion 1980 (1) and (5).) Although textual amendment has largely superseded indirect amendment, it has not entirely done so. In any case, we still have a considerable legacy of statute law produced by this discredited method.

Indirect amendment produces the vice of scatter. An Act amended textually can be reprinted as a single text. Every time an Act is amended indirectly, an additional text is produced. The texts must then remain separate until brought together by a process of text manipulation such as consolidation or Composite Restatement.

Doubt-resolving

Having described the factors that induce subjective blocks on text-comprehension, we turn to the factors that cause objective doubt as to the meaning of legislative texts.

Chapter Fifteen

Doubt-factor I: Ellipsis

One instrument used in the legislative drafter's everlasting pursuit of brevity is the technique of ellipsis. A passage will be shorter if you omit to state the obvious. That can be left to be inferred. But what seems obvious to the drafter, skilled and experienced in statute law, may not be obvious to the statute user. Hence doubt arises.

Ignorance of drafting methods has meant that doubt of this kind is not discussed in terms of the technique of ellipsis. Indeed no attention whatever has been paid to the technique, and the doubts have been resolved in random ways. It is suggested that for anyone concerned to resolve such a doubt, it would help to analyse it in terms of this technique. I begin by describing the technnique, and go on to give examples of its use and treatment.

The technique of ellipsis

The drafter does not wish to to use unecessary words. Words are unnecessary where, although the proposition they embody is intended to have effect, interpreters will accord that effect without its being spelt out. As Coleridge J said in an early case: 'If . . . the proposed addition is already necessarily contained, although not expressed, in the statute, it is of course not the less cogent because not expressed' (*Gwynne* v *Burnell* (1840) 7 Cl & F 572, 606). Effect may be given to unexpressed words for one of three reasons. The first is that it is the known and accepted practice to treat the words as implied: they are there *by operation of law*. The second reason is that the implication arises as a matter of grammar or syntax from the words that are *expressed*. The third reason is that the implication arises from the legal or political *context* of the Act.

An example of the first type of ellipsis is the following. Many Acts create criminal offences. They do so in general terms: 'A person who does so-and-so is guilty of an offence, and shall be liable on summary conviction to a fine of so much.' It is not usual to add that an offender is not liable to be convicted unless he is over the age of criminal responsibility, and is of sound mind. Nor are other general rules of criminal law referred to. Yet all these rules are taken to apply. As Stephen J said in *R* v *Tolson* (1889) 23 QBD 168, 187:

In all cases whatever, competent age, sanity and some degree of freedom from some kinds of coercion are assumed to be essential to criminality, but I do not believe they are ever introduced into any statute by which any particular crime is defined.

Many other general defences may be imported by operation of law; for example necessity, provocation or self-defence. Criminal statutes are to be construed with regard to the accused's right of silence (see *A* v *H M Treasury* [1979] 1 WLR 1056).

In whatever field of law the Act operates, it will import so far as relevant the basic principles of that field of law. Thus if a market is set up by statute, the common law of markets applies to it (*Wakefield City Council* v *Box* [1982] 3 All ER 506). If a tribunal is set up by statute, the common law governing tribunals applies to it (*Anisminic Ltd* v *Foreign Compensation Commission* [1969] 2 AC 147), and so on. Lord Diplock said in relation to statutory provisions defining the offence of arson (ie s 1(1) and (3) of the Criminal Damage Act 1971):

Those particular provisions will fall to be construed in the light of general principles of English criminal law so well established that it is the practice of parliamentary draftsmen to leave them unexpressed in criminal statutes, on the confident assumption that a court of law will treat those principles as intended by Parliament to be applicable to the particular offence unless modified or excluded (*R* v *Miller* [1983] 2 AC 161, 174).

An important category of implication by operation of law is *statutory* implication, for example by virtue of the Interpretation Act 1978.

This type of ellipsis is referable to the fact that an Act of Parliament, even where it is a principal Act, is but one unit in the *corpus juris*. The law consists of many elements, both statutory and non-statutory. Except where a new statute alters these elements, it takes its place among them and operates with due regard to their provisions. Doubt may arise where the existence or extent of one of the provisions is itself doubtful.

The second type of ellipsis relates not to standing rules of the *corpus juris* but to the particular language used by the drafter. It is rare that language is totally free from implications. The drafter relies on them to do his work for him. The more obvious they are, the readier he is to leave what they say unexpressed. In creating a statutory office for example, he will regard it as obvious that the office is to be vacated on the death of the holder; and only slightly less obvious that the holder can resign, or may be dismissed for misconduct. Sometimes he will confirm such implications by indirect references (for example, while not thinking it necessary to provide an express power of resignation he may refer to a vacancy in the office 'on resignation or otherwise').

Another example is provided by the rule that where an Act creates a power, this will be taken to include whatever may be necessary to make the power effective. In *Cookson* v *Lee* (1854) 23 LJ Ch 473, a private Act vested lands in trustees for the purpose of sale as building land. The Act omitted the usual provision empowering the use of purchase money for laying out roads on retained land and otherwise rendering it suitable for later sale as building land. The court held that this provision should be taken as implied.

The way a word is employed by the drafter may irresistibly suggest an implication. Thus when the drafter of s 57 of the Offences against the Person Act 1861 said that 'whosoever, being married, shall marry any other person during the life of the former husband or wife' was guilty of felony, he irresistibly suggested that he was using the word 'marry' in a very odd and unusual way. Under our monogamous system, a person who is already married cannot marry. Yet the only concern of s 57 is with the case where he or she does 'marry'. To give the section any effect the word has to be treated as by implication modified. So in *R* v *Allen* (1872) 1 CCR 367 the court held that it meant 'go through the form and ceremony of marriage'.

The law has adopted maxims regarding the implications to be drawn from certain types of grammatical construction. The leading principles of this kind are explained in chapter 12.

The third type of ellipsis brings in the context or setting of the Act. It cannot be looked on as a piece of prose standing alone. It must be construed in the light of its legislative history, the conditions of its time, and the earlier state of the law. It is well known, said the eighteenth-century lawyer Daines Barrington, that in the exposition of a statute the leading clue is the history of the times (Barrington 1767, p 4).

Abbreviated terms

In search of brevity, the drafter will choose a term he takes to comprehend meanings that might otherwise have to be spelt out. Section 29(4) of the Prices and Incomes Act 1966 imposed a wage-freeze by prohibiting an employer from paying remuneration 'at a rate which exceeds the rate of remuneration paid to him for the same kind of work before July 20th 1966.' It was held in *Allen* v *Thorn Electrical Industries Ltd* [1968] 1 QB 487 that the word 'paid' meant either actually paid or contracted to be paid (though *not* actually paid).

The need for compression forces the drafter to state many propositions without crossing all the t's and dotting all the i's. The interpreter is forced to do that for himself. In *Khan* v *Khan* [1980] 1 WLR 355, the court considered the power to make matrimonial orders conferred by s 2(1) of the Matrimonial Proceedings (Magistrates' Courts) Act 1960. This says that an order may contain one or more specified provisions, including 'a provision that the husband shall pay to the wife such weekly sum as the court considers reasonable . . .'. Nothing is said about whether such a maintenance order may be either unlimited in time or limited in time. Sir John Arnold P said (at p 359):

In my view the word 'such' is not limited to defining the amount of the weekly sum but carries with it an ability to qualify that sum in every relevant respect, in terms of duration in particular so far as this case is concerned, as well as amount. Nor does there seem to me to be anything inconsistent with that provision in making the weekly payments of a variable nature, in relation to successive periods.

The reports are full of instances where the court proved ready to fill out statutory propositions by taking them to imply necessary detail. Here are just a few:

(1) Where an onerous lease is disclaimed by a trustee in bankruptcy, the lease shall 'be deemed to have been surrendered' on the date of adjudication.
Held: words should be read in restricting this so that it only applied as between lessor and bankrupt. Where the bankrupt had sublet the lessor could therefore distrain for non-payment of rent, which after a genuine surrender he could not do (*Ex parte Walton* (1881) 17 Ch D 746).
(2) Witnesses who attest 'any will or codicil' under which they are beneficiaries shall be treated as good witnesses, but the gifts made to them shall be void.
Held: the words 'of real estate' should be implied after the quoted words since, under the then state of the law, wills of personalty did not require attestation (*Brett* v *Brett* (1826) 3 Add 210).
(3) All drug shops 'shall be closed . . . at 10 pm on each and every day of the week'.
Held: Although it does not say so, this means also that they shall *stay* closed until morning. It is not therefore sufficient compliance for a drug shop to close for a few minutes and then open again (*R* v *Liggetts-Findlay Drug Stores Ltd* [1919] 2 WLR 1025, cited Driedger 1974, p 15).
(4) It is an offence to 'stab, cut or wound' any person.
Held: this did not extent to biting off a person's nose, because use of a weapon or instrument is implied (*R* v *Harris* (1836) 7 C & P 416).
(5) Every person who fraudently harbours uncustomed goods shall forfeit a specified sum, 'and the offender may either be detained or proceeded against by summons'.
Held: this included an *apparent* offender, since otherwise guilt would have to be conclusively determined before action could be taken

(*Barnard* v *Gorman* [1941] AC 378, *Wiltshire* v *Barrett* [1966] 1 QB 312).

Ellipsis often gives rise to doubt, by its very nature. But it is some help for the interpreter to be aware that it is frequently employed, and why. He can then be on the look-out for it, and not fall into the trap of thinking that some rule of literalism has the effect of excluding implications. *A legislative text contains both what is expressed and what is implied.*

While we have referred to the *technique* of ellipsis it has to be admitted that implications are sometimes found by the court where they were not consciously intended by the drafter. Quite often a drafter does consider a specific point and then decide to deal with it by raising an implication. Sometimes however an implication may be drawn which was probably never considered by the drafter, but is nevertheless held to arise from the language used.

An example is given by Blackstone when he says of the statute 1 Car 1 c 1 that it 'does not prohibit, but rather impliedly allows' innocent Sunday amusements after the time of divine service (Blackstone 1765, iv 52). In *Ex parte Johnson* (1884) *Law Times* Vol L 214 the court considered the requirement in s 8 of the Bills of Sale Act 1878 that a bill of sale to which the Act applies 'shall set forth the consideration for which such bill of sale was given'. Bowen LJ said that s 8 'means—it does not say so in words, but it says so impliedly—that the consideration must be *truly* set forth' (p 217; emphasis added). Inference may occasionally be restored to by the court in order to resolve a difficulty caused by drafting error.

References to ellipsis

Cases in which judges have referred in terms to the use of ellipsis in statutes include the following: *Inland Revenue Commrs* v *Hinchy* [1959] 1 QB 327, 335 (s 48 of the Income Tax Act 1952 expresses in clearer and lengthier language 'what is intended to be conveyed by the elliptical expression in s 25(3), "the tax which he ought to be charged" '); *Commonwealth of Australia* v *Bank of New South Wales* [1950] AC 235, 295 ('It is a somewhat elliptical but by no means an impossible use of language to speak of a decision upon a certain question when what is meant is a decision in a suit, which cannot be decided without the determination of that question, or, more shortly, a decision involving a certain question or involving the determination of a certain question'); *Lord Advocate* v *AB* (1898) 3 Tax Cases 617 (the words 'in any other manner' in s 21(4) of the Taxes Management Act 1880 refer back to the preceding subsection 'though perhaps it may he said that the words are a little elliptical'); *British Railways Board* v *Dover Harbour Board* [1964] 1 Lloyd's Rep 428, 439 ('the wording is, on any possible interpretation elliptical and it seems to me to result from seeking to compress within a single sentence the limitations of the duration of existing and future liability on existing and future guarantees'); *Robertson v Day* (1879–80) 5 App Cas 63, 69 ('It is doing no violence to the words to read them as if they were slightly elliptical . . .').

Judicial reluctance to recognise ellipsis

In view of the undoubted, and very common, use by drafters of ellipsis, as explained above in this chapter, it is remarkable that some judges have denied that statues contain implied terms. In a famous dictum, Rowlatt J said of taxing Acts: 'Nothing is to be read in, nothing is to be implied' (*Cape Brandy Syndicate v IRC* [1921] 1 KB 64, 71). Lord Goddard CJ appeared to rule out implication in Acts of every description when he said that the court 'cannot add words to a statute or read words into it which are not there' (*R v Wimbledon JJ, ex parte Derwent* [1953] 1 QB 380). More common however are dicta going the other way. Thus in *R v Ettridge* [1909] 2 KB 24, 28 the court held itself entitled, in reading an Act, to 'reject words, transpose them, or even imply words'.

In *Wills v Bowley* [1983] 1 AC 57 the House of Lords gave a firm rebuttal to such dicta as that of Lord Goddard CJ set out above. The case concerned s 28 of the Town Police Clauses Act 1847, a very long section running to some three pages. In explaining the case it is helpful to make use of the technique of *comminution* mentioned above (p 218). What we need here is a refinement of the technique, which we may call *selective* comminution. Retaining the words of the section, we limit the restatement of them in broken-up form to those that are relevant to the facts of the case in question. Further to assist exposition, we number the grammatical clauses. If they deal with more than one matter, we divide them into Parts accordingly. Applied to the facts of *Wills v Bowley*, this technique produces the following version of s 28:

Part I
(1) Every person who in any street
(2) to the annoyance of the residents or passengers
(3) uses any obscene language
(4) shall be [guilty of an offence].

Part II
(5) [Any constable] shall take into custody without warrant
(6) and forthwith convey before a justice
(7) any person who within the constable's view commits any such offence.

This selective comminution reproduces the relevant wording of s 28, except that the passages in square brackets simplify provisions as to which there was no dispute between the prosecution and the defence in *Wills* v *Bowley*. The facts of the case were as follows. The female appellant was charged with two offences. The first ('the s 28 offence') was an offence under the provision restated above as Part I. The second ('the assault offence') was the offence of assaulting, while in the execution of their duty, the constables who (under Part II) arrested her for the s 28 offence. The appellant was acquitted of the s 28 offence because, although she had used obscene language in a street (clause (3) above), no residents or passengers were proved to have been annoyed by it (clause (2)). The question for the House of Lords was whether, in the light of this acquittal, her conviction of the assault offence could be upheld.

There was no doubt that the appellant had assaulted the constables in the course of her arrest: so violent was she that it took three of them to get her into the police van. But only if it was authorised by the provision restated above as Part II was the arrest lawful. Only if the arrest was lawful could the appellant be guilty of assaulting the police in the execution of their duty. If the arrest was unlawful they were not executing their duty in carrying it out, and she was entitled to resist them with all reasonable force.

The key lies in clause (7) of the above restatement. If it is restricted to its literal meaning, the appellant is not guilty of the assault. The arrest was unlawful because she did not commit the s 28 offence within the view of the constables. She did not commit it at all, whether within their view or not.

To sustain the assault conviction, the prosecution were obliged to argue that clause (7) had a further implied meaning. This could be spelt out by rewording clause (7) as follows:

(7) any person who within the constable's view commits any such offence *or so acts as to cause the constable reasonably to believe that he is committing any such offence.*

The House of Lords held that this further meaning was indeed to be implied. They thus confirmed that dicta to the effect that words are never to be read into an enactment cannot be relied on. If enactments are frequently elliptical, as is undoubtedly so, they must equally often contain implications. That is the nature of an ellipsis. (For a fuller treatment of this case see pp 306–309 below).

Chapter Sixteen

Doubt-factor II: The Broad Term

In the previous chapter we saw how, in a search for brevity, the legislative drafter is forced to create doubt by leaving out what it is not essential to state. Now we examine another technique of brevity. By use of a word or phrase of wide meaning, legislative power is delegated to the processors whose function is to work out the detailed effect. Again, doubt is necessarily created. Until the details are worked out, it will be doubtful what exactly they are. The statute user must use his own judgment. Moreover, under our system there is rarely if ever a point at which it can be said that the detail is complete. Even such detail as can be discerned tends to be obscured by the inexact methods used by processors, particularly judges.

A broad term may consist either of a single word or a phrase. In *Regan & Blackburn Ltd* v *Rogers* [1985] 1 WLR 870, 873 Scott J said of the phrase 'pending land action' in the Land Charges Act 1972, s 17(1): 'those words are very broad and cannot be given their full literal meaning'. They were what may be described as a multiple broad term.

A broad term may perform the function of a verb, adverb, adjective or substantive. If a substantive, it is what was described in *Hunter* v *Bowyer* (1850) 15 LTOS 281 as a *nomen generale*. Other descriptions of the broad term include 'open-ended expression' (*Express Newspapers Ltd* v *McShane* [1980] 2 WLR 89, 94), 'word of the most loose and flexible description' (*Green* v *Marsden* (1853) 1 Drew 646), and 'somewhat comprehensive and somewhat indeterminate term' (*Campbell* v *Adair* [1945] JC 29, 23).

The drafter selects a broad term which is either a processed term or an unprocessed term. Either way it is likely to have a core of certain meaning and a penumbra of uncertainty. It may be mobile or static. Its meaning will be coloured by the context, and the legislative purpose.

An implied intention that an unqualified broad term shall be construed as if a narrowing provision had accompanied it will not be found where the absence of such a provision is explicable only on the ground that it was not intended. Thus in *Puhlhofer* v *Hillingdon LBC* [1986] AC 484 the House of Lords declined to treat the term 'accommodation' in the Housing (Homeless Persons) Act 1977, ss 1

237

and 4 as qualified by an implied epithet such as 'appropriate' or 'reasonable' because if Parliament had intended such a narrowing of its meaning it would surely have said so. Moreover such a narrowing ran contrary to features of the Act. The Act did not increase the stock of housing available to authorities governed by it, and was clearly not intended to enable persons to jump the queue of those whose names were on the waiting list for housing.

Processed and unprocessed terms

When the drafter decides to attain brevity by using a broad term, he looks for one which has been processed. If the courts have already worked out the meaning of a term, and that meaning corresponds with the drafter's intention, the term is suitable for adoption. Instead of there being uncertainty about whether subsequent processors will adopt the meaning he desires, the drafter can be reasonably sure that the established meaning will be followed.

Usually, the processed term will be one used in previous legislation. Only rarely will a term whose meaning has been worked out solely at common law present itself as suitable for adoption. The drafter of AP Herbert's Divorce Act, the Matrimonial Causes Act 1937, used a processed verb when he expressed as a ground of divorce that the respondent 'has deserted the petitioner without cause' for three years. The verb 'deserted', used by itself, is a typical broad term. There are many different acts which might be held to fall within it. One is a simple refusal of sexual intercourse. But it had been held in *Jackson* v *Jackson* [1924] P 19 that such refusal did not constitute desertion within the meaning of an earlier Act. When the point was raised under the 1937 Act Tucker LJ took the same line: 'I think the Legislature in . . . refraining from defining desertion must be taken as accepting the tests which had hitherto been applied in the courts . . .' (*Weatherley* v *Weatherley* [1946] 2 All ER 1, 8).

Doubt may arise as to whether use of a processed term in a new Act brings in the processed meaning or the ordinary (dictionary) meaning. Often there is no significant difference. Where there is a difference, the point may turn on whether the new Act is *in pari materia* with the earlier Acts in which the term appeared. The rule was thus laid down by Lord Buckmaster in *Barras* v *Aberdeen Steam Trawling and Fishing Co* [1933] AC 402, 411:

It has long been a well-established principle to be applied in the consideration of Acts of Parliament that where a word of doubtful meaning has received a clear judicial interpretation, the subsequent statute which incorporates the same word or the same phrase *in a similar context* must be construed so that the word or phrase is interpreted according to the meaning that has previously been ascribed to it (emphasis added).

Two points should be noted. It is not the practice of drafters (who tend to be over-cautious) to attract processing by saying expressly in the new Act that the term has the same (undefined but processed) meaning as in the previous Act. This renders unrealistic the remark by Lord Simon of Glaisdale that 'If Parliament wishes to endorse the previous interpretation it can do so in terms' (*Farrell* v *Alexander* [1977] AC 59, 90). Second, the courts will be reluctant to attach previous processing to the term in its new use if they think the processing defective (eg *Royal Crown Derby Porcelain Co* v *Russell* [1949] 2 KB 417, 429).

While the borrowing by the drafter of a term already processed may be convenient, it can give rise to a conceptual difficulty. A word or phrase used in an Act is to be construed in accordance with the purpose of that Act. Decisions on its meaning may be misleading if it is borrowed for another Act with a different purpose (eg *Hanlon* v *The Law Society* [1981] AC 124).

Core and penumbra

Doubt arises from the drafter's use of a broad term only where its meaning is to some extent uncertain. There are terms which are broad in the sense that they cover many different cases, but whose meaning is certain in virtually every case: for example 'mammal' or 'moving'. We are not here concerned with these.

On the other hand, it is unlikely that the application of a statutory term will be doubtful in *every* case. Selection by the drafter of such a term would almost certainly be an error, since it would mean that the entirety of the legal rule in question was founded upon uncertainty; which is not the nature of law. A will may be declared void for uncertainty, but this rule does not apply to Acts of Parliament. Nevertheless a modern Act whose application was uncertain in every case would certainly be considered ill-drawn: at least if drafted on common-law lines.

It follows that what we are in practice concerned with is the broad term whose application to some cases is clear and to others doubtful. A *penumbra* is defined as a partial shade bordering upon a fuller or darker one; in other words a twilight. This is a good description here because we are all familiar with the difficulty caused by a phrase such as 'during the hours of darkness'. Midnight is clearly within it, and noon equally clearly outside it. But there are periods around dawn and sunset during which it must be debatable whether darkness has ceased or fallen.

The drafter tries to choose phrases whose penumbra of doubt is as small as possible. At common law, burglary was committed when a dwelling-house was broken and entered *by night* with intent to commit a felony. Night was understood as the period between sunset and sunrise. A later common-law refinement held it not to be night if there was sufficient light from the sun to tell a person's face. Finally, when statute intervened, night was precisely defined as the period between 9 pm and 6 am. Although the penumbra remained in nature, it vanished from the law of burglary.

An unnecessarily wide penumbra is an instance of bad drafting. A standard example used in juristic discussions of what Hart calls the 'open texture' of language is the notice reading 'No vehicles allowed in the park' (see Twining and Miers 1982, p 205). We can depict the uncertainty this causes by a diagram in which the inner circle depicts the core of certain meaning while the space between the circles marks the penumbra of doubt about what is allowed in the park. Outside this penumbra the meaning is once again certain—in the opposite sense. Not everyone would agree with the

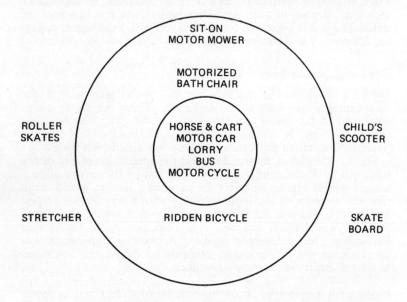

exact placing of these objects, but assuming it to be roughly correct we have three doubtful cases. There could be genuine argument with the park-keeper over whether it is allowed to take into the park a ridden bicycle, a motorised bath chair, or a sit-on motor mower. Other doubtful objects can readily be imagined, and we can vary the condition of the ones mentioned. Does it make a difference if the bicycle is pushed instead of ridden, or the motor mower belongs to the council? Is an ambulance allowed in to take away the victim of an accident on the slide? Suppose a car chassis, minus wheels and engine, is carried in by mischievous youths? The possibilities of doubt are endless.

Greater precision can be achieved by detailed wording, but then we end up with the closely-printed park notice that nobody reads.

Even the park-keeper may not read it, and so lack conviction in trying to repel the practical villains: motorists and motor cyclists. The modern legislative drafter goes into as much detail as he considers practicable. For the rest, he relies on ellipsis or selects broad terms with the smallest penumbra of doubt.

Cutting down the broad term

Sometimes, by usage or judicial decision (or a combination of both) the width of a broad term is drastically cut down. The term 'immoral purposes' is very wide. Yet as used in s 1(1) of the Vagrancy Act 1898 (reproduced in s 32 of the Sexual Offences Act 1956) it has been held to be doubly limited. First, it excludes all forms of immorality except sexual immorality. Second, even as respects sexual immorality, it excludes all but homosexual acts. (See *Crook* v *Edmondson* [1966] 1 All ER 833). This illustrates that the term selected by the drafter as his 'broad term' may itself be elliptical. Here the courts have processed the term 'immoral purposes' as if it were 'purposes involving sexual immorality of a homosexual nature'.

Static and mobile terms

Broad terms can be divided into two types. First there is the case where the content of the term is static or constant, in both place and time. The circumstances that fall within it are basically the same wherever they happen, and at what historic moment. An example is the term 'accident'. Secondly there is the *mobile* phrase. What falls within it may differ according to time or place (or both). For instance one person may or may not be regarded as belonging to another person's 'family' according to the place, or the period, in which they live.

We now consider the two categories in turn, examining these and other examples from decided cases. We shall see later that failure by the drafter to understand the distinction between the categories can have important consequences.

The static broad term

The term 'accident' has been frequently employed in legislation. One famous example of its use was in the Workmen's Compensation Acts, which gave a workman a right to compensation for 'an accident arising out of and in the course of his employment'. This is a multiple broad term of epic proportions. Many thousands of judicial decisions proved necessary to process it. The process began with the first case to reach the House of Lords under the 1909 Act. This concerned a workman suffering from a form of heart disease induced by natural causes, an aneurism. The aneurism might have burst and killed the workman at any time—even while he was asleep in bed. In fact it did so while he was at work, engaged in manual labour of a by no means strenuous kind. Was this an 'accident'? Yes, said the House of Lords in a judgment we are not surprised to find lacked unanimity.

The fact was that the policy of the Act plainly required the term 'accident' to be given a wide meaning. As Kennedy LJ said in deciding that it even covered the murder of a cashier by a thief:

An historian who described the end of Rizzio by saying that he met with a fatal accident in Holyrood Palace would fairly, I suppose, be charged with a misleading statement of fact . . . But whilst the description of death by murderous violence as an 'accident' cannot honestly be said to accord with the common understanding of the word, wherein is implied a negation of wilfulness and intention, I conceive it to be my duty rather to stretch the meaning of the word from the narrower to the wider sense of which it is inherently and etymologically capable . . . (*Nisbet* v *Rayne and Burn* [1910] 2 KB 689).

This neatly illustrates the difference between the case where the drafter has selected a term which is etymologically capable of the wide meaning it should bear and the case where he has erred by making his wording narrower than the object (as to the latter see pp 264–266 below).

Other examples of static broad terms are the following:

Repairing Rules made under the Railway Employment Prevention of Accidents Act 1900 protected workers engaged in 'relaying or repairing' the permanent way. Did this include the routine oiling and maintenance of apparatus working the points? In *London and North Eastern Railway* v *Berriman* [1946] AC 278 the House of Lords, by a majority of three to two, held that it did not. [Here the wording was *narrower than the object*, a frequent drafting defect: see p 264].

Supply Section 1(1) of the Finance Act 1972 introduced a new tax in these words: 'A tax, to be known as value added tax, shall be charged . . . on the supply of goods and services in the United Kingdom . . .'. In *Customs and Excise Commissioners* v *Oliver* [1980] 1 All ER 353, 354, Griffiths J said: 'There is no definition of "supply" in the Act itself, but it is quite clear from the language of the Act that "supply" is a word of the widest import'.

Many more instances could be given of static broad terms, but this is not necessary. The terms are 'static' in the sense that, by processing, detailed rules can be worked out which will be of universal application despite differences of time or place.

The mobile broad term

Section 4(1) of the Obscene Publications Act 1959 provides a defence against a charge of publishing an obscene article 'if it is proved that publication of the article in question is justified as being for the public good on the ground that it is in the interests of science, literature, art or learning, or of other *objects of general concern* (emphasis supplied). In *R* v *Jordan* [1976] 2 WLR 887, 893, Lord Wilberforce said that the italicised phrase 'is no doubt a mobile phrase; it may, and should, change in content as society changes'.

Changes of this kind may occur in time or in place. Often they occur in both. Since an Act is always speaking, it must be worded so as to accommodate them. The drafter of the Obscene Publications Act 1959 assumed that, throughout the life of the Act, science, literature, art and learning would be of general concern. It was safe therefore to specify them (and helpful to do so, since they gave shape and colour to his proposition). But other topics were to be judged not on what was of general concern in 1959 but on what was of general concern at the time of an alleged offence. If the Act lasted 50 years, and a prosecution was brought at the time of its golden jubilee, the drafter intended the case to be judged by what was of general concern in 2009 not 1959.

Let us take some other examples, first of changes in time and then in place.

Suppose it is desired to impose control over firearms but exempt any antique weapon. The term 'antique' is vague. The drafter might seek precision by referring instead to a weapon 'manufactured more than 100 years before the passing of this Act'. But that would be illogical. If the Act were passed in 1968 a gun made 105 years earlier would be exempt. By 1978 however, a gun made 105 years earlier would not be exempt, because it would have been made only 95 years before the passing of the Act. What is wanted is a rolling period, so that at any moment the Act will exempt guns which *at that moment* are 100 years old. The drafter of s 58(2) of the Firearms Act 1968 did not adopt this. Instead, he provided a flurry of broad terms: 'Nothing in this Act relating to firearms shall apply to an antique firearm which is sold, transferred, purchased, acquired or possessed as a curiosity or ornament.' No definitions were provided for 'antique', 'curiosity' or 'ornament'.

The question of the meaning of 'antique' in s 58(2) came before the Divisional Court of the Queen's Bench Division in *Bennett* v *Brown* (1980) *The Times*, 12 April. The prosecutor appealed from magistrates' acquittal of a defendant in relation to three guns 'dating from possibly 1886, and after 1905 and 1910'. He told the court that prosecuting authorities needed guidance on what was 'antique' for this purpose. Eveleigh LJ said it was a question of fact, but guns manufactured in the present century 'could not be antique'. The court directed the magistrates to convict in relation to the guns made after 1905 and 1910. Regarding the gun possibly made in 1886, Eveleigh LJ said that the magistrates were entitled to come to their conclusion, though he would not have done so himself. This judgment seems to put excessive weight on the arbitrary division of time into centuries.

Is 'book' a mobile term? It might not seem so. Everyone knows what is and is not a book. Or do they? Section 9 of the Bankers' Books Evidence Act 1879 defines 'banker's book' as including ledgers, day books, account books, 'and all other books used in the ordinary business of the bank'. In 1879 it was no doubt unthinkable that banks would keep their records in anything but bound books. One cannot blame the drafter for failing to envisage the invention of microfilm. Yet in seeking to make copies of all bank records admissible in evidence he might have managed to find a phrase of more general meaning. In *Barker* v *Wilson* [1980] 1 WLR 884, the Divisional Court had no hesitation in coming to the drafter's rescue. They treated 'book' as a mobile term wide enough to embrace microfilm—and indeed 'any form of permanent record kept by the bank by means made available by modern technology'. It did not worry Caulfield J that a microfilm 'is not normally called a book'.

Another technological development came before the court in *Aerated Bread Co* v *Gregg* [1873] LR 8 QB 355. At the time of the passing of the Bread Act 1836 a certain type of bread, of a certain shape, was widely sold as 'fancy bread'. The Act used this term without definition. Quain J held that 40 years later the term could be applied to bread of the same kind, even though of a different shape and produced by an altered mode of baking.

Social change has frequently to be accommodated by the mobile term. When 'single woman' was first used in Affiliation Acts it referred solely to an unmarried woman. The growing frequency with which marriages broke up led to its ultimate extension to a married woman living apart from her husband—even where they shared the same roof (*Watson* v *Tuckwell* (1947) 63 TLR 634).

It follows that a judicial decision on the meaning of a term will be disregarded if the meaning changes. The Rent Acts give protection, where the tenant dies, to a member of the tenant's 'family'. In 1950 it was held by the Court of Appeal that this did not include the tenant's common law husband (*Gammans* v *Ekins* [1950] 2 KB 328). In another case 25 years later the same court reversed its ruling. The case was *Dyson Holdings Ltd* v *Fox* [1976] QB 503, where Bridge LJ said (p 513):

If the language can change its meaning to accord with changing social attitudes, then a decision on the meaning of a word in a statute before such a change should not continue to bind thereafter, at all events in a case where the courts have constantly affirmed that the word is to be understood in its ordinary meaning.

By this Bridge LJ clearly referred to the fact that a mobile term is to be applied to facts arising at a particular time in accordance with its meaning *at that time*.

Another matrimonial term of long standing is 'cruelty' as a ground of divorce. Here we see the effect of a social change attributable to advancing civilisation. As the times become less rough and barbarous, and the standard of comfort advances, people will put up with less hardship. What was once part of the give-and-take of marriage becomes 'cruelty'. Mental cruelty enters the scene, alongside physical ill-treatment. There is a similar progression with broad terms like 'riotous', 'disorderly', 'indecent' and 'insulting' as descriptions of public behaviour. A dog may now be held 'dangerous' within the meaning of the Dogs Act 1871 even though its behaviour is something less than savage or ferocious (*Keddle* v *Payn* [1964] 1 WLR 262).

Sexual *mores* are notoriously mobile in time. Section 32 of the Sexual Offences Act 1956 (a consolidation Act), reproducing s 1(1) of the Vagrancy Act 1898, makes it an offence for a man to solicit for 'immoral purposes'. In *Crook* v *Edmondson* [1966] 2 QB 81, this was held to mean purposes considered immoral by 'the majority of contemporary fellow citizens' (*per* Winn LJ at p 90).

Here are two other examples of broad terms whose content varies from place to place:

Section 59 of the Highways Act 1980 gives a highway authority power to recover compensation from an operator responsible for damage 'caused by *excessive* weight passing along the highway, or other *extraordinary* traffic thereon'. Both these broad terms are modified by reference to the average maintenance expenses of highways in the *neighbourhood*. Here the variability of the content is expressed in the statute.

In the other example the variability is not expressed, but has been held by the courts to be implied. Section 74(4) of the Licensing Act 1964 (reproducing earlier legislation) empowers justices to extend permitted licensing hours for the sale and consumption of alcoholic liquor on a 'special occasion.' No definition of this term is provided. In a case decided under earlier legislation, Lord Coleridge CJ said 'the question what is a special occasion must necessarily be a question of fact in each locality'. He added: 'Each locality may very well have its own meaning to those words, and it is for the justices in each district to say whether a certain time and place come within the description' (*Devine* v *Keeling* (1886) 50 JP 551, 552). Thus the Saturday before a bank holiday may be a 'special occasion' in a seaside holiday resort but not in an industrial town (*R* v *Corwen Justices* [1980] 1 WLR 1045).

Static term—mobile concept

Not only should the processor be alert to the distinction between the static and mobile broad term, but the drafter needs to be aware of it too. It is really a distinction between static and mobile *concepts*. If the concept for which the drafter needs a term is static, then he should select a static term, and vice versa. If he fails in this he may create unnecessary difficulties of interpretation.

The commonest error, and the most troublesome, is where the

drafter with insufficient imagination thinks his concept is fixed when it is in fact mobile. The Canadian Criminal Code made it an offence to trade or traffic in 'any bottle or syphon' which had upon it the trade mark of another person, or fill it with any beverage for sale, without his consent (cited Driedger 1974, p 86). It is obviously possible for beverages to be sold in other forms of container, such as cartons. By looking only at the conditions prevailing at the time he was writing, and failing to exercise his imagination, the drafter made his text unnecessarily and unjustifiably narrow. He could easily have written 'container' instead of 'bottle or syphon'. We saw earlier how a similar difficulty arose in connection with bankers' books.

The reverse error, of using a mobile term for a static concept, creates unnecessary vagueness. It would not have been sensible to say 'container' instead of 'bottle' in a provision intended to guard against danger from broken glass.

The broadest term

As we have seen, the wider the penumbra of doubt attached to a broad term the greater the discretion effectively delegated to the processor. There is an important class of cases where, because the limiting framework is virtually non-existent, delegation occurs practically across the whole field. In effect the legislator abdicates completely. For his judgment is substituted that of the processor, guided only by vague concepts such as what is 'reasonable' or 'just' or 'fit and proper'.

There are many examples of this form of delegation. Here is one, drawn from the Consumer Credit Act 1974. In this instance the processor is an official, the Director General of Fair Trading. Section 25(1) states that a licence to carry on a credit or hire business shall be granted on the application of any person if he satisfies the Director General that he is 'a fit person to engage in activities covered by the licence'. If this stood alone, as it well might have done, it would empower the Director General to set his own standards of fitness. Parliament has thought it right to lay down guidelines however, and the section goes on to instruct the Director General to have regard to specified factors—such as whether the applicant has a record of dishonesty or violence.

Parliament has been more ready to entrust unfettered discretion to judges than officials. In the early days of divorce law for example, the court was empowered in relation to the children of dissolved marriages to 'make such provision as it may deem just and proper' with respect to their custody, maintenance and education (Matrimonial Causes Act 1859, s 35).

The modern tendency is for judges to receive (and indeed expect) more positive guidance. When the grounds for divorce were recast in 1969–70 elaborate criteria were laid down for maintenance, including the momentous requirement to put the parties as nearly as possible in the position they would have been in if the marriage had not broken down (Matrimonial Proceedings and Property Act 1970, s 5(1) and (2)); see now Matrimonial Causes Act 1973, s 25(1)).

Guides to meaning

Sometimes, as we have seen, guides to the interpretation of the broad term are stated expressly in the legislative text. Even where this is not done, the meaning is not left completely at large. Under the *noscitur a sociis* principle (pp 195-196), terms are recognised to gain colour from their context.

The context may not always furnish assistance. The Housing Act 1980 laid down the repairing covenants that are to apply where the secure tenant of a flat exercises his statutory right to acquire a long lease (see Sched 2, paras 13 to 17). It enabled the landlord to charge the tenant a 'reasonable' proportion of the cost of non-structural repairs. Often when the broad term 'reasonable' is used, as with the concept of a 'reasonable' rent, the factors by reference to which it is to be applied are obvious. Here they are not. The Act imposed on the landlord the duty to repair whether or not it was 'reasonable' that he should be saddled with this. It then enabled him to transfer to the tenant such part of the duty as might be 'reasonable'. If, from an objective viewpoint it was wholly *un*reasonable in a particular case to saddle the landlord with repairs, how could it be 'reasonable' to transfer only a part of the cost to the tenant? The courts are forced to grope for a meaning in such cases, without guidance from the legislature. (For further details see Bennion 1981(6)).

Above all, the broad term must be construed so as to further the purpose and intention of the instrument in which it is used. The ways in which broad terms are processed in this way are examined in Part IV.

Chapter Seventeen

Doubt-factor III: Politic Uncertainty

The final deliberate doubt-factor is seldom used, and so requires only brief discussion. There are various reasons why it may be considered politic to shroud a legislative text in obscurity. They can be condensed into the following propositions:

(1) If the parties to a proposal cannot agree, it may be necessary to fall back on putative agreement by propounding an imprecise formula to paper over the cracks.
(2) Where a government's proposal is politically contentious the government may sneak it on to the statute book under a cloak of bland and harmless phraseology.
(3) On some politically sensitive issues certain forms of words acquire the quality of a shibboleth, which it is felt *must* be advanced regardless of resulting obscurity.
(4) Officials who desire a free hand in administering a regulatory Act favour imprecise language. If no one can be sure what the Act means, there can be no proof that the officials have exceeded their powers.

Treaty provisions

The commonest example of the first proposition is the international treaty. As the Renton Committee remarked, in such documents 'clarity is sometimes sacrificed to expediency' (Renton 1975, para 9.11). When representatives of many nations seek to hammer out agreement they may feel bound to resort to spurious compromise. Either there is agreement or there is not. To pretend to agreement by the use of ambiguous language is ignoble. But it is done. As Brinkhorst and Schermers say in *Judicial Remedies in the European Communities* (p 22): 'Political compromises are often attained by the use of ambiguous words' (quoted Renton 1975, para 9.11).

Every treaty contains compromise of this sort. If the treaty is converted into municipal law, the ambiguity is spread. That is one objection to the idea of making the European Convention on Human Rights part of domestic law. To secure agreement, many important principles were watered down when the wording of the Convention was settled.

248

An example of an international treaty converted directly into municipal law is the Warsaw Convention, as amended at the Hague in 1955. This is given the force of law in the United Kingdom by s 1 of the Carriage by Air Act 1961. The result is to apply directly a number of obscure provisions. Article 18(3) is an example. It begins by saying that the period of the carriage by air does not extend to 'any carriage by land, by sea or by river performed outside an aerodrome'. Then it qualifies this by saying that if such carriage does in fact take place 'any damage is presumed, *subject to proof to the contrary*, to have been the result of an event which took place during the carriage by air' (emphasis added). The italicised phrase seems to contradict the purpose of the qualification.

A case where treaty obligations were implemented indirectly was the Oil in Navigable Waters Act 1955. Reproducing the obscure wording of the treaty, s 1 of the Act said that if oil were unlawfully discharged from a British ship 'the owner or master' of the ship would be guilty of an offence. In *Federal Steam Navigation Co* v *Department of Trade and Industry* [1974] 1 WLR 505, *both* the owner and the master of a ship were convicted. In dismissing their appeals, the House of Lords split three to two.

An extraordinary example of deliberate obscurity induced by a treaty concerns the 1961 Vienna Convention on Diplomatic Relations. By the Diplomatic Privileges Act 1964, certain articles of this are made part of the law of the United Kingdom. One of them is art 31, which gives immunity from jurisdiction except in the case of a 'real action' relating to private immovable property. Now (Admiralty jurisdiction excepted) there are no such things as real actions in English law, so what can this exception conceivably mean? We have an Act of Parliament solemnly legislating about things that simply do not exist. It is as if the Act gave immunity in respect of 'dodos, unicorns and gryphons'. For a valiant attempt by the court to grapple with this difficulty see *Intpro Properties (UK) Ltd* v *Sauvel* [1983] 2 WLR 1 (reversed [1983] 2 WLR 908).

Politically contentious provisions

Enactments which 'paper over the cracks' are not limited to the field of international conventions. For a domestic example relating to the Marine Insurance Act 1906 see p 75 above. Another possible example was referred to by Lord Wilberforce in the 1982 case about the cheap London fares policy, *Bromley London Borough Council* v *Greater London Council* [1983] 1 AC 768. Speaking of the duty imposed by s 1 of the Transport (London) Act 1969 to provide 'integrated, efficient and economic' facilities, Lord Wilberforce said (p 814): 'There has been a good deal of argument as to the meaning of these words, particularly of 'economic'; no doubt they are vague, possibly with design.'

An acutely controversial point may be left deliberately uncertain despite the fact that MPs debating the Bill point to the doubt. This happened on the question of whether the 1968 Race Relations Bill applied to working men's clubs. Lord Simon of Glaisdale said in 1981 that it was notorious that such clubs practised racial discrimination but Parliament shrank from making clear whether the Bill applied to them or not because 'a decision either way was bound to attract some odium' (HL Deb 9 March 1981 col 77).

Craies includes among the causes of defective statute law: 'More or less intentional obscurities, perplexities, or imperfections, inserted or permitted with a view to facilitate the passage of the Bill through Parliament' (Craies 1971, p 28). Sir Courtenay Ilbert explained how in his day counsels of perfection urged by the drafter from the legal view were ignored by politicians. He added that 'whether the Minister who had to decide between the risk of losing his Bill and responsibility for leaving the law obscure adopted the right course is a nice question of political ethics' (Ilbert 1901, pp 18, 22).

It might be a nice question of political ethics, but no realist would suppose for a moment that a minister would be prepared to lose his Bill, or have it delayed, on any grounds except political ones—and then only when they were compelling. This highlights a central paradox: the true arbiters of legal change and content are not lawyers but politicians, whether they be ministers or back-benchers. So it is not surprising that the *corpus juris* assumes erratic shapes.

Another political factor is the party shibboleth. This has been particularly obvious in the protracted battles over trade unionism. Labour hatred of the Industrial Relations Act 1971 was so acute and bitter that it distorted the Act which followed, the Trade Union and Labour Relations Act 1974. Although Labour wished to retain many features of the 1971 Act, its *total* repeal had been a leading general election issue. How do you repeal an Act totally, while retaining large parts of it?

The way it can be done is to be seen in s 1 of the 1974 Act:

(1) The Industrial Relations Act 1971 is hereby repealed.
(2) Nevertheless, Schedule 1 to this Act shall have effect for re-enacting . . . the under-mentioned provisions of that Act, that is to say . . .

Simple, when you know how!

Another party-political distortion in the 1974 Act derived from Labour adherence to the historic fact that trade unions were unincorporated associations and not bodies corporate. Although for practical reasons unions needed to be given most of, if not all, the attributes of corporate status, the drafter was not allowed to turn unions into corporations. How the resultant contradictions misfired was recounted on pp 183–185 of the second edition of this book (now omitted).

Sir Harold Kent, a former drafter, has described in his book of reminiscences *In on the Act* the conflict of interest between the drafter on the one hand the the Minister and his department on the other. The drafter seeks to confine the Bill strictly to matters requiring an alteration of the law. On the other hand:

The department is conscious that the Minister would like to make a Parliamentary splash; it also knows that administration is sometimes helped by being able to refer to an Act of Parliament; so it wants to put as much as possible into the Bill' (Kent 1979, p 44).

Kent goes on to point out that other occasions of conflict are when the Minister wants a clause to look as attractive politically as possible, or is 'impatient of the detail needed for precision'.

Convenience of officials

The development of legislation as an instrument of social policy has brought a corresponding increase in bureaucracy. Regulatory legislation requires officials to administer it. They are then in the public eye, and the subject of constant probing and attack. Everything they do is open to challenge, and often is challenged. So it is not surprising that the officials take advantage of what refuge they can find. If the Act which officials administer is obscure, their antagonists have less opening for attack. Even when not afflicted with megalomania (and few officials are) it is more comfortable to be covered by wide, vague powers. Then you can get on with the job without fear of challenge.

The departmental official has a guiding hand in the preparation of legislation. Usually its shape is a reflection of his views. They are not idiosyncratic personal views; but the demands of his work colour his approach. The official does not think it important that the statute user should be able to understand the law from the text alone: he is always ready with advice.

The legislative drafter opposes this view. If not particularly concerned about the plight of the statute user, he does at least want to express the law he intends to make. Sir Harold Kent describes the conflict by recollecting occasions in his own experience 'when the department wants its administrative powers drawn widely, or even obscurely, so as to avoid risk of legal challenge, an attitude which hardly pleases a self-respecting draftsman'.

Kent's last word on this really says it all. 'I remember a clause of mine receiving the dubious compliment of "nice and vague" from a bureaucrat of seasoned experience' (Kent 1979, p 45).

It should perhaps be added in conclusion that the rise of judicial review since the above was written in 1979 has rendered it less likely that challenge will be avoided by the use of obscurity in drafting.

Chapter Eighteen

Doubt-factor IV: The Unforeseeable Development

As we saw from the discussion of updating construction (pp 181–186), the longer a statute remains in operation, the more likely it is that doubts will arise as to its application. It is a static text amid constant flux. Changes in language, technology, social practice and in the surrounding law are bound to be continual.

The static text

We may usefully consider some examples. It is truly remarkable how long-lived English statutes are. In magistrates' courts throughout the land, people are still being bound over to keep the peace under an Act passed more than six centuries ago. It is still 'speaking'. Can its voice be comprehensible today? This is how it begins:

Primement q̃ en chescun Countee Dengletre soient assignez, pᵣ la garde de la pees, un Seignᵣ, & ovesq lui trois ou quatre des meultz vauez du Countee, ensemblement ove ascuns sages de la ley, & eient poer de restreindre les mesfesours, riotoᵣs, & touz auts barettoᵣs . . .

Even that is not the oldest criminal statute operative. The law of treason, an offence still carrying the death penalty, is embodied in an Act of 1351. This begins as follows:

Auxint pᵣceo q̃ divses opinions ount este einz ces heures qeu cas, qᵃnt il avient doit estre dit treson, & en quel cas noun, le Roi a la requeste des Seignᵣs & de la Cõe, ad fait declarissement q̃ ensuit, Cest assavoir; qᵃnt hõme fait compasser ou ymaginer la mort nr̃e Seignᵣ le Roi, ma dame sa compaigne, ou de lour fitz primer & heir . . .

It is true that for both these fourteenth-century statutes an official translation is provided. But the wording, even in translation, is redolent of times long past. There can be no justification for a modern state still expressing its law against attacks on the head of state by imposing sanctions 'when a man doth compass or imagine the death of our lord the King, or of our lady his companion or of their eldest son and heir; or if a man do violate the King's companion, or the King's eldest daughter unmarried, or the wife of the King's

252

eldest son and heir; or if a man do levy war against our lord the King in his realm, or be adherent to the King's enemies in his realm, giving them aid and comfort in the realm, or elsewhere . . .' (Treason Act 1351).

Nor can there be any justification for subjecting today's citizens to the risk of binding-over by saying that 'in every country of England shall be assigned for the keeping of the peace one lord, and with him three or four of the most worthy in the county, with some learned in the law, and they shall have power to take of all them that be [not] of good fame, where they shall be found, sufficient surety and mainprise of their good behaviour towards the King and his people . . .' (Justices of the Peace Act 1361).

Apart from obvious archaisms, the texts of these two Acts abound with doubts and defects. It is doubtful whether the word 'not' is really present in the passage just cited, there being a respectable argument for saying that not only was that negative never included but that other words (not cited above) render its omission necessary! Blackstone it is true felt confident that 'not' was properly included. He gives us an engaging picture of the sort of people who in his day fell within the ambit of a provision that was already more than 400 years old:

Under the general words of this expression, *that be not of good fame*, it is held that a man may be bound to his good behaviour for causes of scandal, *contra bonos mores*, as well as *contra pacem*: as, for haunting bawdy-houses with women of bad fame; or for keeping such women in his own house; or for words tending to scandalize the government, or in abuse of the officers of justice, especially in the execution of their office. Thus also a justice may bind over all night-walkers; eaves-droppers; such as keep suspicious company, or are reported to be pilferers or robbers; such as sleep in the day, and wake in the night; common drunkards; whore-masters; cheats; idle vagabonds; and other persons whose misbehaviour may reasonably bring them within the general words of the statute, as persons not of good fame: an expression, it must be owned, of so great a latitude, as leaves much to be determined by the discretion of the magistrate himself.' (Blackstone 1756, IV 268. See further 133 SJ (1989) 498. As to broad terms generally see chapter 16 above.)

Other Acts still in our statute book, though not as ancient as the two just mentioned, nevertheless govern today's citizens by the language of the past. Here are just a few examples at random. All are in force today.

The Pedlars Act 1871 contains a definition of 'pedlar' stating that it means 'any hawker, pedlar, petty chapman, tinker, caster of metals, mender of chairs, or other person who, without any horse or other beast bearing or drawing burden, travels and trades on foot . . .'.

Section 4 of the Vagrancy Act 1824, still in constant use, punishes 'every person wilfully, openly, lewdly, and obscenely exposing his person with intent to insult any female'. It was decided only in

1972 that the reference to a person exposing his 'person' means the penis and nothing else: *Evans* v *Ewels* [1972] 1 WLR 671. The section goes on to penalise the carrying of any gun, pistol, hanger, cutlass or bludgeon, and renders such weapons forfeit to the King's Majesty. Then the section says that anyone apprehended as an idle and disorderly person and violently resisting any constable or other peace officer shall be deemed a rogue and vagabond. We are not surprised to find that such a rogue and vagabond is to be committed 'to the house of correction'.

Section 4 of the Statute of Frauds 1677 remains an important element in the law of contract. It provides that 'noe action shall be brought whereby to charge the defendant upon any speciall promise to answere for the debt default or miscarriages of another person unlesse the agreement upon which such action shall be brought or some memorandum or note thereof shall be in writeing and signed by the partie to be charged therewith . . .'

The Gaming Act 1710 is still important to gamblers and those who exploit them. It renders void any security given in respect of 'gaming or playing at cards dice tables tennis bowles or other game or games whatsoever or by betting on the sides or hands of such as do game at any of the games aforesaid . . .' The effect is somewhat reduced by the Gaming Act 1835.

How doubts arise

It is clear that the static text, enduring through changing conditions, must raise uncertainty as to how it is to be interpreted at a given time. Looking only at examples quoted above, we feel doubt as to how they are to be construed today. Is it really punishable to 'imagine' the death of a monarch? Suppose the monarch's heir is not the 'eldest son' but the eldest daughter, or the second-born son? Does 'violating' the consort mean only taking her by force, and exactly what sexual conduct is proscribed? Can a person who *is* 'of good fame' be bound over? What does 'surety and mainprise' mean? Does the *ejusdem generis* rule (p 196) apply to the 1871 definition of 'pedlar' and if so to what effect? Does s 6(*b*) of the Interpretation Act 1978 ('words importing the feminine gender include the masculine') now mean that it is an offence for a person to expose his person with intent to insult a *male*? What conduct is 'idle and disorderly' today? The way courts deal with such questions is described above in the discussion of updating construction (pp 181–186).

Chapter Nineteen

Doubt-factor V: The Fallible Drafter

Statute law consists of words. The words are put together by an anonymous being formerly called the draftsman. In the present edition, out of deference to the fact that this task is nowadays performed by both sexes, I have substituted 'drafter'.

Under the British system there is usually one person who composes the text, and can be regarded as its author. Yet, as we have seen, the drafter is far from being a free agent. Much constraint bears upon him before he begins to compose. Then his careful composition is liable to be distorted by various factors. Within the instructing government department, administrators and their collaborating lawyers will intervene. Government ministers then have their say. In Parliament, lobbyists exert pressure. Opposition members gain concessions, according to the magnitude of their political clout. The result may be a hotch-potch. The drafter's original concept can be bent out of shape. The extent of this distortion depends on a number of considerations, including the political content of the measure, the degree of government control, and the force of the drafter's own resolution. He can do much if determined to fight for the integrity of his contribution to the statute book; little if uninterested.

It is not widely understood that doubtful passages in statute law often owe their uncertainty to drafting errors. Books on statutory interpretation devote little space to this. Yet the truth is that if the meaning of a legislative text is objectively obscure this is due either to one of the factors discussed in the four preceding chapters or to inadequate drafting. Here let it be made clear once and for all that in referring to drafting error we do not necessarily impute blame to the drafter himself. Often he is helpless, overcome by forces which are, or seem to be, of greater strength. By drafting error we refer to all defects in the text which need not have been there.

Drafting errors are of many types. In this chapter I attempt to describe them, one by one. For convenience, the discussion is in terms of *Acts*, though it applies equally to statutory instruments. As the exemplar of the legislative unit, we refer to a *section* (meaning one not broken into subsections; in other words a single proposition). Again, what is said about sections applies equally to subsections, or paragraphs in a Schedule, or any other legislative units. We are concerned with drafting errors that cause doubt as to meaning or application, and we aim to relate varieties of doubt to types of error. We begin with errors confined to the section itself. Later we discuss errors that involve another part of the Act. Finally we deal with errors related to other Acts.

Errors confined to the section itself

We consider first errors that make the text defective or garbled, including printing errors and punctuation mistakes. Next we deal with defects in meaning, including syntactic ambiguity. Logical defects follow, and then cases where the literal meaning fails to carry out the intention. Next we examine two common instances where the drafter's intention itself is at fault, and his words go narrower or wider than the mischief or object. Following this we look at the problem of the incomplete text, where the drafter has failed to say enough. Finally we consider cases where the project is misconceived through some mistake of fact, or the drafter mounts a faulty hypothesis. (See further the section on *disorganised composition* at pp 312–314 below.)

Garbled texts

Not infrequently, errors creep into the texts even of modern Acts. We saw in the previous chapter how there is doubt about the presence of the word 'not' in the Justices of the Peace Act 1361. In s 2 of the Justices Protection Act 1848 there is doubt about whether the words 'or order' have been omitted. The section gives certain rights where 'any conviction or order' is based on insufficient jurisdiction. The proviso states that 'no action shall be brought for anything done under such conviction or order until after such conviction shall have been quashed'. It seems obvious that 'or order' has been accidentally omitted after 'such conviction'. This view is strengthened by a later reference to a time 'after such conviction or order shall have been so quashed as aforesaid'. Yet in *O'Connor* v *Isaacs* [1956] 2 QB 288, 328 it was held that it could not be assumed the missing words were omitted in error, nor could they be implied.

A well-known example of a garbled text is s 8 of the Prescription Act 1832, where 'convenient' has crept in instead of 'easement' in the opening passage referring to 'any land or water upon, over or from which any such way or other convenient watercourse or use of water shall have been or shall be enjoyed'. In *Laird* v *Briggs* (1881) 19 Ch D 22, 23, Jessel MR thought 'convenient' could be ignored as an absurdity.

Another familiar example occurs in s 6 of Lord Tenterden's Act, which is still in force (the Act is now called the Statute of Frauds Amendment Act 1828). The section requires production of a signed memorandum before an action can be brought 'to charge any person upon or by reason of any representation or assurance made or given concerning or relating to the character . . . of any other person, to the intent or purpose that such other person may obtain credit, money or goods *upon*'. In *Lyde* v *Barnard* (1836) 1 M & W 101 the judges disagreed as to whether the italicised word should be rejected as nonsensical or the words 'such representation or assurance' should be implied as following it.

In *Green* v *Wood* [1845] 7 QB 178, 185, it was suggested that 'or execution issued' in s 2 of the Warrants of Attorney Act 1822 should be read as 'and execution levied' but the court declined to do this, preferring to say that the words had no meaning at all. On the other hand it was held in *R* v *Oakes* [1959] 2 QB 350 that 'and' should be read as 'or' in a passage making it an offence where a person 'aids or abets *and* does any act preparatory to the commission' of another specified offence. Lord Parker CJ said that the passage as it stood was 'unintelligible'. In *Jubb* v *Hull Dock Co* (1846) 9 QB 443, 455 the court found it necessary, in order to make sense of a section, to read in the words 'to the owner or party interested' between 'the sum of money to be paid' and 'for the injury done to the lands of any such party'.

A similar omission occurred in s 33 of the Fines and Recoveries Act 1833, which provided that if the protector of a settlement should be convicted of felony or an infant, the Court of Chancery should be the protector 'in lieu of the infant'. In *Re Wainwright* (1843) 1 Ph 258 the court supplied the omission by reading in a reference to the convict also.

A section may be garbled by punctuation errors. It is well-known that Sir Roger Casement was said to have been hanged by the last comma in the passage from the Treason Act 1351 quoted on pp 252–253 (*R* v *Casement* [1917] 1 KB 98). A comma was omitted after 'justice' in s 10 of the Fugitive Offenders Act 1881. This authorised extradition to be refused if it would be unjust 'by reason of the trivial nature of the case, or by reason of the application for the return of a fugitive not being made in good faith in the interests of justice or otherwise'. By inserting the missing comma before 'or otherwise', the court in *R* v *Governor of Brixton Prison, ex parte Naranjansingh* [1962] 1 QB 211 greatly widened the stated grounds for refusal of extradition.

Other misplaced punctuation marks may cause difficulty. In a Canadian case the court was faced by an errant full stop which rendered the passage meaningless. They accordingly read '. . . judicial district in this Province. The statement of claim may issue . . .' as if it said '. . . judicial district. In this Province the statement of claim may issue . . .' (cited Driedger 1974, p 112).

By garbling of the text we refer to mistakes which have crept in by some form of crude mishap, often a printer's error. They are not something the drafter can ever have intended. We pass now to cases where the drafter himself has gone wrong, and used a form of words inapt to convey his meaning.

Defects in meaning

Inefficient construction of the sentence is a prime cause of doubt. In particular, failure to make clear which words a modifier modifies and which it does not gives rise to ambiguous modification or syntactic ambiguity. Thornton gives the following examples, among others, in his book *Legislative Drafting*:

a public hospital or school (is the school 'public'?)
a registered dentist or medical practitioner (is the medical practitioner 'registered'?)
a teacher or student of mathematics (is mathematics the teacher's subject too?)
an owner of gold bullion in New Zealand (does 'in New Zealand' qualify 'owner' or 'bullion'?)

A famous syntactic ambiguity related to the words 'if need be' in the statute 4 Edw 3 c 14. By applying them to the whole sentence, instead of to the last part only, medieval kings constantly disregarded the law requiring annual Parliaments to be held (see Erskine May 1976, p 57). For an alleged syntactic ambiguity in s 49(4)(*b*) of the Race Relations Act 1976 see *R* v *Racial Equality Commission, ex parte Hillingdon London Borough Council* [1981] 3 WLR 520, 532; 126 Sol J 167. A remarkable example of *two* syntactic ambiguities in one phrase is to be found in rule 8(6) of the Industrial Tribunals (Labour Relations) Regulations 1974. This gives a tribunal chairman power to correct 'clerical mistakes or errors arising from accidental slip or omission'. If (which is denied) there is any difference between a 'mistake' and an 'error', does this require an error to be 'clerical'? Clearly an omission may be made otherwise than by accident (as where it is deliberate). Can the chairman correct it?

It is surprising that, despite the publicity given to the vice of syntactic ambiguity, drafters still fall into it so often. Section 20(1) of the Sexual Offences Act 1956 contains an elementary example. Replacing the provisions relating to abduction in s 55 of the Offences against the Person Act 1861 (which used the term 'unlawfully'), s 20(1) speaks of abduction 'without lawful authority or excuse'. Does the latter mean any excuse or only a 'lawful excuse'? It took the Court of Appeal decision in *R* v *Tegerdine* [1983] Crim LR 163 to give us the answer. It means a lawful excuse only. Even then, as Professor Smith remarks (*ibid*), the meaning remains obscure. What would amount to a lawful excuse that would not also be a lawful authority? No one has any idea.

Thornton quotes a remarkable example of faulty relation of a pronoun to its antecedent: 'And when they arose early in the morning, behold, they were all dead corpses' (2 Kings 19, 35). As Thornton says, 'Ambiguity caused by faulty reference is almost always no more than the result of carelessness' (Thornton 1987, p 30). Twining and Miers say the same: 'Syntactic ambiguity is almost always a defect that can and should be avoided at the formulatory/drafting stage' Twining and Miers 1982, p 212.

Another instance, frequently found, is misuse of the word 'any'. Section 50 of the Town Police Clauses Act 1847 gives power to revoke the licence of a hackney carriage proprietor or driver upon conviction for the second time for *any* offence under that Act or other specified legislation. This could either mean that the second conviction must be for the *same offence* as the first, or that it need merely be for an offence of the same class. In *Bowers* v *Gloucester Corporation* [1963] 1 QB 881 the latter interpretation was preferred. On a similar point under different legislation, the court came to the opposite conclusion in *R* v *South Shields Licensing Justices* [1911] 2 KB 1.

Such defects in meaning are due to sloppy construction, where the drafter does not stop to consider whether he has been deluded by a spurious appearance of sense. Section 65 of the County Court Act 1888 gave power to send certain cases for trial in the court in which the action might have been commenced 'or in any court convenient thereto'. In *Burkill* v *Thomas* [1892] 1 QB 99 it was held that the drafter had put down a phrase which may have seemed sense to him at first sight but was in fact meaningless. One court cannot be 'convenient' to another.

Sometimes sloppy construction leads to downright contradiction within the section. Section 2(2) of the Married Women (Maintenance) Act 1949 gave the court power to extend certain child maintenance orders which would otherwise expire when the child reached 16. In logic you cannot 'extend' an order which has already expired, so in *Norman* v *Norman* [1950] 1 All ER 1082 the court were prepared to reject an application initiated after the child had reached this age. It was then pointed out that the section gave power to extend if it appeared that the child '*is or* will be engaged' in a training course after attaining 16. The italicised words could only apply where the child was already 16 at the date of the application (in other words when the order had already expired). Faced with this contradiction, the court held that Parliament must have intended that 'continuation' of the order could be granted after an interval had elapsed since its expiry.

The technique of overlap Where an Act states a proposition in tautologous phrases there may be interpretation difficulties if the nature of the drafting process is not understood. With modern precision drafting the tautology is likely to be partial rather than complete. The purpose is to *build up* an enactment by overlapping expressions, each contributing its share to a rounded statement. One expression used alone may be doubtful, but with two or more used in conjunction the doubts as it were cancel each other out. A simple example is provided by the Motor Car Act 1903. This, the first of the Acts regulating the driving of motor vehicles, made it an offence to drive a car 'recklessly or negligently'. Here the drafter took two imprecise terms with overlapping meanings and put them together. The overlap meant that at the centre the imprecision disappeared. There could be no argument that a piece of driving was 'reckless' rather than 'negligent' (or vice versa) because the same consequences followed either way. This advantage was lost when in a later more complex enactment, the Road Traffic Act 1930, s 11(1), the concept of recklessness was used on its own (see Bennion 1981(5)).

Humpty-Dumptyism Another example of defect in meaning concerns the case where the drafter decides to flout an established definition. Since he is composing what is to be overriding law, he possesses a power denied to other authors. Occasionally this fact goes to his head. He employs a word with one meaning to denote something quite different. This may be called Humpty-Dumptyism, after the Lewis Carroll character who boasted: 'When *I* use a word, it means just what I choose it to mean—neither more nor less' (*Alice Through the Looking Glass*, chapter 6).

What is the difference between nullity and dissolution? Most people would say that a null thing is void from the outset, while a dissolved thing exists until its dissolution. That established view was departed from in the drafting of the Nullity of Marriage Act 1971 (re-enacted in the Matrimonial Causes Act 1973, ss 11-16). Section 5 of the 1971 Act (now s 16 of the 1973 Act) provides that a decree in respect of a voidable marriage 'shall operate to *annul* the marriage only as respects any time after the decree has been made absolute and the marriage shall, notwithstanding the decree, be treated as if it had existed up to that time'. Thus was the distinction between nullity and dissolution abolished at a stroke. Humpty-Dumptyism asserted itself.

In *Re Roberts decd* [1978] 1 WLR 653 the Court of Appeal held that this change in the law might very possibly give rise to anomalies, but that could not justify interpreting the statutory language otherwise than in accordance with its plain terms. One anomaly was that a will could now be automatically revoked by a 'marriage' of the testator to which he was mentally incapable of consenting. Buckley LJ said that whether that effect had been appreciated by Parliament was doubtful, but it was the inescapable effect of the legislation. This illustrates the danger of departing from established meaning. Humpty-Dumptyism by drafters is to be deprecated.

Having considered the garbled text, and the text defective in conveying the drafter's meaning, we now turn to the case where the drafter's proposition is logically deficient.

Logical flaws

Doubt is inevitably raised by a logical failure in the drafting of the section. An example is the leaving of a lacuna in a recital of alternatives. This breaks one of the logical rules of division, namely that the constituent species must together exhaust the genus. The division must not leave gaps, or 'make a leap' (*divisio non facit saltum*).

In *R v Secretary of State for the Home Department, ex parte Zamir* [1979] QB 688 the Divisional Court had to consider an immigration rule which provides that a passenger holding a current entry clearance duly issued to him is not to be refused leave to enter unless the Immigration Officer is satisfied that:

(*a*) false representations were employed or material facts were concealed . . . for the purpose of obtaining the clearance, or
(*b*) a change of circumstances since it was issued has removed the basis of the holder's claim to admission.

One circumstance which may remove the basis of the holder's claim to admission is his marriage, as occurred in this case. He married six weeks after the issue of the clearance, and the Court had no difficulty in applying the rule. But suppose he had married six weeks *before* the issue of the clearance, but after submitting an application for the clearance stating (correctly at the time) that he was unmarried. This might easily have happened, since nearly three years elapsed between the making of the application and the issue of the clearance.

Now the error made by the drafter of the rule set out above becomes obvious. Paragraph (*a*) relates to what was said or omitted in the application. Paragraph (*b*) relates to what happens after the application is granted. There is a lacuna as to the period between the making and granting of the application. Instead of 'since it was issued' in paragraph (*b*) the drafter ought to have written 'since it was applied for'.

Self-defeating text

Sometimes it is clear what the intention is, and equally clear that it has misfired. In 1965 JD Davies pointed out in the *Law Quarterly Review* that the drafter of the Perpetuities and Accumulations Act 1964 (who was myself) had fallen into an elementary error over the repeal of s 163 of the Law of Property Act 1925 (81 LQR 346). Section 4 of the 1964 Act replaced s 163 by improved provisions, expressed in terms of what the position would be 'apart from this section'. This would have worked perfectly but for the fact that the consequential repeal of s 163 was placed in s 4 itself (as seemed natural to the drafter). Apart from s 4 therefore, s 163 would remain operative and this put the hypothesis wrong. The guilty drafter managed to engineer a correction later by the insertion of a provision in another Act he was drafting (for fuller details see Bennion 1976(2)).

Another type of misfiring of intention is the erroneous reference to a related enactment. Section 66(2)(b) of the War Damage Act 1943 was intended to authorise capital to be raised under s 30 of the Universities and College Estates Act 1925 for defraying war damage contributions. Instead of referring to s 30 however, it referred to s 31. This also deals with raising money on mortgage. The mistake passed unnoticed. It misled the drafter of an Act passed nearly 20 years later into giving a similarly erroneous reference (see Town and Country Planning Act 1962, s 206(1)). Both errors were finally corrected by the Universities and College Estates Act 1964, s 4(1) and Sched 3.

A parallel case arose in *R* v *Wilcock* (1845) 7 QB 317, which concerned a reference to an Act described as having been passed in 13 Geo 3. Lord Denman CJ said:

A mistake has been committed by the Legislature; but, having regard to the subject matter, and looking to the mere contents of the Act itself, we cannot doubt that the intention was to repeal 17 Geo 3, and that the incorrect year must be rejected (p 338).

A similar error occurred in s 42 of the Stannaries Act 1869, which referred to 6 & 7 Vict c 106 instead of 6 & 7 Will IV c 106.

The mistakes we have so far dealt with can be described as slips, which do not go to the root of the legislative intention. Now we venture into deeper waters.

Error of law

The drafter is not likely to produce a satisfactory text if he is mistaken about the law he is attempting to alter. Such mistakes are rendered more frequent by the chaotic state of our statute book. A famous example is *IRC* v *Ayrshire Employers' Mutual Insurance Association. Ltd* [1946] 1 All ER 637. The intention of s 31 of the Finance Act 1933 was to subject mutual insurance companies to income tax on the surplus arising from transactions with contributors who were their members. The drafter attempted to achieve this by saying that for tax purposes such a surplus was to be included in the company's profits or gains as if it arose from transactions with non-members. He failed to realise that in law the surplus was immune from tax for a different reason. Under the terms of the contracts with the contributors (which the Act did not deem to be altered) the surplus belonged not to the company but to the contributors. The House of Lords declined to alter the statutory language so as to remedy this error. As Lord Buckmaster had said in an earlier case, the subject ought not to be made liable to tax 'by an elaborate process of hair-splitting arguments' (*Ormond Investment Co* v *Betts* [1928] AC 143, 151).

Lord Diplock criticised the *Ayrshire* decision by saying that if the courts can identify the target of legislation 'their proper function is to see that it is hit; not merely to record that it has been missed' (cited Cross 1976, p 93). The problem in such cases is that it is far from obvious what form the legislation would have taken if the drafter had not misunderstood the existing law. Various courses would have been open, some involving a greater incidence of tax in certain cases than others. Courts may legislate, but they certainly cannot tax.

A case that went the opposite way is *Salmon* v *Duncombe* (1886) 11 App Cas 627. The Judicial Committee of the Privy Council held that the drafter of a Natal Ordinance had clearly mistaken the relevant law. The preamble recited that it was expedient to exempt British-born settlers from the local law relating to testamentary dispositions of real and personal property. Section 1 said any such settler could exercise the rights given by English law 'as if [he] resided in England'. Under private international law, real property passes according to the *lex situs* and personal property according to the law of the domicil. In neither case is the place of residence material.

It was held that s 1 should be construed as if it had been worded on a correct understanding of the relevant law, in other words as if the hypothesis had not related to residence in England but to the location there of the real property devised and (in relation to personal property) the domicil there of the testator. The Judicial Committee said it would be 'a very serious matter to hold that when the main object of a statute is clear, it shall be reduced to a nullity by the draftsman's . . . ignorance of law' (*ibid*, p 634).

The drafter of an important constitutional statute, the Parliament Act 1911, made a minor error of constitutional law. In ss 1(1) and 2(1) he speaks of a Bill passed under the procedure laid down by the Act as becoming law 'on the Royal Assent being signified'. Yet Bills become law not on the date when assent is signified but on the date (which could be later) when it is communicated to both Houses of Parliament (see Bennion 1981(11), p 137).

Drafters have occasionally perpetrated errors of law by not studying with sufficient care an Act they were engaged in amending. Thus the drafter of the Nuisances Removal Act 1860 'must have forgotten that in the [Nuisances Removal Act 1855] there was power given not only to the local authority but to an inhabitant to initiate proceedings' (*Cocker* v *Cardwell* (1869) LR 5 QB 15, 17 *per* Cockburn CJ, who remarked that this was 'one of the most remarkable specimens of legislative incuria of the many that are daily brought before us').

We now go on to consider cases where, through drafting error, either the section goes narrower or wider than the object or the text is incomplete.

Narrower than the object

It is common to refer to the problem or deficiency intended to be remedied by the section as 'the mischief' (see the discussion, on pp 159–163, of the rule in *Heydon's Case*). The *object* of the section is to remedy this mischief. If it does not go wide enough there is a *casus omissus*. Usually the object is not stated or described, but manifests itself by implication from the text. This means that where there are cases that the section does not cover, but apparently ought to cover, doubt arises.

The 'a fortiori' case

Sometimes a case not covered by the words of the section has a claim stronger even than the cases that are covered. The interpreter feels surprise. The doubt raised by the wording is acute.

The statute 22 & 23 Car 2 c 25 restricted possession of guns for taking game to 'the son and heir apparent of an esquire, or other person of higher degree'. This is a good example of ambiguous modification. Every person (with certain exceptions) is prohibited from having guns for taking game. It is clear that one exception is the son and heir apparent of an esquire. The other exceptions may be either A or B:

    A Any person of higher degree than the son and heir apparent
      of an esquire

or

    B the son and heir apparent of any person, where that person
      is of higher degree than an esquire.

Since the test clearly turns on social rank, it seems obvious that A is to be preferred (though both A and B are defective in not covering persons of *equal* degree to the rank specified). Yet the court in *Jones* v *Smart* (1785) 1 TR 44 preferred B, even though this had the absurd result of favouring a son and heir at the expense of his father.

The court was equally reluctant to remedy a defect in *A-G* v *Sillem* (1864) 2 H & C 431. Section 7 of the Foreign Enlistment Act 1819 made it an offence to 'equip, furnish, fit out or arm' a ship for the warlike service of a foreign prince. Obviously it was an *a fortiori* case if a person actually went to the length of building a new ship for this purpose, yet the section did not mention building. Pollock CB elected to treat the omission as deliberate, though no reason for it was suggested. If providing arms to warring foreign states is regarded by Parliament as a mischief, then greater acts are more in need of remedying than lesser ones. It was left to Parliament itself to achieve this in the replacing s 8 of the Foreign Enlistment Act 1870, where a prohibition of building leads the way.

In *Adler* v *George* [1964] 2 QB 7 the court considered an appeal against conviction under a section prohibiting obstruction 'in the vicinity of' any prohibited place (Official Secrets Act 1920, s 3). Obviously obstruction *within* a prohibited place is more serious than obstruction in its vicinity. Lord Parker CJ robustly held that 'in or' must be treated as inserted before 'in the vicinity of'. The conviction was upheld accordingly.

The 'in pari materia' case

While the *a fortiori* case is relatively rare, there are many instances where a section does not cover cases which seem to be just as qualified for inclusion as those it does cover. Here are a few examples.

In *Whiteley* v *Chappell* (1868–9) 4 LRQB 147 a statute aimed to prevent electoral malpractice made it an offence to personate 'any person entitled to vote'. The accused was charged with personating X, whose name was still on the register although he was dead. The court found that no offence had been committed. The personation was not of a person entitled to vote because a deceased person is not entitled to vote. He does not exist, and can have no rights.

R v *Dyott* (1882) 9 QBD 47 concerned a section which said that a local church rate would not be valid unless notice of it was affixed on or near the door of the church or chapel. Although a rate could otherwise have been made for Hopwas Hays, an extra-parochial place, it possessed neither church nor chapel. The court held that this invalidated the rate.

In *R* v *Symington* (1895) 4 BCR 323 a Canadian court considered an Act exempting 'any resident farmer' from liability for killing deer in his cultivated fields. The court held that although there was no mention of a resident farmer's *agent*, he was to be treated as included in the exemption.

The court in *Christopherson* v *Lotinga* (1864) 33 LJCP 121 refused a corporation leave to file an affidavit under wording empowering a judge to order discovery of a document upon the application of either party to a cause 'upon an affidavit by such party'. Although the corporation was indeed a party to the cause, it was of course incapable of swearing an oath.

Section 2(1) of the Inheritance (Family Provision) Act 1938 provided that an order under the Act should not be made 'save on an application made within six months from the date on which representation in regard to the testator's estate for general purposes is first taken out'. This overlooked the possibility of a hidden will being found some time after issue of a grant of administration as on intestacy. Such a contingency occurred in the case of *Re Bidie* [1949] Ch 121, where the court's rejection of jurisdiction to make a late order was reversed on appeal.

Any person over the age of ten is capable in law of committing murder or manslaughter, and not infrequently children do this. Yet s 3 of the Homicide Act 1957, in laying down the test of provocation, speaks of the effect the conduct in question would have on a reasonable *man*. In *Director of Public Prosecutions* v *Camplin* [1978] AC 705, the House of Lords held that where a boy accused of murder raised the defence of provocation his age and other characteristics should be taken into account.

Wider than the object

While sometimes the drafter goes narrower than the object, at other times he may raise doubt by going wider. Where the Act is penal, or has other adverse effects on those subject to it, this gives rise to unjustified hardship or inconvenience. Here are some examples:

Section 39(3) of the Powers of Criminal Courts Act 1973 deals with criminal bankruptcy orders. Where an order is made in respect of more than one offence, it requires the judge to apportion the sum in question accordingly. The purpose is to quantify what is owed to each creditor. It follows that it is not necessary to carry out an apportionment when the same person is the creditor under every debt subject to the order. Yet the Act still requires it to be done. Lord Widgery CJ described this as 'purely an exercise of futility' (*R* v *Saville* [1981] QB 12, 17).

The Redundancy Payments Act 1965 was passed so as to compel employers to pay compensation to employees made redundant. It was held in *Lee* v *Nottinghamshire County Council* (1980) *The Times*, 28 April, that since the Act was in broad terms it covered the case of a teacher who took a short-term engagement knowing perfectly well that through a fall in the birth-rate his sector of employment was rapidly diminishing and there was no chance of his engagement being extended.

The Companies Act 1867 said that a prospectus 'shall specify the date and the names of the parties to *any contract* entered into by the Company or the promotors . . . before the issue of such prospectus' (emphasis added). In terms this would cover any contract made by the promotors at any time in their lives. In *Twycross* v *Grant* (1877) 46 LJCP 636 the Court of Appeal disagreed on just where the obviously necessary line of demarcation should be drawn.

Section 161 of the Income Tax Act 1952 aimed to tax benefits in kind received by company directors. It treated as a director's own taxable income any expense incurred by the company 'in or in connection with the provision of living or other accommodation or of other benefits or facilities of whatsoever nature'. There was a saving for expense incurred by the company in the 'acquisition or production' of an asset which remained its own property. To prevent hardship from the width of the main provision, the House of Lords strained these saving words to include *repairs* of a kind normally executed by a landlord (*Luke* v *Commissioners of Inland Revenue* [1963] AC 557).

Wider and narrower

A legislative instrument often has more than one object. This is true even of a single section. It is possible for a section to go wider than one of the objects and at the same time go narrower than another. The main object of the Leasehold Reform Act 1967 was to enable lessees under long leases at a ground rent to purchase their freeholds. It was desired however to except family arrangements under which a lease can be brought to an end at the death of the tenant. That was the 'object' of the proviso to s 3(1), which excepts 'a tenancy granted so as to become terminable by notice after a death or marriage'. The wording goes wider than this object however, since it is not limited to a death or marriage in the family in question.

The wording was found to provide a major loophole by which lessors granting new leases could deny the lessee a right to enfranchisement which Parliament intended to give him. All that was necessary was to insert a provision in any ordinary lease whereby the lessee had a right to determine the lease on say the death of the last survivor of the descendants of King George V alive when the lease was granted.

The lessee would never exercise the right, since it would not be in his interest to do so. No one else could exercise it against him, since it was conferred only on him (and his heirs and assigns of course). So by going wider than its own limited object, the proviso to s 3 produced the result that the Act as a whole went narrower than its principal object.

It is obvious that whenever a proviso or exception goes wider than its object this will result in the provision to which it is attached going narrower than its object, because too much will be excluded from it. *Patterson* v *Redpath Brothers Ltd* [1979] 1 WLR 553 concerned reg 9(1) of the Motor Vehicles (Construction and Use) Regulations 1973. This stated that the overall length of an articulated vehicle must not exceed 15 metres. A proviso excepted vehicles constructed for the conveyance of indivisible loads of exceptional length. This was obviously to deal with the well-known case where a large boiler or other such item has to be transported from where it was manufactured to the place of use.

In *Patterson* the respondents were conveying a purpose-built container for livestock. This fell within the literal meaning of the definition of an indivisible load, but the court held it was not excepted by the proviso. It would be simple to evade the length restriction by constructing special containers which were 'indivisible'. That was not what the proviso was designed for, and would reduce the effectiveness of the restriction.

Incomplete text

Akin to going narrower than the object, is failing to say enough to deal with the case legislated about. This may sometimes be viewed as a misuse of the techniques described in chapters 15 and 16, namely ellipsis and the broad term. Yet the appropriateness of their use must largely be a matter of opinion, and opinions may legitimately differ.

One of the commonest drafting errors is the missed consequential. It is a principle of good drafting that the law should not be changed in a way which leaves the effect of the change on any existing rule uncertain. NA Bastin has drawn attention to a remarkable missed consequential in the Partnership Act 1890 ((1978) 128 NLJ 1021). The Act is usually regarded as a model of drafting, but s 3 contains a lacuna which should surely have been avoided. The section deals with the case where money is lent to the owner of a business under a contract whereby the lender is entitled to a rate of interest varying with the profits. If the owner becomes insolvent the section provides that the lender 'shall not be entitled to recover anything in respect of the share of profits contracted for, until the claims of the other creditors . . . have been satisfied'.

But suppose the lender has taken security—for example a mortgage on land? If he forecloses to recoup his share of the profits, does this conflict with s 3? The point has given considerable trouble in practice, and the answer the courts have attempted to give is far from clear. To state the effect of s 3 on the general law of mortgages and security was a duty which surely should have been obvious to the drafter. In parallel circumstances, the Consumer Credit Act 1974 makes it clear that the Act is not to be evaded by the use of security, and s 113 spells out exactly what this means.

Bacon's remark that to choose time is to save time might have been directed to drafters who deal with matters where the time of an event is relevant, yet fail to pinpoint its significance. They do not choose which is to be the significant time, and so waste the time of unfortunates obliged to grope for their presumed but probably non-existent intention.

Jackson v *Hall* [1980] AC 854 provides an example of this, based on the Agriculture (Miscellaneous Provisions) Act 1976. The Act states that on the death of an agricultural tenant any eligible person may within the relevant period apply for a direction by a tribunal entitling him to a tenancy of the holding. The term 'eligible person' is defined by s 18(2) as a survivor of the deceased in whose case certain conditions 'are satisfied', but the *time* when they must be satisfied is not stated. It could be the time of death, or the time of the application, or the time of the hearing by the tribunal. Or it could be all three. By four to one, reversing the Court of Appeal, the House of Lords held that it was all three. If the drafter had decided on this construction, and stated it, he would not merely have saved people's time. Lord Dilhorne said 'it is to be regretted that this lengthy *and no doubt expensive* litigation has been brought about by the inadequacy of the drafting of this Act' (p 885).

Time also caused problems in *Grant* v *Allen* [1981] QB 486. Here the question was whether, in conferring power on county court judges to settle the terms of agreements relating to the use of a site for a mobile home, the Mobile Homes Act 1975 enabled agreements to be made retrospective. Brandon LJ commented that 'the Act is not as clear about this as it might be' (p 495).

Such defects are often caused by failure to foresee what should be obvious. In *Grunwick Processing Laboratories Ltd* v *Advisory, Conciliation and Arbitration Service* [1978] AC 655, the report on the Grunwick dispute by the Advisory, Conciliation and Arbitration Service (ACAS) was declared void by the House of Lords because ACAS had not complied with its statutory duty to 'consult all parties who it considers will be affected' and 'ascertain the opinion of workers to whom the issue relates by any means it thinks fit' (Employment Protection Act 1975, ss 12(1) and 14(1)). How can you consult people who refuse to be consulted? It might have been foreseen by the framers of the Act, knowing the heated atmosphere often engendered by labour disputes, that an employer would, like Mr Ward, refuse to supply lists of his workers and that workers would, like those who braved the Grunwick picket lines, refuse to be interviewed. It might have been foreseen, and the Act might have said what then was to happen—thus saving the expense, trouble and delay of appeals up to the House of Lords. In fact it was not foreseen, or if it was the framers of the Act preferred to remain silent as to the intended consequences.

Drafters seem to have a blind spot for the fact that people often own or occupy land or buildings jointly rather than singly. In 1980 the House of Lords was concerned with two examples of this. *Tilling* v *Whiteman* [1980] AC 1 involved a provision in the Rent Act 1968. Case 10 of Pt II of Sched 3 gives the court jurisdiction to make a possession order where a person who occupies a dwelling-house as his residence lets it on a regulated tenancy and later wishes to live in it again. The Act is silent about the position where joint occupiers let, though it is obvious that in such a case one or more (but not all) of them may desire to reoccupy. That in fact happened in *Tilling* v *Whiteman*, and much judicial disarray ensued. In the end the House of Lords, by four to one, reversed the Court of Appeal and decided that one of two joint owners could obtain a possession order—even though the other did not wish to reoccupy.

In *Jackson* v *Hall* [1980] AC 854 the question concerned the transmission of an agricultural tenancy on the death of the holder. A survivor of the deceased was eligible if he satisfied certain statutory conditions, including not being 'the occupier' of any other commercial unit of agricultural land. The Act says nothing about the possibility, which arose in this case, of an applicant being one of two joint occupiers of another unit (the other occupier being ineligible, and therefore not applying, for a tenancy of the first unit).

Again the House of Lords reversed the Court of Appeal by four to one, and ruled that being such a joint occupier disqualified the claimant. Lord Dilhorne complained that the lengthy and expensive litigation had been brought about by inadequate drafting of the Act (the Agriculture (Miscellaneous Provisions) Act 1976).

In each of these cases the drafter no doubt relied on the Interpretation Act, which since Lord Brougham's Act of 1850 has provided that unless the contrary intention appears 'words in the singular include the plural' (see now Interpretation Act 1978, s 6(c)). But this simple formula is manifestly inadequate to deal with the complexities that may arise in real life. The cases cited each concerned the problem of how a condition to be satisfied in relation to 'the occupier' is to be taken to operate where there are two joint occupiers and only one of them satisfies the condition. Would it be an answer for the Interpretation Act to be amended so that it spelt out the detailed consequences of its simple provision? It is doubtful whether it is possible for one formula to comprehend all cases. There is no substitute for care by the drafter. He needs to ask himself if a joint or other plural case may arise, and if so how he intends his provision to apply to it.

This is, incidentally, an example of the difficulties attached to use of the definite article. The simple definite article may be inadequate where the Interpretation Act makes a singular substantive include the plural. In *Jackson* v *Hall* it was not enough to say that a person is qualified to succeed to a tenancy if 'he is not the occupier of a commercial unit'. The drafter needed to go on to add such words as 'or (in the case of a commercial unit occupied jointly) he is not one of the occupiers'. Similarly in *Tilling* v *Whiteman* it was insufficient merely to speak of 'the owner-occupier' desiring to reoccupy. It was necessary to deal with the possibility of joint owner-occupiers and say either that they all had to desire reoccupation or that it was sufficient if one of them did.

We see that, as so often happens, a drafting point masks a point of substance. In each of the cases cited there was a substantial policy difference between the two alternative constructions.

'As usual our parliamentary draftsmen did not display the skill expected of them.' This harsh judgment was passed in an article on the drug laws by WT West (122 SJ 322). It was called forth by the fact that s 1 of the Drugs (Prevention of Misuse) Act 1964 makes it an offence for a person to have a specified substance in his possession but says nothing about the possessor's mental state. In *R* v *Warner* [1969] 2 AC 256 the House of Lords was called upon to decide whether, in the words of Lord Reid, the offence created by s 1 'is an absolute offence in the sense that the belief, intention or state of mind of the accused is immaterial and irrelevant' (p 271). In a later case on the possession of drugs, Lord Reid said of the necessity for *mens rea* in offences by statute: 'In a very large number of cases there is no clear indication either way' (*Parsley* v *Sweet* [1970] AC 132). Continuing his attack, Mr West said that here Lord Reid was 'trying wearily to spell out the message to our parliamentary draftsmen'. Drafters may get the message (they are not stupid), but can do little in isolation.

The mental state required for the commission of crime is one of the most complex areas of law. It was the subject of a Law Commission study in 1978 (*Criminal Law: Report on the Mental Element in Crime* (Law Com No 89)). Annexed to the report was a draft Criminal Liability (Mental Element) Bill. On its appearance Professor Glanville Williams said: 'Here is the long-awaited Report; and we can only surmise from the delays attending it what fearful impediments have been placed in its way by parliamentary counsel and departmental draftsmen' ([1978] Crim LR 588).

Unfortunately the 'fearful impediments' were not removed on publication, and the report is still blocked. The new Interpretation Act would have been a suitable vehicle for implementing it, but innovations were not on offer there.

Those who oppose general formulas in this field do have some justification. Professor Williams criticises the fact that the Law Commission's draft Bill confines itself to intention *as to results*. He mentions *Cotterill* v *Penn* [1936] 1 KB 53 where the question was whether a person who shot a house pigeon without knowing it to be such was guilty of 'wilfully' shooting a house pigeon. The defendant knew it was a pigeon, but believed it to be wild. He was convicted. Professor Williams says that as a matter of common sense the conviction was wrong, and rejoices that under the Law Commission's draft the defendant would not have been convicted 'unless he realised that the bird might be a house pigeon' (*ibid* p 590). But common sense might reject that also.

The truth is that there is no substitute for careful provision by the drafter of the individual measure. If one is trying to protect house pigeons from being shot, one needs to ask oneself precisely what state of mind is to attract guilt. The marksman may not 'realise that the bird might be a house pigeon' if he is unaware of the law protecting house pigeons. The question will be irrelevant to him unless it matters for some other reason (eg because he likes the flavour of cooked house pigeons). Ignorance of the law will not count as an excuse, but clearly it may affect the actual state of mind. The drafter should think out the result he wants to achieve and then express it. There would be few problems about a provision worded: 'It is an offence for a person to shoot a house pigeon knowing or suspecting it to be a house pigeon, or not believing it to be something other than a house pigeon'. This would exclude a case Professor Williams mentions, the man who shoots a house pigeon believing it to be a clay pigeon.

There is a clear order of preference here. The carefully worded individual provision is best because it is tailor-made. The general off-the-peg formula is second best. Worst of all is what we usually get. As the Law Commission report says: '. . . where Parliament does not indicate to what extent an offence requires a certain mental element or negligence, the courts are often placed in a position of great difficulty, resulting in protracted and expensive litigation'.

Mens rea has probably given the courts more trouble than any other aspect of statutory interpretation. Lord Devlin once complained that Parliament had continually shown that it had no intention of troubling itself with the problem. It is a problem by no means confined to Britain. An example came before the Supreme Court of Victoria in *Pallero v Gladman* [1979] VR 197. Under s 85 of the Motor Car Act 1958, a person is guilty of an offence in that state if 'by any false statement' he obtains or attempts to obtain a driving licence. (In passing it may be mentioned that the reference to attempt was probably otiose, since under general criminal law principles it is only necessary to create the substantive offence: related inchoate offences follow automatically.)

What state of mind is required for commission of this offence? The doctrine of *mens rea* calls for knowledge that the statement is false, or recklessness as to its truth. The defendant (an immigrant) here pleaded that although his answer was false (ie incorrect) he misunderstood the question. As an answer to what he *thought* the question was it would have been correct. Lush J dismissed this argument on grounds based on the context of the words in s 85. In other words he held the offence to be one of strict liability.

Often drafters, and those instructing them, simply do not know what intention they mean to require when offences are created. In the past *mens rea* has been imported by words such as 'wilfully' or 'knowingly'. These are archaic in view of judicial development of the topic. A phrase like 'wilfully or recklessly' is slightly better. The opposite, importing strict liability, could be expressed by saying 'whether wilfully or recklessly or not'. It might appear clumsy, but if used consistently would be some improvement on the present position. The phrase 'whether knowingly or not' has been used (see Performers' Protection Act 1963, s 2).

We now turn to the case where the legislative project is misconceived in whole or part.

Project misconceived

If the drafter makes a mistake over the factual situation he is legislating about, the result will be a travesty. The mistake may relate to a single factual situation, or the *type* of situation his provision will encounter. Where an Act legislates about a single factual situation, but gets it basically wrong, the Act is likely to be abortive. A nineteenth century Act made detailed provision about the exploitation of a certain tract of land in Labrador. It was believed that the land was owned by the Labrador Company, and this was the basis on which the Act operated. It later appeared that this may have been mistaken, and that the land was not owned by the Labrador Company at all. (See *Labrador Company* v *The Queen* [1893] AC 104.) Of course the drafter himself is unlikely to have been in any way to blame for this particular error.

More common is the case where the drafter has failed to get into his head the true nature of the factual situations with which the Act will in future have to deal. His wording is therefore inappropriate. Here are some examples.

Section 1(1) of the Race Relations Act 1968 defined racial discrimination by reference to the grounds on which discriminatory treatment is based. It specified the grounds of 'colour, race, or ethnic or national *origins*'. Yet some discrimination of this type is based on the *current* nationality of the victim, whether or not it is his nationality of origin. In *Ealing Borough Council* v *Race Relations Board* [1972] AC 342 the Council gave priority to British subjects when allocating housing. A Polish national resident in Ealing was not placed on the housing list for this reason. The House of Lords accepted that such discrimination was contrary to the object of the Act, but held that it was outside the wording. By misunderstanding the factual basis of the Act the drafter had gone narrower than its object.

Section 74 of the Harbours, Docks and Piers Clauses Act 1847 renders the owner of every vessel liable 'for any damage done by such vessel . . . to the harbour, dock or pier'. But a ship is not capable in itself of 'doing' anything. Only the human beings controlling it can 'do' things, and the Act should have been worded accordingly. This would have saved much litigation, including the famous case of *River Wear Commissioners* v *Adamson* (1877) 2 App Cas 743 (in which strangely this point does not appear to have been raised). See further Holmes 1881, p 29.

Section 186 of the Customs Consolidation Act 1876 subjected a person who fraudulently harboured uncustomed goods to a penalty. It continued: 'and the *offender* may either be detained or proceeded against by summons'. This clearly operates upon a misunderstanding of the factual situation. At the arrest stage, it may not be known by the customs officer whether or not the person under suspicion is actually guilty. In *Barnard* v *Gorman* [1941] AC 378 a seaman arrested on suspicion of offending against s 186 was tried and acquitted. He then sued for damages for assault on the ground that it was thus demonstrated that he did not fall within the description 'the offender'. The House of Lords, reversing the Court of Appeal, found for the defendants. Lord Romer said:

That the ordinary meaning of the word 'offender' is a person who has in fact offended must be conceded, but the context in which a word is found may be, and very often is, strong enough to show that it is intended to bear other than its ordinary meaning and such a context is in my opinion to be found in the present case for the section provides that the offender may be proceeded against by summons, and to give the word 'offender' in this connection its ordinary meaning would be to render the provision nonsensical. It would mean that before issuing the summons the magistrate would have to decide that the offence had in fact been committed.

A similar mistake was made by the drafter of s 6(4) of the Road Traffic Act 1960, which dealt with drunken driving. It empowered a constable to arrest without warrant 'a person committing an offence under this section'. On a claim for damages for assault, the Court of Appeal held in *Wiltshire* v *Barrett* [1966] 1 QB 312 that this must be read as 'a person *apparently* committing an offence under this section'. It is unfortunate that on the consolidation of these provisions in 1972 the opportunity was not taken of correcting the error (see Road Traffic Act 1972, s 5(5)).

The Road Traffic Acts have since their inception been full of mistakes caused by drafters' inability to visualise the likely factual situation and provide properly for it. The breathalyser provisions are a notorious example. Section 8 of the Road Traffic Act 1972 said: 'A constable in uniform may require any person *driving or attempting to drive* a motor vehicle on a road or other public place to provide a specimen of breath . . .'. The natural meaning of 'driving' suggests that the vehicle is in motion, but the mind boggles at the picture of a constable administering a breath test to a driver who is steering a moving car. Equally, as DJ Birch comments, it would undoubtedly seem odd to a layman to say that a person could be 'driving' a car with no ignition key and the steering locked. Yet it was so held in *Burgoyne* v *Phillips* [1983] Crim LR 265 (Birch's comment is at p 266). Since the word 'driving' plainly does not carry its normal meaning here, what exactly does it mean? The courts have spent much time, and litigants much money, in spelling it out. (See further on misconceiving the project, Bennion 1962, p 344.)

Defective deeming

The final type of drafting mistake we consider before going on to examine errors relating to multiple texts can be described as defective deeming, or asifism gone wrong. As we have seen, common-law drafting makes extensive use of hypotheses. A certain situation is to be treated 'as if' it were something else. Or, to be more precise, a certain legal rule (statutory or otherwise) is applied to a novel situation 'as if' it were one to which the rule already applied directly. This has many advantages for the drafter. It saves him spelling out again (usually with modifications) statutory provisions which may be lengthy and complicated. In his constant search for brevity he jumps at it. Yet it contains the dangers which lurk in any form of pretence. W A Wilson goes so far as to say that there is always doubt as to the extent of a statutory hypothesis (Wilson 1974, p 503). If asifism is to work properly it requires the drafter to consider every aspect of the applied provisions and check that (with any modifications he may prescribe) they fit exactly. This task, which may be laborious, is often skipped.

Section 52 of the Licensing Act 1953 provided that for the purposes of the Act the City of London and the administrative county of London should each be deemed separate counties. The drafter overlooked s 37 of his own Act, which provided for costs to be paid 'out of the county fund'. The City of London has no county fund. (See report of the Joint Committee on the Licensing Act 1964, pp 15–17.)

Ex parte Walton (1881) 17 Ch D 746, another example of defective deeming, has already been mentioned (p 233). In that case James LJ stressed that 'when a statute enacts that something shall be deemed to have been done, which in fact and truth is not done, the court is entitled and bound to ascertain for what purposes and between what persons the statutory fiction is to be resorted to' (p 756). The court's intervention is only required where the drafter has erred in his deeming. Courts are inclined to be impatient with this technique anyway. The judicial attitude showed through in the following words of Romer J in *Robert Batchellor and Sons Ltd* v *Batchellor* [1945] Ch 169, 176:

It is, of course, quite permissible to 'deem' a thing to have happened when it is not known whether it happened or not. It is an unusual but not an impossible conception to 'deem' that a thing happened when it is known positively that it did not happen. To deem, however, that a thing happened when not only is it known that it did not happen, but it is positively known that precisely the opposite of it happened, is a conception which to my mind . . . amounts to a complete absurdity.

Unfortunately for his robust common sense, Romer J was reversed on appeal. Perhaps the last word should lie with AP Herbert's Lord Mildew, who said 'there is too much of this damned deeming' (cited Megarry 1955, p 361).

Multi-textual errors: (1) Conflicts within the same instrument

So far in the account given in this we have dealt with drafting errors within a single proposition, taking a section of an Act as an exemplar. Now we move on to consider contradiction or disharmony between different parts of an Act or other instrument. A section may be clear and plain if taken by itself. Yet doubt must inevitably arise if elsewhere in the Act there is found a provision inconsistent with it. The interpreter is then forced to decide between the two. If the contradiction is between two sections (treating as part of a section any Schedule induced by the section) the problem is most serious, since these are the operative provisions of an Act (sometimes misleadingly called the enacting provisions). Less difficult is a conflict between a section and a non-operative provision such as a preamble or heading. We take the former case first.

In *Curtis* v *Stovin* [1899] 22 QBD 513 the court ruled on a contradiction in the County Courts Act 1888. Section 65 allowed a contract claim not exceeding *100 pounds* brought in the High Court to be transferred to any county court 'in which the action might have been commenced'. But under another provision of the Act, only claims not exceeding *50 pounds* could be commenced in the county court. The court resolved the logical contradiction in favour of the reading clearly intended by the legislature. Bowen LJ said: 'I think we must introduce some words to this effect, "*if it had been a county court action*"' (*ibid*, p 518).

A contradiction which has caused difference of opinion among lawyers engaged in the criminal courts is contained in the Criminal Law Act 1977. The story begins with s 1 of the Criminal Damage Act 1971. Subsection (1) creates the offence of destroying or damaging property belonging to another, while subs (2) creates a more serious offence where a person destroys or damages property belonging to himself or another *with intent to endanger life*. The 1971 Act made the latter offence punishable only on indictment, but the former punishable either on indictment or (with consent of the accused) summarily. Then along came the 1977 Act, with its concept of the offence 'triable either way'. Section 16 of that Act made offences under s 1(1) of the 1971 Act triable either way. It left untouched offences under s 1(2), which remained triable solely on indictment. This was in accordance with the original scheme of the 1971 Act, and with common sense. Unfortunately the 1977 Act then went on to contradict itself. Section 23 said that if an offence charged involved a sum not exceeding £200, and was mentioned in Sched 4, 'the court shall proceed as if the offence were triable only summarily'. Schedule 4 includes offences 'under s 1 of the Criminal Damage Act 1971' (excluding arson), and thus in terms includes the serious crime created by s 1(2). For the confusion that resulted see [1979] Crim LR 266 and 607–8; and [1980] Crim LR 68–9. The controversy ended with an acknowledgment from Professor Glanville Williams that the contradiction had led him to state the law erroneously in his *Textbook of Criminal Law* (see [1980] Crim LR 69). It will not have escaped the reader that this is one more example of trouble involving asifism.

Another contradiction in a criminal Act is found in the Metropolitan Police Act 1839. Section 63 gives a general power of arrest for offences against the Act, but applies only where the offender's name and address are unknown and cannot be ascertained. A duplicate power of arrest, *without these words of limitation*, is contained in s 54 in relation only to the offence of obstruction created by that section. In *Gelberg* v *Miller* [1961] 1 WLR 153 the contradiction was resolved by reading the general words of s 63 as if they contained an exception for s 54.

Driedger mentions a contradiction in an Ontario byelaw directed against owners of wandering dogs. It prohibited 'the running at large' of any dog. This appears to contemplate the appearance in any place of a dog not under control. Another provision of the byelaw however said that 'a dog shall be deemed to be running at large when found in a street or other public place and not under the control of any person'. Did this mean that a stray dog *not* in a public place was excluded from the prohibition? The court observed that such a reading would have the result that:

Being pursued on the road, he would, if he were a wise dog, dodge through the fence upon a farm and forthwith cease to be running at large . . . A dog traversing the country would alternatively be, and not be, running at large, as he crossed the road or got through fences.

It was held that the repugnancy between the two provisions should be resolved in favour of the wider one, the narrower being treated as intended only to deal with cases where the stray dog was in a public place (Driedger 1974, p 39).

A case of conflict between a preamble and an operative provision was adjudicated upon in *AG* v *Prince Ernest Augustus of Hanover* [1957] AC 436. The preamble to an Act of Anne stated that with the object that the Electress Sophia:

and the heirs of her body and all persons lineally descended from her may be encouraged to become acquainted with the laws and constitutions of this realm it is just and highly reasonable that they *in your Majesty's lifetime* should be naturalised.

This wording suggests that the naturalising operation of the ensuing words is to be limited to persons born in the lifetime of Queen Anne. A moment's reflection will show however that this is another example of ambiguous modification. The italicised phrase was intended to indicate that the naturalising operation (extending to descendants whenever born) was desirably to be effected while the Queen lived. This was demonstrated by the ensuing words. The naturalised descendants of the Electress 'born or hereafter to be born', without limit of time. The House of Lords confidently held that they should prevail. Lord Normand said (p 467):

The courts are concerned with the practical business of deciding a *lis*, and when the plaintiff puts forward one construction of an enactment and the defendant another, it is the court's business . . . after informing itself of what I have called the legal and factual context including the preamble, to consider in the light of this knowledge whether the enacting words admit of both the rival constructions put forward. If they admit of only one construction, that construction will receive effect even if it is inconsistent with the preamble, but if the enacting words are capable of either of the constructions offered by the parties, the construction which fits the preamble may be preferred.

These words apply to any discrepancy between operative words and other parts of an Act.

Such discrepancies often arise between a definition contained in the interpretation section and an operative provision in which the defined term occurs. Definitions are usually stated to apply only where the context does not otherwise require. Even this caveat may not be enough to avoid doubt, as occurred in *Old Grovebury Manor Farm Ltd* v *W Seymour Plant Sales and Hire Ltd (No 2)* [1979] 1 WLR 1397. The drafter of s 140 of the Law of Property Act 1925 broke the rule that the definite article is properly used only where the substantive to which it is attached is unique. He defined 'lessee' as including persons deriving title under a lessee. Then he said that a right of forfeiture for breach of covenant could not be enforced until the lessor served a notice on 'the lessee'. If the breach is of a convenant against assignment of the lease without the lessor's consent there must be at least two people who fall within the definition: the assignor and the assignee. Which of them is 'the lessee'? The Court of Appeal found little difficulty in answering this question. They held in effect that the phrase 'the lessee' in s 146 is elliptical. Its full meaning is 'the current lessee'.

Where there are conflicts within an instrument, the rule as we have seen is to reconcile them by reference to the instrument read as a whole and its overall policy (see also *Nugent-Head* v *Jacob (Inspector of Taxes)* [1948] AC 321). In the very last resort, where this does not produce the answer, the courts will adopt the rule of thumb that a provision nearer the end of the instrument is taken to prevail over one nearer the beginning. Thus in *A-G* v *Chelsea Waterworks* (1731) Fitzg 195 it was laid down that a proviso should be taken to repeal the purview (ie the words to which it is a proviso) 'as it speaks the last intention of the makers'. (A sounder ground, at least with the modern proviso, would be that the proviso is intended to contradict a part of the purview.) In *R* v *Ramsgate* (1829) 6 B & C 712, 717 Holroyd J said that the disputed words 'must be construed, according to their nature and import, *in the order in which they stand in the Act of Parliament*'. See also p 189 above.

Multi-textual errors: (2) Conflicts between different instruments

If there is inconsistency between two Acts, the later prevails. This rule robs such inconsistencies of much of their difficulty. Nevertheless problems can still arise where the two Acts are by an express provision to be construed as one, or are otherwise *in pari materia*. Then, if it appears that the drafter of the later Act intended not to contradict the earlier Act, but has nevertheless produced an inconsistent provision, the position may be very like that prevailing where there is inconsistency within the same instrument.

The Interpretation Act is to be read as one with every later Act, though it does not apply where the contrary intention is shown. The trouble is that it may be doubtful whether there is a contrary intention on the part of the drafter of the later Act. Drafters are instructed to be constantly aware of the provisions of their Interpretation Act. Lord Thring went so far as to say 'it is the duty of every draftsman to know it by heart' (Thring 1902, p 14).

Another source of conflict is the amending Act. This may alter the wording of the earlier Act in ways which seem contrary to the basic intention of the amending Act. Thus it seemed that the purpose of an Act amending the County Courts Admiralty Jurisdiction Act 1868 was to confer on county courts certain powers corresponding to the jurisdiction of the High Court of Admiralty. One provision however conferred jurisdiction to try claims not exceeding £300 arising out of agreements for the use or hire of any ship. The Admiralty Court possessed no such jurisdiction. (See *Brown & Sons* v *The Russian Ship 'Alina'* (1880) 42 LT 517 and *The Queen* v *The Judge of City of London Court* [1892] 1 QB 273.)

Acts which make textual amendments sometimes leave the amended text in a defective condition. Driedger gives a good example from Canada, concerning an Act dealing with appeals from magistrates' decisions in small debt cases. Before amendment, the Act required an appellant to do the following:

(*a*) serve notice of appeal on the magistrate within *five* days after the date of judgment, and then

(*b*) serve a copy of the notice (on which the magistrate would have meanwhile endorsed the amount of security required) on the clerk of the district court within *ten* days after the date of judgment.

The amending Act changed 'five' to 'twenty' in paragraph (*a*) but left paragraph (*b*) untouched. In *Fleming* v *Luxton* (1968) 63 WWR 522, the judge treated this as a 'draftsman's error' and read 'ten' in paragraph (*b*) as 'thirty' (Driedger 1974, p 51).

Conclusion

In this chapter we have surveyed a considerable number of different types of drafting error, but we have merely scratched the surface. The truth is that it is extremely common for drafters to produce a text which raises doubt unnecessarily.

Lord Reid, who made a considerable contribution to elucidating problems of statutory interpretation, once said: 'Fortunately draftsmen do not often make mistakes but I cannot suppose that every draftsman is entirely free from that ordinary failing' (*Connaught*

Fur Trimmings Ltd v *Cramas Properties Ltd* [1965] 1 WLR 892, 899). Lord Reid used the language of courtesy, as was his wont, but he was far too kind.

Sometimes, as we know in other connections, excessive kindness is harmful. The harm here is that, by treating drafting error as a rarity rather than a commonplace, the courts have inhibited the development of adequate techniques to deal with it.

Part IV

Dynamic and Static Processing of Texts

Chapter Twenty

The Nature of Dynamic
Processing

Dynamic processing is the authoritative resolving of *doubt* as to the meaning and application of a legislative text. In the previous Part we surveyed the need for processing raised by the user's problems of text collation, text comprehension and doubt resolving. The first two are tackled by static processing, to which we turn later in this Part. First, because it is juristically more important, we look at the dynamic process of doubt resolving.

It was pointed out above that there are two aspects to this question. The law on a topic may need to be stated as a whole (and cannot be satisfactorily stated if areas of it are infected by doubt). Or the doubt may arise in connection with the application of an enactment to a particular set of facts. The doubt is unlikely to relate to that set of facts alone; it will probably exist whenever facts of that type occur. Dynamic processing operates on both aspects, which of course interact. But the processor tends to be working with the latter aspect, whether as the administrative official handling an application for the exercise of his discretion, or as the judge hearing a particular case, or otherwise. For convenience we refer to these two aspects of processing as wide and narrow processing respectively.

The doubt-factors

Before examining the nature of dynamic processing, we need to weigh up the doubt-factors explored in the last five chapters. This is necessary because we cannot understand the processor's function unless we understand the basis of the authority possessed by him, and this relates closely to the nature of the doubt-factors. Where the doubt-factors are *intentional* there can be no doubt that the processor has authority to resolve them. Difficulty arises where a doubt-factor is *unintended*. It is a difficulty that lies at the heart of our long-standing problems with statutory interpretation. The intentional doubt-factors were explained in chapters 15 to 17. By use of ellipsis or the broad term, or by politic uncertainty, the legislature openly delegates the function of resolving doubt to the processor. He must therefore proceed to carry out that function, acting within the legal framework governing the exercise of his functions generally.

But what of the case where the legislator did not intend to delegate? As we have seen, this may arise where unforeseen developments have overtaken the text (chapter 18) or where the drafter has erred (chapter 19). Either way the text is defective as an expression of currently operative law. Can Parliament be taken to have given a general delegation covering such defective texts? There is no sign of it. Or does the processor's function, particularly where the processor is a court, necessarily involve tidying-up operations of this kind? Judges have given few indications that they think so, and many that they do not.

Two things stand as obstacles to processing as a cure for defective texts. One is the predictability principle. This states that the statute user is entitled to be able to rely on the letter of the legislative text. The other is the reluctance of modern judges to usurp the legislative function, which in a democracy belongs only to elected representatives assembled in Parliament. These considerations, while of fundamental importance and worthy of the highest respect, are not sufficient to dispose of the matter. Faced with a defective text, both statute user and processor are necessarily obliged to surmount the defects as best they can. The defects put the user on enquiry. Unless they have been already processed, he must seek guidance from what it may be expected future processors will do to resolve the doubts they arouse. Basically, he needs to know whether the processor's approach to the defective text will be literal or remedial.

Back to the duplex approach

In understanding the juristic nature of dynamic processing of defective tests, we need to return to the discussion in chapter 1 of the duplex approach to legislative meaning (pp 14–15). The dichotomy between text-creation and text-validation was there outlined, together with a suggested reconciliation of the conflict between the idea of the infallible legislature and the fact of the fallible drafter.

Into the gap between the clear commands of the ideal legislature and the defective texts of actual law the processor steps. His function is to perfect the texts with due regard to the predictability principle and to democratic propriety. This is a difficult task, requiring to be scientifically approached.

Who are the processors?

Statute law itself appoints the processors; they do not intervene from outside. Even a written constitution is an emanation of statute law; Britain of course does not possess one. The principal processors are the judges. In British constitutional theory judicial power, like executive power, originates with the monarchy: 'All jurisdiction exercised in these kingdoms that are in obedience to our King is derived from the Crown' (Bacon's Abridgment, 'Prerogative' (D)(1)). The judges stand in the place of the sovereign in whose name they administer justice (*John Russell & Co Ltd* v *Cayzer, Irvine & Co Ltd* [1916] 2 AC 298, 302).

Nevertheless it is by statute that modern courts are set up and administered. Little is said directly in the Acts about the nature of the judicial function. The Supreme Court Act 1981, reproducing provisions originating in the Judicature Act of 1873, confers jurisdiction indirectly. The High Court is given the jurisdiction formerly vested in the Court of Queen's Bench, the Court of Common Pleas at Westminster, and so on (s 19(2)(*b*)). The Court of Appeal succeeds to the powers of the Court of Appeal in Chancery and the Court of Exchequer Chamber (s 15(2)(*b*)).

Other statutes conferring jurisdiction are slightly more illuminating. The House of Lords, when hearing an appeal, is required to 'determine what of right, and according to the law and custom of this realm, ought to be done in the subject-matter of such appeal' (Appellate Jurisdiction Act 1876, s 4). County court jurisdiction is conferred item by item. For example, s 16 of the County Courts Act 1984 gives jurisdiction to 'hear and determine' any action for the recovery of money due under any statute where the amount claimed does not exceed a specified sum.

An Act dealing with a particular matter often confers jurisdiction expressly in relation to that matter. For example, Pt IX of the Consumer Credit Act 1974, headed 'Judicial Control', confers detailed functions on county courts as to the settlement of disputes under the Act. Either because of a general provision conferring jurisdiction, or under some specific enactment, a court finds itself with the function of determining a dispute governed by a statutory text. If it considers the meaning doubtful, the court, even if it is only a court of first instance, is not permitted to say 'Non liquet' (it is not clear). Provided the doubt is relevant to the cause before it, so that the cause cannot be determined without resolving the doubt one way or the other, the court cannot dodge resolving it. By his judicial oath or affirmation, the judge has bound himself to 'do right to all manner of people *after the laws and usages of this realm*' (Promissory Oaths Act 1868, s 4). Where a relevant law is doubtful the judge must make up his mind what it is. His *ratio decidendi* has the effect of declaring the law.

Under the doctrine of *stare decisis*, accepted in our system, the law is not declared for that case alone. To stand by things decided is:

to abide by former precedents, *stare decisis*, where the same points come again in litigation, as well to keep the scale of justice even and steady and not liable to waver with every judge's opinion, as also because, the law in that case being solemnly declared and determined, what before was uncertain and perhaps indifferent is now a permanent rule which it is not in the breast of any subsequent judge to alter or vary from according to his private sentiments, he being sworn to determine, not according to his own private judgment, but according to the known laws and customs of the land, not delegated to pronounce a new law, but to maintain and expound the old one, *jus dicere et non jus dare' (Broom's Legal Maxims*, (1st edn, 1845), p 61).

Administrative authorities

Judges are not the only processors of statute law, though they are the ultimate ones. Any public official charged with the function of administering an Act or statutory instrument must resolve relevant doubt as to its meaning. Where by a broad term it confers on him a discretion, the way he uses the discretion may have the effect of setting up detailed rules of law. The official differs from the judge in being 'on the inside'. He is part of the government system that originated the law in question. His function is not judicial and impartial, but administrative. It is his duty to help ensure that the Act achieves its governmental aim.

Professional and academic commentators

Vitally connected with dynamic processing of legislative texts are the experts who write textbooks, learned articles and other commentaries. The busy judge has little time for reflection: it is his main duty to decide the case before him. The official too is distracted by the need to ensure that the administrative machine works efficiently, and that he does not arouse political criticism of his actions.

The commentator, whether a practitioner writing from the depths of his experience or an academic accustomed to handle theoretical considerations, performs as an invaluable auxiliary to the processor. Few modern judges share the opinion of Lord Hanworth MR, who once said that problems of statutory interpretation 'cannot be solved by reliance upon the opinions of writers of text-books, however able, who are yet living' (*Re Ryder and Steadman's Contract* [1927] 2 Ch 62, 74). The current view was expressed by Lord Denning in an article written in 1947. He said that the notion that academic lawyers' works are not of authority, except after the author's death, has long been exploded. He added: 'Indeed, the more recent the work, the more persuasive it is' (63 LQR 516). We have discussed above (p 21) the status of commentaries by the drafter himself.

The contribution made by the commentator to the process of doubt-resolution has several aspects. First, he can present a rounded explanation of the object aimed at by the Act. For this he can draw on materials not permitted to be directly cited in court. Next, the commentator can analyse the nature of the doubt and suggest ways of resolving it. The higher the academic or professional standing of the commentator the more weight will be attached to his observations.

Finally, the commentator can marshal the cases bearing on a disputed point and by doing so demonstrate how far processing has already got. He can convert narrow processing to wide. All this can be of great help to the profession. In the field of criminal law, for example, the *Criminal Law Review* has proved itself invaluable in this way. Indeed, if dynamic processing is defined as the authoritative resolving of doubt it is arguable that the commentator himself qualifies as a processor.

Nevertheless, reserving the term for those charged by law with this duty, we will now examine in more detail the role of the administrative and judicial processor respectively.

Chapter Twenty-One

Dynamic Processing: The Administrative Processor

Modern statute law often leaves it to officials to resolve doubts as to its meaning. It does so despite the citizens' antipathy to this, noted by Sir Courtenay Ilbert: 'Englishmen prefer to be governed (if they must be governed) by fixed rules rather than by official discretion' (Ilbert 1901, p 209).

The most formal way of effecting this delegation is by conferring on the Minister in charge of the appropriate government department power to spell out detail by statutory instrument. We saw above (p 242) how vague is the key word 'supply' as a basis for value added tax. The Finance Act 1972, which imposes the tax, does not leave the matter there however. Section 5 lays down guidelines as to what is and is not to be treated as a supply of goods or services for the purposes of the Act. Even this is not enough. Subsection (7) adds:

Subject to the preceding provisions of this section, the Treasury may by order provide with respect to any description of transaction—

(a) that it is to be treated as a supply of goods and not as a supply of services; or

(b) that it is to be treated as a supply of services and not as a supply of goods; or

(c) that it is to be treated as neither a supply of goods nor a supply of services.

This is an example of what may be called *peripheral drafting*, which is a most useful technique. The reason for the name is that the drafting pays special attention to the periphery, where doubts are particularly likely to arise (see the section headed 'Core and penumbra' on p 239 above). Peripheral doubt may be dealt with by the drafter in either of two ways, one bad and one good. The bad way, which is unfortunately the most common, is to lay down complex provisions over the whole field. The good way is to use peripheral drafting, which confines the drafting complexity to the area where it is needed.

Take for example a concept like theft. Peripheral drafting would say 'It is an offence to steal' and then go on to deal in detail with peripheral cases where the meaning of this might be doubtful (for example where the defendant has a claim of right). The other way, followed by the Theft Acts 1968 and 1978, is to make the definition of theft complex *in every case*. Nine out of ten cases are likely to be straightforward, but to find out the law the statute user has to plough through the complexity every time. Greater use of peripheral drafting would simplify the law. Its main principles could be stated briefly, and separately. One would need to consult the fine print in difficult cases only.

To give a minister power to resolve doubt by regulations is really to usurp the function of the courts, but it is increasingly done as a matter of convenience. It is justified on Chalmers' principle that legislation is cheaper than litigation. Under s 5(7) of the Finance Act 1972, set out above, the Treasury determined that a gratuitous loan of goods by a taxable person in the normal course of business should be treated as neither a supply of goods nor a supply of services (Value Added Tax (Treatment of Transactions) (No 1) Order 1972, SI 1972 No 1170). By this the Treasury set at rest doubts which had arisen among certain traders. Without such machinery, the doubts could have been resolved only by the courts in the course of litigation.

This form of doubt-resolving is mentioned here for completeness. As we have seen, it is not strictly a form of processing, but a type of legislation. Processing of doubts arises through the piecemeal exercise of judgment or discretion in particular cases. By this the doubtful provision is underpinned by sub-rules lending exactness.

The processors

Many different types of official are vested with processing authority. This may be conferred directly or indirectly. It is conferred directly when the official is named in the enactment. (The naming is by office rather than personal identification.) It is conferred indirectly when the official who actually exercises the judgment or discretion does so as an employee in the department of the named officer. As before, we take as an example the Consumer Credit Act 1974. This demonstrates the hierarchical nature of the arrangements commonly made.

Section 1 of the Act confers on the Director General of Fair Trading the duty:

(*a*) to administer the licensing system set up by the Act, and
(*b*) to exercise the adjudicating functions conferred on him by the Act in relation to the issue, renewal, variation, suspension and revocation of licenses, and
(*c*) generally to superintend the working and enforcement of the Act.

Section 2 empowers 'the Secretary of State' to regulate the carrying out by the Director General of his functions under the Act. (By virtue of Sched 1 to the Interpretation Act 1978 this means 'one of Her Majesty's Principal Secretaries of State', the one in question being selected by the Prime Minister.) Section 3 places the adjudicating functions of the Director General under the supervision of the Council on Tribunals. By virtue of Sched 1 to the Fair Trading Act 1973, anything authorised or required by or under the Consumer Credit Act to be done by the Director General may be done by any member of his staff. The Director General and his staff are collectively known as the Office of Fair Trading.

The result of these provisions is that central administration of the Consumer Credit Act is divided between officials of the Department of Trade and officials of the Office of Fair Trading. Local enforcement of the Act is entrusted to officials of local authorities. This follows the usual pattern of central and local administration, repeated with numerous regulatory Acts. Other types of Act confer processing powers on central and local officials. The most important of these Acts are the ones relating to income tax, customs and excise duties, value added tax and other forms of taxation, those containing health, social security and welfare provisions, and those concerned with education, employment and registration. The police too possess processing powers, together with similar functionaries such as traffic wardens and immigration officers.

Whenever relatively junior officials exercise judgment or discretion they are likely to do so in accordance with guidelines laid down by their superiors. The superior may or may not be the office holder on whom the statutory authority is directly conferred. The Director General of Fair Trading is such an office holder, and duly issues guidelines to his staff. But a police constable may be given direct authority by being mentioned as such in the statute. Yet he is obliged to carry out his statutory duties in accordance with the instructions of his superior officers.

Such policy guidelines or instructions are not likely to be regarded by a court as prejudging individual cases or improperly fettering the official's discretion, provided they do not preclude fair consideration of all relevant issues (see *R* v *Port of London Authority, ex parte Kynoch Ltd* [1919] KB 176, 184; *Stringer* v *Minister of Housing and Local Government* [1970] 1 WLR 1281). Any such policy must be reasonable and not capricious (*Cummings* v *Birkenhead Corpn* [1972] Ch 12). Where a proper policy has been laid down, exercise of judgment or discretion in accordance with the policy cannot be regarded as a failure to exercise it, and thus tantamount to a refusal entitling a person aggrieved to appeal.

It is important to bear in mind that the scope for official processing is cut down where judicial processing of the point has already occured. Official processing mainly takes place in areas not considered by the court. Once the court has resolved the doubt in question, officials (like everyone else) must abide by the court's decision. The recent rise of judicial review has enhanced the court's power to supervise administrative processing.

Processing intentional doubt-factors

We now look at some examples of how officials process the various kinds of intentional doubt-factor discussed in chapters 15 to 17.

Ellipsis

When government inspectors seek to enter premises under statutory powers they need to be quite sure that they conform to the statutory requirements. Where these are or may be elliptical, a policy judgment by the department concerned must be taken. Thus until the courts decided that the common phrase 'has reasonable cause to believe' was elliptical, and meant 'has reasonable cause to believe *and does believe*', departments in charge of an inspectorate had to reach their own judgment on the meaning of the phrase and instruct their officials accordingly. To be on the safe side, the tendency in such cases is to adopt the meaning which ensures legality whichever way the doubt is resolved. This was done in *R* v *Adams* [1980] QB 575. Here the police mistakenly relied on an ellipsis by which (if it had existed) a search warrant could have been used more than once. The result was that their second entry of premises under the warrant turned out to be unlawful.

Safety-first tactics are often impracticable. If the dock officials had adopted them in *London and India Docks* v *Thames Steam Tug and Lighterage Co Ltd* [1909] AC 7 there would have been a loss of revenue from lighter owners which the House of Lords ultimately held to be payable. The police had considerable difficulty with the breathalyzer provisions before the necessary sub-rules were worked out by the courts (p 274 above). Safety-first interpretation by the police would have rendered the legislation inoperative from the start.

Broad terms

Section 62 of the Highways Act 1959 entitled a highway authority to recover expenses incurred through repairing damage caused by 'excessive' weight passing along a highway, or other 'extraordinary' traffic thereon. The only clue given by the Act as to what these broad terms were intended to mean was that the entitlement must appear to the authority 'by a certificate of their surveyor'. 'Surveyor' here is also a broad term, since it lacks exactness. The provision derived from an earlier Act, and much processing was required to establish the necessary sub-rules. Must the surveyor be on the staff of the authority? If so must he hold an established post? Can his certificate apply to more than one road? Must it particularise the roads included? Is its issue a condition precedent to recovery of the expenses? Must it contain an estimate and apportionment of the expenses? These questions and many more had ultimately to be determined by the courts. Meanwhile highway authorities and their surveying staff grappled with them as best they could, adopting their own provisional sub-rules. The Highways Act 1959 has been repealed and replaced by the Highways Act 1980, s 59 of which reproduces s 62 of the 1959 Act. The phrase 'by a certificate of their surveyor' has now become 'by a certificate of their proper officer', another broad term.

The Tribunals and Inquiries Act 1971, s 12 requires tribunals to give 'the reasons' for their decisions if asked. Various courts have held that this implies that proper and adequate reasons must be given, that they must be in clear intelligible form, that they must deal with all substantial points raised, and so on. Subject to these rulings the clerks to the tribunals have had to work out for themselves just what the requirement involves in the way of practical administration.

Part II of the Housing Act 1957 gave wide powers to local authorities in relation to houses 'unfit for human habitation', a good example of a mobile broad term (see pp 242–246). Although there has been the usual amount of judicial processing of the phrase, in the main it has been for housing authorities to work out the effective sub-rules. In this, as often happens, they are aided by central advisory sources such as relevant government departments, associations of local authorities and professional housing management organisations.

Politic uncertainty

We saw in chapter 17 how officials responsible for instructing the drafter usually like to see their powers expressed in vague terms, so as to minimise effective challenge. In some policy areas however officials may dislike administering an Act so flexible that it leaves wide scope for criticism of their practice. An example of wide discretion is given by the town and country planning legislation. Although in theory this places decision-making in the hands of elected local government representatives, in practice planning officials determine policy. Moreover this is an area where processing by the courts has been of relatively little importance.

Unintentional doubt-factors

We turn now to examples of administrative processing of doubts which are caused by unforeseeable developments or drafting error.

Unforeseeable developments

We considered unforeseeable developments in chapters 11 (pp 181–186) and 18. One example given there should not have arisen, since it was really due to drafting error. This was *The Longford* (1889) 22 QBD 239. When the Judicature Act of 1873 amended the courts system the drafter should have made consequential amendments in the earlier Act referred to in that case. It was one more instance of the 'missed consequential', a common occurrence. Parliamentary changes do not properly belong in the category of unforeseeable developments because when they occur Parliament has the opportunity to make the necessary adjustments in existing legislation.

Another example *A-G* v *Edison Telephone Co* (1880) 6 QBD 244, was a triumph for the drafter. He managed to find words which were apt to include the telephone although it had not yet been invented! The Post Office officials who considered that on policy grounds their monopoly powers should cover telephone messages were vindicated in their practice.

Official practice may have to change to correspond with social change, as occured in relation to rent officers over developments in the meaning of 'family' (p 244).

Drafting errors

Officials are frequently put in difficulty by mistakes of the kind described in chapter 19. What is the rate collector to do if he cannot fix a notice of the rate on the church door because the district has no church? (*R* v *Dyott* (1882) 2 QBD 47). How can the official administering the hackney carriage licensing system proceed if he does not know whether a proprietor convicted of a second offence under the Licensing Act is or is not liable to have his licence revoked? (*Bowers* v *Gloucester Corporation* [1963] 1 QB 881). What does ACAS do when the Act tells it to consult a party who refuses to be consulted, or to ascertain the opinion of workers whose identity is not discoverable? (*Grunwick Processing Laboratories Ltd* v *Advisory, Conciliation and Arbitration Service* [1978] AC 655). What does the City of London treasurer do when the City is liable for costs directed to be paid out of the 'county fund' and he knows perfectly well that the City does not possess such a thing? Resort can be had to the courts, but that is time-consuming and expensive. Usually the official makes his own mind up.

The nature of offical processing

The answer to questions caused by doubtful drafting depends on whether the offical processing is ante-judicial or not. By ante-judicial processing I mean processing which anticipates judicial processing. Even though judicial processing of the point may never in fact occur, the official (often with the aid of legal advice) attempts to forecast what a court would decide. It follows that ante-judicial processing can happen only if, and to the extent that, a court would have jurisdiction to entertain a case in which the doubt could be settled. Sometimes the department may bring a test case for this purpose.

Processing which is not ante-judicial occurs where the court does not have jurisdiction to resolve the doubt, or its jurisdiction is peripheral. The main category is where the doubt-factor is the use of a broad term. The Competition Act 1980 is based on the concept of what it calls 'an anti-competitive practice'. No definition of this broad term is given, except the obvious (and almost equally broad) statement that it concerns the restricting, distorting or preventing of competition in connection with the production, supply or acquisition of goods or the supply or securing of services (s 2). The result is that it is for the Office of Fair Trading to process the phrase and supply a network of sub-rules underpinning it. Before this process began there were many questions. Would it include the giving of loyalty rebates or discriminatory discounts? Would it extend to full line forcing or the refusal to supply goods to price cutters? The trade did not know until the Office of Fair Trading chose to tell it. An Opposition attempt to add to the Bill a list of 26 practices to be treated as anti-competitive was defeated.

The body of sub-rules which emerges in such cases is given the description 'practice'. In introducing estate duty, the Finance Act 1894, s 8(1) perpetrated an appalling piece of asifism:

The existing law and practice relating to any of the duties now leviable on or with reference to death shall, subject to the provisions of this Act and so far as the same are applicable, apply for the purposes of the collection, recovery, and repayment of Estate duty . . . as if such law and practice were in terms made applicable to this Part of this Act.

The result of this disgraceful evasion of the drafter's duty (for which the drafter himself may well not have been personally responsible) was that throughout the eighty years estate duty endured it was never possible to consolidate the enactments relating to it. This was so even though they were supplemented by almost every annual Finance Act from 1894 onwards.

Official practice changes from time to time, and it is often very difficult for the outsider to discover exactly what the practice of an earlier time was. Unlike judicial processing, much administrative processing takes place out of public view and its results are not embodied in accessible records. The way a doubt is officially resolved may remain unknown unless the officials concerned choose to reveal it. Equally, a *change* in the official interpretation of a doubtful statute may pass unnoticed if not revealed. Some government departments include such matters in their annual or other reports. Thus a 1979 report by the Civil Service Department revealed a reinterpretation of s 8(2)(*a*) of the Pensions (Increase) Act 1971. As a result of this, the report said, 300,000 files would need to be reviewed at a cost of some £250,000 (*Legal Entitlements and Administrative Practices* (1979), para 31 and App 2; cited Miers and Page 1982, p 241).

Policy handouts

Government departments frequently issue booklets, leaflets and other guides informing interested parties how doubt-resolving processing is carried out and what its results are. The former Supplementary

Benefits Commission published a *Handbook* explaining how its various discretionary powers were exercised and the way it resolved doubts on the wording of the parent Act. In *Supplementary Benefits Commission* v *Jull* [1980] 3 WLR 436, the court referred to para 16 of the *Handbook* in support of its view on how such a doubt should be determined. Another example is furnished by the planning circulars issued by the relevant government department, eg the circular entitled *The Use of Conditions in Planning Permissions* issued in 1968 by the Ministry of Housing and Local Government (the circular is referred to in *Newbury DC* v *Secretary of State for the Environment* [1981] AC 578, 600).

Where a non-governmental body has statutory functions it may issue similar guidance. An example is the Notes for Guidance issued by the Law Society in connection with the legal aid scheme administered by it (*Hanlon* v *The Law Society* [1981] AC 124). Some Acts *require* the administering department to issue guidance of this kind. Thus s 4 of the Consumer Credit Act 1974 requires the Director General of Fair Trading to arrange for the dissemination of information and advice about the operation of the Act. Section 12 of the Housing (Homeless Persons) Act 1977 required housing authorities to have regard, in exercising their discretion, to guidance issued by the Secretary of State. A Code of Guidance was accordingly issued by the Department of the Environment (*A-G* v *Wandsworth LBC* [1981] 1 WLR 854).

An important publication of this kind is the booklet issued by the Board of Inland Revenue which details the extra-statutory concessions made by the Board in relation to income tax, corporation tax, capital gains tax etc. These concessions are an important method of mitigating the literal effects of taxing Acts where these are contrary to current government policy. The concessions also serve to indicate, where doubts exists on the meaning of a particular taxing provision, that the authorities have adopted the practice of collecting tax in accordance with the less onerous reading.

Judicial control

The courts retain some degree of control even over processing that is not ante-judicial. The usual principles of judicial review apply to restrain abuse of power by orders of certiorari or prohibition, or compel the carrying out of statutory duties by orders of mandamus. These prerogative orders do not exhaust the courts' powers of control over administrative authorities. The doctrine of *ultra vires* can always be resorted to by those who claim that an authority has gone too far or has failed to exercise a judgment or discretion in accordance with the terms of the empowering statute.

In *Lally* v *Kensington and Chelsea RB* (1980) *The Times*, 27 March, Browne-Wilkinson J considered the practice of the borough council in setting up a sub-rule with regard to the exercise of its discretion under the Housing (Homeless Person) Act 1977. The sub-rule was that in all cases an intentionally homeless persons would be granted temporary accomodation for a period of 14 days only. The judge, while accepting that he was not sitting as a court of appeal from the local authority, nevertheless made an order against the council. He pointed out that the court could intervene 'only if the local authority had misdirected themselves and had reached a conclusion that no reasonable council could have reached'. They had done this by applying a rigid 14 day rule instead of allowing in each case a period suited to the circumstances of the family in question.

The courts will not hesitate to cut down powers given by wide wording if they consider this necessary to give effect to the purpose of the Act. A well known example concerns the imposition of conditions on the grant of planning permission. Section 29(1) of the Town and Country Planning Act 1971, reproducing earlier legislation, authorises a local planning authority to grant planning permission 'either unconditionally or subject to such conditions as it thinks fit'. In broad terms this gives power to impose any condition at all, but the courts have curtailed this width. The following statement of law by Lord Denning in *Pyx Granite Co Ltd* v *Ministry of Housing and Local Government* [1958] 1 QB 554, 572 has been approved by the House of Lords in several subsequent cases (see *Newbury DC* v *Secretary of State for the Environment* [1981] AC 578, 599):

Although the planning authorities are given very wide powers to impose 'such conditions as they think fit', nevertheless the law says that those conditions, to be valid, must fairly and reasonably relate to the permitted development. The planning authority are not at liberty to use their powers for an ulterior object, however desirable that object may seem to them to be in the public interest.

This is one more example of ellipsis. Unexpressed in the planning permission formula are words having the effect of this statement by Lord Denning.

Formerly, Acts of Parliament not infrequently contained provisions ousting the jurisdiction of the courts to carry out judicial review. The exclusionary clause was to the effect that an exercise of the administrative judgment or discretion should be 'final' or 'conclusive', or should not be questioned in any legal proceedings (*Ridge* v *Baldwin* [1964] AC 40). The courts resisted such provisions, and they are not used in current legislation. Their death-knell came in s 11(1) of the Tribunals and Inquiries Act 1958, which provided that existing provisions of this kind should not prevent judicial review (see s 14(1) of the Tribunals and Inquiries Act 1971).

Chapter Twenty-Two

Dynamic Processing: The Judicial Processor

For sound reasons, the courts have been reluctant to acknowledge their processing function in relation to legislation, since it is itself legislative, rather than strictly judicial, in nature. However, it would be of considerable help to the clarity of the law if judges could bring themselves openly to accept this undoubted function, and refine their technique accordingly.

How would a distinct judicial technique for processing operate? Let us begin with the case where judicial processing of the point in question has not occurred before. The judge has a clean sheet. As soon as he realised that determination of the *lis* required resolution of a doubt as to the meaning or operation of a legislative text, he would proceed accordingly. If his judgment was likely to be reported, he would, with the aid of counsel in the case, make sure that it contained a passage appropriately worded for adding a new sub-rule. If he thought fit, he might then *direct* that the judgment should be reported.

It would be helpful, though not essential, if judgments in such cases could assume a more structured and standardised form. If a sub-rule is to be laid down by a quasi-legislative process it would assist the statute user if it were in rule form. It would also assist future processors of the same text, including appellate courts deciding whether to overrule or approve the sub-rule. Here it may be convenient to remind the reader that these sub-rules are of varying degrees of complexity. As we have seen in relation to lotteries, highway repairs and other matters, a broad term may be so broad as to produce a complex network of sub-rules when it is processed. If codified, they would occupy considerable space in a statute setting them forth exactly. That such codification has not occurred in British-type statute law is mainly due to unsystematic formulation of sub-rules by judges.

Sometimes the courts seize on the processing opportunities conferred on them by Parliament and fashion an important principle, worthy of a more dignified description than 'sub-rule'. This is particularly likely to happen in an area in which judges have been prominent historically. One such area concerns the welfare of wives and children. We are not surprised to find that the courts have used neutrally-expressed statutory powers to make maintenance orders in favour of divorced wives as a means to create the important principle of the 'clean break'. In *Minton* v *Minton* [1979] AC 593, 608, Lord Scarman described the effects of this important piece of judicial processing when he said:

> The law now encourages spouses to avoid bitterness after family breakdown and to settle their money and property problems. An object of the modern law is to encourage the parties to put the past behind them and to begin a new life which is not overshadowed by the relationship which has broken down.

This type of processing is an important judicial contribution to statute law. It strengthens the case for a more orderly treatment in judgments. The statute user should not have to guess whether the judge intended to create a sub-rule. Nor should he have to guess what its content and effect are.

Interstitial articulation

The judges could go much further than is suggested above in framing sub-rules with precision. They could supplement the work of the drafter by including in their judgment on an Act an *interstitial articulation*. This may be defined as a judicial sub-rule framed in a way which codifies it, and fits it textually into the body of the Act.

The ideal requirement   In explaining this technique, it is convenient to start with what it is that the parties ideally need when an enactment has to be applied to the facts of their own case. They ideally need a version of the enactment that fits like a glove, or in other words is *tailored to the shape of those facts*. The parties are not interested in how the enactment might apply to any other facts but their own. Blackstone gives an example when he frames this syllogism: 'against him who has rode over my corn, I may recover damages by law: but A has rode over my corn, therefore I shall recover damages against A' (Blackstone 1765, III 399). Obviously the relevant law would not be framed in terms merely of riding over corn, but more widely. The parties here are only interested in riding over corn however.

Take a modern example. Suppose a person is charged with the offence of using his house as a retreat for the consumption of dangerous drugs by addicts. Both defence and prosecution wish to know whether, if the defendant is convicted, his house can be forfeited. The Misuse of Drugs Act 1971, s 27(1) says that:

> . . . the court by or before which a person is convicted of an offence under this Act may order *anything* shown to the satisfaction of the court to relate to the offence to be forfeited (emphasis added).

The parties might think that here they have their answer. No word could be wider than *anything:* it must include a house. That however is an argument. It is a very strong argument, but the position is not as clear as it would be if s 27(1) had said '. . . may order any *house* . . . to be forfeited'. That is the sort of wording the parties in that particular case really want. It avoids all argument, and is absolutely conclusive.

Now of course they cannot have that wording. If passed in that form the enactment would have been incomplete. The nearest they could have hoped for is something like '. . . may order anything (of whatever nature, whether corporeal or incorporeal) . . . to be forfeited'.

It may be argued that the drafter of s 27(1) should have worded his enactment in such a way. In the context of the present discussion, that argument is not available. We have accepted as a general proposition that the drafter cannot say everything. Suggestions about how he might have said a bit more when drafting a particular enactment are beside the point.

Any competent lawyer will know that the parties in our drugs case would be unwise to assume that, for the purposes of s 27(1) as actually drawn, a house really is 'anything'. Research will reveal to them that in *R v Beard (Graham)* [1974] 1 WLR 1549 Caulfield J said (without giving any reason) that the word 'anything' in s 27(1) is a very general description of *personal* property and would not include a house. (See also *R v Cuthbertson* [1981] AC 470 and *R v Khan* [1982] 1 WLR 1045.)

In this example, the gap in the express wording of the enactment was the absence of any statement of whether or not 'anything' included anything in the nature of a house. The court in *Beard* closed, or at least narrowed, this gap; and it did so in the usual way. Parties in future such cases (who might be concerned with a flat or a shop—or even a ship) will, in the usual way, need to try and work out for themselves the *ratio decidendi* of *Beard,* or decide whether Cauldfield J's dictum was merely *obiter*.

Assertion or articulation?   There are two ways a court can deal with a gap in the express wording of an enactment, as it applies to the particular facts under consideration. The first is the usual way, namely simply to *assert* (as in *Beard*) that the enactment 'means' (or does not 'mean') so-and-so. (For a critical account of this judicial technique of *assertion* see Murphy and Rawlings 1981.) The other way would be for the judge to fill the gap by spelling out in his judgment a legislative formula that fits more closely to the facts of the instant case. In other words to *restate* the enactment in an expanded version which includes the expression (in relation to such facts) of precisely what it was that Parliament, or in practical terms the drafter, left unsaid. The precision of modern drafting nowadays makes such restatement practicable.

The starting point is formally to isolate those of the express words of the enactment that are relevant to the facts of the instant case. Few enactments are as brief and simple as s 27(1) of the Misuse of Drugs Act 1971. The technique of compression used by modern drafters leads to long sections, often divided up into complex and indigestible subsections. Here is a typical example. Section 5 of the Public Order Act 1936 (as substituted by s 7 of the Race Relations Act 1965) runs as follows:

Any person who in any public place or at any public meeting—
(a)   uses threatening, abusive or insulting words or behaviour, or
(b)   distributes or displays any writing, sign or visible representation which
       is threatening, abusive or insulting,
with intent to provoke a breach of the peace or whereby a breach of the peace is likely to be occasioned, shall be guilty of an offence.

This one section contains a very large number of different enactments. Each one constitutes an offence on its own, and can be stated separately without departing from the language Parliament has used. For example one of the many offences created by s 5 can be expressed in this way: 'Any person who in any public place uses insulting behaviour, whereby a breach of the peace is likely to be occasioned, shall be guilty of an offence.'

Here a word of caution is required. Although this brief formula is extracted from the section without alteration, it cannot necessarily be treated as if it formed the entirety of the section. Other words located elsewhere in the section, or in other parts of the Act, may colour its meaning: an Act is to be construed as a whole. Subject to this caveat, the application of which is not likely to make much difference in the general run of cases, it is helpful to abbreviate a section in this way. It should always be possible to produce an abbreviation of this kind. Even if not actually produced to the court, notionally it forms the subject of the enquiry into meaning. What needs to be grasped is that an enactment is less a specific portion of an Act than a *proposition* which, though always to be gathered from the words of the Act (and not significantly departing from them), fluctuates in its composition according to the point at issue. The statute user has to develop a technique of skimming through a provision and mentally picking out the bits that matter in the case he has before him. If his mind can learn to blot out the irrelevant words, the remainder will read continuously and make sense.

The need to do this is accepted by judges. Lord Scarman cited an enactment in a form he described as 'trimmed of words inessential for present purposes' in *Riley* v *A-G of Jamaica* [1983] 1 AC 719, 739. In *Ludlow* v *MPC* [1971] AC 29, 38, Lord Pearson used the technique in relation to r 3 of Sched 1 to the Indictment Act 1915 (revoked and replaced by the Indictment Rules 1971). The rule allowed joinder of charges in an indictment 'if those charges are

founded on the same facts, or form or are a part of a series
of offences of the same or a similar character'. Lord Pearson said
of the two offences charged in *Ludlow:*

This question can be narrowed, because these two offences were not
presented as being part of some larger series of offences and they were
not of the same character. Thus the question comes to be whether these
two offences formed a series of offences of a similar character.

The technique is the one we have called *selective comminution*
in describing it above (p 235). Its usefulness has been recognised
by other writers. For example, JR Spencer used it to telling effect
when exposing weaknesses in s 22 of the Theft Act 1968 (Spencer
1981(2)). A refinement of the technique where *defined terms* are
included in the relevant enactment was suggested by Donaldson
MR in *Bland* v *Chief Supplementary Benefit Officer* [1983] 1 WLR
262, 265, where he called it reconstructing the relevant subsection
'to make it slightly more intelligible'. The refinement was to set
out in the selective comminution, the full meanings of the defined
terms included in the enactment.

Here is a more complex example. D is charged with making without
lawful excuse a threat to kill V, contrary to s 16 of the Offences
against the Person Act 1861. D admits making the threat, but argues
that he had a lawful excuse in that the threat was uttered to prevent
a crime. He relies on s 3 of the Criminal Law Act 1967, a selective
comminution of which reads:

(1) A person may use such force as is reasonable in the circumstances
(2) in the prevention of crime
(3) Clauses (1) and (2) above replace the rules of the common law on the
question when force used for the purpose of the prevention of crime is
justified by that purpose.

In clause (3) of this there has been some necessary rewording. As
well as dealing with force used in the prevention of crime, s 3(1)
of the Criminal Law Act 1967 covers force used in making an arrest.
Section 3(2) of the Act (the relevant effect of which is reproduced
in our clause (3)) says that s 3(1) 'shall replace the rules of the
common law on the question when force used for a purpose
mentioned in the subsection is justified by that purpose'. Rewording
of this limited nature (described by drafters as 'carpentry') is
necessary to achieve the purpose of selective comminution, but it
must never depart more than is requisite from the statutory wording.
Nor of course must it in any way change the meaning.

The prosecution counter D's argument by saying that s 3 refers
to the actual use of force, and does not mention threats. D retorts
that statutes are to be construed with logic and common sense, and
that in logic and common sense the greater includes the less. He
puts forward the following as an elaborated version of clause (1):

(1) A person may use such force *or threat of force* as is reasonable in the circumstances.

The judge accepts D's argument and directs the jury accordingly. His direction omits any reference to actual force because on the evidence that is irrelevant. He prefaces his direction by saying 'I am not going to attempt a comprehensive definition because you will be considering purely this case'. He directs the jury that the law says: 'A person may use such threat of force as is reasonable in the circumstances in the prevention of crime.' The above is based on the decision of the Court of Appeal in *R* v *Cousins* [1982] 2 WLR 621. The quoted preface to the direction was used by the Crown Court judge in that case (see p 625). It illustrates how in practice courts are concerned only with opposing constructions of an enactment *as it applies to particular facts*. Where does the Crown Court judge get this statement of the law from? As we have seen, it is not what s 3 of the Criminal Law Act 1967 says. It can scarcely be what the common law says, because s 3(2) has abolished common law rules in this field. There are two possibilities in such cases. One is that the judge is making express a meaning that is implied in the words Parliament has used. The other is that the judge is treating Parliament as having delegated to him some degree of legislative power.

Articulating the implied meaning   It is submitted that the true answer is an amalgamation of these possibilities. While one might accurately describe what the judge does as an exercise of delegated legislative power, in essence he is making express an implied meaning. Certainly that is the analysis the judiciary themselves prefer. Here it needs to be borne in mind that in the origins of our law judicial authority and legislative authority are, as Richardson and Sayles put it, 'but two facets of law-giving' (Richardson and Sayles 1934, p 555). To this day Parliament remains both the supreme legislature and the supreme judicial authority.

In a significant phrase, Lord Bridge referred to the mid-nineteenth century as 'an age when Parliament was less articulate than it is now' (*Wills* v *Bowley* [1983] 1 AC 57, 104). The precision of modern drafting means that Parliament nowadays clearly articulates many details that in former times were left to be spelt out by the courts. Nevertheless, as we have seen, this unavoidably falls far short of articulating all the detail necessary to decide every case.

When the court in effect supplies this missing detail, it does not usually say that that is what it is doing. (For an instance where it did do so, see the remark by Viscount Kilmuir LC in *Inland Revenue Commissioners* v *Hinchy* [1960] AC 748, 762 that the effect of a previous decision of the House of Lords was to 'rewrite' the relevant section.) As we saw above in relation to *R* v *Beard (Graham)* [1974] 1 WLR 1549, the court usually contents itself with explaining in informal language that the enactment 'means' whatever is necessary to decide the case. The court does not attempt to articulate what might be described as the invisible wording of the enactment. Its beam for a moment rescues this from darkness, but then passes on.

The same is true of counsel, when they advance to the court their opposing constructions. They argue that the enactment 'means' one thing or the other, but rarely attempt to draft (as if it were a part of the Act) the wording their argument requires to be taken as implied. It is true that they receive little judicial encouragement to do so.

It may be helpful if we now examine one of the occasional exceptions to the usual judicial way of proceeding. In *R* v *Schildkamp* [1971] AC 1 the prosecution went to the House of Lords over a point on the meaning of s 332(3) of the Companies Act 1948. A selective comminution of this reads:

(1) Where any business of a company is carried on
(2) with intent to defraud creditors of the company
(3) every person who was knowingly a party to the carrying on of the business in manner aforesaid
(4) [shall be guilty of an offence].

The question for the House of Lords was whether this enactment applied literally or was, by an implication arising from its context, confined to the case where the company was in liquidation. By three to two, the House held that it was so confined and that the appeal of the prosecution failed. Dissenting, Lord Guest said (p 15):

One of my difficulties in giving effect to the respondent's contentions is to understand what words of limitation are to be imported in subsection (3). As the subsection creates a criminal offence, this must be a matter of precision. Mr Hawser, for the respondent, suggested that subsection (3) should commence with the following words:
'If in the course of the winding up of a company it appears that the business of the company has been carried on with intent to defraud creditors of the company or creditors of any other person or for any fraudulent purpose . . .'
This would be a clumsy section to construe and the [prosecutor] would have considerable difficulty in drafting an indictment in line with such a provision.

Lord Hodson, for dismissing the appeal, said he was not impressed by the argument that on the majority view some rewriting of the enactment was necessary (p 11). Lord Upjohn, who delivered the main majority opinion, pointed the way to how the rewriting might best be achieved (while purporting to do the opposite).

The Court of Appeal had framed the point of law for decision by the House of Lords as being 'what, if any, words of limitation must be imported in s 332(3)?' Lord Upjohn rejected this formulation as not disclosing the real point of law. He said: 'The real point is whether before a prosecution can be initiated . . . the company must be in liquidation' (p 28). He dismissed the difficulties raised by Lord Guest on the ground that s 332(3) itself required no alteration: 'it stands as it is, plain and unambiguous, but in the context in which it is found it requires a limitation in its application . . .' (p 26).

In a sense both sides were right. Lord Upjohn was right in saying that it was not necessary for the House of Lords to formulate a textual amendment of s 332(3) in order to rule that it did not mean what it said. Lord Guest was right in saying that the majority ruling involved the necessity of some notional amendment of the literal meaning even if it was not put into exact words. (The decision was reversed by s 96 of the Companies Act 1981).

There are many different ways of saying a thing. The professional drafter's motto is that 'anything is draftable', though it may have to be drafted as an overriding provision rather than one that neatly slots into the passage it modifies. Lord Diplock went too far when he said in *Jones* v *Wrotham Park Settled Estates* [1980] AC 74, 105, that a departure by the court from the literal meaning is not legitimate unless it is 'possible to state with certainty what were the additional words that would have been inserted by the draftsman'. No two drafters will draft a proposition in the same words, but draft it they will. Lord Upjohn's speech suggests that as good a way as any of articulating the effect of the decision in *Schildkamp* would be to treat it as adding the following proviso to s 332(3): 'Provided that no prosecution shall be instituted for an offence under this subsection unless the company is being, or has been, wound up.'

It is submitted that it would substantially improve the clarity of legal reasoning if judges openly accepted that when they construe a statute, what they are in substance doing is *declaring* or making explicit certain of its implied provisions. As Neil MacCormick puts it, the statute is *concretised* through the process of judicial interpretation (MacCormick 1978, pp 188, 218).

As a corollary of such acceptance, it would be helpful in many ways if judges would further accept a responsibility to *articulate* what seems to them an appropriate version of those implied provisions which their judicial function requires them to concretise. The judiciary would thus, to a limited extent, resume its ancient drafting function. Within the verbal interstices provided by the express wording of an Act or statutory instrument, there would then grow, decision by decision, the concrete details needed to spell out its meaning in particular cases. Holmes J said in *Southern Pacific Company* v *Jensen* (1916) 244 US 205, 221: 'I recognise without hesitation that judges do and must legislate, but they do so only interstitially . . .'

Whether or not judges who necessarily fill up gaps in statutes can properly be described as legislating, they do what they do interstitially. As Miers and Page put it in their book *Legislation:* 'Judges make law interstitially, within the limits of existing rules, precedents and doctrine . . .' (Miers and Page 1982, p 205). Elsewhere they say:

To the extent that judges do make law, for example where there is no appropriate rule available, they do so only interstitially within the context of the discharge of their primary function (of settling disputes in accordance with pre-existing rules). *(Ibid* p 1.)

The interstices identified in these passages vary in their nature. The term *interstitial articulation* alludes to what can almost literally be regarded as cracks, clefts or crevices between verbal propositions in statutes. The OED defines *interstice* as:

An intervening space (usually, empty); especially a relatively small or narrow space, between things or the parts of a body (frequently in plural, the minute spaces between the ultimate parts of matter); a narrow opening, chink or crevice.

As Cardozo said in an important section of his book *The Nature of the Judicial Process,* how far the judge may go 'without travelling beyond the walls of the interstices' is governed by complex factors (Cardozo 1921, p 141). It would be of advantage for the product of this activity to be clear and precise rather than, as so often under our system, tangled and diffuse.

The ratio decidendi   The first obvious advantage of interstitial articulation by judges is that where applied it would put an end to the well-known difficulties about working out the *ratio decidendi* of a relevant case. This working out is not a task to be shirked, as Lord Reid sternly reminded us in *Nash* v *Tamplin & Sons Brewery (Brighton) Ltd* [1952] AC 231, 250:

It matters not how difficult it is to find the *ratio decidendi* of a previous case, that *ratio* must be found. It matters not how difficult it is to reconcile that *ratio* when found with statutory provisions or general principles, that *ratio* must be applied to any later case which is not reasonably distinguishable.

Whatever difficulties may remain in finding the *ratio* of a decision at common law, there could be no doubt of the *ratio* of a case turning on statutory interpretation where the judge had articulated the provision in question.

Sir Rupert Cross defined the *ratio* as 'any rule of law expressly or impliedly treated by the judge as a necessary step in reaching his conclusion. . .' (Cross 1977, p 76). Holdsworth said that 'the authority of a decision is attached, not to the words used, nor to all the reasons given, but to the principle or principles necessary for the decision of the case' (Holdsworth 1928, p 46). Where an enactment governed the decision, and any relevant implied terms of the enactment were articulated by the judge, there could be no doubt that the resulting form of the words was the rule of law upon which the decision was based. The authority of the decision then would be, *pace* Holdsworth, attached to the words used.

It should perhaps be stressed that it would be necessary for the articulation to confine itself to *ratio* and not stray into the realm of *dicta*. What under the present system is expressed in the form of an *obiter dictum* should, under the proposed system, continue to be so expressed.

The gain in certainty about what is the *ratio* of a case would in itself be a considerable advantage. Cross remarked on the confusion caused by difficulty in arriving at this:

. . . every English law student is familiar with the difficulty of differentiating those parts of the leading judgments that are *ratio* from those that are mere *dicta*, and disagreements over the distinction lie at the root of a number of legal controversies. These difficulties and disagreements are largely, if not entirely, due to the elaborate and varied forms in which English judgments are delivered. (Cross 1977, p 49; Hart 1961, p 95).

Elsewhere Cross quotes with approval the remark by Paton and Sawer that the function of a court is not only to give judgment, but also to lay down a principle consistent with that judgment (*ibid,* p 99.) He ends his chapter on the *ratio decidendi* saying: 'there is no doubt that unnecessary uncertainty may be occasioned by the discursive nature of the judgments in appellate courts, and those sitting in such courts should take every possible step to avoid it' (p 102).

Adoption of the practice of interstitial articulation is certainly a 'possible' step. It would of course require the advocates presenting argument to the court to set the ball rolling by offering their own respective articulations of the contested enactment. As Lord Radcliffe said, 'a court decision is formed out of the work of those who prepare a case, those who argue it before the court and those who ultimately explain and record their view' (cited Zander 1989, p 275). Such articulation would appropriately form part of the 'skeleton arguments' now required to be submitted in advance to the court.

A worked example   It may be helpful at this point to give an example of the working of this technique of interstitial articulation coupled with selective comminution. Almost any case involving statutory interpretation would serve for this purpose. The following is based on *Wills* v *Bowley* [1983] 1 AC 57, which we have already used as an example in explaining comminution (see p 235 above). The example indicates some of the things imaginary judges and counsel might do if using the technique, but does not purport to say what any actual judge or counsel involved in that case really did.

Mr P is briefed to prosecute D (a female) at a magistrates' court. She is charged with two offences. One is an offence under s 28 of the Town Police Clauses Act 1847 ('the s 28 offence'). The other is the offence of assaulting three police officers in the execution of their duty of arresting her without a warrant ('the assault offence'). The facts are that the constables saw and heard D using obscene language in a street. When they tried to arrest her she became violent.

Mr P looks up s 28. It is a long section, running to some three pages. He makes a selective comminution which reduces this to a mere 48 words. It runs as follows:

Part I
(1) Every person who in any street,
(2) to the annoyance of the residents or passengers,
(3) uses any obscene language
(4) shall be [guilty of an offence].

Part II
(5) Any constable shall take into custody, without warrant,
(6) and forthwith convey before a justice,
(7) any person who within his view commits any such offence.

(This selective comminution is presented in two parts because the relevant portions of s 28 constitute two independent propositions and it is convenient to be able to refer to them separately.)

Mr P perceives that in order to succeed on the assault charge he needs to show that the power of arrest conferred by Part II had really arisen. If the arrest was not lawful D was justified in resisting it. Mr P finds there is some doubt about whether the evidence will establish what is required by clause (2). He realises that if the case goes to appeal he may have to uphold a conviction for the assault offence without his argument being supported by D's conviction for the s 28 offence. Indeed D may by that time have been acquitted of the s 28 offence.

Mr P then sees that, to obtain (and retain) a conviction for the assault offence, it may be necessary to convince the court that clause (7) is wide enough to include a case where the constable reasonably believes the accused to be committing a s 28 offence even though this is not actually the case. Mr P therefore prepares the following articulated version of clause (7):

(7) any person who within his view—
(a) commits any such offence, or
(b) does any act which he reasonably believes constitutes such an offence.

Miss Q is briefed for the defence. She prepares a similar selective comminution to that prepared by Mr P. She appreciates the point that has troubled him, and prepares an articulation of clause (7) that strengthens the wording in her client's favour. It runs as follows:

(7) any person who within his view does an act which actually constitutes any such offence.

The bench acquit D of the s 28 offence. In relation to the assault offence, Mr P and Miss Q argue for their respective versions of clause (7). The bench prefer Mr P's version. They convict D of the assault offence on the ground that her behaviour fell within Mr P's clause (7)(b) and rendered her arrest lawful. D appeals by case stated to the Divisional Court, who dismiss her appeal. She then appeals to the House of Lords, who by three to two also dismiss the appeal. The majority agree that a slightly different version of Mr P's clause (7) is appropriate. It runs as follows:

(7) any person
(a) who within his view commits any such offence, or
(b) whom he honestly believes, on reasonable grounds derived wholly from his own observation, to have committed an offence within his view.

Through the effort of thinking out their respective articulations, counsel on each side formed a more exact appreciation of what the enactment provides. This helped them to prepare a full and clear formulation of what, in the contention of each, the relevant law really was. The process of preparing his or her articulation, and the resulting ability to refer to these formulations in argument before the court, clarified counsels' minds and assisted the cogency and certainty of their arguments. This was a distinct gain. The difficulty of *correct* formulation of any legal argument based on statute law is formidable, and often underrated. Gordon Woodman has remarked that its intellectual difficulty is a characteristic of such argument not often explicitly discussed (Woodman 1982, p 135).

The court too is enabled by this means to concentrate on the exact point at issue. The final version of clause (7) given above is based on Lord Bridge's answer to the certified question in *Wills* v *Bowley* [1983] 1 AC 57, 104. It is respectfully submitted however that Mr P's version is preferable to that of Lord Bridge. The former slots properly into the structure of s 28, and correctly identifies the nature of the offence. Lord Bridge's version refers to 'an offence' in general terms. In stating that the grounds of belief must derive wholly from the constable's observation, Lord Bridge is more restrictive than the wording of s 28 appears to justify.

These defects (if such they be) are probably due to the fact that under the present system argument is not directed to the precise wording of the key passage in the judgment. Indeed counsel before the House of Lords in *Wills* v *Bowley* are unlikely to have had an opportunity to comment on Lord Bridge's formulation of the answer to the certified question. In most cases before the courts there is not even the concentration of argument provided by a stated case. By including the articulation in its judgment, the court would give *precise* guidance as to what the law on the point is. This would help the parties in considering whether to bring or resist an appeal. If an appeal is brought, the articulation would help the appellate court to decide whether or not the court below had erred.

From the point of view of the law generally, the articulation by the court of the relevant provision would make the enactment clearer for the future. This would assist potential litigants, and indeed all who are concerned to, administer, expound or alter the enacted law in question.

Prevention of error   Perhaps the most powerful argument in favour of interstitial articulation is that it can hardly fail to reduce the number of cases that are wrongly decided. This is because it requires the argument to be thought through with a stringency and thoroughness not necessitated by conventional methods.

As a further example of this advantage we may take the hire-purchase case of *Porter* v *General Guarantee Corporation* (1982) CCLR 1; *The Times,* 15 January. Here the High Court came to a plainly wrong decision on s 75(2) of the Consumer Credit Act 1974. These were the facts.

A car dealer represented to the plaintiff that a certain car was in excellent condition. In fact it was in poor condition. Acting on this misrepresentation, the plaintiff agreed to buy the car on hire-purchase. To enable him to do so, the dealer introduced the plaintiff to a finance company, to whom the dealer sold the car. The finance company in turn sold it on hire-purchase to the plaintiff.

On contract law principles, the plaintiff later rescinded the agreement. He claimed that by virtue of s 56(2) of the Consumer Credit Act 1974 the dealer's misrepresentation was to be treated as made by the seller (the finance company). In respect of the loss suffered by it because of this rescission, the finance company claimed to be indemnified by the dealer under s 75(2) of the 1974 Act.

In claiming this indemnity the finance company was clearly in error. There is no indemnity under s 75(2) in a case like this. The statutory indemnity only arises where the creditor and the supplier are different persons. Here the finance company was both creditor and supplier, a situation which (under the definition of 'supplier' in the 1974 Act) is always the case with a hire-purchase agreement. It might be said that there was no necessity to go to the length of working out an articulation in order to discover this error. Obviously that is true. But if the judge had been presented with an appropriate articulation he could hardly have failed to reach the correct result. Indeed the point can be pushed further back. If counsel for the finance company had first sat down to prepare such a formula he would so clearly have seen the true legal position that he could never have brought himself to advance to the court the argument he did. The fact is that modern statutes are so complex that techniques of this sort are essential. The process of working them out enables counsel to make sure he is on the right track. Having the formula before him in court ensures that his argument does not stray from that track.

Codification   Over a long period, the judicial articulations of implied provisions of an Act would collectively form a codification. Their existence in reported judgments would greatly ease the problems, described above (pp 74–77), of carrying out a codification of processed enactments on conventional lines.

Conclusion   The need for interstitial articulation (coupled usually with selective commination) arises from the immense complexity of modern statute law. The opposing constructions put forward in actual cases usually represent but a tiny fraction of the possible meanings inherent in an enactment. Other possible factual situations (of which the range is infinite) will, if and when they arise, call forth other pairs of opposing constructions of their own. The potential in the case of a particular enactment may be without limit. So it is not at all surprising that statutes are difficult to construe, and that great care and thought are required to arrive at their correct meaning in any one case.

The best way to deal with this, both for arriving at the correct decision in the instant case and for optimum use of that case as a precedent, is to treat the words of the enactment as supplemented by a number (in some cases infinitely great) of notional or implied words. By the technique now suggested, such of these words as are needed to decide a particular case are picked out and declared by the court, acting on the advice of the advocates appearing before it. The words are not confined to the facts of the case, but are generalised so as to apply to facts of that kind (the factual outline). Thereafter the words are on record as a piece of dynamic processing of the enactment in question. Just as we now have precision drafting, so by this means we could enjoy precision judging. (For further examples of interstitial articulation see Bennion 1982(3), 1983(1) and 1983(3)).

Awareness of drafting technique

It has been said that a judge engaged in dynamic processing needs to be aware of relevant techniques of text-creation and text validation. To supplement what is said about these in chapters 1 and 2, we now describe how legislative drafting has become more precise in modern times.

Precision drafting   Legislative drafting in Britain has now reached a high degree of precision. This warrrants the deployment of corresponding precision by judges and practitioners when legislation is dealt with in court. As we have seen, drafters occasionally fall short of this demanding standard. Such inevitable human failure should not prevent statute users from understanding how fully-developed the current drafting technique is, and what benefits can be gained from it.

This high level of precision in modern drafting is recognised by the judiciary. Thus Lord Reid said in *Luke* v *Inland Revenue Commissioners* [1963] AC 557, 577, that 'our standard of drafting is such that [the need to do violence to the words] rarely emerges'. In *Wills* v *Bowley* [1983] 1 AC 57, 104, Lord Bridge referred to 'a modern statute, using language with the precision one expects'. In *Jennings* v *United States Government* [1982] 3 All ER 104, 116, Lord Roskill remarked that until comparatively recently 'statutes were not drafted with the same skill as today'.

In this respect we have gone full circle. The earliest medieval statutes were mostly drafted by the judges. The king's justices were of the Council and of the Parliament. Hazeltine regarded this judicial membership as by far the most important element of Parliament from the point of view both of adjudication and legislation (see Plucknett 1922, p xviii). Holdsworth said of these early statutes:

The statutes were concisely and clearly drawn, and do not seem to have given rise to many difficulties of construction. This is due not only to the fact that they were drafted by the best lawyers of the day, but also to the fact that the prevailing style of legal draftsmanship was good. (Holdsworth 1924, XI 366).

The telling factor however was the complete control the early medieval executive had over the wording of statutes. In this respect we have also turned full circle.

The executive lost this control early in the fifteenth century, when a crucial change came. The Commons, growing more powerful, rejected the system under which, when the king had granted their petition, a judge put the result into 'legal language'. The Commons complained that the ensuing statute often did not correspond to what they had asked for. The remedy was obvious. The Commons themselves should draw the proposal in 'legal language', and present the result to the king for ratification when they (and the Lords) were satisfied with its wording. Thus the Parliamentary Bill was born. (See Holdsworth 1924, pp 439–40.)

The judges, usually as members of the king's Council, continued to play a large part in the drafting of statutes. As the House of Lords grew to be a separate body, it claimed the right to use the services of the judges. Ilbert notes that after the Restoration the judges habitually assisted the House of Lords in their legislative business and drafted Bills or clauses. He adds:

Sometimes the heads of a Bill were agreed to by the House, and a direction was given either to the judges generally or to particular judges to prepare a Bill. In other cases a judge would attend a grand committee of the House as a kind of assessor, and do such drafting work as was required (Ilbert 1901, p 78).

In 1758 the House of Lords had before it a Bill to amend the Habeas Corpus Act 1679. The House consulted the judges as to the existing law and the effect on it of the proposed Bill. The judges responded adversely, whereupon the House threw out the Bill and ordered the judges to draft a new one (Holdsworth 1924, XI 375). Lord Hardwicke made a significant point in his contribution to the debate. The judges, he said, were asked 'not whether it is fit upon political reasons to pass such a Bill—that is a legislative consideration—but to inform your lordships in law' *(Ibid)*. Down to the present century the judges have on occasion drafted legislation (for example Lord Halsbury LC drew part if not the whole of the Companies Act 1900: *Hilder* v *Dexter* [1902] AC 474, 477-8). Nevertheless, from the sixteenth century onwards, more and more statutes were drawn by private practitioners.

Disorganised composition   The unified control essential to clarity had, as stated above, been lost at an early stage in the emergence of the Houses of Parliament. It was not to be fully regained until the present century. This was a gap of some 500 years, during which the distinguishing feature of the statute book was *disorganised composition.*

Thus early on in this interval we find Coke complaining that the Acts of his time are 'overladen with provisoes and additions, and many times on a sudden penn'd and corrected by men of none or very little judgment in the law' (Co. Rep: Preface to Part ii). This state of affairs, said Coke, meant that learned men were often required to 'perplex their heads to make attonement and peace by construction of law between insensible and disagreeing words'. Ruffhead, in his eighteenth century edition of the statutes, described the enactments of the fifteenth and sixteenth centuries as 'hastily drawn up without Order and without Precision'. (Preface to Ruffhead's Edition of the *Statutes at Large* (1763) I v.)

Holdsworth says of the position towards the end of the seventeenth century:

Thus the style in which the statutes were drawn became more and more variegated. The result was increased difficulty in interpreting them, and sometimes in ascertaining their relations to one another. And since, during this period, the style of legal draftsmanship, which was used in the drawing of pleadings, conveyances, and other documents, was tending to become more verbose, the statutes which these lawyers drew exhibited the same quality; and so the difficulties of understanding and applying the growing body of statute law were increased. (Holdsworth 1924, XI 370.)

The position worsened in the eighteenth century. Not only was the statute book inevitably growing bulkier, but the scope of legislation widened. It was an age of technicalities. Conveyancers drafting statutes were paid by the folio, and had no inducement to be brief. 'The result' says Holdsworth 'was that the statute book became not only so heterogeneous and so uncorrelated, but was also so bulky, that, by the middle of the eighteenth century, it was becoming unmanageable' (Holdsworth XI 374).

The transformation came with the establishment of the Parliamentary Counsel Office under Thring in 1869 (see chapter 2 above). Holdsworth said that there could be no doubt as to the 'enormous improvements' effected by this change in the drafting of statutes (Holdsworth 1924, XI 387). A single government department came to be responsible for the drafting of all government Bills not solely relating to Scotland or Ireland. A uniform technique was adopted, which to the present day has steadily improved in precision.

It is important to grasp the essence of this transformation. The difference, as has been said, is between organised and disorganised composition. With disorganised composition there is in reality no coherent meaning. One statement contradicts another. Within a single statement there are glaring defects. As Grove J politely put it in *Ruther* v *Harris* (1876) 1 Ex D 97, 100, the language 'is not strictly accurate and grammatical'.

The enactment with which *Ruther* v *Harris* was concerned, s 21 of the Salmon Fishery Act 1861, furnishes a typical example of disorganised composition. It says that between certain hours no person 'shall fish for, catch, or kill, by any means other than a rod and line any salmon'. (Note that syntactical ambiguity is avoided only by the comma after 'kill', a breach of the rule that punctuation should not affect meaning. The headnote to the report makes the mistake of failing to include this vital comma, thereby demonstrating the validity of the rule.)

The mention in s 21 of both fishing for and catching salmon clearly indicates that the unsuccessful as well as the successful fisherman contravenes the section. Yet it continues with these words: 'and any person acting in contravention of this section shall forfeit all fish taken by him, and any net or moveable instrument used by him *in taking the same*' (emphasis added). The court robustly held that the net of a person who had caught no fish was forfeited.

That particular error is likely to have been the fault of the original drafter. An error probably caused by an ill-considered amendment in Parliament also fell to be dealt with by Grove J in the year 1876. Section 78 of the Highway Act 1835 was a very long section concerned with improper driving of horsedrawn vehicles. It was equipped with no less than three sidenotes, all of which referred only to *drivers*. In the middle of the section however there is inserted a prohibition of furious *riding* of any 'horse or beast'. The machinery provisions of the section, imposing penalties and dealing with the refusal of an offender to disclose his name, are solely in terms of 'drivers'. Again the court was robust. Grove J refused to hold that the legislature had made the 'absurd mistake' of creating riding offences without affixing any punishment for them. (*Williams* v *Evans* (1876) 1 Ex D 277, 282.)

Yet in fact the legislature had indeed made that absurd mistake. What the court did was come to the rescue of the legislature by correcting its error. That regularly had to be done with the sort of disorganised composition the courts were constantly required to grapple with before the advent of modern precision drafting. (As to the contribution formerly made by ill-considered parliamentary amendments to disorganised composition see the remarks by Lord James in *Garbutt* v *Durham Joint Committee* [1906] AC 291, 297. While such errors can still happen today, they are very rare.)

Changing the drafting technique   While complex precision drafting of the common law type has its critics, their objections can mostly be got round by subsequent textual processing of the kind described in chapter 23 below. We had better make the most of the virtues of our drafting techniques, for they are firmly established and resistant to change. Certainly the Law Commission have failed to make any impression on them. Their first programme, following the establishment of the Commission in 1965, contained this pregnant passage:

It is evident that a programme of law reform, which must necessarily use the instrument of legislation, depends for its successful realisation on the interpretation given by the courts to the enactments in which the programme is embodied. The rules of statutory interpretation . . . are often difficult to apply, particularly where they appear to conflict with one another and when their hierarchy of importance is not clearly established.

The Commission accordingly recommended 'that an examination be made of the rules for the interpretation of statutes', to which the Lord Chancellor agreed. A working paper followed, on which there was exhaustive consultation. The resulting recommendations were published in 1969 (Law Com No 21). They proved abortive. One reason was the steadfast oppostion of Parliamentary Counsel (who are well aware of the close link between rules of interpretation and drafting technique). As we have seen, a like fate befell the Renton Report (p 48) and the Law Commission report on drafting in relation to criminal responsibility (p 271).

Apart from perhaps abandoning the technique of indirect amendment (p 229), the Parliamentary Counsel Office has maintained its techniques unaltered in the face of continuous recent criticism. Yet they are far from being the only techniques that could be applied for the purpose. We have discussed at some length the claims of civil law drafting (pp 23–26). Now for further comparison let us glance at a third system, that prevailing in the United States. For those not familiar with it, there are some surprises in store.

Legislative drafting in America

Every principle of drafting now observed in Britain is overturned in the United States. The executive does not have its legislation drafted by its own expert officials in a central office. It has no expert officials, and no central office. Drafting is not regarded as a refined art, to be mastered only after many years' full-time practice. Much federal and state legislation is drafted by law students at Harvard or Yale. There is no pressure for a scientific statute book, arranged under titles. Few people have shown concern at the flaws revealed by this passage from Reed Dickerson's classic book *Legislative Drafting:*

In the rush to meet the exigencies of particular problems, laws are proposed and frequently enacted that do not show how far they amend or supersede pre-existing laws. Others are proposed that do not dovetail adequately with related or companion legislation. Many show little regard for the need to develop a reliable means of communication between the legislator and the persons the legislation is addressed to. Common usage is too readily perverted by short cuts that save the draftsman's time but sooner or later lose untold hours for the individuals, agencies and courts that have to determine what the law means (Dickerson 1954, p 5).

The last sentence at least has a convincing ring in Britain!

While there are official federal and state legislative counsel in the United States, no one is obliged to use them or take their advice. Bills that become law are drafted by the personal staff of Congressmen and Senators, by specialists attached to Congress committees, by freelance drafting agencies, by lobbyists and by agencies of the executive. As we have seen, some are even drafted by law students.

The Harvard Legislative Research Bureau was founded in 1952 to provide governmental and public service groups with technical services in the preparation and drafting of legislation. In 1964 it began publishing the Harvard Journal on Legislation, which still flourishes. Reed Dickerson contributed to the first issue, an article on 'diseases of legislative language'. The journal was seen as a vehicle for disseminating the drafting work of the Bureau, including model bills on key issues of current public interest. Two recent models were a bill to protect the confidentiality of a newsman's sources (a 'shield' bill) and a bill to require periodic evaluation of governmental agencies (a 'sunset' bill).

Requests for the services of these Harvard units come mainly from three areas:

(1) Congressional and state legislative committees, agencies and legislative counsel.
(2) Lobbying organisation that attempt to represent the public interest.
(3) Legislators wishing to obtain a first draft, or initial picture,

of what a legislative response to their particular concern would look like.

Harvard makes no charge for these services, since it believes that supplying them (under expert supervision) enhances the students' educational development. I queried with Russell Isaia, a third-year student who was the current president of the Bureau, whether Harvard students could provide draft Bills of comparable standard to those produced by Parliamentary Counsel in Britain (who are not regarded as fully qualified until they have had at least ten years' fulltime drafting experience). He replied: 'We do not pretend to achieve the mastery that ten years' full time experience would provide, but it is usually sufficient to meet the standards of American legislatures.'

This digression on American legislation has been included to emphasise that the British way is not the only way (even if it is the best way currently on offer). It may also remind our judges that there are different drafting methods, and that it is therefore important to know which one is operating in the judge's jurisdiction— and what its detailed characteristics are.

The way forward

Was Lord Wilberforce right to say that law reform cannot grapple with statutory interpretation, and that it is merely a matter of 'educating the judges and practitioners and hoping that the work is better done' (HL Deb 6 November 1966, col 1254)? It depends what you mean by law reform. The question is how judges should treat the five doubt-factors which prevent legislation operating as direct communication with the statute user. Can the judges themselves rectify the system? Might they pass a resolution effectively updating the resolution passed by the judges of the Court of Exchequer Chamber four centuries ago (*Heydon's Case* (1584) 3 Co Rep 7a)? Or must Parliament step in to confirm a delegation which after all is no more than implied, and therefore disputable? We return to this question below.

Differential readings

Even where no doubt-factor is present, and static processing (dealt with in chapter 23 below) has rendered all the assistance it can, there may still be disagreement about meaning. This is because of the limits to semantic precision where general rules are formulated. When judges differ it may be because they take different views on how to resolve a doubt-factor. On the other hand it may be because, while no doubt-factor is present, they disagree about how a general formula applies to particular facts. Different minds, confronted with a formula using inexact language (as most language is), will sometimes arrive at different results. The mental process of applying the rule to the facts can only end in a 'feeling' that one interpretation or another is correct. Such feelings are justified in presentation by advancing supporting arguments and denigrating counter-arguments. The weight to be attached to each supporting argument, and the offsetting weight of each counter argument, are in the last resort a question of 'feel'. This is abundantly illustrated in the reports. It is well described in the following passage from the speech of Lord Simonds in *Kirkness* v *John Hudson & Co Ltd* [1955] AC 696, 712. He begins by describing the task of the five Law Lords in the case:

Each one of us has the task of deciding what the relevant words mean. In coming to that decision he will necessarily give great weight to the opinion of others, but if at the end of the day he forms his own clear judgment and does not think that the words are 'fairly and equally open to divers meanings' he is not entitled to say that there is an ambiguity. For him at least there is no ambiguity and on that basis he must decide the case.

This is an important concept, which needs to be clearly grasped by interpreters. If, on an informed approach, no real doubt is felt about the meaning, there is no room for the application of any interpretative criteria (see *Director of Public Prosecutions* v *Ottewell* [1970] AC 642, 649). But then it has to be remembered that, as explained above, (pp 105–107), these criteria must be kept in mind in deciding whether or not doubt exists.

Examples of differential readings

A remarkable example arose in *Newbury DC* v *Secretary of State for the Environment* [1981] AC 578. The case concerned aircraft hangars on a former aerodrome. They had been used by the Home Office for the storage of fire-pumps. Subsequently they were used by a company for storing synthetic rubber. The question was whether these uses made the hangars 'repositories' within the meaning of a Town and Country Planning (Use Classes) Order. The differential readings at various stages of the case are well summarised by Lord Dilhorne (at pp 596–597):

All the members of the Divisional Court (Lord Widgery LJ, Michael Davies and Robert Goff JJ) and all the members of the Court of Appeal (Lord Denning MR, Lawton and Browne LJJ) agreed that the use of the hangars by the Home Office was not use as a repository. Despite the unanimity of judicial opinion and despite the strong view expressed by Lord Denning MR that 'no one conversant with the English language would dream of calling these hangars a 'repository' when filled with fire-pumps or synthetic rubber' and that of Lawton LJ that—

'As a matter of the ordinary modern usage of the English language . . . no literate person would say that the use to which the Home Office had put the hangars in the 1950s was, or that the company are now, using them as a repository'

I feel compelled to say that to describe the use of the hangars when so filled as use for a repository is, in my opinion, a perfectly accurate and correct use of the English language. They were when used by the Home Office used as repositories for fire-pumps and so to describe them is just as correct as it is to describe a burial place as a repository for the dead.

The other four Law Lords agreed with Lord Dilhorne. It was six judges against five, but the five had the last word.

Nothing could have been clearer in some eyes than the capital gains tax enactment applicable in *O'Brien* v *Benson's Hosiery Ltd* [1980] AC 562. A company entered into a seven-year contract of service with a Mr Behar. It thereby acquired what many people would call an 'asset' (the term used in the enactment). So valuable was the asset that after 18 months Mr Behar paid the company £50,000 for his release. Was not this a gain accruing to the company on the 'disposal' of its asset?

The Court of Appeal (consisting of Buckley LJ, Bridge LJ and Sir David Cairns) did not think so. The drafter of the Act had not relied only on common sense to do his work. He went to great trouble to spell out that 'asset' included all forms of property, including options, debts and incorporeal property generally. He added that there was a 'disposal' of an asset where a capital sum was received in return for forfeiture or surrender of a right. None of this satisfied the Court of Appeal. They allowed counsel for the company to lead them along byways of argument designed to show that the plain words should be given an artificially restricted meaning because of a House of Lords decision 25 years earlier on entirely different legislation. Five unanimous present-day Lords of Appeal corrected their error.

In *Bourne* v *Norwich Crematorium Ltd* [1967] 1 WLR 691 the court had to consider tax provisions later consolidated in the Capital Allowances Act 1968. Allowances were granted for expenditure on construction of an industrial building or structure, the relevant definition referring to a building or structure 'in use for the purposes of a trade which consists in . . . the subjection of goods or materials to any process'. Did this include the furnace chamber and chimney tower of a crematorium? No, said the court. It would be a distortion of the English language to describe dead bodies as 'goods or materials'. The decision was perverse, since the policy of the Income Tax Acts clearly indicates that the allowance should have been given. The Law Commission, when pronouncing on the decision, blamed what it called an unsatisfactory body of interpretative principles, or in other words 'literalism' (Law Com No 21 (1969) para 8).

The same thing happened in *Buckingham* v *Securitas Properties Ltd* (1979) 124 SJ 17. Slade J denied capital allowances to a security company on the ground that making up wage packets was not the subjection of goods to a process. The term 'goods' did not extend to coins and notes treated as currency or a medium of exchange. But why should not coins and notes be treated as 'materials' and so qualify? The report is silent on this point.

In both these cases the taxpayer was deserving of sympathy. Should the drafter be blamed? No, because in referring to the subjection of goods and materials to any process he was using a phrase going as wide as the language permits. Anything movable and concrete is within these words on any reasonable construction. Was the Law Commission right in blaming a rule of interpretation requiring 'literalism'? No, because on a literal construction both corpses and currency notes are materials. So one can only blame the courts for failing to apply a straightforward enactment in a straightforward way. But is this fair either? Neither judge felt any doubt.

The drafter's dilemma

The phenomenon of differential readings places the drafter in a difficulty. He knows that what seems plain to him may not be found plain by others—even where their intellect is not clouded by extraneous factors such as sympathy for the plaintiff. The drafter's feelings are on record in one case, namely s 1 of the Wills Act 1968. In the Heap Report this is criticised for saying that attestation of a will by a beneficiary is to be disregarded 'if the will is duly executed without his attestation' (Statute Law Society 1970, para 84). The report states that a witness to the Heap Committee complained:

The use of the word 'without' suggests that the attestation is not there whereas the whole point of it is that it *is* there. Modern usage would call for 'apart from', and if those words had been substituted for 'without', it would not be necessary to read the section several times in order to find out what it is trying to say.

Rarely in modern times are we privileged to know the views of the drafter on criticism of this sort. Here we have that privilege. The drafter was no less a person than the head of the United Kingdom drafting office, Sir Noël Hutton. In a session of the Renton Committee (of which he was a member) Sir Noël said to representatives of the Statute Law Society (which appointed the Heap Committee): 'this seems to be so plainly mistaken as a criticism that I wondered again if you yourselves had actually read the Act before publicising this as a criticism of it' (Statute Law Society 1979, p 11).

Differentials across the border

Where judges produce differential readings of the same words as applied to the same, or similar, facts, the normal result is that the

reading preferred by the highest court trumps the rest. An exception
may arise where the Act applies in two different jurisdictions.

Section 1 of the Road Traffic Act 1972 created the offence of
causing death by reckless driving. It applied both in England and
Scotland. In *R* v *Murphy* [1980] Crim LR 309 the Court of Appeal
(Criminal Division) held that in this connection the test of the
existence of the recklessness was *subjective*. The required mental
element of indifference to the need to drive with due care had to
be proved by the prosecution.

On the other hand in *Allan* v *Patterson* (1980) 124 SJ 149, the
High Court of Justiciary in Scotland applied what it called 'a totally
objective test' in construing the same provision. They held that it
is the quality of the driving that matters. In this context ' "recklessly"
. . . plainly means a piece of driving which, judged objectively, is
eloquent of a high degree of negligence'. Since there is no appeal
to the House of Lords from decisions on criminal matters in Scotland,
the two countries would have continued to operate a different law
of reckless driving if in *R* v *Lawrence* [1982] AC 510 the House
of Lords had not brought English law into line with the Scottish
decision. While unfortunate, this would have been an inevitable
consequence of having two jurisdictions, coupled with the inexorable
phenomenon of differential readings.

Conclusion

We see that the 'feel' by which judges arrive at differential readings
is subjective. It may be possible to ascribe an erroneous reading
to a conspicuous factor, such as an over-persuasive advocate or a
party who arouses sympathy. Alternatively, there may be no obvious
reason. In some respects legal doctrine is decided on purely subjective
grounds. The line may not be easy to draw. Some might treat
'repository' and 'materials' as broad terms, and argue that the cases
we have cited concerning them merely illustrate resolution of a doubt-
factor, as described in chapter 16. That does not appear to have
been the view of the judges concerned.

The position is obscured by the fact that judges are not accustomed
to approach problems of interpretation in this way, and so do not
frame their judgments in appropriate terms. There is a clear
conceptual difference between delegation by use of a broad term
objectively capable of alternative meanings in a given connection,
and subjective disagreement on meaning where no doubt is felt.

A processing Act?

Parliament has shown itself unwilling to deal with the correction
of errors in statutes by any formal procedure short of ordinary
legislation. The House of Commons Select Committee on Procedure
received coolly the Renton Committee's suggestion of a streamlined

procedure for correcting errors in Bills discovered between the passing of the Bill and royal assent (Renton 1975, para 18.36; First Report from the Select Committee on Procedure Session 1977–78, para 2.44). A similar reception was accorded to the Government's Acts of Parliament (Correction of Mistakes) Bill 1977. The Select Committee on Procedure commented on this that 'we believe the public are entitled to have such corrections drawn to their attention by means of an amending Act' (*Ibid*, para 2.45; see Miers and Page 1982, p 106).

In these circumstances it would be helpful for an Act to be passed codifying what it is submitted are the existing judicial powers.

Terminology

It is convenient to begin with some defined terms to be used in the proposed Act. We propose that the Act should apply to the interpretation both of Acts of Parliament and statutory instruments. We may use the term 'legislative text' to cover both these, producing the following definition: 'legislative text' means a provision of an Act or statutory instrument, and references to the enactment of a text shall be construed accordingly.

It will be necessary to refer to 'the legislator', and the following is suggested: 'the legislator' in relation to an Act means Parliament, and in relation to a statutory instrument means the person or body by whom it was made. Difficulties arise in relation to the concept of the legislator's *intention*. The duplex approach calls for recognition of the drafter's role as well as Parliament's. It does not seem proper to refer in the Act to 'the drafter' bearing in mind that there may not be a single drafter, that the drafter may change in the course of the Bill's progress, that text creation is also the business of administrative officials and others, and that amendments may be added of which the drafter does not approve (for an example see Bennion 1976 (3)). Nevertheless some reference, even though oblique, needs to be made to the duplex approach.

There is also the vexed question of allowing citation of travaux préparatoires and other external materials, including reports of Parliamentary debates. While full allowance ought to be made for the objections to this, it is submitted that judges should be permitted a discretion here. They should always have in mind the predictability principle, and the need to avoid prolonging proceedings unduly, so the Act should contain reminders to this effect. Subject to this, it would be desirable to avoid the artificiality of requiring a ruse such as the reading out in court of a passage from a textbook which cites forbidden material. Judges can surely be trusted not to let the facility of citing external sources get out of hand or be misused.

Less difficult is the problem of the connection between the intention of the Minister in making a statutory instrument and the intention of Parliament in conferring the power to do so. It seems desirable to deal with all these questions by a special provision, as follows:

Intention of the legislator.	(1) In construing any reference in this Act to the intention of the legislator, the court shall have regard to the principles set out in this section.

(2) The intention is primarily to be derived from the legislative text itself (including any source referred to in the text).

(3) The court may refer to any other source in addition if it thinks fit to do so having regard to the requirements of justice, including –

(*a*) the desirability of persons being able to rely on the meaning conveyed by the text itself, and

(*b*) the need to avoid prolonging legal proceedings without compensating advantage.

(4) The court shall have regard, so far as may be relevant, to the procedures by which, in accordance with constitutional practice, the text may be taken to have been created and validated as law.

(5) In the case of a statutory instrument the court shall, so far as may be relevant, have regard to the intention of Parliament in delegating power to make the instrument as well as to the intention of the person or body by whom it was made.

Although it is convenient to refer to a 'court', the Act should apply to any functionary charged with applying a legislative text. The following is suggested for this: ' "court" includes a tribunal, arbitrator or other person or body with the function of interpreting a legislative text.'

Having completed the interpretative provisions, we now turn to the substance.

Substantive provisions

How far is it necessary or desirable to give statutory recognition to judicial processing? We need to distinguish here between intentional and unintentional doubt-factors. Deliberate delegation to the courts by ellipsis, the use of broad terms or politic uncertainty scarcely needs mention in our new Act. The trouble is that these techniques are not openly recognised now. It would help if the Act could refer to them in some way. The drafter's method in such cases is to operate indirectly by including a passing reference to the matter in question. The phrase 'without prejudice . . .' is useful here.

Another point concerns just how far the new Act should

go. Should it refer to processing as such, and confer or imply power to make sub-rules? Or should it merely confer or imply power to deliver judgments in particular cases? Then, by the doctrine of *stare decisis*, the judgments would form precedents from which sub-rules could be postulated in the way familiar in the development of common law doctrines. Since these are innovatory concepts they are more likely to gain acceptance if we move cautiously. So we adopt the latter course.

These considerations lead us to suggest an introductory clause, as follows:

> Powers of the court.
>
> Without prejudice to a court's implementation of a legislative text under which (whether expressly or by an implication arising from a deliberate omission or use of a term of wide meaning or otherwise) any power is conferred on or delegated to the court, it is hereby declared, for the avoidance of doubt, that a court has the powers referred to in sections   to   in relation to a legislative text relevant to the case before it.

It will be noticed that this operates, not by conferring any new power, but as a declaration of existing law. It is my contention that all these powers already exist, and that the new Act is not strictly necessary to enable the courts to proceed in the ways suggested in this book. The Act is simply a desirable measure to overcome the reluctance of the judiciary to exercise the powers they are in fact given by the wording of individual texts.

The first of the main clauses will deal with obsolescent Acts of the kind discussed in chapter 16 (in relation to terms mobile in time) and in chapter 18. Difficult problems await us here. It is suggested that we could usefully establish the 'always speaking' principle, subject to any indication to the contrary in the text. If the original mischief has disappeared altogether, the Act may have become spent. This possibility needs to be recognised, but subject to it the court should apply the Act in relation to what remains, updating the text as necessary. Here is the suggested provision:

> Obsolescent text.
>
> (1) This section applies where it appears to the court that, through the passage of time since the enactment, or original enactment, of the text, its effect is doubtful.
> (2) If the mischief or object at which the text was directed has changed its nature, the court shall apply the text, subject to such modifications as may be requisite, to the changed mischief or object.
> (3) Subsection (2) does not apply where the change is such that the interests of justice require that the text be treated as spent.

This enables the obsolescent language to be updated so far as necessary, provided the original mischief or object has not virtually disappeared (in which case it would be right to treat the enactment as spent). The words 'or original enactment' in subs (1) allow for the possibility that the original text has been consolidated.

Next we turn to cases of drafting error. Here it would be very valuable to have parliamentary recognition of the possibility of error, with express power to the courts to deal with it. At the same time it does not seem necessary or desirable to go into much detail about the possible types of error. The predictability principle requires the power to rectify not to be given unless the error is obvious. It should also be reasonably obvious what the correct version is (though the exact wording may not matter). It seems worth distinguishing the defective text from the text which fails to carry out the legislator's intention. The following two clauses are suggested:

Defective text.

(1) This section applies where it appears to the court that, through grammatical error, syntactical ambiguity, omission, transposition or intrusion, logical error, punctuation mistake or other formal defect, the effect of the text is doubtful.

(2) Where it is clear what form the legislator intended the text to take, the court shall apply it in that form.

(3) In any other case the court shall apply it in the form best suited to serve the object of the text as intended by the legislator.

Unintended effect.

(1) This section applies where it appears to the court that, because the text goes narrower or wider than the object, or is based on an error of law or fact, or is otherwise misconceived, it does not carry out the legislator's intention, or goes wider than the intention.

(2) Where it is clear what the effect of the text should have been in order to carry out the legislator's intention and no more, the court shall give the text that effect.

(3) In any other case the court shall apply the text as it stands apart from this section.

These provisions, arranged in the form of a Bill, are set out in Appendix A (p 343).

Chapter Twenty-Three

Static Processing of Texts

Aiding text collation

The statute user's problem of text collation was described briefly in chapter 13 (pp 210–211). In order to discover what statute law provides for a factual situation, it is necessary, as we have seen, for the user to find out which are the relevant texts, and then make sure he has them in up-to-date form. In Britain the tools officially provided for this purpose are of high quality. This is one respect in which we are in advance of some other Commonwealth countries. The basic need is for an *index* arranged under topics (from which to compile a list of relevant texts) and a *table* in which texts so compiled are listed chronologically, with annotations showing amendments, commencement dates etc. Both these are provided by the British authorities.

The nearest we have to a keeper of the statute book in Britain is the Statute Law Committee. This was set up in 1868 by Lord Cairns. Its chairman is the Lord Chancellor of the day, who appoints the remaining members. Its current terms of reference are as follows:

To consider the steps necessary to bring the Statute Book up to date by consolidation, revision and otherwise, and to superintend the publication and indexing of Statutes, Revised Statutes and Statutory Instruments. (Renton 1975, paras 5.1 and 5.2.)

In 1870, shortly after the setting up of the Statute Law Committee, the first official index was published under its direction. This was in response to a suggestion made by Lord Cairns to the then Lord Chancellor, Lord Chelmsford. The title of the work was *Index to the Statutes in Force*. In 1876 Lord Thring prepared a paper of instructions, laying down improved principles. The scheme of the index, nowadays called the *Index to the Statutes*, continues to be to group, under appropriate headings, entries relating to the whole of the general statute law in force. Lord Cairns' suggestion also extended to the production of a chronological table, and this too began publication in 1870. It still continues, under the title *Chronological Table of the Statutes*.

In 1887 Alexander Pulling sent a memorandum to the Statute Law Committee. In it he made suggestions for remedying the inconvenience arising from the lack of an official system of indexing or collating what Pulling called 'statutory rules and orders' (a name which stuck). In the result Pulling was asked by the Committee to prepare the first of an annual series of volumes of S R & O's. They also desired him to compile a comprehensive index. The initial annual volume appeared in 1889. It has been repeated in each year since. The first index produced by Pulling was published in 1891. He also compiled the first collected edition of S R & Os. It contained instruments of a public and general character issued before 1890, and ran to eight volumes.

In 1893 the Rules Publication Act was passed. This required rule-making authorities, as the Act called them, to send the rules and orders they made to the Queen's Printer to be registered, numbered and printed. In the following year the Treasury made regulations governing the details of this process. In 1895 Pulling was placed in charge of indexing both statutes and what are now known as statutory instruments. The Statutory Publications Office was born, but has never itself been a publisher. That function continues to be in the hands of Her Majesty's Stationery Office (HMSO).

The *Index to the Statutes* is published 'annually', though publication difficulties in recent years have meant that this aim is not always realised. The *Index* covers in two volumes all public general statutes in force, including ante-Union Scottish Acts. A corresponding work relating to Northern Ireland is published less frequently. There is also an index to local Acts. These give local authorities special powers in relation to such matters as highways and streets, public utilities etc. This publication is called *Index to Local and Personal Acts.*

The Chronological Table of the Statutes also aims (though not always successfully) at annual publication, also in two volumes. It lists all public general Acts passed since 1235, whether or not they are still in force. If an Act remains operative, the *Table* lists the amendments which have been made to it. Again, there is a corresponding publication for Northern Ireland. At the end of the second volume of the *Chronological Table of the Statutes* there is a chronological table of local and personal Acts. This was instituted by a direction of the Statute Law Committee in 1974, and shows all amendments to local and personal Acts after 1973.

In relation to statutory instruments, there are two useful official publications. The *Index to Government Orders* is a biennial publication showing under appropriate subject headings the powers to make statutory instruments, together with titles of instruments made under those powers and still in force. The *Table of Government Orders* is a cumulative annual publication. It lists general statutory instruments in chronological order, showing whether each instrument is still in force and, if it is, giving details of any amendments which affect it. The *Table* also includes instruments made under the Royal prerogative. The information given by these two publications is updated by *Annual, Monthly* and *Daily Lists of Statutory Instruments* issued by HMSO. Another useful feature is the supplementary material given in the annual volume of public general Acts passed during the year. This includes tables of short titles and effects of legislation, subject index, tables of derivations and destinations of consolidation Acts and a table of textual amendments made to Acts by statutory instruments.

In an account of the work of the Statutory Publications Office by a former Editor, AB Lyons, it is stressed that 'our function is to make the laws available to all, not to make them intelligible' (Lyons 1969, p 2). Intelligibility belongs to the realm of text-comprehension, also discussed in chapter 13 (pp 211–212). As we saw in chapter 14, there are specific factors that cause impaired intelligibility in the drafting of legislation. It remains to consider a further aspect related to the subject of this chapter. Can the drafting of Acts be improved to render text-collation easier?

Since an Act changes the law, it often has to include what are called transitional provisions. It cannot be brought fully into force with immediate effect, but must spell out precisely how its substantive parts are modified for pending cases and other transactions already in train. The Act also has to specify relevant dates. Usually these transitional provisions are quickly spent. Thereafter, their dead words cumber the Act, obscuring its substance.

Later on, the Act is likely to be amended by a further Act. Let us hope this is done by direct textual amendment, and not indirectly. The original Act can then be reprinted as amended, and endures as one coherent text. Even if the amendments are textual however, there is still a transitional problem. It is the same problem as arose with the original Act—of dealing with pending cases (and other transactions already in train) and specifying relevant dates. It means that further transitional provisions are needed to deal with the amendments made by the new Act.

Each time the original Act is amended, the same thing happens. Let us take as a model Principal Act 1960 and Amending Acts 1965, 1970, 1975 and 1980. Suppose that each Amending Act amends Principal Act 1960 textually and contains its own transitional provisions (which, following the usual practice, are not textually incorporated into Principal Act 1960). Suppose further that Principal Act 1960 is reprinted as textually amended. To get the whole story the user still needs to consult *five* documents, as follows:

(1) Substantive provisions of Principal Act 1960 (as textually amended by Amending Acts 1965, 1970, 1975 and 1980) plus transitional provisions 1960.
(2) Transitional provisions 1965.
(3) Transitional provisions 1970.
(4) Transitional provisions 1975.

(5) Transitional provisions 1980.

To deal with this problem I devised a special type of Schedule when drafting tax legislation for the Jamaican Government in the early 1970s. Using the above model, the device works as follows. Principal Act 1960 would have contained a schedule on the following lines (which later came to be known as a Jamaica Schedule). Paragraph 1 of the schedule states the commencement date for every provision of the Act not specified in any subsequent paragraph of the schedule ('the master commencement date'). Subsequent paragraphs deal seriatim with substantive provisions of the Act for which the master commencement dates does not apply, or for which transitional provisions are required (setting them out). Subsequently, each Amending Act (as well as amending the substantive provisions of Principal Act 1960) also textually amends the Jamaica Schedule to Principal Act 1960 as necessary to incorporate transitional provisions for the new amendments.

The result is that once Principal Act 1960 is reprinted as amended textually, the whole story is to be found in one document instead of five. It should be added that amendments to the Jamaica Schedule would also include repealing provisions, with operative dates. The Jamaica Schedule thus operates as a complete historical file on the substantive provisions of the principal Act. (For additional details see Statute Law Society 1972, pp 12 and 32). At least one academic commentator has welcomed the aid given by the Jamaica Schedule (Samuels 1974, p 534).

A further refinement ought to be mentioned. Where, as frequently happens, commencement dates are not specified in the Act itself but are left to be prescribed by order, the power to make commencement orders would include a requirement that each order should amend the Jamaica Schedule textually so as to write in the commencement date. As we have seen (p 49), a comparable procedure was adopted for the Consumer Credit Act 1974.

The great utility for computer use of equipping Acts with a Jamaica Schedule or historical file was fully spelt out in an article I wrote for the New Law Journal in 1981 and supplemented in a subsequent letter (see Bennion 1981(3) and (4)). The need for this reform is demonstrated by the flow of cases concerned with doubt as to the commencement of enactments (for examples see [1983] Crim LR 255-6).

Text manipulation

Our final task is to examine ways of easing the statute user's problems of text comprehension, which were outlined in chapter 13 (pp 211–212). We saw in chapter 14 the factors that cause legislative texts to be drafted in ways inimical to understanding. If we accept that these factors are ineluctable, and are content to take drafting methods as they are, what remedies can we devise? The clue is given in

Access to the Law, a study conducted for the Law Reform Commission of Canada in 1975. As the author, Dean Friedland of the University of Toronto, says: 'The challenge is to simplify the manner of presentation, not necessarily to simplify the law itself' (Friedland 1975, p 65).

How can this challenge be met? First let us see exactly what is involved. We rule out summaries and paraphrases, whether official or unofficial. They have their uses, but they are not ways of presenting the text. An unfortunate consequence of the complication of legislative texts is that people despair of understanding them and resort to substitutes. Yet as we saw from the remark of Sir William Dale quoted in chapter 2 (p 26) 'when once one understands a United Kingdom Act, one can usually ascertain the answer to one's question.'

It is of course the *authoritative* answer to the question, direct from the horse's mouth. It is not the opinion of someone else (however expert he may be), but the pronouncement of the legislator. That is why it is worth going to a good deal of trouble to find it out. Modern drafters take care to spell out the detail of their provisions in a logical and consistent way. Usually, if not always, they succeed. If the matter goes to court, the court usually arrives at the result the drafter intended. The fact that we have spent time in this book analysing the deficiencies of this system ought not to obscure that.

So we must work with the official text, and the whole of it. But the official text is arranged in the way required by parliamentary procedure, its shape perhaps distorted by factors extraneous to its meaning. The language is compressed by the need for brevity, and the text is deficient in headings and other signposts. It may be only of several texts that the user needs to fit together or conflate.

The first question in meeting the challenge posed by Dean Friedland is this. Can we, so as to 'simplify the manner of presentation', as it were play about with the official text? Can we juggle the order of sections, or mix up provisions from an Act with provisions from a statutory instrument? This is not as straightforward as might appear.

The doctrine of the free-standing Act

It has been customary in Britain to regard each Act as a self-contained entity. It was drafted as a whole, and is to be read as a whole. It is a rounded piece of work, standing alone. Its author has not designed it to slot into some larger structure, created by other hands. This principle partly explains the inveterate opposition of parliamentary counsel to the textual amendment method. The doctrine was also responsible for the hostility by some drafters to publications such as *Statutes Revised*, which print the text in amended form and not as originally enacted. For convenience we will call it the doctrine of the free-standing Act.

If the doctrine has any substance in law it may form an impediment to the idea of shuffling the textual units around in an effort to 'simplify the method of presentation'. Has it any substance?

We saw in chapter 3 (p 48) how the draftsman of the Criminal Law Act 1977 may have felt inhibited by one manifestation of the doctrine. This is the rule in *A-G* v *Lamplough* (1878) 3 Ex D 214. We can illustrate the point now by a simplified example.

An Act prohibits certain conduct 'where condition A, B or C is satisfied'. It goes on to say that 'in any other case' the conduct is permissible if specified requirements are observed. A later Act repeals the reference to condition B. Do the words 'in any other case' now include B, although they clearly did not do so before?

It is arguable that *A-G* v *Lamplough* lays down a rule to the contrary. An Act amended by the repeal of certain words is not to be read in future by closing up the gaps and pretending the words were never there. In our model the phrase 'in any other case' did not include condition B when enacted. The repeal does not alter this (unless of course there are other words in the amending Act to indicate that the alteration is intended). So the repeal removes conduct satisfying condition B from control altogether.

It will be seen how inconvenient this rule is. The literal meaning of the amended text cannot be followed. Indeed to show the true meaning it is necessary to print the text with the repealed words included. The reader must be alert to remember that they have been repealed but he needs to know what they are because they affect the meaning of the words that remain. This is the triumph of the old-fashioned view. You must read each Act as originally enacted. No one must come to your aid by processing the text. So the statute book, instead of presenting a jigsaw picture with the pieces interlocking, resembles a pack of cards. Each Act trumps the one before. Fortunately the rule in *A-G* v *Lamplough* is not firmly established. It is little known, and if it ever comes up for review one hopes the courts will overrule it. We can do without unnecessary traps and obstacles to simplification.

The opposite of the doctrine of the free-standing Act may be called the doctrine of the continuous text. The drafter, whether of an Act or a statutory instrument, regards his text (so far as text-validation procedures allow) as something to be slotted into the existing legislation rather than as an independent entity. But he does not make the mistake involved in the now discredited practice of providing that an Act is to be 'construed as one' with various other Acts. (For the confusions caused by this see Craies 1971, pp 138-9, 223 and 360-1).

The drafter using the continuous-text method makes clear the relationship of his text to other texts with which it is 'continuous'. He does not set any traps or puzzles in relation to other texts, but he does enable helpful rearrangements to be made by processors. It is believed that most modern drafters now follow this method, and that it is firmly enough established to enable us to devise processing methods which rely on it. We aim therefore to 'simplify the manner of presentation' while retaining the entirety of the official language, juggling it around as may seem convenient. What methods shall we use?

A text that lays down a series of alternatives operating according to the particular factual situation can be presented sequentially. This converts a generalised statement into a method by which the user can trace out the answer to his own problem without stumbling over provisions that for him are irrelevant. Moreover he is saved from having to work out which provisions *are* irrelevant. All he need do is answer a series of factual questions.

This presentation of a legislative text is called an algorithm. The following diagram is an algorithm I devised for my book *Consumer Credit Control*. It uses nothing else but unabbreviated provisions of the Consumer Credit Act 1974. The idea is to inform a trader of his statutory duties in relation to certain agreements governed by the Act. It will be seen that the algorithm gives only partial relief. Before using it the trader must decide that the agreement in question is not a 'cancellable agreement'. This involves applying a definition in the Act. (A different algorithm is provided for cancellable agreements.)

While this algorithm retains the complete statutory language, thus satisfying the condition under which we are operating in searching for ways of simplifying the manner of presentation, it is far from telling the *whole* story. Many terms used in it are defined terms, and for completeness the user needs to look in the Act for the definitions. There are references to certain regulations, and again the user needs the text of these. This illustrates the limitations of algorithms. They are useful, but only where some detailed set of alternatives is involved. The more alternatives there are, and the more clear-cut the factual situation involved in each one, the more effective and useful will the algorithm be.

Where texts in machine-readable form are stored in a computer data base, they can be accessed by various techniques for search and retrieval. Examples are key words in context (KWIC) and lists giving words used and numbers of occurrences. Hard copy (printouts) can be obtained, and texts can be scanned visually using VDUs.

So far the legal texts stored in computer data bases throughout the English-speaking world have consisted of archival material designed originally for conventional print media. Law reports, textbooks, even statutes are in a form designed for another age. There is little sign as yet that the significance of this has been grasped. The service rendered by the computer is only as good as the materials put into it. In time they will be designed for the purpose.

The boldest idea in this regard is to begin with the law itself, and frame it from the start in a logical symbolism. Instead of storing

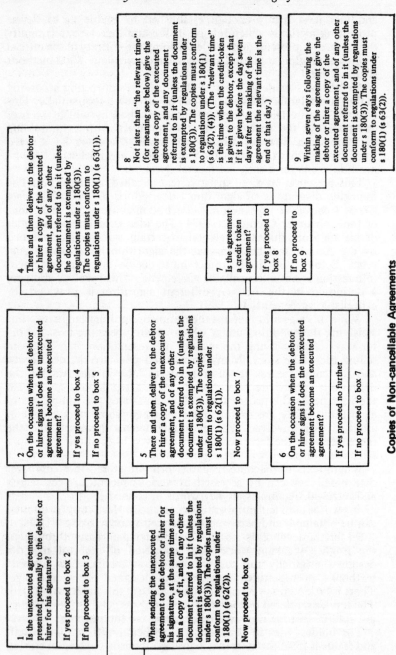

1
Is the unexecuted agreement presented personally to the debtor or hirer for his signature?

If yes proceed to box 2

If no proceed to box 3

2
On the occasion when the debtor or hirer signs it does the unexecuted agreement become an executed agreement?

If yes proceed to box 4

If no proceed to box 5

3
When sending the unexecuted agreement to the debtor or hirer for his signature, at the same time send him a copy of it, and of any other document referred to in it (unless the document is exempted by regulations under s 180(3)). The copies must conform to regulations under s 180(1) (s 62(2)).

Now proceed to box 6

4
There and then deliver to the debtor or hirer a copy of the executed agreement, and of any other document referred to in it (unless the document is exempted by regulations under s 180(3)). The copies must conform to regulations under s 180(1) (s 63(1)).

5
There and then deliver to the debtor or hirer a copy of the unexecuted agreement, and of any other document referred to in it (unless the document is exempted by regulations under s 180(3)). The copies must conform to regulations under s 180(1) (s 62(1)).

Now proceed to box 7

6
On the occasion when the debtor or hirer signs it does the unexecuted agreement become an executed agreement?

If yes proceed no further

If no proceed to box 7

7
Is the agreement a credit token agreement?

If yes proceed to box 8

If no proceed to box 9

8
Not later than "the relevant time" (for meaning see below) give the debtor a copy of the executed agreement, and any document referred to in it (unless the document is exempted by regulations under s 180(3)). The copies must conform to regulations under s 180(1) (s 63(2), (4)). (The "relevant time" is the time when the credit-token is given to the debtor, except that if it is given before the making of the agreement the relevant time is the end of that day.)

9
Within seven days following the making of the agreement give the debtor or hirer a copy of the executed agreement, and of any other document referred to in it (unless the document is exempted by regulations under s 180(3)). The copies must conform to regulations under s 180(1) (s 63(2)).

Copies of Non-cancellable Agreements

within a data base formulations in ordinary language, which can then be accessed as a book is taken down from a library shelf, the computer is given the means of working out problems for itself, and delivering the answers. LEGOL, a linguistic system developed at the London School of Economics, points the way (see Bennion 1981(10)).

From the point of view of the citizen, if not perhaps of the legal profession, the prospect opened up by LEGOL is exciting. The citizen is required to obey the law. Ignorance of it, however excusable, is not excused. Moreover ignorance of what has become all-pervasive statute law can be a considerable handicap in a person's business and private activities. To be able to interrogate a desk-top electronic counsellor about one's income tax, or one's duty in respect of a traffic accident, or one's right of recourse against a recalcitrant travel agency, will be of distinct advantage. There is a long way to go before the entire body of law can be made available in this way, but a start has been made.

No doubt there will always be areas where a judicial or administrative discretion must be exercised before the definitive answer can be known. Here all the computer can do is provide the citizen with information on how, in the light of relevant factors, the functionary entrusted with the discretion is likely to decide. Information so made available might indeed influence the decision itself. After all, the functionary will have a desk-top terminal too!

As well as assisting the individual citizen in this way, linguistic techniques like LEGOL may be expected to enhance the general quality of law. Logical consistency and certainty of operation are not conspicuous features of our present legal system, yet they are highly desirable. Use, for example, of 'entities' tested and refined in expression by the LEGOL technique need not be confined to the Act for which they were devised. An entity of general application (as many are) becomes available to be used over and over again as required in subsequent legislation. In time, the availability of what might be called prefabricated legislative units will shorten and simplify the drafting process, as well as furthering consistency of treatment in the law generally.

After that flight into the future, we return to the present day. Even within the limitations of our existing legal system, what is good for the computer is good apart from the computer. The computer will give more effective service if archival material can be rationalised *before* it is entered in the data base. No software yet written can achieve rationalisation by itself.

So what we need, both for the computer and apart from it, is manipulation of legislative texts to overcome the vices described in chapter 14. While retaining the official language, we need to present it in the most helpful way possible. That is the purpose of composite restatement.

Composite restatement

For the statute user, it is a matter of indifference whether the law on the point he is concerned with is contained in an Act of Parliament or a statutory instrument. He just wants to know what the law is; and he would like to find it in one place. He needs a simple system to direct him to the place. Once there, he wants the point dealt with as simply and comprehensively as the subject matter allows. He also needs the provision to be in up-to-date form.

These needs are self-evident, and scarcely need confirmation. One example of such confirmation is furnished by a note in what is perhaps the legal practitioner's most used publication, the Supreme Court Practice or White Book. This regrets that as a result of the enactment of s 31 of the Supreme Court Act 1981 (dealing with judicial review) the advantage has been lost of enabling a relevant rule of procedure 'to be found in one instrument instead of partly in a statute and partly in rules' (1982 edn, para 53/1-14/2). Composite restatement is designed to meet all these needs, while retaining the official wording in its entirety. As will be seen, it provides an answer to all the vices of statute law examined in chapter 14. A restatement is far easier to understand than the source material it processes; it is far more reliable than any summary, precis, digest or abridgement.

The Composite Restatement method outlined

Choice of topic   A topic is selected which is largely regulated by statute law. (The method does not cover codification of common law rules.) Restatement is more useful the more Acts and statutory instruments are involved in the topic. Topics largely dealt with by ancient Acts, or by a short Act standing alone, are unsuitable. So are topics dealt with by formal Acts, Acts only of concern to officials, Acts relating to overseas territories, Statute Law Revision Acts and other special categories. Otherwise all legislation is suitable.

The restater   The person constructing the restatement (whom we may call the restater) should have some experience of legislative drafting. He needs to have a thorough understanding of text creation, text validation and general principles of legislation. This includes use of the Interpretation Act, styles of drafting and techniques of commencement, amendment, repeal etc.

Text-collation   The restater assembles the original official texts of all Acts and statutory instruments to be included in the restatement, including of course amending Acts and instruments.

Structure of the restatement   There are a number of ways a restatement might be arranged but this account follows the system

I myself have devised and used. The basic textual unit is the *paragraph*. Groups of paragraphs dealing with an aspect of the topic are arranged in *divisions*, the first division consisting of *definitions*. A paragraph may stand alone or may consist of two or more *sub-paragraphs*. A paragraph or sub-paragraph usually consists of a single sentence, but unless very short the sentence is broken up spatially into *clauses*.

Numbering Divisions are numbered from 1 onwards. In numbering paragraphs allowance is made for future additions, so they are numbered in fives. The sign § is used as a prefix, so the first paragraph in Division 1 is referred to as 1 § 5. If § 5 is broken up into sub-paragraphs they are referred to as § 5A, § 5B, etc. Clauses are given marginal numbers (1), (2) etc, so clause (2) of § 5B is referred to as § 5B(2).

Headings Each division is given a heading, and if convenient there are cross-headings within the division. Each paragraph and sub-paragraph is also given a heading. Again if convenient, cross-headings are supplied within a paragraph or sub-paragraph.

Example Division 6 of my book *Consumer Credit Control* (Bennion 1976 (4)) begins as follows:

CURRENCY OF AGREEMENTS
6§5 Variation of regulated agreement under power contained in agreement
6§5A Notice requirements (general rule)

INTRODUCTORY
(1) Where under a power contained in a 'regulated agreement' other than a 'non-commercial agreement'
(2) the 'creditor' or 'owner' varies the agreement
(3) the variation does not take effect before clauses (4) to (6) below are satisfied (or by virtue of *6§5B* or *6§5C* are treated as satisfied).

STATEMENT OF RULE
(4) A notice in 'writing' setting out particulars of the variation
(5) must be 'given' to the 'debtor' or 'hirer' (or to each of them if more than one)
(6) not less than *seven days* before the variation takes effect.

Source notes Following each sub-paragraph its source is stated. The source note to the example given above cites five different provisions of the Consumer Credit Act 1974 and three different sets of regulations.

Typography   As the example shows, different typefaces and other typographical devices are used to aid clarity. Understanding is assisted by splitting up the clauses so that the reader does not have to work out for himself where the breaks in sense occur. Single quotation marks are used to indicate defined terms, the definitions being set out alphabetically in Division 1. Another typographical device is to italicise key words or phrases to draw them to attention (see clause (6) of the example).

Restater's task   The structure in which the restated texts are arranged is designed to present the relevant statutory provisions to the reader in the most logical and helpful manner possible. The restater must at the start work out the best way to do this. Then he takes the official texts and fits them together accordingly. He is not inhibited about mixing provisions of an Act with those of a statutory instrument. For this purpose the two are of equal rank, and the restater's function is to carry out once and for all the task of conflation that otherwise needs to be attempted by each user who comes to the topic. In doing so he must be careful not to change the official language more than is strictly necessary for purposes of 'carpentry'.

A modern Act removes detail from the body of the Act, and avoids repetition, by alloting a label to detailed provisions and using that instead. The restater can sometimes improve on the Act or instrument in this respect. He can further simplify the substantive provisions of the restatement by devising additional definitions. This does not involve any change in meaning, but aids the reader who seeks only the main outline.

Another simplification is to omit provisions of no immediate interest to the user, such as regulation-making powers or provisions not yet operative. Ideally the restatement should be published in looseleaf form so that it can be updated as legislative changes occur. It should consist of all currently operative law on the topic, but not law which is not yet in force or has ceased to operate.

A further aid is the spelling-out in detail of applied provisions, thus curing the difficulty referred to on pp 220–221.

Textual notes   Sometimes the preparation of the restatement brings to light ambiguities, obscurities or omissions. Unless the true intention is so plain that the restater feels no doubt that a court would give effect to it, the errors must be reproduced. Either way, the restater's treatment of the point is explained in a *textual note*.

The Analysis   Preparation of the restatement as a logical structure produces a valuable by-product. If the headings of divisions, paragraphs and sub-paragraphs are printed by themselves in numerical order, they form a useful *outline* of the legislative provisions applying to the topic.

Since the restatement presents the current statutory provisions in logical order, suitably conflated, it serves as a sound basis for explanation and commentary. We are accustomed to annotated Acts and statutory instruments, but the notes are themselves rendered inadequate by the inadequacies in presentation of the official texts. Now the expert commentator can do a more effective job.

The annotator There is no reason why the restater and the annotator should be the same person. The skills required are different. A restater needs no special knowledge of the topic with which his restatement deals. The annotator on the other hand should be knowledgeable in the topic. He need not wait for completion of the restatement to begin work. The essence of the composite restatement method is that the official language is retained, and this of course is available to the annotator from the outset.

Method To achieve maximum utility, a composite restatement needs copious annotation. As we have seen, the statutory text by itself is but the dry bones. It needs to be fleshed out by explanations and examples. While notes on sources, and any textual notes, need to be drafted by the restater, the other notes, as we have said, can be compiled by a different person. Apart from general introductory explanations, it is best if these notes follow each paragraph or sub-paragraph.

Appendix B gives extended examples of the Composite Restatement method. Part I sets out the portion of the Analysis section of *Consumer Credit Control* relating to Division Nine. Part II sets out the beginning of Division Nine omitting all annotations except those giving the sources and interpretation references.

An official restatement?

All statute users would gain if the main body of statute law were made available in the Composite Restatement form. There are three ways this might be done:
(1) By Parliament itself (the restatement might be enacted in the form of an Act of Parliament).
(2) By one or more private bodies, such as commercial publishers or university law departments.
(3) By a body, such as a Statute Law Commission, which has an official status (perhaps conferred by Act of Parliament) but has no power to override legislation.

In some ways an enacted restatement would be better than any other. It would itself constitute the law, and would repeal the Acts and subordinate legislation restated by it. The possibility of conflict between the enacted law and the restatement would be avoided, as would the need for anyone to consult both texts. Yet there are serious problems about an enacted restatement. First, the restatement must include not only Acts of Parliament but also statutory instruments the making of which Parliament has delegated to ministers. It has done this because statutory instruments concern matters of detail which Parliament has not time to consider itself or because they relate to topics on which speedy action may be needed, or for similar reasons. Having delegated this responsibility Parliament ought not to be asked to take it back by passing statutory instruments in the form of an Act of Parliament.

Second, Parliament is unlikely to agree to enact the restatement without either being satisfied that it exactly reproduces the existing law (apart from formal or trifling departures) or allowing itself an opportunity to debate and amend it. Either of these would be destructive of the object of the restatement. The history of the process of consolidation (always well behind requirements) shows the danger of insisting on slavish reproduction of the existing law, with all its obscurities and ambiguities. Even the freedom given first by the Consolidation of Enactments (Procedure) Act 1949 and later (to a wider extent) by the system of 'consolidation with Law Commission amendments' has not enabled the output of consolidation in Britain to keep pace with requirements, partly because even the abbreviated parliamentary procedures are time and effort-consuming for the drafter. To allow parliamentary debate and amendment on the other hand would be unworkable. Parliament has insufficient time for substantive legislation, and we should in any case be back with the problem of distortion of the legislative structure by amendments made in Parliament.

The third objection to an enacted restatement is that it would have to take the form of a parliamentary Bill, so that the improvements in structure and signposting effected by the restatement would be lost. This might be obviated by making the restatement a schedule to an Act, rather as some constitutions were treated in the days when Westminster provided constitutions for other countries. This is a clumsy device however. Of course if parliamentary procedure were changed so that the forms of Acts could be improved, that might get round the difficulty.

Fourthly, it would interfere with the exercise by ministers of their delegated power of legislation if their regulations and orders were crystallised into legislation. Statutory instruments should remain under the control of those with power to make them (subject of course to overriding powers of annulment or affirmation retained by Parliament). Government departments would not relish seeing their regulations picked up and remodelled without their control, and such control, if given, would be another delaying factor. Furthermore, the amendment of statutory instruments would be difficult if they had become embedded in an enacted restatement. The text of the restatement would not distinguish between the origins of its provisions, and problems of *vires* might become acute.

It is true that the objections listed above did not prevent the enactment by Congress of the United States Code in 1926, described as 'the official restatement in convenient form of the general and permanent laws of the United States'. Clearly the possibility of an enacted Restatement is worthy of investigation.

There is of course nothing to prevent a university law department, commercial publisher or other private body from producing and publishing a restatement in some field of enacted law. It will have the value indicated by the skill and effort which has gone into it, but that will be difficult for outsiders to assess. It is true that many private compilations have won high renown — *Halsbury's Statutes* being a notable example. Ideally the restatement should be fully comprehensive, and the effort required might be beyond the reach of any one British publisher — though a consortium of commercial publishers and others might accomplish the task.

My own view is that it would be best for the restatement to be produced and promulgated by an official body such as the Law Commission, or a body set up for the purpose. The law restated would remain fully in force in its original form, and would be amended by Act of Parliament or statutory instrument in the ordinary way. It would be for the body responsible for the restatement to follow suit and issue its own amending material in accordance with such changes in the statute law. Similarly, the courts would retain their full authority to pronounce upon the meaning and effect of any enactment in the form in which it was passed by Parliament or made by a minister. The courts would no doubt treat the restatement as being of persuasive authority, but in any conflict the actual law would prevail — the restatement would not in itself be law. It may be asked what is the use of the restatement if it is subordinate to statute law. Will it not be necessary for the practitioner to look at the statute law as well, so that his burden, far from being lightened, is actually doubled? I regard this question as the crux of the whole problem of whether a restatement is worth while.

The restatement is intended as a tool for practitioners who need to find out what the statute law on a particular subject is. I believe it is also capable of being used by lay persons — at least in the form of the Analysis and as an outline exposition (ie without investigating defined terms). Tools of this kind are in common use by practitioners and lay persons. For practitioners they take the form of annotated texts (such as *Halsbury's Statutes* or the *Supreme Court Practice*) or textbooks (such as Stone's *Justice Manual* or Archbold's *Criminal Pleading, Practice and Procedure*). Very often the busy practitioner relies on statements of law which are not in the official form, and courts nowadays are ready to follow suit. The restatement, if issued by an official body, would merely give a better and more authoritative substitute source. In practice, reference to the official text would rarely be necessary. The position would become like that of the American Law Institute and its restatements, which in time attained far greater authority than at the outset was thought possible (Lewis 1945). (As to the possibility of setting up on similar lines a British Statute Law Institute, which could perform the function of producing composite restatements, see pp 68–69 above.)

To yield its full value, the text of the restatement would need to be annotated. Statutory texts, however well drafted, require copious explanations and illustrations to become fully accessible to the reader. Should the official body responsible for the restatement also be responsible for the annotations? My answer is no. To produce the full range of annotations would greatly enlarge the task of the official body — already heavy if it is to be discharged adequately. It would be best if the official body gathered the best talent available to produce the actual restatement but left it to commercial publishers and others to produce annotated editions. Indeed for the restatement to succeed it would be necessary for the efforts now devoted by commercial publishers to producing annotated texts of statutes to be switched to the restatement.

We can now attempt to answer the questions posed above. If the restatement were produced by an official body, as I have suggested, it would have strong persuasive authority but the enacted law would remain paramount. In practice it should be possible to proceed by consulting the restatement *instead* of the enacted law, especially if published commentaries cited the restatement rather than the enacted law. Only if difficulty arose over some obscurity or ambiguity would it be necessary to compare the texts. In such cases the existence of the restatement would be a valuable adjunct.

Commercial versions of the restatement with annotations might well become the most commonly used source books for statute law. I believe they would serve a useful public purpose in bringing statute law fully before those to whom it is directed in a form they could consult easily and understand.

It would of course be an immense task for a single organisation, even when financed by the state, to produce a restatement of the entire body of statute law. I would propose that a programme of restatement should take the place of the programme of consolidation of enactments, so that the former could use the services of drafters who would be otherwise engaged on consolidation. Composite restatement is far more useful than consolidation. Even so, it is obvious that the restatement would have to be carried out by instalments. Fortunately its value does not depend on completeness. As I hope to have shown with my own restatement of consumer credit law, the method is useful even when confined to a single topic. For further information see the video cassette *Composite Restatement* (Longman 1982).

Appendices

Draft Processing Bill

A
BILL

To declare the powers of courts and other persons or bodies in relation to the interpretation of Acts and statutory instruments.

BE IT ENACTED by the Queen's most Excellent Majesty, by and with the advice and consent of the Lords Spiritual and Temporal, and Commons, in this present Parliament assembled, and by the authority of the same, as follows:-

1. Powers of the court

Without prejudice to a court's implementation of a legislative text under which (whether expressly, or by an implication arising from a deliberate omission or use of a term of wide meaning or otherwise), any power is conferred on or delegated to the court, it is hereby declared, for the avoidance of doubt, that a court has the powers referred to in sections 2 to 4 below in relation to a legislative text relevant to the case before it.

2. Obsolescent text

(1) This section applies where it appears to the court that, through the passage of time since the enactment, or original enactment, of the text, its effect is doubtful.

(2) If the mischief or object to which the text was directed has changed its nature, the court shall apply the text, subject to such modifications as may be requisite, to the changed mischief or object.

(3) Subsection (2) does not apply where the change is such that the interests of justice require the text to be treated as spent.

3. Defective text

(1) This section applies where it appears to the court that, through grammatical error, syntactical ambiguity, omission, transposition or

343

intrusion, logical error, punctuation mistake or other formal defect, the effect of the text is doubtful.

(2) Where it is clear what form the legislator intended the text to take, the court shall apply it in that form.

(3) In any other case the court shall apply it in the form best suited to serve the object of the text as intended by the legislator.

4. Unintended effect

(1) This section applies where it appears to the court that, because the text goes narrower or wider than the object, or is based on an error of law or fact, or is otherwise misconceived, it does not carry out the legislator's intention, or goes wider than the intention.

(2) Where it is clear what the effect of the text should have been in order to carry out the legislator's intention and no more, the court shall give the text that effect.

(3) In any other case the court shall apply the text as it stands apart from this section.

5. Intention of the legislator

(1) In construing any reference in this Act to the intention of the legislator, the court shall have regard to the principles set out in this section.

(2) The intention is primarily to be derived from the legislative text itself (including any source referred to in the text).

(3) The court may refer to any other source in addition if it thinks fit to do so having regard to the requirements of justice, including —

> (a) the desirability of persons being able to rely on the meaning conveyed by the text itself, and
>
> (b) the need to avoid prolonging legal proceedings without compensating advantage.

(4) The court shall have regard, so far as may be relevant, to the procedures by which, in accordance with constitutional practice, the text may be taken to have been created and validated as law.

(5) In the case of a statutory instrument the court shall, so far as may be relevant, have regard to the intention of Parliament in delegating power to make the instrument as well as to the intention of the person or body by whom it was made.

6. Interpretation

In this Act —

'court' includes a tribunal, arbitrator or other person or body with the function of interpreting a legislative text;

'legislative text' means a provision of an Act or statutory instrument and references to the enactment of a text shall be construed accordingly;

'the legislator' in relation to an Act means Parliament, and in relation to a statutory instrument means the person or body by whom it was made.

7. Short title
This Act may be cited as the Legislation (Powers) Act 19 .

Appendix B

Illustration of the Composite Restatement Method

(Consumer Credit Control Division 9:
Information on Credit Reference Agency Files)

Part I: Analysis

9§5   Duty to disclose names and addresses of agencies consulted
        9§5A   Duty of creditor
        9§5B   Duty of owner
        9§5C   Duty of credit-broker where goods sold by him to creditor
        9§5D   Duty of credit-broker in other cases
        9§5E   Duty of connected supplier
        9§5F   Breach of duty an offence in certain cases
        9§5G   When request valid

9§10   Duty of agency to give consumer copy of his file
        9§10A   Nature of duty
        9§10B   Requirements to be observed by consumer
        9§10C   Breach of duty an offence

9§20   Duty of agency where no file kept
        9§20A   Nature of duty
        9§20B   Breach of duty an offence

9§30   Alternative procedure for business consumers (section 160 direction)

9§40   Section 160 direction: giving of information to consumer
        9§40A   Nature of duty
        9§40B   Breach of duty an offence

9§50   Section 160 direction: obtaining of further information by consumer
        9§50A   Nature of duty
        9§50B   Breach of duty an offence

9§60   Notice requiring amendment of file

9§70   Response to notice requiring amendment of file

9§80 Requirement to add notice of correction to file
    9§80A   Nature of requirement
    9§80B   Period for serving requirement

9§90 Response to requirement to add notice of correction to file
    9§90A   Where agency considers notice of correction unsuitable
    9§90B   Duty to notify consumer
    9§90C   Consumer's right when not notified
    9§90D   Duty to notify clients of agency

9§100 Order by Director General as to notice of correction
    9§100A   Making of order
    9§100B   Duty to notify clients of agency

Part II: Restatement

9§5 Duty to disclose names and addresses of agencies consulted
9§5A *Duty of creditor*
(1) The 'creditor' under an actual or prospective 'consumer credit agreement' (being a 'regulated agreement' or 'prospective regulated agreement') must comply with the following provisions as from 16 May 1977.
DUTY TO INFORM CREDIT-BROKER
(2) Not later than he informs a 'credit-broker' that he is not willing to make the agreement, the creditor (if he is a 'licensee')
(3) unless he informs the 'debtor' directly that he is not willing to make the agreement
(4) must inform the credit-broker of the name and address of any 'credit reference agency'
(5) from which the creditor has during the 'antecedent negotiations' applied for information about the financial standing of the debtor.
DUTY TO INFORM DEBTOR
(6) Within seven 'working days' after receiving a *valid* request to that effect from the debtor
(7) the creditor must 'give' the debtor a notice in 'writing'
(8) stating the name and address of any credit reference agency
(9) from which the creditor has during the antecedent negotiations applied for information about the financial standing of the debtor.

Source
Consumer Credit Act 1974, ss 26, 147, 157 and 189(1); Consumer Credit (Conduct of Business) (Credit References) Regulations 1977, reg 2.

Interpretation
'creditor' see 1§920   'debtor' see 1§1020
'consumer credit agreement'   'credit reference agency'

see 1§500
'regulated agreement' see 1§2560
'prospective regulated agreement'
  see 1§2440
'credit-broker' see 1§760
'licensee' see 1§1860

see 1§840
'antecedent negotiations'
  see 1§100
'working day' see 1§3200
'give' see 1§1500
'writing' see 1§3220

9§5B *Duty of owner*
 (1) The 'owner' under an actual or prospective 'consumer hire agreement' (being a 'regulated agreement' or 'prospective regulated agreement') must comply with the following provisions as from 16 May 1977.
      DUTY TO INFORM CREDIT-BROKER
 (2) Not later than he informs a 'credit-broker' that he is not willing to make the agreement, the owner (if he is a 'licensee')
 (3) unless he informs the 'hirer' directly that he is not willing to make the agreement
 (4) must inform the credit-broker of the name and address of any 'credit reference agency'
 (5) from which the owner has during the 'antecedent negotiations' applied for information about the financial standing of the hirer.
      DUTY TO INFORM HIRER
 (6) Within seven 'working days' after receiving a *valid* request to that effect from the hirer
 (7) the owner must 'give' the hirer a notice in 'writing'
 (8) stating the name and address of any credit reference agency
 (9) from which the owner has during the antecedent negotiations applied for information about the financial standing of the hirer.

Source
Consumer Credit Act 1974, ss 26, 147, 157 and 189(1); Consumer Credit (Conduct of Business) (Credit References) Regulations 1977, reg 2.

Interpretation
'owner' see 1§2160
'consumer hire agreement' 'hirer'
  see 1§560
'regulated agreement' see 1§2560
'prospective regulated agreement'
  see 1 §2440
'credit-broker' see 1§760

'licensee' see 1§1860
'hirer' see 1§1620
'credit reference agency' see 1§840
'antecedent negotiations' see 1§100
'working day' see 1§3200
'give' see 1§1500
'writing' see 1§3220

9§5C *Duty of credit-broker where goods sold by him to creditor*
 (1) As from 16 May 1977, a 'credit-broker' engaging in 'antecedent negotiations' falling within 1§100B
 (2) within seven 'working days' after receiving a *valid* request to that effect from the 'debtor'

(3)   must give the debtor a notice in 'writing'
(4)   stating the name and address of any 'credit reference agency'
(5)   from which the credit-broker has during the antecedent negotiations applied for information about the financial standing of the debtor

or

(6)   of which the credit-broker has been informed under 9§5A (4).

Source
Consumer Credit Act 1974, ss 26, 147, 157 and 189(1); Consumer Credit (Credit Reference Agency) Regulations 1977, reg 3; Consumer Credit (Conduct of Business) (Credit References) Regulations 1977, reg 3.

Interpretation

'credit-broker' see 1§760

'antecedent negotiations'
    see 1§100

'working day' see 1§3200

'debtor' see 1§1020

'writing' see 1§3220

'credit reference agency'
    see 1§840

Table of References

Allen Sir Carleton 1964, *Law in the Making* (7th edn), Oxford University Press.

Australia 1982, 'Extrinsic Aids to Statutory Interpretation', Australian Government Publishing Service, Canberra.

Barrington Daines 1767, *Observations upon the Statutes* (2nd edn).

Barwick Sir Garfield 1961, 'Divining the Legislative Intent' 35 Australian Law Journal 197.

Bennion F A R 1962, *The Constitutional Law of Ghana*, Butterworths.

1969, *Professional Ethics: the Consultant Professions and their Code*, Charles Knight.

1970, *Tangling with the Law: Reforms in Legal Process*, Chatto and Windus.

1971 (1), *Second Report from the Select Committee on Procedure*, Session 1970-71 HC 538 p 223 (oral evidence).

1971 (2), *Proceedings of the Ninth International Symposium on Comparative Law*, University of Ottawa Press, 115.

1975 (2), 'The Renton Report', 119 SJ 346.

1975 (3), 'The Renton Report', 125 NLJ 660.

1975 (4), 'A Computer Experiment in Legislative Drafting', *Computers and Law* Nov 1975.

1976 (1), 'Our Legislators are "CADS"', 120 SJ 390.

1976 (2), 'Correcting a Defect in the Perpetuities and Accumulations Act 1964', 120 SJ 498.

1976 (3), ' "First Consideration": A Cautionary Tale', 126 NLJ 1237.

1976 4), *Consumer Credit Control: an annotated Composite Restatement of the Consumer Credit Act 1974 and regulations etc made under it*, Longman.

1976-77, 'Computers and Law in Canada', *Computers and Law* Nov 1976 & Feb 1977.

1977 (1), 'Improvements in Legislative Techniques', *Proceedings & Papers of the Fifth Commonwealth Law Conference* p 53.

1978 (1), 'Statute Law Obscurity and the Drafting Parameters' (1978) *British Journal of Law and Society* 235.

1978 (2), *First Report from the Select Committee on Procedure*, Session 1977-78 HC 588-III p 87 (written evidence).

350

1979 (1), 'Legislative Technique', 129 NLJ 748.
1979 (3), 'Legislative Technique', 129 NLJ 1170.
1980 (1), 'Legislative Technique', 130 NLJ 56.
1980 (2), 'Statutory Sanity', (1980) *Professional Administration* 8.
1980 (3), 'Statute Law Processing: the Composite Restatement Method', 124 SJ 71, 92.
1980 (4), 'Legislative Technique', 130 NLJ 243.
1980 (6), 'Drafting Practice', 124 SJ 195.
1980 (7), 'The Science of Interpretation', 130 NLJ 493.
1980 (8), Review of *Legislative Drafting: A New Approach* by Sir W Dale (full version), [1980] Stat LR 61.
1980 (9), 'Framing the Crime of Attempt', 130 NLJ 725.
1980 (10), 'Drafting Practice', 124 SJ 567.
1980 (11), 'Principal Acts and Textual Amendment', 130 NLJ 913.
1980 (13), 'The Literal Rule of Interpretation', 130 NLJ 1156.
1981 (1), 'Ambiguity by Misuse of Homonyms', 131 NLJ 192.
1981 (2), 'Drafting Practice', 125 SJ 139.
1981 (3), 'Bringing Acts into Force: The Computer Dimension', 131 NLJ 356.
1981 (4), Letter amplifying 1981 (3), 131 NLJ 586.
1981 (5), 'Leave My Word Alone', 131 NLJ 596.
1981 (6), 'Drafting Practice', 125 SJ 420.
1981 (7), 'Can there be an Infringing Copy without a Copyright Infringement?', 131 NLJ 749.
1981 (8), 'Another Reverse for the Law Commissions' Interpretation Bill', 131 NLJ 840.
1981 (9), 'Credit or Theft: The Lambie Case', 131 NLJ 1041.
1981 (10), 'LEGOL and the Electronic Home Lawyer', 1981 *Law Society's Gazette* 1334.
1981 (11), 'Modern Royal Assent Procedure at Westminster', 1981 Stat LR 133.
1982 (1), 'The Need for Training in Statute Law', 1982 *Law Society's Gazette* 219.
1982 (2), Follow-up letter to 1982 (1): 1982 *Law Society's Gazette* 664.
1982 (3), 'Penalty Points—a Transitional Problem' (pseudonymous), 1982 *Law Society's Gazette* 1622.
1983 (1), 'Making Off Without Payment' (letter), [1983] Crim LR 205.
1983 (2), 'Founding of Statute Law Society' (letter), 1983 Stat LR 63.
1983 (3), 'Scientific Statutory Interpretation and the Franco Scheme', [1983] *British Tax Review* 74.
1983 (4), 'The Controversy over Drafting Style', 1983 *The Law Society's Gazette* 2355, 3211.
1984 (1), *Statutory Interpretation*, Butterworths.

1984 (2), 'Propositions of Law in Conviction Appeals' [1984] Crim LR 282.

1985 (1), 'Mass Picketing and the 1875 Act' [1985] Crim LR 64.

1985 (2), 'Trade Descriptions, or How to Tackle a Problem of Statutory Interpretation', 135 NLJ 953.

1986 (1), *Information Sources in Law*, edited by R Logan (chapter 3), Butterworths.

1986 (2), *The All England Law Reports Annual Review 1985* (chapter entitled 'Statute Law'), Butterworths.

1986 (3), 'The Technique of Codification' [1986] Crim LR 295.

1986 (4), 'A Point on the Companies Consolidation', 130 SJ 736.

1987, *The All England Law Reports Annual Review 1986* (chapter entitled 'Statute Law'), Butterworths.

1988 (1), *The All England Law Reports Annual Review 1987* (chapter entitled 'Statute Law'), Butterworths.

1988 (2), *The Law Commission and Law Reform*, edited by G Zellick (pages 60 to 66), Sweet & Maxwell.

1988 (3), 'Statutory Exceptions: A Third Knot in the Golden Thread?' [1988] Crim LR 31.

1989 (1), *The All England Law Reports Annual Review 1988* (chapter entitled 'Statute Law'), Butterworths.

1989 (2), Supplement to *Statutory Interpretation*, Butterworths.

1989 (3), 'Statute law reform: is anybody listening?', 133 SJ 886.

Bentham Jeremy 1775, *A Comment on the Commentaries* (1928 edn), Oxford.

Blackstone Sir William 1765, *Commentaries on the Laws of England*, edited by R M Kerr (4th edn 1876).

Braithwaite J 1979, *Inequality, Crime and Public Policy*, Routledge and Kegan Paul.

Brooke A W 1981, 'Section 3 of the Wills Act 1837: a Reminder', 125 SJ 368.

Burton I F and Drewry G 1970, *Public Legislation: a Survey of the Session 1968/69*.

Cardozo Benjamin N 1921, *The Nature of the Judicial Process*.

Carr Sir Cecil 1926, 'Citation of Statutes', 126 *Cambridge Legal Essays* 71.

Chalmers Sir M D 1894, Introduction to the first edition of *Chalmers' Sale of Goods Act 1893*.

Clarence Smith 1972, *Proceedings of the Ninth International Symposium on Comparative Law*, University of Ottawa Press, pp 155-178.

Collins Lawrence 1980, *European Community Law in the United Kingdom* (2nd edn), Butterworths.

Corry J A 1935, 'The Interpretation of Statutes', (as reprinted in Driedger 1974, p 203).

1954, 'The use of legislative history in the interpretation of statutes', 32 Canadian Bar Review 624.

Craies W F 1971, *Statute Law* (7th edn), Sweet & Maxwell.
Cross Sir R 1976, *Statutory Interpretation*, Butterworths.
1977, *Precedent in English Law* (3rd edn), Oxford.
1987, *Statutory Interpretation* (2nd edn by Dr John Bell and Sir George Engle), Butterworths.
Curtis Charles P 1949, 'A better theory of legal interpretation', 4 *The Record of the Association of the Bar of the City of New York* 321.
Dale Sir W 1977, *Legislative Drafting: a New Approach*, Butterworths.
Devlin Lord 1965, *The Enforcement of Morals*, Oxford.
1979, *The Judge*, Oxford.
Dicey A V 1939, *Law of the Constitution* (9th edn), Macmillan.
Dickerson R 1954, *Legislative Drafting*, Little Brown.
1981, *Materials on Legal Drafting*, West Publishing Co, St Paul.
Diplock Lord 1965, 'The courts as legislators' (address to the Holdsworth Club of the University of Birmingham).
Driedger E A 1971, 'Statutory Drafting and Interpretation', *Proceedings of the Ninth International Symposium on Comparative Law*, University of Ottawa, p 71.
1974, *The Construction of Statutes*, Butterworths.
Field D D and Bradford A W 1865, 'Introduction to the Completed [New York] Civil Code' reprinted in Honnold *The Life of the Law* 1964 (Macmillan).
Fitzgerald P J 1971, 'Are Statutes Fit for Academic Treatment?', 11 *Journal of the Society of Public Teachers of Law* 142.
Frankfurter Justice 1947, 'Some reflections on the reading of statutes', 2 *The Record of the Association of the Bar of the City of New York* 213.
Friedland M L 1975, *Access to the Law*, Carswell/Methuen.
Friedmann W 1949, *Legal Theory* (2nd edn), Stevens.
Gower L C B 1960, *Report of the Commission of Enquiry into the Company Law of Ghana*, Government Printer, Accra.
Gowers Sir E 1973, *The Complete Plain Words* (2nd edn).
Graham Harrison Sir William 1935, 'An Examination of the Main Criticisms of the Statute Book and of the Possibility of Improvement' *Journal of the Society of Public Teachers of Law* (1935) 9.
Hailsham Lord 1978, *The Dilemma of Democracy*, Collins.
Hart H L A 1961, *The Concept of Law*, Oxford University Press.
Holdsworth Sir W 1924, *History of English Law* (2nd edn).
1928, 'The Case-Law System: Historical Factors which Controlled its Development', reprinted in Honnold *The Life of the Law* (1964) Macmillan 44.
Holmes Oliver Wendell Jr 1881, *The Common Law* Boston: Little, Brown.
1898-1899, 'The Theory of Legal Interpretation', 12 Harv LR 417.

Hutton N K 1961, 'Mechanics of Law Reform', 24 MLR 18.
1967, 'Preparation of Acts of Parliament', 1967 *Law Society's Gazette* 294.
1979, 'Legislative Drafting Technique in the United Kingdom', LX *The Parliamentarian* No 4.
Ilbert Sir C 1901, *Legislative Methods and Forms*, Oxford University Press.
Jamieson N J 1976, 'Towards a Systematic Statute Law', 3 *Otago Law Review* No 4.
Kent Sir H 1979, *In on the Act*, Macmillan.
Kerr R M 1876, editorial additions to Blackstone *Commentaries on the Laws of England* (4th edn).
Leitch W A 1965, 'The Interpretation Act—10 years later', XVI *Northern Ireland Legal Quarterly* 237.
and Donaldson A G 1955, 'A Commentary on the Interpretation Act (Northern Ireland) 1954', XI *Northern Ireland Legal Quarterly* 45.
Lewis W D 1945, 'How We Did It' *History of the American Law Institute and the First Restatement of the Law* Philadelphia: American Law Institute.
Lyons A B 1969, 'The Statutory Publications Office, Past, Present and Future', unpublished.
MacCormick Neil 1978, *Legal Reasoning and Legal Theory*, Oxford.
Mackinnon LJ 1942, 'The statute book' (presidential address to the Holdsworth Club of the University of Birmingham).
Maine Sir Henry 1883, *Early Law and Custom*.
Maitland F W 1908, *The Constitutional History of England*, Cambridge.
1911, 'English Law', IX *Encyclopædia Britannica* (11th edn).
Maxwell P B 1969, *The Interpretation of Statutes* (12th edn), Sweet & Maxwell.
May Erskine 1976, *The Law, Privileges, Proceedings and Usage of Parliament* (19th edn), Butterworths.
Megarry Sir R E 1973, *A Second Miscellany-at-Law*, Stevens.
Mellinkoff D 1963, *The Language of the Law*, Little Brown.
Miers David R and Page Alan C 1982, *Legislation*, Sweet & Maxwell.
Mill J S 1838, 'Bentham' *London and Westminster Review* August 1838.
Miller A S 1956, 'Statutory Language and the Purposive Use of Ambiguity', 42 *Virginia Law Review*, Jan 1956).
Odgers Sir Charles E 1967, *Construction of Deeds and Statutes* (5th edn by G Dworkin), Sweet & Maxwell.
Pepy D 1971, 'Statutory Drafting and Interpretation', *Proceedings of the Ninth International Symposium on Comparative Law*, University of Ottawa Press, p 94.
Plucknett T F T 1944, 'Ellesmere on Statutes' 60 LQR 242.
1980, *Statutes & their Interpretation in the First Half of the Fourteenth Century*, Willam S Hein & Co, Buffalo.

Porter Lord 1940, 'Case Law in the Interpretation of Statutes' Presidential address to the Holdsworth Club of the University of Birmingham.

Radin Max 1930, 'Statutory Interpretation', 43 *Harvard Law Review* 863.

Radzinowicz 1948, *History of English Criminal Law.*

Renton Lord 1975, *The Preparation of Legislation*, report of a committee appointed by the Lord President of the Council, Cmnd 6053.

1980, 'Form and Structure', 10 *Professional Administration* No 1.

Richardson H G and Sayles George 1934, 'The Early Statutes', 50 LQR 201 and 540.

Robinson, Richard 1952, *Definition*, Oxford.

Russell Sir A 1938, *Legislative Drafting and Forms* (4th edn), Butterworths.

Samuels A 1974, 'Improving the Quality of Legislation', 3 *Anglo-American Law Review* 523.

Select Committee 1971, *Second Report from the Select Committee on Procedure*, Session 1970–71 HC 538.

Simon of Glaisdale Lord and Webb J V D 1975, 'Consolidation and Statute Law Revision' 1975 *Public Law* 285.

Spencer J R 1981 (1), 'The Mishandling of Handling', 1981 Crim LR 682.

1981 (2), 'When is a Law not a Law?', 131 NLJ 644.

Statute Law Society 1970, *Statute Law Deficiencies*, report of a committee chaired by Sir D Heap, Sweet & Maxwell.

1972, *Statute Law: the Key to Clarity*, report of a committee chaired by Lord Stow Hill, Sweet & Maxwell.

1974, *Statute Law: A Radical Simplification*, report of a committee chaired by H Marshall, Sweet & Maxwell.

1979, *Renton and the Need for Reform*, containing evidence submitted to the Renton Committee by the Society and by F A R Bennion, Sweet & Maxwell.

Thornton, G C 1987, *Legislative Drafting* (3rd edn), Butterworth.

Thring Lord 1902, *Practical Legislation* (2nd edn).

Twining W and Miers D 1976, *How To Do Things With Rules*, Weidenfeld and Nicholson.

1982, *How To Do Things With Rules* (2nd edn).

Williams G 1945, 'Language and the Law, 61 LQR 179, 293, 384; 62 LQR 387.

1982, *Learning the Law* (11th edn), Stevens.

Willis J 1938, 'Statutory Interpretation in a Nutshell', 16 *Canadian Bar Review* 1.

Wilson W A 1974, 'The Complexity of Statutes', 37 MLR 497.

Woodman Gordon 1982, 'Dworkin's "Right Answer" Thesis' 45 MLR 121.

Zander Michael 1989, *The Law-Making Process* (3rd edn), Weidenfeld and Nicholson.

Zellick 1988, *The Law Commission and Law Reform*, ed by G Zellick, Sweet & Maxwell.

Note. An exhaustive Bibliography of materials on statute law is published by the Commonwealth Secretariat, Marlborough House, London SW1.

Index